Dark Thoughts

Philosophic Reflections on Cinematic Horror

Edited by
Steven Jay Schneider
Daniel Shaw

The Scarecrow Press, Inc.
Lanham, Maryland, and Oxford
2003

SCARECROW PRESS, INC.

Published in the United States of America
by Scarecrow Press, Inc.
A Member of the Rowman & Littlefield Publishing Group
4501 Forbes Boulevard, Suite 200, Lanham, MD 20706
www.scarecrowpress.com

PO Box 317
Oxford
OX2 9RU, UK

British Library Cataloguing-in-Publication Information Available

Library of Congress Cataloging-in-Publication Data

Dark thoughts : philosophic reflections on cinematic horror / edited by
Steven Jay Schneider, Daniel Shaw.
    p. cm.
 ISBN 0-8108-4792-2 (alk. paper)
 1. Horror films—History and criticism. I. Schneider, Steven Jay,
1974– II. Shaw, Daniel, 1951–
PN1995.9.H6D27 2003
791.43'6164—dc21   2003008100

Contents

Philosophical (Horror) Investigations

Horror and Reality

Bibliography

Index

About the Contributors

Acknowledgments

The editors would like to thank Cynthia A. Freeland, and Westview Press, for permission to reprint "The Slasher's Blood Lust," a chapter from her book *The Naked and the Undead: Evil and the Appeal of Horror* (2000); Noël Carroll, and Routledge, for permission to reprint "The General Theory of Horrific Appeal," an excerpt from his book *The Philosophy of Horror; or, Paradoxes of the Heart* (1990); and Matt Hills and Sara Gwenllian Jones, editors of *Intensities: The Journal of Cult Media*, as well as Andy Black at Noir Publishing, for the right to reprint Steven Jay Schneider's essay "Murder as Art/The Art of Murder: Aestheticizing Violence in Modern Cinematic Horror."

Our personal thanks go out to Richard Allen, Karen Gray, William Irwin, Rebecca Massa, Melissa Ray, Mel Thompson, and Dana Polan for their helpful advice and assistance along the way.

Introduction

Steven Jay Schneider and Daniel Shaw

Philosophers getting excited about horror films may seem incongruous to the average intellectual reader, and saying that one has a "philosophy of horror" may simply sound pretentious. Maybe it's the bad critical reputation of most monster movies, a perennially popular genre (especially with teenagers) that has always taken its lumps, both aesthetically and morally. Plato wanted to ban all representations of the monstrous from his ideal Republic, and his successors have condemned such depictions ever since. The editors of this volume believe that there is ample reason for philosophers to become interested in horror films, for they raise a number of complex and interrelated questions that lie at the heart of philosophical aesthetics.

Primary among these is the question of horror-pleasure. Why are those of us who enjoy the genre so attracted to watching things that, in real life, would be repellent to us? Like the more traditional aesthetic issue concerning tragic pleasure, there is something puzzling about enjoying in fiction what is painful in reality. Freudian film scholars Laura Mulvey and Robin Wood offered the first compelling solution to this puzzle, and it has been tough to beat. Wood's thesis that monsters represent a return of the repressed, gratifying the instinctive drives of the id in a cathartic fashion, had almost no serious rival in critical literature from the mid-1970s until 1990.[1] Elizabeth Cowie offers an elaboration on that long-dominant paradigm in her essay for this collection.

Serious philosophical discussion of horror theory was triggered by Noël Carroll's seminal treatise, *The Philosophy of Horror; or,*

Paradoxes of the Heart (1990), a brief excerpt from which is included here.[2] Carroll's cognitivist approach to solving what he calls "the paradox of horror pleasure" was painstakingly modeled on David Hume's theory of tragedy. We do *not* take pleasure in the painful and repugnant monster, according to Carroll, but rather in having our curiosity satisfied about its impossible nature, and whether and how the narrative's human protagonists will dispatch it successfully. His denial that we take pleasure in the monster itself, along with his requirement that the object of horror must be an impossible being—one not believed capable of existing according to the tenets of contemporary science—have generated a good deal of critical ink. The dialogue continues here, in essays by Cynthia A. Freeland (who defends realistic, "slasher" horror as a legitimate subgenre of horror cinema generally), Matt Hills (see below), and co-authors Deborah Knight and George McKnight (who categorize Mary Harron's *American Psycho* [2000] as a horror film, despite its quite possible human protagonist).

As with tragedy, the major philosophic challenge of horror theory is to come up with a suitable definition of the genre, which to our minds comes down to defending your estimation of what instances of it you believe to be the best and most central. Genre definitions are serious recommendations about what to look for and how to look at examples of the genre, as well as being exercises in rhetoric, designed to convince the reader to see such examples as the writer does. This, indeed, is the intent of the essay by co-editor Daniel Shaw, advancing as it does a Nietzschean theory of horror to understand our seemingly endless fascination with the figure of Hannibal Lecter. The genre reflections of Michael Grant are aptly grounded in the philosophy of Ludwig Wittgenstein. Matt Hills proposes an event-based (as opposed to Carroll's mere "entity-based") definition of art-horror, and Angela Curran argues that particular horror films succeed in approaching the lofty status of Aristotelian tragedy.

Closely associated with defining the genre is an analysis of the emotion of "art-horror" (Carroll's term), used to distinguish this feeling from the real horror with which we respond to horrifying events that we believe to be nonfictional. Robert C. Solomon addresses this distinction in his moving reflections on the World Trade Center attacks, where he asks what our responses to the events on 9/11/2001 can tell us about some of the issues surrounding the experience of cinematic horror. Two other essays in the volume illustrate and analyze the differences between art-horror, which has a definite monstrous object, and art-dread, which does not.

It may be asked what differentiates *philosophizing* about horror cinema from the more common practices of horror film criticism, notably the psychoanalysis of the genre. Freud's theory of the uncanny has been highly influential in discussions of the horror film, including work by one of the present editors. Curtis Bowman proposes an alternative, Heideggerean account of the elusive concept of the uncanny, and demonstrates how useful it can be in evaluating the horror films of Jacques Tourneur (*Cat People* [1942], *I Walked with a Zombie* [1943], *The Leopard Man* [1943], and *Curse of the Demon* [1957]). Aaron Smuts, meanwhile, draws on John Dewey's concept of emotion-charged spaces to explain the dread so many of us feel when watching Robert Wise's 1963 version of *The Haunting*. Ken Mogg sees a Schopenhauerian worldview embodied in the films of Alfred Hitchcock, especially that philosopher's unique conception of Will. Coeditor Steven Jay Schneider discusses the art of murder, and the rise of films that depict murder as an art form pursued by mad artists of the macabre. J. P. Telotte mobilizes Paul Virilio's ideas concerning the visible and the invisible, of spectacular illusion and "reality," to help plumb the deeper themes in Paul Verhoeven's underappreciated *Hollow Man* (2000). These essays ably illustrate the value of bringing distinctively *philosophical* concepts and problematics to bear on the interpretation and evaluation of both particular horror films and directorial careers.

Another similarity between tragedy and horror is that both genres raise philosophical questions about the meaning and purpose of human existence. That is surely one of the main reasons why both attract so many philosophers. Is horror fundamentally a nihilistic genre, or does it affirm *anything* in its depictions of mayhem and evil? Do monster movies have a deleterious moral effect on their viewers, or does a catharsis occur that is of positive social worth? Our fascination with horror cinema, and the pleasure we take in it, is in the end simply a natural extension of a philosopher's inclination to wonder.

Notes

1. See Robin Wood, "An Introduction to the American Horror Film," reprinted in *Movies and Methods, Volume 2*, ed. Bill Nichols (Berkeley: University of California. Press, 1985), 195-219.

2. Noël Carroll, *The Philosophy of Horror; or, Paradoxes of the Heart* (New York: Routledge, 1990).

The General Theory
of Horrific Appeal

Noël Carroll

[A]n awareness of the paradox of horror had already dawned on 18th-century theorists. The question they asked about tales of terror . . . was in fact part of the more general aesthetic question of how it is possible to derive pleasure from any genre—including not only horror but tragedy as well—whose objects were things that ordinarily cause distress and discomfiture. That is, encountering such things as ghosts or Desdemona's massacre in "real life" would be upsetting rather than entertaining. And, of course, what is disgusting on-screen or or on the page is genuinely disgusting. It is something we would ordinarily seek to avert. So why do we seek it in art and fiction? How does it give us pleasure and/or why does it interest us?

In order to answer these questions, I think it is quite helpful to return to some of the very authors that first asked them—to see what they have to say. I will undoubtedly have to modify and amplify their accounts. However, a review of their thoughts will serve to orient us toward what I believe is at least part of a comprehensive answer to the paradox of horror.

In order to appreciate the way Hume's observations on tragedy can contribute to answering the paradox of horror, it is important to keep in mind that the horror genre, like that of tragedy, most generally takes a narrative form. . . . That horror is often narrative suggests that with much horror, the interest we have and the pleasure that we take may not primarily be in the object of art-horror as such (i.e., in the monster for its own sake). Instead, the narrative may be the crucial locus of our

1

interest and pleasure. For what is attractive—what holds our interest and yields pleasure—in the horror genre need not be, first and foremost, the simple manifestation of the object of art-horror, but the way that manifestation or disclosure is situated as a functional element in an overall narrative structure.

That is, in order to give an account of what is compelling about the horror genre, it may be wrong to ask only what it is about the monster that gives us pleasure, for the interest and pleasure we take in the monster and its disclosure may rather be a function of the way it figures in a larger narrative structure.

Speaking of the presentation of melancholy events by orators, Hume notes that the pleasure derived is not a response to the event as such, but to its rhetorical framing. When we turn to tragedy, plotting performs this function. The interest that we take in the deaths of Hamlet, Gertrude, Claudius, et al. is not sadistic, but is an interest that the plot has engendered in how certain forces, once put in motion, will work themselves out. Pleasure derives from having our interest in the outcomes of such questions satisfied. Hume writes:

> Had you any intention to move a person extremely by the narration of any event, the best method of increasing its effect would be artfully to delay informing him of it, first to excite his curiosity and impatience before you let him into the secret. This is the artifice practiced by Iago in the famous scene of Shakespeare; and every spectator is sensible that Othello's jealousy acquires additional force from his preceding impatience, and that the subordinate passion is here readily transformed into the predominant one.[1]

Hume's idea is that once a tragic, unsettling event is housed in an aesthetic context, with a momentum of its own, the predominant feeling response, in terms of pleasure and interest, attaches to the presentation as a function of the overall, narrative structure. That is, the ostensibly "subordinate passion", but the one keyed to the structure, becomes predominant. Hume notes:

> These instances (and many more might be collected) are sufficient to afford us some insight into the analogy of nature, and to show us, that the pleasure which poets, orators and musicians give us, by exciting grief, sorrow, indignation, compassion, is not so extraordinary and paradoxical as it may at first sight appear. The force of imagination, the energy of expression, the power of numbers, the charms of imitation; all these are naturally of themselves delightful to the mind:

and when the object presented lays also hold of some affection, the pleasure rises upon us by the conversion of this subordinate movement into that which is predominant. The passion, though perhaps naturally, and when excited by the simple appearance of the real object, it may be painful; yet is so smoothed and softened and mollified, when realised by the finer arts that it affords the highest entertainment.[2]

With tragedy, the "affection" Hume thinks takes hold is narrative expectation, which certainly hearkens back to Aristotle's observations about the audience's anticipation of recognition and reversal in plays of that sort. Thus, it is not the tragic event in itself that imparts pleasure, but rather, the way it is worked into the plot...

[T]he mechanics of Hume's transition of a subordinate passion to a predominant one are somewhat unfathomable, if not wrong (since the tragedy of the event and our predictably distressed reaction to it seems to me to be an inseparable element of the narration). However,...the notion that that the aesthetic contrivance of normally upsetting events depends upon their contextualization in structures like narrative, is particularly suggestive with respect to the paradox of horror.

For, as noted, a great deal of the horror genre is narrative. Indeed, I think it is fair to say that, in our culture, horror thrives above all as a narrative form. Thus, in order to account for the interest we take in and the pleasure we take from horror, we may hypothesize that, in the main, the locus of our gratification is not the monster as such but the whole narrative structure in which the presentation of the monster is staged. This, of course, is not to say that the monster is in any way irrelevant to the genre, nor that the interest and pleasure in the genre could be satisfied through and/or substituted by any old narrative. For...the monster is a functional ingredient in the type of narratives found in horror stories, and not all narratives function exactly like horror narratives...

[T]hese stories, with great frequency, revolve around proving, disclosing, discovering, and confirming the existence of something that is impossible, something that defies standing conceptual schemes. It is part of such stories—contrary to our everyday beliefs about the nature of things—that such monsters exist. And as a result, audiences' expectations revolve around whether this existence will be confirmed in the story.

Often this is achieved, as Hume says of narrative "secrets" in general, by putting off the conclusive information that the monster exists for quite a while. Sometimes this information may be deferred till the very end of the fiction. And even where this information is given to the audience right off the bat, it is still generally the case that the human characters in the tale must undergo a process of discovering that the monster exists, which, in turn, may lead to a further process of confirming that discovery in an ensuing scene or series of scenes. That is, the question of whether or not the monster exists may be transformed into the question of whether and when the human characters in the tale will establish the existence of the monster. Horror stories are often protracted series of discoveries: first the reader learns of the monster's existence, then some characters do, then some more characters do, and so on; the drama of iterated disclosure—albeit to different parties—underwrites much horror fiction.[3]

Even in overreacher plots, there is a question of whether the monster exists—i.e., of whether they can be summoned, in the case of demons, or of whether they can be created by mad scientists and necromancers. Furthermore, even after the existence of the monster is disclosed, the audience continues to crave further information abut its nature, its identity, its origin, its purposes, and its astounding powers and properties including, ultimately, those of its weaknesses that *may* enable humanity to do it in.

Thus, to a large extent, the horror story is driven explicitly by curiosity. It engages the audience by being involved in the processes of disclosure, discovery, proof, explanation, hypothesis, and confirmation. Doubt, skepticism, and the fear that belief in the existence of the monster is a form of insanity are predictable foils to the revelation (to the audience or to the characters or both) of the existence of the monster.

Horror stories, in a significant number of cases, are dramas of proving the existence of the monster and disclosing (most often gradually) the origin, identity, purposes, and powers of the monster. Monsters, as well, are obviously the perfect vehicles for engendering this kind of curiosity and for supporting the drama of proof, because monsters are (physically, though generally not logically) impossible beings. They arouse interest and attention by being putatively inexplicable or highly unusual vis-à-vis out standing cultural categories, thereby instilling a desire to learn and to know about them. And since they are also outside of (justifiably) prevailing definitions of what is, they understandably prompt a need for proof (or the fiction of a proof) in the face of skepticism. Monsters are, then, natural subjects for curiosity, and they straightforwardly warrant the ratiocinative energies the plot lavishes upon them.

All narratives might be thought to involve the desire to know—the desire to know at least the outcome of the interaction of the forces made salient in the plot. However, the horror fiction is a special variation on this general narrative motivation, because it has at the center of it something which is given as in principle *unknowable*—something which, *ex hypothesi*, cannot, given the structure of our conceptual scheme, exist, and that cannot have the properties it has. That is why, so often, the real drama in a horror story resides in establishing the existence of the monster and in disclosing its horrific properties. Once this is established, the monster, generally, has to be confronted, and the narrative is driven by the question of whether the creature can be destroyed. However, even at this point, the drama of ratiocination can continue as further discoveries—accompanied by arguments, explanations, and hypotheses—reveal features of the monster that will facilitate or impede the destruction of the creature.

To illustrate this briefly, let us consider Colin Wilson's novel *The Mind Parasites*. The story is presented as a compilation of the chronicle of humanity's confrontation with the mind parasites. This chronicle has been drawn from a number of sources. So, from the perspective of the order of the presentation of the fiction, it begins with the presupposition that the mind parasites—called Tsathogguans—exist. But the exposition proceeds by laying end-to-end the successive discoveries of the existence of these creatures, among other things (such as the discovery of the ruins of an ancient city—a red herring, it turns out). The major character, Gilbert Austin, first discovers his friend's—Karel Weissman's—discovery of the Tsathogguans, which itself comprises a narrative of discovery. Austin then goes through his own process of discovery. In the course of both discoveries, the possibility that the discoverer is insane has to be disposed. Austin then proceeds to convince his colleague Reich of the existence of the mind parasites; this is not difficult, but it allows for more ratiocination and the compiling of a little more evidence.

Austin and Reich then impart their discoveries to a select group of other scientists, many of whom are killed by the mind parasites. But enough survive to share their discoveries eventually with the President of the United States. The plot, in other words, proceeds by means of the revelation of the existence of the Tsathogguans to increasingly larger groups of people. But even when Austin has secured sufficient government aid to confront the mind parasites, further discoveries are mandated by the story. Austin says:

> It was maddeningly frustrating. We possessed the great secret; we had warned the world. And yet, in a fundamental sense, we were as ignorant as ever. Who were these creatures? Where did they come from? What was their ultimate aim? Were they really intelligent, or were they as unintelligent as the maggots in a piece of cheese?

Of course, the reader wants to know the answers to these questions as well, and we stay on board to get them till the end of the plot. Moreover, it is not until then that we learn of the properties of the Tsathogguans (and their relations to the Moon) that make possible their final destruction.

The Mind Parasites contains a good deal more "philosophizing" than many horror fictions, employing a somewhat mystical brand of phenomenology as a weapon against the Tsathogguans in a way that ought to provoke Husserl's return from the dead. But by virtue of being what might be called a narrative of continuous revelation or disclosure, it is representative of a large body of horror fictions.

What is revealed and disclosed, of course, are monsters and their properties. These are appropriate objects of discovery and revelation, just because they are unknown—not only in the sense that the murderer in a detective fiction is unknown, but also because they are outside the bounds of knowledge, i.e., outside our standing conceptual schemes. This, as well, accounts for why their revelation and the disclosure of their properties is so often bound up with processes of proof, hypothesis, argument, explanation (including sci-fi flights of fancy and magical lore about mythological realms, potions, and incantations), and confirmation. That is, because horror fictions are predicated on the revelation of unknown and unknowable—unbelievable and incredible—impossible beings, they often take the form of narratives of discovery and proof. For things unknown in the way of monsters obviously are natural subjects for proof.

Applied to the paradox of horror, these observations suggest that the pleasure derived from horror fiction and the source of our interest in it resides, first and foremost, in the processes of discovery, proof, and confirmation that horror fictions often employ. The disclosure of the existence of the horrific being and of its properties is the central source of pleasure in the genre; once the process of revelation is consummated, we remain inquisitive about whether such a creature can be successfully confronted, and that narrative question sees us through to the end of the story. Here, the pleasure involved is, broadly speaking, cognitive. Hobbes, interestingly enough, thought of curiosity as an appetite of the mind; with the horror fiction, that appetite is whetted by the prospect of knowing the putatively unknowable, and then satisfied through a continuous process of revelation, enhanced by imitation of (admittedly simplistic) proofs, hypotheses, counterfeits of causal reasoning, and explanations whose details and movement intrigue the mind in ways analogous to genuine ones.[4]

Moreover, it should be clear that these particular cognitive pleasures, insofar as they are set in motion by the relevant kind of unknowable beings, are especially well served by horrific monsters. Thus, there is a special functional relationship between the beings that mark off the horror genre and the pleasure and interest that many horror fictions sustain. That interest and that pleasure derive from the disclosure of unknown and impossible beings, just the sorts of things that call for proof, discovery, and confirmation. Therefore, the disgust that such beings evince might be seen as part of the price to be paid for the pleasure of their disclosure. That is, the narrative expectations that the horror genre puts in place is that the being whose existence is in question be something that defies standing cultural categories; thus, disgust, so to say, is itself more or less mandated by the kind of curiosity that the horror narrative puts in place. The horror narrative could not deliver a successful, affirmative answer to its presiding question unless the disclosure of the monster indeed elicited disgust, or was of the sort that was a highly probable object of disgust.

That is, there is a strong relation of consilience between the objects of art-horror, on the one hand, and the revelatory plotting on the other. The kind of plots and the subjects of horrific revelations are not merely compatible, but fit together or agree in a way that is highly appropriate. That the audience is naturally inquisitive about that which is unknown meshes with plotting that is concerned to render the unknown known by processes of discovery, explanation, proof, hypothesis, confirmation, and so on.

Of course, what it means to say that the horrific being is "unknown" here is that it is not accommodated by standing conceptual schemes. Moreover, if Mary Douglas's account of impurity is correct, things that violate our conceptual scheme, by (for example) being interstitial, are things that we are prone to find disturbing. Thus, that horrific beings are predictably objects of loathing is a function of the ways that they violate our classificatory scheme.

If what is of primary importance about horrific creatures is that their very impossibility vis-à-vis our conceptual categories is what makes them function so compellingly in dramas of discovery and confirmation, then their disclosure, insofar as they are categorical violations, will be attached to some sense of disturbance, distress, and disgust. Consequently, the role of the horrific creature in such narratives—where their disclosure captures our interest and delivers pleasure—will simultaneously mandate some probable revulsion. That is, in order to reward our interest by the disclosure of the putatively impossible beings of the plot, said beings ought to be disturbing, distressing, and repulsive in the way that theorists like Douglas predict phenomena that ill fit cultural classifications will be.

So, as a first approximation of resolving the paradox of horror, we may conjecture that we are attracted to the majority of horror fictions because of the way that the plots of discovery and the dramas of proof pique our curiosity, and abet our interest, ideally satisfying them in a way that is pleasurable.[5] But if narrative curiosity about impossible beings is to be satisfied through disclosure, that process must require some element of probable disgust since such impossible beings are, *ex hypothesi*, disturbing, distressful, and repulsive.

One way of making the point is to say that the monsters in such tales of disclosure have to be disturbing, distressful. and repulsive, if the process of their discovery is to be rewarding in a pleasurable way. Another way to get at this is to say that the primary pleasure that narratives of disclosure afford—i.e., the interest we take in them, and the source of their attraction—resides in the processes of discovery, the play of proof, and the dramas of ratiocination that comprise them. It is not that we crave disgust, but that disgust is a predictable concomitant of the disclosing of the unknown, whose disclosure is a desire the narrative instills in the audience and then goes on to gladden. Nor will that desire be satisfied unless the monster defies our conception of nature which demands that it probably engender some measure of repulsion.

In this interpretation of horror narratives, the majority of which would appear to exploit the cognitive attractions of the drama of disclosure, experiencing the emotion of art-horror is not our absolutely primary aim in consuming horror fictions, even though it is a determining feature for identifying membership in the genre. Rather, art-horror is the price we are willing to pay for the revelation of that which is impossible and unknown, of that which violates our conceptual schema. The impossible being does disgust; but that disgust is part of the overall narrative address which is not only pleasurable, but whose potential pleasure depends on the confirmation of the existence of the monster as a being that violates, defies, or problematizes standing cultural classifications. Thus, we are attracted to, and many of us seek out, horror fictions of this sort despite the fact that they provoke disgust, because that disgust is required for the pleasure involved in engaging our curiosity in the unknown and drawing it into the processes of revelation, ratiocination, etc.

Notes

1 David Hume, "Of Tragedy," in *Of the Standard of Taste and Other Essays*, ed. John W. Lenz (Indianapolis: Bobbs-Merrill, 1965), 33–34.

2 *Ibid.*, 35.

3 See J. P. Telotte, "Faith and Idolatry in the Horror Film," in *Planks of Reason: Essays on the Horror Film*, ed. Barry Keith Grant (Metuchen, N.J.: Scarecrow Press, 1984), 25–26.

4 In claiming that the pleasures derived from horror are cognitive in the broad sense—of engaging curiosity—I am attempting to explain why the genre often engages us. I am not attempting to justify the genre as worthy of our attention because it appeals its appeal is cognitive. Nor by saying that it is cognitive, in the special sense of engaging curiosity, am I even implicitly signaling that I think it superior to some other genres whose appeal might be said to be more exclusively emotive.

5 "Ideally" here is meant to take note of the fact that not all such horror fictions are successful.

The Mastery of Hannibal Lecter

Daniel Shaw

> You can't reduce me to a set of influences. You've given up good
> and evil for behaviorism, Officer Starling. You've got everybody in
> moral dignity pants—nothing is ever anybody's fault. Look at
> me…can you stand to say I'm evil?
>
> —Hannibal Lecter[1]

The phenomenon that is Hannibal Lecter is unmatched in the history of
Hollywood. Never has an evil (but clearly mortal) character been so
popular. *Hannibal* (2001) set box office records for a non-holiday
weekend release, and it was one of the few live action films to do over
$200 million in domestic gross. Though *Red Dragon* (2002) didn't do
as well, despite giving Hannibal a much bigger role than he had in the
original Thomas Harris novel, sales of the new DVD version of
Manhunter (1986) are brisk (unlike its original box office take), and a
Criterion edition of *The Silence of the Lambs* (1991) was brought out in
tandem with the much heralded video release of *Hannibal*.

How has such a character enthralled the world? What makes
Lecter's brand of evil so palatable and attractive? Lecter is transformed
from a ruthless serial killer into a beloved protagonist by the third entry
in the series. This essay will examine all three Lecter films (and the
novels on which they are based), seeking to explain our great
fascination with "Hannibal the Cannibal" in terms of the almost
preternatural power he exerts over everyone with whom he comes in
contact.

Previously, and at greater length than is possible here, I have
proposed a catharsis theory of horror-pleasure that focuses on the
vicarious feelings of power that horror films provide their audiences.[2]

10

Influenced as I am by Friedrich Nietzsche's philosophy of the Will to Power, I believe that much of our pleasure in horror films comes from our dual identification with both the threatening antagonists and human protagonists in such works. The astounding feats of the monster or human psychotic are what most attracts us to them, for they exhibit powers and abilities far beyond those of mortal men. It is precisely for this reason that we revel in their penchant for wreaking immeasurable havoc. Sharing in their superhuman acts, we are exhilarated and alarmed by our enjoyment of the forbidden. Our ambivalence is grounded in this tension between our guilty enjoyment of such power and the true terror we would feel if it were us that were being victimized, as well as this dual identification with both the monstrous force and with those who seek to conquer it.

In my view, then, a battle for mastery between human and monster is at the heart of most horror narratives. Following Nietzsche, I will highlight three senses of power in my account of horror-pleasure: power over the self, over the environment, and over one's inferiors. Wresting control in these major areas of our lives is essential to human happiness, which Nietzsche thought of as resulting from a feeling of increasing power. That feeling is most intense when great resistance is overcome. My major thesis is that Hannibal Lecter is one of the most *powerful* human characters in the history of horror and *that* is the primary reason why we are so drawn to him. This essay will analyze the evolving role of Lecter in the trilogy of novels and movies, where he develops from an interesting sidelight into almost the sole narrative and emotional focus.

Red Dragon / Manhunter

In *Manhunter*, Hannibal Lecter plays a relatively peripheral role in the goings on. Will Graham (William Peterson, in his first major role as a crime scene investigator) is unambiguously the protagonist, a tormented man who must identify with the psycho-killers that he targets in order to catch them. Graham tracked Lecter down initially, and Hannibal wants revenge. Graham reconnects with his nemesis in order to get the scent of a psychotic and possible clues as to how to catch Francis Dolarhyde, the so-called Tooth Fairy (named for his habit of biting his victims with his saw-toothed dentures). Lecter sends Graham's address to Dolarhyde, and the hunter becomes the hunted.

The Thomas Harris novel and Michael Mann film diverge at this point. Mann depicts Graham as the traditional male hero, crashing through a picture window to save the life of the blind woman who had become Dolarhyde's lover. In the book, Francis stages his own death for her benefit, then unexpectedly ambushes his adversary at Graham's Florida Keys home (led there by an address sent by Hannibal Lecter). Graham would have died but for his wife, who hooks Dolarhyde with a massive Rapala lure and then blows the intruder away with a handgun. Mann's macho ideology, and traditional Hollywood conventions, apparently would not permit such a gender reversal.

A narrative pattern is set in *Red Dragon* and followed (with interesting variations) in *The Silence of the Lambs*. The protagonist consults Lecter for help in catching *another* serial killer who is on the loose and must be stopped. Will Graham and Clarice Starling are relatively traditional law enforcement officers—the "good guys" after the "bad guys." Both the Red Dragon and Buffalo Bill are undergoing psychic transformations, which drive them to their murderous pursuits.

Agents Graham and Starling have an intuitive link to those they seek, enabling them to anticipate what will happen next. This link troubles Graham, who was institutionalized after his last case and is clearly putting his sanity (as well as his family) on the line in this one. Lecter taunts him with the notion that he *enjoyed* gunning down the target of his last investigation, a particularly violent fellow by the name of Hobbes. Deeply shaken by the experience, Graham retired, only to be reluctantly coaxed back into service by Jack Crawford, his former boss at the FBI. In their first interview, Hannibal tweaks his captor's deepest fear: "The reason you caught me is that we are *just alike*. If you want the scent, *smell yourself*" (that last line was added by screenwriter Michael Mann).

Graham's work on the case reveals that Lecter isn't too far from right. When examining the first crime scene, Graham speaks of his quarry in the third person. As he gets into the criminal's mindset, he shifts to the second person ("you did this, then you did that"). Finally, when he checks out the Jacobi house, he uses first person pronouns exclusively ("The house is mine . . . children mean nothing to me . . . I see you there, and I see me desired by you"), adopting the perspective of the murderer to understand the psychotic dream that motivates such horrific acts.

In creating a narrative momentum that never lets up, *Red Dragon* is the best novel of the trilogy. Dolarhyde is far more threatening, powerful, and sympathetic than either Buffalo Bill or *Hannibal's*

Mason Verger. Born with a severely cleft palate, and unimaginably abused as a child, Francis harbors feelings of total inadequacy that lead him to transform himself into the Red Dragon. His murders are twisted expressions of a desperate need to be loved and accepted. He places mirrors in the eyes of his victims, so that he may see himself triumphant in their eyes. His dominant image, tattooed across his chest, is the eponymous William Blake painting, *The Great Red Dragon and the Woman Clothed with the Sun* with the Dragon depicted as rampant and exalting in its power. Focused almost solely on the visual, Dolarhyde chooses his victims from the home movies his photographic studio develops. He also films his intrusions, so that he may relive the atrocities over and over again (echoing the central theme of Michael Powell's *Peeping Tom* [1960]).

But Francis becomes peculiarly sympathetic when he gets emotionally involved with a blind fellow employee at his photographic plant. Not put off by his imposing size and facial deformity, she responds to his attraction to her, and is deeply moved when he takes her to the zoo to pet a tranquilized tiger (photographing nocturnal creatures there is his explanation for seeking film that works in total darkness, which led to his meeting her). Reba McClane (Joan Allen in the film) makes the first move when he invites her over for dinner, and Francis has what is apparently the only satisfying sexual encounter with another person he ever enjoyed. As a result, his psyche bifurcates into Francis and the Dragon, who fight it out for the life of Reba.

Tom Noonan's performance in *Manhunter* heightens our ambivalence; his soft, almost effeminate voice provides a striking contrast to his menacing appearance. The Tooth Fairy is, by turns, ruthless and touching, and we never lose sight of his tortured upbringing once it is revealed. By contrast, Mann's film only alludes to the etiology of Dolarhyde's psychosis in Graham's passing admission to Crawford (Dennis Farina) that while he feels for the abused child, he will not hesitate to shoot the crazed adult.

A phone conversation between Lecktor *sic* and Graham (which does not take place in the novel) is explicit about the theme on which I am focusing. After gleefully rehearsing the details of the latest church collapse, and how many of the faithful had been slaughtered as they prayed (the old Problem of Evil, one of his favorite themes), Lecktor puts it this way:

> L: We don't invent our natures, they're issued to us along with our lungs and our pancreas and everything else. Why fight it?

G: Fight what?

L: Did you really feel so depressed when you shot Mr. Garrett Jacob Hobbes? I didn't know you then, but I think that you probably did. But it wasn't the act itself that got you down. Didn't you really feel so bad because killing him felt so good? And why shouldn't it feel good? It must feel good to God, he does it all the time . . .

G: Why does it feel good, Dr. Lecktor?

L: It feels good, Will, because God has power and if one does what God does enough times, one will become as God is. God's a champ...he always stays ahead.

In the novel, Will is denied the pleasure of slaying the Dragon himself. Graham deduces that Dolarhyde saw the home movies of his victims, and traces him to the St. Louis plant where they were developed. But rather than save Reba, he is tricked into complaisance. The Dragon stages his own fiery death for Reba's sake, leaving behind a uniquely characteristic set of dentures. He then uses the information Lecktor provided to track Graham down in his turn. Pouncing just when Graham feels most secure, the Dragon drives an Army knife through his cheek, and would have finished him off but for the wife's timely intervention.

Mann's film provides the more conventional climax, with Graham mastering the Dragon in a final shootout. Lecktor disappears after the previously quoted dialogue, and remains in his whitewashed institution. Deftly underplayed by Brian Cox, Hannibal is a presence throughout both the film and the novel. Though his appearances were severely limited, his ability to strike at Graham (through Dolarhyde) from his prison cell, and his focus on the great ironies of existence that raise the Problem of Evil, left an indelible impression. Despite the commercial failure of *Manhunter*, Harris's next novel (which focused on Lecter to a much greater extent) was to be adapted by Jonathan Demme and Ted Tally into the most successful and critically acclaimed horror film in Hollywood history.

The Silence of the Lambs

Though Dr. Lecter was depicted as thoughtful, cunning, and resourceful in *Manhunter*, he truly came into his own in *Silence*. Anthony Hopkins' Oscar-winning performance as Lecter is the sick heart and soul of the film, "in his own way, as riveting and influential as Anthony Perkins in *Psycho*."[3] Ostensibly a detective thriller about catching a serial killer, *Silence* is really more focused on the relationship between Hannibal and Clarice Starling (Jodie Foster, also deservedly rewarded with the Oscar). Mentor, substitute father figure, potential lover, and psychoanalyst, Lecter probes Starling's mind, demanding personal revelations in return for hints as to how to capture Buffalo Bill. Their four face-to-face confrontations, and the telephone conversation that forms the coda to the film, are absolutely engrossing and reward countless viewings.

On first impression, Lecter describes her as being "one generation away from poor white trash," dismissing her out of hand until a fellow inmate defiles her with his semen. Outraged at this unmannerly act, Lecter recompenses her with the clue that leads to the discovery of the head of Benjamin Raspail, Bill's first victim in the film version. As she elatedly relates her discovery, Lecter offers to help her catch Bill, in return for a transfer to a cell with a view. Throughout their exchanges, in extreme close-up, he is (in the words of Teresa de Lauretis), a being "awesome to behold, whose power to capture vision, to lure the gaze, is conveyed in the very etymon of the word 'monster.' "[4]

In that third dialogue, Lecter goes straight for the emotional jugular, asking Starling about her most painful memory from childhood (a psychoanalyst's question, indeed). When she frankly describes the death of her father (going against Jack Crawford's express warning not to let Lecter into her head), Hannibal is immediately impressed: "I think it would be quite something to know you in private life."

In her insightful discussion of *Silence* in *The Naked and the Undead: Evil and the Appeal of Horror*, Cynthia Freeland explains our fascination with Lecter in three ways: 1) he functions as both mentor and suitor to our heroine, 2) he is so exceptionally successful in bucking the system, and 3) he possesses striking aesthetic sensibilities.[5] I agree with her on all counts, but would like to augment her explanation by claiming that it is Lecter's complete control over every situation in which he finds himself that is the real key to his magnetism.

Only the extreme watchfulness of Barney (Frankie Faison), the orderly assigned to Lecter's case at the state hospital, had kept the monster imprisoned for all those years. What Hannibal achieves in the course of the film takes one's breath away. The wily doctor gets masturbator Miggs to kill himself by swallowing his tongue, wheedles Starling's deepest secrets out of her (while helping her catch Buffalo Bill in the process), escapes from a maximum security lockup that is crawling with police and FBI agents, kills five people without sustaining a scratch, and tracks down his nemesis, hospital director Dr. Frederick Chilton (Anthony Heald), in a remote Caribbean locale. His last chilling words to Clarice are that he must hang up the phone because "I'm having an old friend for dinner."

It is crucial to appreciating his attraction to note that, in the course of all three films (with the exception of Mason Verger's flashback), Lecter kills only when it is necessary for his escape, or in retaliation against his captors and pursuers, and never simply for the sheer pleasure of it. His ambush of the two guards is executed with a dancer's grace, expressive of his much commented-upon aesthetic taste. Stripping off Pembry's face and placing it over his own head is a brilliant stroke. Everything he does is effortless; his heart rate barely accelerating when he eats the tongue of the infirmary's nurse early on during his period of confinement. This absolute self-possession under pressure is awesome, and is generally thought to be an admirable quality.

Like Nietzsche's *Übermensch*, Lecter is ruthless without being needlessly sadistic (much more on this theme later). He doesn't enjoy lording it over the weak or innocent. Having gone beyond all conventional notions of good and evil, he develops a personal code of honor that leads him to respect outsiders like himself. When practical, he targets only those who deserve it—the "free-range rude" as he described them to Barney in *Hannibal*. His victims are uniformly unsympathetic.

Freeland, too, acknowledges the affinity with Nietzsche: "Lecter has consciously formed himself and aimed to transvalue values in the Nietzschean sense, putting himself outside of conventional morality with an omnivorous aesthetic all his own."[6] As a feminist film theorist, however, she is most concerned with condemning the sexist and patriarchal nature of the relationship between Clarice and Lecter, refuting a critic who had called *Silence* "the perfect feminist movie." But it is precisely Lecter's paternalistic *control* that bothers her so much. Lecter's complete mastery of every situation skews the dramatic weight of the film too far in his favor. When he disappears for its final half hour, only to resurface in the coda, his absence is glaring. Clarice's climactic descent into the labyrinthine maze of Bill's lair was gripping, but the shootout itself came off as unrealistic because the viewer has been denied the crucial background information (provided in the novel) that Starling could squeeze off more rounds per minute than anyone in her class.

By contrast, the final crane shot of a red-haired Anthony Hopkins disappearing into a South American crowd in the wake of his next meal (Dr. Chilton) made the hairs on the back of my neck stand on end when I first saw it. My intense pleasure at his survival is one of my fonder memories of the cinema of the 1990s. It was clear from the cheers in the audience that I wasn't the only one who was rooting for Lecter and welcomed his escape.

Much has also been made of Hannibal's black humor, and his "fava beans" threat became one of the most popular taglines of the decade. Relishing his existence, he embodies a willingness to live dangerously and a witty lightness of which Nietzsche could only have approved. His discriminating aesthetic and culinary tastes, increasingly foregrounded as the trilogy develops, also mark him as a uniquely civilized serial killer.

Hannibal

Both Thomas Harris's novel and Ridley Scott's film suffer by comparison to their distinguished predecessors. Forced by Lecter's escape to abandon his previous narrative template, Harris had no triangular plot with which to fascinate us. Crucially, Starling and Lecter only meet at the end of the novel, and then hook up in a fashion that generated so much controversy that the powers that be decided to exorcize it from the film version.

Clarice, clearly the focus of our identification in *Silence*, can only seek Lecter from afar for most of *Hannibal*, while busily defending herself from being targeted by Justice Department honcho Paul Krendler (Ray Liotta). Krendler wants to sell Lecter to Mason Verger for five million dollars in Congressional campaign funds. Verger offered the bounty because the good doctor (who was his therapist at the time) slipped him a hallucinogen and convinced him to cut off his face in strips and feed it to his dogs. Florentine Inspector Rinaldo Pazzi (Giancarlo Giannini) wants the money to drench his young wife in luxuries. The Sardinians hired by Verger to capture Hannibal want to get rich by feeding him to the pigs, while recording his consumption on video in the process. Dr. Lecter (a more playful though less sleek Anthony Hopkins) triumphs easily, leaving their slaughtered bodies in his wake.

The aesthetic set piece of this film (correlate to the bludgeoning of the guards in *Silence*) is Lecter's confrontation with Pazzi and his

Sardinian henchmen. Applying for the directorship of the library of the Uffizi gallery, Hannibal gives an inspired lecture on the classic punishment for avarice, hanging and disembowelment. He shows slides of a painting of Pazzi's Renaissance forbear, who met just such a fate outside the very room in which Lecter was then speaking. After wowing his distinguished interviewers, he guts the Inspector like a fish and dangles him out the same window as his traitorous ancestor.

Far less satisfying is the Grand Guignol ending where Hannibal feeds Krendler his own brain one slice at a time, with Clarice voicing encouragement and the victim's higher functions going haywire in a manner reminiscent of the dismantled Hal in *2001: A Space Odyssey* (1968). Part of the problem with *Hannibal* is the one-sidedness of the contest. Other than Agent Starling, Lecter makes fools out of all who chase him. It his only her intricate, computerized scheme to track his highly expensive tastes that permits them to anticipate that he will bring her a particularly expensive bottle of wine for her birthday (its vintage was her birth year) and set their trap. Lecter gets tripped up when he gets whimsical, and he is tranquilized and abducted as he tries to slip the bottle of wine into Clarice's high-powered Mustang. Verger's henchmen are poised to feed Hannibal to a host of man-eating pigs until Clarice bursts upon the scene. She cuts him loose and helps slay his enemies, though he must carry her unconscious body away from the Verger farm after she is shot with two tranquilizer darts.

If anything, Lecter is more superhuman in *Hannibal* than in *Silence*. He doesn't utter a sound when shocked with a cattle prod in the eye, or burnt with a red-hot poker. As he is escaping with Starling in his arms, he stares down the wild and ferocious swine, who sense no fear within him. By the end, he has slain his predecessor at the library, Pazzi the Italian inspector, Mason Verger (and all but one of his Sardinian henchmen), and Paul Krendler of the Justice Department. No one is left to continue the hunt.

In Harris's novel, Lecter and Starling become lovers in a conclusion that many found utterly implausible (reportedly Jodie Foster refused to do the sequel because she loathed the book, which was understandable considering the degree to which her character is marginalized). Hannibal treats Clarice with an array of therapeutic psychochemicals, and exorcizes the demon of her father by exhuming his bones for her to see. After a second helping of brain ("Please, may I have some more?"), she drips wine on her naked breast and proffers it to him.

Dr. Doemling, the psychoanalyst that Verger consulted to analyze the workings of Lecter's mind, discounted the possibility of a true relationship developing between the detective and her quarry (Barney was right to ridicule the pompous fool). But he did make one insightful observation:

> I'm not proposing a kind of sympathy between two orphans, Mr. Verger. This is not about sympathy. Sympathy does not enter here. And mercy is left bleeding in the dust. Listen to me. What a common experience of being an orphan gives Dr. Lecter is simply a better ability to understand her, and ultimately control her. This is all about control.[7]

My initial reaction to their coupling was as skeptical as Doemling's (and most of the critics) but upon reflection I find this turn of affairs to be a natural one. Their relationship always had sexual undertones, with Lecter constantly interjecting jibes about Crawford "fucking" her, or asking if her Montana guardian forced her into sodomy or fellatio. When she visits him in the lockup in Memphis, he quips "people will think we're in love," and their touch at the end of that emotionally intense interview is electrifying. To those who believe that Starling would never have done it, one can only note that Lecter was bending her will with hypnotism and chemicals. Starling's total disillusionment with the FBI, resulting (with Krendler's help) from her failure to achieve the advancement for which she longed, would also make her vulnerable to such influence.

On Lecter's part, his infatuation had existed at least as long as the comment in *Silence* that it would be really something to get to know her. Impressed with both her intelligence and her honesty, Lecter recognizes that she is the only character in his experience that is even close to being his equal. Sexually active in his former life as a Baltimore analyst, he left behind several female acquaintances that had nothing but good things to say about him, and all showed a discretion that seemed to testify to the personal charisma of the man. One must also remember how long it had been since Lecter had seen a woman of any kind, and how much is made of Clarice's beauty throughout both novels. Besides, Lecter is never depicted as the kind of out-of-control schizo that is likely to be impotent as well.

No doubt the studio, and director Ridley Scott, backed off from Harris's original conclusion because of the howls of outrage such a development might have raised among the champions of political correctness (a similarly disastrous omission, of Verger's butch sister Margot, was motivated by Scott's professed unwillingness to deal in controversial lesbian stereotypes). Lecter's psychological and chemical seduction of Starling is the final act of a man totally in control of his situation. Naturally, this is an outrage to feminists, but when we are talking about a cannibalistic serial killer, it seems somewhat odd to excoriate him for his sexism.

Both the novel and the film version of *Hannibal* are inferior in conception to *Silence*, in part because Lecter seems to lose a lot of the aura of evil that made him so fascinating. Everyone he kills (save the library director that preceded him) deserves it, and when first we see him in Florence, all he wants is to be left alone in his archives. He had even stopped murdering for pleasure in order to be less conspicuous. He only acts in self-defense, and if he retains his macabre sense of how best and most aesthetically to dispose of his adversaries, that only makes him more endearing. What is missing is that sense of unmotivated evil, that Satanic streak present in *Silence* (not to mention that fact that Hopkins had turned into a somewhat pudgy sexagenarian in the intervening decade).

Lecter as Übermensch: Master Morality

Nitimur in vetitum (We strive for the forbidden)[8]

There are a plethora of Nietzsche commentators to choose from (more every day), but one of my favorites has always been Harold Alderman, and his little book *Nietzsche's Gift*. There, he offers one of the best glosses on the concept of Master Morality that I have ever read, and his contrasting typology of the virtues of Slave and Master morality is very useful in the present context. But first, a fundamental distinction on the level of metaethics must be drawn, which marks that typology as more than simply an outline of competing sets of personal virtues.

Alderman notes that one of the basic differences between these two value systems is that masterly types recognize (and embrace the fact) that they are the source of their own values, while slaves seek some absolutist structure (grounded in God or a benign concept of nature) that underlies their evaluations, unable to shoulder the heavy burden of self-creation. While admitting the artificiality of boiling down Nietzsche's conception to a checklist of character traits, Alderman offers the following catalogue:

The primary distinguishing features of master morality are:
1. expresses anger directly
2. creative
3. self-directive
4. this-worldly
5. self-aware
6. proud (*not* vain)
7. egoistic
8. experimental
9. aristocratic
10. discrete (masked)
11. morality of persons
12. strong willed
13. good (strength) vs. bad (weakness)[9]

Two other traits are needed to complete the list. Ruthlessness is crucial to the successful master (i.e., the willingness to do what is necessary to achieve one's goals) even when this involves harm to others. A masterly figure is impervious to the moral demand not to use others merely as a means to an end, so he also avoids the paralyzing burden of guilt and regret. Having seen through the conventional nature of all moral values, he pursues his own priorities without hesitance or remorse.

Dr. Lecter is most creative in the aestheticization of violence, and in the clever ways he enacts his own brand of poetic justice. In a scene omitted from the film, he sees a video at a gun show of an obnoxious hunter known to the game wardens as a poacher. Coming upon the lawbreaker carving up a deer killed before the start of the season, Lecter puts a crossbow dart in the unfortunate man's brain, then dresses the hunter out more artfully than the deer.

Certainly, Hannibal expresses his anger directly. Rather than repressing his vengeful urges, he visits them on *all* who have crossed him, whether it be Will Graham, Dr. Chilton, Rinaldo Pazzi, Mason Verger, or Paul Krendler. No one could be more self-directed. His cannibalism flaunts one of the most basic taboos in all culture. He revels in his unconventionality and in his total refusal to submit to any system, cultural, or institutional.

Decidedly this-worldly, Lecter scoffs at faith in God. Like many dark characters before him, he is fascinated with the problem of evil. He sees only two possibilities:: either a highly imperfect and bloodthirsty creator God exists, or the universe is mere random chance and entropy. In either case, no absolute moral standards can be justified, and one is free to live as one likes, subject only to the necessity of arbitrary physical laws. As Barney succinctly responds when asked by Clarice what Lecter believes in: "Chaos."[10]

Hannibal is extremely self-aware. He makes no apologies for his conduct, caring only for what he himself thinks, and (at least in *Silence*) proudly owning his responsibility for the evil that he does. His world view seems to correspond to Friedrich Nietzsche's in *Beyond Good and Evil*, especially in this (in)famous passage from the Ninth Part, "What Does 'Distinguished' Mean?":

> Here one must think radically to the very root of things, and ward off all weakness of sensibility. Life itself is essentially assimilation, injury, violation of the foreign and weaker, suppression, hardness, the forcing of one's own forms on something else, ingestion and—at least in its mildest form—exploitation.[11]

Lecter's proud and aristocratic bearing is the mark of a soul that feels it is superior, and makes no bones about acting as such. He does not suffer fools gladly, seldom responding to the many visitors that sought to pick his brain in the basement of the Baltimore State Hospital for the Criminally Insane.

Lecter meant it when he said it would be something to get to know Starling, and in *Hannibal* he once again proved to be a man of his word. Dr. Doemling makes too much of an "avuncular" attitude the doctor was supposed to have toward Starling, while Barney gets at the heart of his attraction to her: "In the asylum, Dr. Lecter responded to her when she held onto herself, stood there wiping come off her face, and did her job. In the letters he calls her a warrior, and points out that she saved that child in the shoot-out. He admires and respects her courage and her discipline."[12]

Though a thoroughly masked individual (at times even more so than when he dons Pembry's face), Lecter has a personal code of conduct that he does not break. An expert dissembler to those unworthy of his respect (the weak), he is the model of honesty and candor to people that matter. Neither Clarice nor Barney ever worried much about Lecter coming after them *because he said he wouldn't*. He has his own brand of courtesy, and nothing angers him as much as crass rudeness. No one has a stronger will or a more stoic ability to endure pain. He may dish it out, but he can take it.

In fact, Lecter in Florence seems natural, since he would have been quite at home dabbling in the Machiavellian intrigues of the Medici palace. In many ways, he is a throwback to that earlier, more bloodthirsty era, which Nietzsche praised for its aesthetic achievements (linking them to the aristocratic ruthlessness of the Florentines). But while Hannibal may have been a masterly individual, he would hardly qualify as the *Übermensch* that Nietzsche sought to herald in the next evolutionary stage in the progress of the human species. Cannibalism is an atavism (to use a favorite Nietzschean epithet) and can hardly be seen as particularly creative, in the positive sense of that term.

This highlights a widespread confusion in Nietzsche interpretation as well. When Nietzsche outlines the essential distinction between slave-type and master-type moralities in *Beyond Good and Evil*, some commentators have misidentifed the traits of the masters as identical to the traits of the *Übermenschen* that he calls "the meaning of the earth" in *Thus Spoke Zarathustra*. They are importantly different (although more similar to each other than either is to any type of slave morality), and Alderman once again elucidates that difference succinctly. After quoting the brilliant passage from *Zarathustra* that discusses a thousand peoples and their diverse goals, he observes: "But these lines also tell us that the goal of master morality is still lacking; we must each discover both the master and the slave within ourselves, so that the master—and thus our human self—can be created."[13] It is not enough to answer the question "Free *from* what?" as Hannibal clearly can. "Free *for* what?" is the really hard question.

Now, I hope it will strike the reader as stating the obvious, but Hannibal Lecter is no role model, nor did his creators intend to portray him as one. My point has been that he is one of the most powerful characters in recent cinema, and our great pleasure in seeing him do what is forbidden comes from our vicariously sharing in that power. Somewhat of a throwback, he puts us in touch with the rare strain of humanity that Nietzsche believed was instrumental in helping found aristocratic societies:

> Let us tell ourselves without indulging ourselves how every superior culture got its *start*. Men whose nature was still natural, barbarians in every frightening sense of the word, men of prey, men still in possession of unbroken strength of will and power drives—such men threw themselves upon weaker, better-behaved, more peaceable races . . . The distinguished class in the beginning was always the barbarian caste; their superiority lay not primarily in their physical but in their

psychic power; they were more whole as human beings (which on every level also means "more whole as beasts").[14]

Such a man wanders like a tiger among the sheep that populate the contemporary cinematic landscape. Though he affirms nothing new, positive or progressive for the human race, Lecter acts as a tonic in an emasculated culture that requires us to apologize whenever our lusts or ambitions are all too obviously showing.

Notes

1. Thomas Harris, *The Silence of the Lambs* (New York: St. Martin's Paperbacks, 1988), 21.

2. Daniel Shaw "Power, Horror and Ambivalence," *Film and Philosophy*, Special Edition on Horror (2001): 1–12.

3. David Thomson, in his profile of Anthony Hopkins for the *Blockbuster Video CD -ROM*.

4. Teresa De Lauretis, *Alice Doesn't: Feminism Semiotics, Cinema* (Bloomington: Indiana University Press, 1984), 109.

5. Cynthia Freeland, *The Naked and the Undead: Evil and the Appeal of Horror* (Boulder: Westview Press, 2000), 205–207.

6. Freeland, *The Naked and the Undead*, 206–207.

7. Thomas Harris, *Hannibal* (New York: Random House, 1999), 268.

8. One of Nietzsche's favorite Latin phrases. Friedrich Nietzsche, *Beyond Good and Evil*, Section 259 in the Ninth Part, "What Does 'Distinguished' Mean?" in *Nietzsche Selections*, ed. Richard Schacht (New York: Macmillan, 1993), 192.

9. Harold Alderman, *Nietzsche's Gift* (Athens: Ohio University Press, 1977), 66.

10. Harris, *Hannibal*, 90.

11. Nietzsche, *Beyond Good and Evil*, 229.

12. Harris, *Hannibal*, 277.

13. Alderman, *Nietzsche's Gift*, 67.

14. Nietzsche, *Beyond Good and Evil*, 228–29.

The Lived Nightmare: Trauma, Anxiety, and the Ethical Aesthetics of Horror

Elizabeth Cowie

The theatre, which holds 2646, was so crowded I had trouble finding a seat. Even dubbed, *Eyes Without a Face* . . . is austere and elegant . . . It's a symbolist attack on science and the ethics of medicine, and though I thought this attack as simple-minded in its way as the usual young poet's denunciation of war or commerce, it is in some peculiar way a classic of horror. . . . Even though I thought its intellectual pretensions silly, I couldn't shake off the exquisite, dread images.
But the audience seemed to be reacting to a different movie. They were so noisy the dialogue was inaudible; they talked until the screen gave promise of bloody ghastliness. Then the chatter subsided again in noisy approval of the gory scenes. When a girl in the film seemed about to be mutilated, a young man behind me jumped up and down and shouted encouragement. "Somebody's going to get it," he sang out gleefully. The audience, which was, I'd judge, predominantly between 15 and 25, and at least a third feminine, was . . . pleased and excited by the most revolting and obsessive images. . . . But nobody seemed to care what the movie was about or be interested in the logic of the plot.

—Pauline Kael[1]

Kael's amusing account of watching Georges Franju's *Les Yeux sans visage* (*Eyes Without a Face*) on its release in America in 1959 deftly articulates the paradox that the enjoyment of the horror film has posed to critics and theorists in her contrast between the film's silly intellectual pretensions[2] and its "exquisite, dread images" whose power she cannot "throw off." It also reproduces the commonplace, and complaisant, assumption of many critics, that there are two kinds of audiences for horror: one, like Kael herself, which is moved not by the story or plot but by the images, and another—the majority at the screening Kael attended—which, while also dismissive of "what the movie was about" or "the logic of the plot" (though she terms this as a matter of not caring, in contrast to her own critical assessment of its silliness!), is not similarly in thrall to its images. Instead, this second audience is pleased and excited by the images, which are now no longer exquisite and dreadful, but "revolting and obsessive." It is as if Kael saw, to use Wittgenstein's famous example, the duck in the image while the rest of the audience saw the rabbit. While Kael can only imagine the rabbit that the other audience sees, she also implies a—moral—superiority in seeing the duck (unable to shake off the "exquisite, dread, images") rather than the rabbit (excited enjoyment of the revolting images). This essay explores the issues Kael raises here about how we may be moved by the horror film, together with assumptions of causality and morality in relation to its pleasures and unpleasures. These two ways to view horror do indeed constitute an illustration of the alternative forms of image recognition that Wittgenstein is concerned with in his example.[3]

Works of horror, and perhaps especially horror films, are singular in their impact on audiences in two opposed ways: successful horror films succeed in horrifying both those who love the horror of horror films and those who loathe the horror of horror films. It is a cult form to a greater extent than perhaps any other popular genre, with a devoted following of viewers who seek and enjoy the experience of horror in the cinema while others—myself included—avoid and abhor the same experience. While much recent discussion has concerned the pleasure or pleasures of the horror film, my starting point will be its unpleasures.

The "horror" of the horror film, just as much as horror in everyday life, involves both objects of horror—the horrible—and a psychical response, but one which is not simply "caused" by the horribleness of the object. Many, but not all, of us are horrified by spiders, or by the sight of blood, while the sight of the horrific—a badly injured car crash victim, for example—can prompt an extreme physical response such as vomiting or fainting, which is a reflex or automatic response triggered by seeing a certain kind of object or scene, or by hearing or touch. Indeed, the first screenings of *Eyes Without a Face* in Edinburgh are reported to have produced fainting among some of the audience.[4]

Neither spiders nor blood are in themselves horrific, yet they may become—in common parlance—phobic objects. In the case of arachnophobia, the victim is often also afraid of *killing* the terrifying object. In feeling horror, we are responding to the object recognized *as horrible*, although it is not so intrinsically, or even universally. The question I want to address, therefore, is how to understand the capacity of humans to experience horror traumatically, to be emotionally affected by the horrific and thus to experience unpleasure. I will draw upon psychoanalytic theories of trauma and anxiety, as two sorts of psychological unpleasure, to explore the attraction of unpleasure in the horror film.

The very term "pleasure" is itself extremely imprecise and frequently imbricated in two problematic assumptions: first, that humans have a straightforward capacity for pleasure that is clearly distinguishable from unpleasure; and second, that freely choosing to do something implies we take pleasure in it (either directly or indirectly). Moral discourses, which draw on these assumptions, involve a characterization of pleasure as proper or improper, as good or evil. Improper and evil pleasures were once just sins, but are now also (or instead) considered to be morally inhuman. Audiences that are drawn to performances of horror are assumed to find satisfaction, pleasure, or enjoyment in the experience. If, as good human beings, we abhor such acts of violence and terror against others, how can we understand such pleasure except as inhuman? Should we adopt the characterization (as moralists have often done) that such behavior is *depraved*, that is, that the brutish possibilities in human nature have gained the upper hand in these instances, either due to ignorance and lack of education, or to an innate human nature that has been insufficiently civilized?

To cheer and clap at the painful and murderous mutilation of another human being is, surely, an obscenity. Yet public performances of horror are also social enactments of community, whether organized as sports or entertainments, as scenes of public justice or as social rituals.[5] As entertainments enacted in reality, the Roman amphitheater, the bullfight, or boxing, each afford an arena for the performance of endeavor and struggle—a mise-en-scene for heroism, fear, and anguish in the face of mutilation and death, or its possibility, within a temporal frame, thus giving rise to suspense. In societies founded and sustained by military conquest and domination, the dignifying of violent death through notions of valor, courage, and skill employed in the struggle to avoid such an outcome may be understood as a sign of humanity rather than inhumanity. In modern Western societies, such performances have increasingly come to be viewed as objectionable, and are no longer identified as practices of the civilized but of the brutish, giving rise to the banning of animal hunting and calls for the ending of sports such as boxing. It is precisely as brutish, however, that counter-movements defending such practices have made their case, with the presumption that men, or at least *real* men, require outlets for the violence and aggression innately predestined by flow of testosterone.

In public punishments, the victims are, of course, justly abused. Here too, nevertheless, contemporary accounts refer to the fortitude—and sometimes the defiance—of the punished as positive and redeeming features, while the exhibition of fear on the part of the thief or murderer is seen as cowardly and hence proof of guilt, and thus also of the justness of the punishment. The presentation of the physical power of the crown or state over its subjects or citizens in the public punishment is no doubt a central reason for such performances, involving a justice that requires penalty in kind, as an eye for an eye, but also as the subjection of the body to salutary torment in a public display, ostensibly as a deterrent to other would-be perpetrators.[6]

It is the cinema that now provides the most widely consumed public performances of horror. While its scenes of horror, as fiction, might be expected to be exempt from the changed ethical view of public performances of the horrifying, in making ubiquitous what was once exceptional and in their very realism, cinema's performances of horror are also deemed depraved and dehumanizing. The moral—and political—requirement to distinguish between the real and the illusory is central to modern Western culture, yet the role of cinema and photography has been equivocal here, enabling both greater realism and greater illusionism. What is held to be execrable in both fiction and reality is the gratuity of the violence and suffering that such public performances orchestrate. That in fiction film no one actually dies, or is hurt,[7] is irrelevant here insofar as fictional violence has no purpose except to entertain! In this view, those who seek such imaginary depictions, are held to be *enjoying the suffering of others* as if they were real.[8] The difference between reality and fiction is elided here, and the corollary of this so-called paradox of fiction is to censor fiction as if it were reality. The assumption here, again, is that our participation as spectators in scenes of violence, real or fictional, is to also enjoy, which is always conventionally understood as a sadistic enjoyment.

Unpleasure and Pleasure in Horror

What, then, is this supposed pleasure we take in horror? Rather than attempt to posit a positive pleasure in horror, such as the gratification of our curiosity proposed by Noël Carroll,[9] I suggest (following Freud) that pleasure, or satisfaction, is dependent on a previous unpleasure in order for a recognizable *change* in the state of the subject, or organism, to be experienced. If we consider the role of *suspense* in narrative, we can see the way that a certain unpleasure leads to pleasure, for the suspenseful places us as subject to the anxiety of not knowing the outcome or effect of events already narrated and known. The suspended answer institutes a path to pleasure in the answer to be known. Narrative suspense introduces a structural unpleasure of the suspended answer—structural in the sense that it is not the *answer* that will assuage unpleasure, but the *answering*. Thus, to finally know the outcome—whether horrible or happy—is itself satisfying. Pleasure is not *caused* by unpleasure, rather pleasure might be described as the cessation of unpleasure. And this is the (cognitivist) theory Freud proposed.

Two distinct types of "recognition" are put forward in Freud's theory. The first is the recognition of unpleasure, such as hunger or pain, which will produce a reflex action or biologically automatic response by the organism, either by resuming feeding or by flinching and moving away from the cause of pain. However, what Freud, and current work on the processes of the brain, are concerned with is not such automatic responses, but rather those which deal with *the anticipation* of either unsatisfaction—the danger of a predator, the potential of hunger—or the perception of a possible pleasure. The cognition, that is, of a possible *altered* state. Such a cognition depends upon memory as a perception of time, of before and after, of *recognition*. The genetic disposition to such remembering or learning and the consequences for "natural selection" arising from such recollections can only be guessed at. This second form of knowing unpleasure/pleasure, which arises with memory, was referred to by Freud as *trieb*, or drive, as distinct from *instinkt*, involving the simplest form of memory, namely repetition in the drive to re-experience satisfaction.

Such a satisfaction, or pleasure, is not emotion as *aesthesis* in the sense traditionally used in aesthetics—as the knowledge derived from the senses together with the sensational or bodily response made to that knowledge or cognition.[10] The term adopted by psychoanalysis here is *affect*, which both descriptively designates the emotional repercussions of an experience, and (more important) recognizes the way in which the emotional response can become detached from the experience and come to be felt in relation to other experiences or objects, or even in the absence of any such objects. Affect is therefore not only the emotion aroused by an experience, but also a feeling that arises as a result of a mental and (perhaps unconscious) process of thought in response and reaction to an experience.[11] Affects are in some sense always unreasonable, that is, not fully justified by the empirical circumstances of the experience.

Anxiety, for example, is different from fear because it exceeds the response proper to the circumstance, or because it is experienced even where there is no ostensible cause for fear or its anticipation. Fear will provoke an instinctual response of flight or a countering aggressive reaction, such as a baring of teeth in animals as a warning response, whereas anxiety gives rise to dread. This excessive or inappropriate aspect to the feeling alerts us to a psychical process through which an ideational representative has arisen—anxiety as the perception of a threat not to the organism, which would be fear, but to the *idea of the self*, the *imaginary ego* (i.e., the self as thought), as the imagined unity and conceptualization of the disparate bodily experiences of the organism. One is no longer an experiencing organism, simply, but an entity that apprehends itself as subject to disparate bodily sensations that are nevertheless experienced within or across a continuous body.

Apprehension is thus now not just of a sensation but of sensing in relation to specific but different sites that are imaginatively apprehended as contiguous and bounded, precisely related *as* bodily. Furthermore, in imagining itself, the subject can imagine itself as experiencing, and imagine the possibility of sensation, of a feeling coming to be apparent on or within the body. Such an anticipation might be cognitively triggered by an assessment of likelihood of outcome—the approaching mother as the probable source of bodily gratifications of feeding, etc., or it might arise in the absence of any such potential empirical sources or causes, namely it might arise as desire. The imagined result anticipated may, of course, be of a dreaded outcome, and hence unpleasurable. Freud distinguished between realistic anxiety as a fear of an anticipated danger and which always has an object, and neurotic anxiety that is "anxiety about an unknown danger."[12]

What characterizes such anxiety is a dreadful anticipation that is experienced as nameless and object-less. The anticipation of danger is accompanied here by the anticipation of a—traumatic—experience of helplessness in relation to this danger. "Anxiety is therefore on the one hand an expectation of trauma, and on the other a repetition of it in a mitigated form." Freud suggests that every anticipated real danger is accompanied by the fear that one will be unable to deal with it—thus there is anxiety about both the real danger and the anticipated helplessness, which may be more or less realistic. It is the latter that appears inexpedient in the human, marking the irruption of irrational "fear." Freud writes, "What it is the ego fears . . . cannot be specified; we know that the fear is of being overwhelmed or annihilated; but it cannot be grasped analytically."[13] It is a signal to the ego of a threat which is not properly external.

Lacan proposed that the ego is formed on the basis of a unifying perceptual *Gestalt*, on the model of the child's mirror image—the imaginary. He thereby also posed a previous state (the "real") of the body in parts, fragmented, which comes into existence at the same time. The splitting of the ego that Freud explores[14] is now shown to be the very condition for the emergence of the ego as such. The external threat is the desire of the Other. It is not properly external, however, because it exists as a threat only insofar as the subject desires the desire of the Other. In his discussion of Lacan's unpublished seminar on anxiety, Roberto Harari describes how Lacan refers to Hegel's classic dialectic between the master and the slave, developed in the *Phenomenology of Spirit*, in which desire is for recognition—the desire of desire, to "be" for the Other.[15] Yet, in this, I become the object of the Other's desire in a recognition that thereby denies me the subjectivity I desire in desiring the Other's desire. Lacan identifies a fundamental asymmetry here, as the result of which a reciprocity of recognition is impossible. Instead, he argues, what I seek in desiring the Other's desire is to find myself in the other, in which I thereby also seek the Other's loss. The reverse is thus that what the Other seeks, desires, in desiring me is to find itself in me, "for which it solicits my loss."[16]

Hence, in desiring the desire of the Other, I confront the Other's desire, which Lacan characterizes as "I love you but, because inexplicably I love in you something more than you—the *objet petit a*—I mutilate you."[17] Harari explains this as follows: "If the Other seeks my loss, it does so because it is trying to restitute its own *object a*. It desires a fragment of myself, which it can appropriate, and that is where the anxious condition appears, when facing the threat of loss of the pound of flesh."[18] Anxiety is signaled when the ego experiences the desire of the Other as its desire for my loss. It is an inescapable experience for, insofar as I am a desiring subject, I desire the desire of the Other, who desires my loss. Anxiety is thus not truly objectless; its object is desire itself, and the fear is "of disappearing in the enjoyment of the Other."[19] Anxiety is a defense against *jouissance*.[20] Psychoanalysis articulates the fascination of the subject with lack of the Other, with being the object–cause of the desire of the Other as the death drive. The subject must move beyond this imaginary captivation in a symbolizing of desire, but where this symbolization always partakes of the real it thereby renders into the world of signs.[21]

The unique role of the horror film here is not its symbolizations as such, but its enjoining the spectator to symbolize.

The Real of Reality and Fiction

The involuntary intrusion of the nightmare in the dreams of the victim of trauma appear opposed to the voluntary submission of the cinephile to the anxieties of the horror film. Can cinema's fictions produce trauma when, after all, we do know that they are, really, unreal?

Freud has challenged the assumption of a simple division between a domain of reality and a domain of imagination, as well as the correlation of fantasy with simple illusion. For the human subject, the unconscious and fantasy are psychically very real and produce effects in reality. Indeed the contagion, as it was often perceived, of shell shock or war trauma amongst soldiers in the First World War was a contingent reality threatening the war effort of the allies and enemy alike.[22] War trauma was the unrepresentable, not only for the soldier but also for conventional psychiatry[23] and psychoanalysis, leading Freud to reorganize his view of the role of the drives and sexuality to account for the compulsion to repeat, and for self-aggression as well as for aggressivity as such. As a result, in a move that appears counter-intuitive in opposing the Darwinian assumption that our desire is for life, Freud posits a human drive to stasis—to death. Freud's initial understanding of the pleasure principle as simply a drive for satisfaction is now qualified by the recognition of the human compulsion to repeatedly return to unpleasure, which nevertheless can only be understood as itself a form of "enjoyment." In Freud's account of his grandson's game of *fort-da*, the aim and ultimate pleasure of this painful performance of "mama gone, mama here" is mastery of unpleasure, as the child controls his mother's coming and going through fantasy play, and thereby also masters his anxiety over her loss and absence in reality.[24] For Lacan, however, the repetition in the child's throwing the reel (mama gone) again and again reveals not a mastering of reality, but a subjection to the compulsion to play and replay the game, which betrays the extent to which the child remains mastered by anxiety and what he terms the "real" (in his tripartite distinction of the symbolic, the imaginary, and the real).

Freud himself, Jean Laplanche has argued, remained a "prisoner of the antithesis of *factual reality* and a purely subjective interpretation close to *fantasy*," in which psychoanalysis is either the discovery through analysis of what is to be understood as the "true" event, or it is the construction by the analyst of an interpretation of the reality—which is not directly knowable—on the basis of the analysand's memories, dreams, and associations."[25] Laplanche argues that Freud lacks a necessary third category, that of the *message* with a meaning that is immanent, and which takes the form of the mostly nonverbal sexual messages conveyed by the adult to the small child. The development of the human individual is to be understood as an attempt to translate these enigmatic, traumatizing messages. "Analysis is first and foremost a method of deconstruction (ana-lysis) with the aim of clearing the way for a new construction, which is the task of the analysand."[26] It is not a factual truth (that has been or can be externally verified) that is important, but the particular yet also contingent translation of the enigmatic, traumatizing messages communicated by the analysand.

Laplanche here reintroduces the analysand as interpreter, and not simply as receiver of the interpretation, in a process of detranslation and retranslation in relation to such messages. In trauma, however, the message remains untranslated and untranslatable. Freud's term *Nachträglichkeit*, translated by Strachey as "deferred action," refers to the "afterwardsness" of trauma whereby an event or experience becomes understood—translated, in Laplanche's terms—traumatically through a subsequent experience. For Lacan, "anxiety is not a symbolic phenomenon, but is situated at the border of the imaginary and the real." Trauma is a symptom of the real, it is not a simply past event, it is "the experience you are awaiting,"[27] namely, an annihilation. It is not the infraction—the wound—as such but the possible *future* wound that will destroy, just as *this* wound might have; it is the unrepresentable of anxiety, whereby the subject herself or himself is placed as lack, as *objet petit a*, in relation to the desire of the Other that the subject desires.[28] Most simply, this translates as: myself enabling the Other's enjoyment, that is also the loss—death of the self to oneself.

The horror film as traumatic does not therefore involve a

remembering of a past trauma as a kind of recovery of an experience. It *is* the experience, and as such may produce a "remembering," *Nachträglichkeit.* Public performances of horror address us as both traumatic and as symbolizing, as translated. Both its compulsive attraction and its ethical dimension lie in this double role of horror. That we can find the fictitious terrors of the horror film traumatic testifies not to the success of its illusionism—its "realism"—nor to the humanist truths of its fabrications, but to the appearance of the uncanny real that is never either reality or fiction.[29]

Squeamishness as the Unethical

> It's an anguish film. It's a quieter mood than horror, something more subjacent, more internal, more penetrating. It's horror in homeopathic doses.
>
> —Georges Franju[30]

Franju's comments here on *Eyes Without a Face* suggest an approach to horror that, perhaps not coincidentally, closely relates to Lacan's view of anxiety: "In my experience, it is necessary to canalise it [anxiety] and, if I may say so, to take it in small doses, so that one is not overcome by it. This is similar to bringing the subject into contact with the real."[31] Homeopathy—established on the principle of "Let likes cure likes"—seeks to heal through the similar, prescribing a remedy that will *cause* the symptom in a healthy person, and thus in the ill body stimulate it to restore itself to health. Yet for psychoanalysis this cannot be a form of inoculation against or resistance to anxiety, or the real, as if it were a pathogen, which could be removed.[32] The experiencing of "small doses" must, rather, bring about some accommodation with the real of anxiety, circumscribing anxiety so that it no longer floods the subject or defines every encounter with others in reality as always being in the service of the *jouissance* of the Other.

The horror film's monstrous figures of abjection and scenes of terrifying destruction and chaos, in engaging us in a compulsive return to look, to watch, to know what we dread, snare us in the uncanny, and in the pleasure/unpleasure of repetition.[33] That is, they snare us in the repeated re-encounter of the *jouissance* of the Other, which I serve insofar as I find my enjoyment, my *jouissance*, in the desire of the Other, and resist by attempting to master the Other—to abject her.[34] What is required is not the destruction of the monstrous Other—as we know, she always returns! Instead, what is necessary is a refiguring of my relation to the desiring Other through symbolization and not as *jouissance*. This is not a matter of rational explanation—which is always so disappointing in a horror film. The processes of thought here might be better described as extra-rational, for they are not without reason, and moreover they produce purposive action and understanding on the part of the subject; nevertheless, they do not accord with the procedures of rational thought established by modern science.

The anthropologist Geoffrey Lienhardt addresses the issue of different kinds of purposive thought in his account of the belief systems of the Dinka peoples of Southern Sudan, and his example seems to me to also suggest a way in which the encountering of "small doses" of the real may be enacted. He writes:

> The Dinka have no conception which at all closely corresponds to our popular modern conception of the "mind," as mediating and, as it were, storing up the experiences of the self. [Footnote in original: And still less of conscious and unconscious elements, of course.] There is for them no such interior entity to appear, on reflection, to stand between the experiencing self at any given moment and what is or has been an exterior influence upon the self. So it seems that what we should call in some cases the "memories" of experience, and regard therefore as in some way intrinsic and interior to the remembering person and modified in their effects upon him by that interiority, appear to the Dinka as exteriorly acting upon him, as were the sources from which they derived. Hence it would be impossible to suggest to the Dinka that a powerful dream was "only" a dream, and might for that reason be dismissed as relatively unimportant in the light of day, or that a state of possession was grounded "merely" in the psychology of the person possessed. They do not make the kind of distinction between the psyche and the world which would make such interpretations significant for them.
>
> A man who had been imprisoned in Khartoum called one of his children "Khartoum" in memory of the place, but also to turn aside any possible harmful influence of that place upon him in later life. The act is an act of exorcism, but the exorcism of what, for us, would be memories of experiences. Thus also do the Dinka call children after Powers, and after the dead, who to the Dinka way of thought are less likely to return to trouble the living if their place and constant presence are thus explicitly acknowledged.[35]

We might dismiss as simple animism the general belief in Powers shown here by this Dinka father, yet it also strikes me, as it may have struck Lienhardt, that it is a process of mourning in which a traumatic past experience is being addressed. Khartoum personifies the traumatic experience enacted upon the man, which is acknowledged and propitiated in giving his child the city's name. It is a process of memorialization, as distinct from remembering, in which a new—and valued—object stands in for and thus also signifies the trauma. This it might strike us as grotesque and cruel if we were to imagine an Auschwitz survivor calling her child by the camp's name. The child would perhaps seem to us to be contaminated and burdened by an unbearable reality of which he or she is innocent. Yet, this burden is precisely one that children of survivors have so lucidly pointed to as being borne by them, and that has been all the more terrifying insofar as it has remained unnamed, unremembered, and unowned by their survivor parent or parents. Instead, for this Dinka father and his child, traumatic memory is made into a process of external enactment and memorialization, it is contained and corralled in a symbolizing naming rather than made abject to return again and again. Lienhardt explains that for the man who called his child Khartoum,

> it is Khartoum which is regarded as an agent, the subject which acts, and not as with us the remembering mind which recalls the place. The man is the object acted upon. Even in the usual expressions of the Dinka for the action of features of their world upon them, we often find a reversal of European expressions which assume the human self, or mind, as subject in relation to what happens to it; in English, for example, it is often said that a man "catches a disease," but in Dinka the disease, or Power, always "seizes the man."[36]

Subjectivity is expressed here as a being subject to the Power (or, for Lacan, the *desire*) of the Other.

The horror film, in enabling us to encounter a modicum of the real and memorialize it, is ethical because it allows us to move from ensnarement by *jouissance* to symbolization (in which the aesthetics, and comedy, of the horror film are also important). What is made possible is a distinction between, rather than an identification of, the horror of violent destruction enacted on our fellow human beings and the traumatic terror of the real of *jouissance*. Squeamishness, I suggest therefore, is not at all an ethical response, but on the contrary a symptom of an anxious enjoyment in unpleasure. Such an ethical as well as aesthetic dimension to horror cinema is suggested by the "tenderness" Raymond Durgnat finds in Franju's violent films:

> It is easy enough to be tender in erotic or amiable circumstances . . .
> Hence the desperate rarity and the almost prophetic power of artists

who, like Franju, can remain tender in the face of brutality and loss, who can maintain a tender pessimism. As Franju has commented, his most violent films are the most tender, because the more tender you are the more you feel the violence, and it's in the face of violence that tenderness is more extreme. Franju's is not at all a savage eye; his toughness is stoic, his vision as tender as can bear the truth.[37]

I had not, however, found such tenderness on my own first viewing of *Eyes Without a Face*. On the contrary, it has figured as a traumatic memory for me.

Eyes Without a Face

The very title of the film is gruesome—its words institute a cruel verbal play, for how does one imagine eyes without a face? Perhaps as separated organs lying on a table,[38] an image where the more horrifying correlative for me is of the empty eye sockets from which these ocular globes have been wrenched. Or should the focus be on the missing face as setting for the eyes? Here, what is meant is not the displacement of the eyes from their proper place/face, but the displacement of the setting itself. But what is behind the face? For me, on seeing the film for the first time, it was a nameless dread. Perhaps, to give it words now: the bloody wound of the left-behind. Actually, it is a lot of scar tissue, maybe suppurating, tight, and uncomfortable, but not *missing*. The punning title still produces an uncanniness for me, as did a recent newspaper headline stating "Healthcare trust to ask patients to donate 'surplus' skin for research at Porton Down"[39]—for how does skin become surplus? The uncanny power of words is evident here, and indeed the visual is no more powerful than the word, for it is not immanent but read, that is, cognitively apprehended through memory, and thus the visual is already coded.

The horror of the film is not merely the ripped face, it is also its suspense story. It is, however, not suspense as such that produces traumatic horror (for suspense is a fundamental feature of narrative in general); it is the threat of, not death itself, and not simply loss, but of a devouring, of the appropriation of the self by another.[40] *Eyes Without a Face* stages the traumatic real of the desire of the Other. The film commences—suspensefully—with a beautiful woman driving at night, nervously watching the road and other cars, as well as a male-attired figure slumped in the back seat. She pulls off the road and drags out what is now clearly a lifeless woman's body, abandoning it to the nearby river's dark waters.

The film suspends the question of whose body it is, instead cutting to a lecture by eminent plastic surgeon, Professor Génessier (Pierre Brasseur), in which he describes extraordinary new possibilities for his craft and art. Afterward, he is called by the police to identify a body that may be his missing daughter, Christiane (Edith Scob). Having suspended the question of who owns the eyes without a face, the film now appears to answer it, for the Professor positively identifies the body, with its awful torn face, as his daughter. As he leaves, he passes the anxious father of another missing woman, who asks for reassurance that it is indeed Christiane. The Professor's affirmative answer is of course a snare—which we may already have conjectured—for the body was in fact the other father's daughter. But the film delays further solutions and cuts instead to Christiane's funeral, which is marked not only by the strangeness of the lighting and camera placings of its mise-en-scene, but also by the appearance of the driver in the opening scene, who is revealed as Louise (Alida Valli), the Professor's "secretary,"[41] and who displays obvious discomfort and an urgent desire to leave.

The subsequent scene resolves these questions while setting in motion the next sequence of actions. We are given Génessier's point of view as he enters a room in his home, seeing first caged doves (marking their initial association with Christiane), then a woman lying on a day bed, her back to the camera. The next shot shows Génessier beside the woman; he turns off a radio and pick s up what is revealed as a notice for his daughter's funeral. "Where did you find this?" he says, "I don't like the way you poke into everything," confirming that the woman is his daughter but also that he has not yet told her what he has done. As she turns to him he suddenly says—realizing its absence— "Your mask, you must get into the habit of wearing it," suggesting his own horror (Christiane later tells Louise in a whisper that "my face frightens me, my mask terrifies me even more"). To Christiane's querying his use of the term "habit," he declares that he will give her a new face, saying "I shall succeed. I promise you." But Christiane retorts, "I don't believe that anymore," to which Génessier angrily responds, "You have no reason to doubt me—I am a man of distinction, am I not? You shall have a real face, I pledge my word."

It is Louise who has sought young women students (as I was on first seeing the film) as potential sources for the new face Professor Génessier seeks for his horribly damaged daughter—injuries she sustained in a car crash which, Christiane claims, he caused by his obsessive need to dominate: "even on the road, he drives like a demon." Instituted here is a relay of desire, for Louise does not seek these women's faces for herself, but for Christiane; nevertheless, in this she doubles not Christiane's but Génessier's desire—both his professional ambitions and his desire to remake his daughter's beauty and thereby erase his own failure.

Christiane's disfigured face represents a challenge to her father's professional skills; if he succeeds, he will also gain the prestige he so much desires. The operation also constitutes the real of his desire, the *jouissance* of his power over the image, eradicating the defacement of time, fate, or nature; it is a fetishizing of the flaw—gone in a (re)making of The Woman Beautiful. Christiane's desire mirrors her father's: wanting the face he will give her and to be beautiful again. However, in also wishing to be beautiful for Jacques (François Guérin), her fiancé, Christiane's desire places her beyond her father's *jouissance*.

Louise, meanwhile, remains enthralled by her desire for the desire of the Other, such that she will act against her own moral feelings. After the transferral of Edna's (Juliette Mayneil) face, Louise reports to Génessier on Christiane's progress, saying, "This time she believes." He replies, "I was so afraid," to which Louise responds, "Don't be. I, too, believe this time." Here, the role of remaking Christiane for Génessier is revealed: it is both the cause of his desire and the catalyst that evokes sheer anxiety in him. He says, "I can only hope. To achieve such a thing . . . God, it would be beyond price. I have done so much wrong to perform this miracle. I have done you a great wrong too." Louise's reply acknowledges this: "I know, but I shall never forget that I owe my face to you" (the only trace remaining of her scars are hidden by the pearl choker she always wears).[42] It is not, however, simple gratitude for her regained beauty that causes Louise to help destroy other women's faces. While the film clearly suggests that she suffers great anguish as a result of her actions, she also enjoys them insofar as she identifies with Génessier's desire: the Woman-Made-Beautiful.

The film's ethics center on showing Christiane as well as Louise to each be complicit in the terror Génessier pursues. Christiane secretly overlooks her father and Louise's kidnapping and drugging of Edna, a new victim for her beauty. While the young woman lies helplessly strapped to an operating table, Christiane enters and approaches her; then, distracted by the sound of dogs, she leaves by a side door and we see her fondly caressing several of them in their adjacent quarters. She returns to the operating room, stopping at a mirror where, removing her mask, she inspects her face, before approaching the drugged girl whom we are now shown through Christiane's optical point of view. As she passes her hands across Edna's face, Christiane (we may infer) is imagining what it might look and feel like on herself. At this, the girl is momentarily roused and we are now given her view of the unmasked Christiane, appearing as just a shadowy patch of black with a band of light across the eyes. The film cuts to the girl's face as she screams and faints, then cuts back to the previous shot of Christiane, who retreats further into shadow as we hear the sound of dogs barking.

The film doubles Génessier and his daughter; both wish for her beauty to be regained. Tellingly, however, it also distinguishes them through their different relation to the animals. For Christiane, the dogs (who later tear her father to pieces) are her friends, and their response to her is one of pleasure. This is in sharp contrast with the later shots of her father who, after completing the operation, also passes through, provoking violent barks and howls from the angry and fearful animals that he prods with his stick. Christiane, like the animals, is merely a means to Génessier's will to power and surgical success, but (and *unlike* the animals) this is only insofar as Christiane finds her being in her desire for his desire—her beauty.

This second operation is revealed as a failure just as its very success is being heralded. As they gather over dinner, Louise comments that Christiane appears "more beautiful than ever,"[43] but when her father, kissing her before he leaves to go out, inspects her face approvingly he suddenly observes what we later understand to be the almost imperceptibly faint marks of the rejection of the graft. A series of still photographs follow, which document the advancing necrosis of the dying transplanted tissue, and Christiane "loses" her face again. It is now that Christiane once again phones Jacques, this time whispering his name. Courting his recognition, she also thereby courts the exposure this might bring. This marks an important shift in Christiane, a shift also signalled by a change in her dress from the stiff silk taffeta housecoat of earlier scenes to the much softer material which drapes her here.

For their third attempt, Genissier and Louise abduct a young patient as she leaves his clinic, on the grounds of which he has his home and research laboratories. The girl has been planted by the police following Jacques' information but she contrives to be released early. Her imminent defacing is prevented not by the representatives of the law, whom she has evaded, but by Christiane. Already prepped for the procedure, the girl awakens and begins screaming, shaking her head from side to side. She is observed by Christiane, who also (but without the same violence) shakes her head, then goes up to the girl and, grasping a scalpel while the girl screams in terror, cuts the tapes restraining her. The dogs start barking and Christiane, whom we may infer expects to be discovered, repositions the scalpel in her hand as a dagger when Louise enters and calls on her to stop. Instead, Christiane stabs her, piercing her throat at the place of the tiny scar that is the only remaining sign of her former mutilation. Passing from the operating room, Christiane releases the caged animals in the adjacent laboratories, and then departs into the wooded grounds outside. At this point, her father returns from speaking with the policemen. Hearing the dogs, Génessier opens the garden entrance to their quarters and they leap out, attacking him and destroying his face. The film closes with Christiane's departure from the house surrounded by white doves, echoing the portrait of her unscarred visage seen earlier but now with her face concealed by her mask.

The story is ethically resolved by Christiane's action in choosing to set free the girl, which is figured by Franju's closing images as also a freedom for herself. But her ethical choice is not only—and perhaps not even primarily—her action to prevent another girl's defacement. Rather, it is to finally turn away from the fascination with the beautiful constituted for her by her father's desire, and accept a self, even a mutilated one, that is her own.

Two distinct horrors are therefore presented in the film. One, quite straightforwardly, is the gruesomeness of the faceless face, made literally visible in the scene where the skin is shown being lifted away from Edna's drugged form. This is straightforward insofar as it draws for its effect on our identification with Edna. The dismemberment of the self, represented by the face, is made viscerally palpable here in the dispossessing of what should be inalienable. It is a matter quite literally of "your face or mine," which is either good black humor or a shocking apprehension in a terrifying encounter with the real that perhaps produced the sudden fainting reported amongst some contemporary audience members.

Here arises the second horror: What the Other of my desire desires of me is this dismemberment of myself in support of the Other's desire. For while Christina's desire doubles that of her father—since each desires a new face for her—nevertheless Génessier desires the *separable* face for his daughter, such that it is the object for him. Christiane, in thus desiring the desire of her father, is also doubled with Edna, who becomes "unfaced" by Génessier just as Christiane has been. What is involved is not, therefore, desire, but an enjoyment by the Other—*jouissance*. The cost of such an enjoyment is my pound of flesh. Edna also serves the desire of Christiane, not only of her father. And in another form of doubling, both women function as support to Génessier's enjoyment, suggested in the repetition of Christiane's movement through the house to observe her kidnapping, now followed in reverse by Edna as she flees, falling to her death (which, her scream notwithstanding, may be suicide). For Christiane, however, there is escape and freedom (although perhaps also madness), while it is her father who dies.

It had been Christiane's mask that subsequently seemed the focus of my distress at this film. This connection was further motivated by the similar role of a mask and a face destroyed in Kaneto Shindô's *Onibaba* (1964), which I saw a few weeks later, with equal horror. No subsequent reflection, even after my intellectual encounter with psychoanalysis, resolved the enigma of my horror. But I have noticed that my sense of horror was also very much like my horror in Voltaire's *Candide* and its story of the girl who must pay for survival with the flesh of her buttock. The horrible mask as the thing of horror has been a kind of fetish standing in for a traumatic real, but its role for me remained unconscious. My squeamish horror was not an ethical response but a traumatic encounter. If my remembered horror remains uncanny for me, but not traumatic, this is notwithstanding my analysis here of *Eyes Without a Face*, which could only offer me the satisfaction of a mastering I must continuously remake.

Notes

1. Pauline Kael, "Are Movies Going to Pieces?" *The Atlantic Monthly* 214.6 (December 1964): 61–81.

2. Others have found as its message a reference to the atrocities of the Nazi concentration camps and the Holocaust. See, in relation to this, Adam Lowenstein, "Films Without a Face: Shock Horror in the Cinema of Georges Franju," *Cinema Journal* 37, no. 4 (Summer 1998): 37–58. Lowenstein's essay valuably explores the role of spectacle and shock and Franju's relation to surrealism.

3. "The picture might have been shewn me, and I never have seen anything but a rabbit in it." Ludwig Wittgenstein, *Philosophical Investigations*, trans. G.E.M. Anscombe (Oxford: Basil Blackwell, 1953), 194.

4. Raymond Durgnat writes that "Alas, when it was presented in the Film Festival at Edinburgh (home of body-snatchers), seven people fainted, and

public and press were outraged." In *Franju* (London: Studio Vista Movie Paperbacks, 1967), 79.

5. Certain forms of public performance of the horrific also implicate us not merely as spectators but also as participants, for example, initiation ceremonies that involve considerable pain and incursion onto the body, or that, as with Halloween celebrations, enact as make-believe the fear of the monstrous and the diabolical dead and undead.

6. I am drawing here upon Michel Foucault's discussion in *Discipline and Punish*, trans. Alan Sheridan (New York: Vintage Books, 1979): "Instead of taking revenge, criminal justice should simply punish" (74). The change in the concepts of justice and punishment in western societies—though not of the sovereignty of state power—whereby the inhumanity of the crime is no longer matched by an inhumanity of punishment, has led, for example, to the widespread (except in the U.S.) abolition of capital punishment.

7. Of course, accidental death has occurred in some cases—for humans as well as animals—in the play acting required in making a film.

8. One may note here St. Augustine's assertion that to sin in mind is to sin in reality.

9. Noël Carroll, *The Philosophy of Horror; or, Paradoxes of the Heart* (New York: Routledge, 1990): "Whatever distress horror causes, as a probable price for our fascination, is outweighed for the average consumer by the pleasure we derive in having our curiosity stimulated and rewarded" (193). The horror film fascinates—aptures our attention—by transgressing boundaries, thereby stimulating our 'inquisitiveness about its surprising properties" (188).

10. "In ancient Greek philosophy, in the texts of the pre-Socratics, Plato and Aristotle, *aisthesis* refers to lived, felt experience, knowledge as it is obtained through the senses, in contrast to *eidos*, knowledge derived from reason and intellection, from which we get the word 'idea'." Clive Cazeaux, in the introduction to his edited collection, *The Continental Aesthetics Reader* (London: Routledge, 2000), xv.

11. Lacan, discussing anger as an affect, writes that while "anger is no doubt a passion which is manifested by means of an organic or physiological correlative, by a given more or less hypertonic or even elated feeling, but that it requires perhaps something like the reaction of a subject to a disappointment, to the failure of an expected correlation between a symbolic order and the response of the real." *The Ethics of Psychoanalysis*, trans. Denis Potter (London: Tavistock/Routledge, 1992), 103.

12. Sigmund Freud, *Inhibitions, Symptoms and Anxiety* (1926 [1925]), in *The Standard Edition of the Complete Works of Sigmund Freud*, trans. James Strachey (London: The Hogarth Press, 1953–74), vol. 19, 57. Subsequent references to Freud will use the abbreviation *SE*.

13. *Ibid.*

14. *The Ego and the Id* (1923), *SE*, vol. 19.

15. Roberto Harari, *Lacan's Seminar on Anxiety* (New York: The Other Press, 2001), 108.

16. *Ibid.*

17. Jacques Lacan, *The Four Fundamental Concepts of Psycho-Analysis,* trans. Alan Sheridan (Harmondsworth, U.K.: Penguin Books, 1979), 263.

18. Harrari, 111.

19. Paul Verhaeghe, "The Riddle of Canstration Anxiety: Lacan Beyond Freud 'Mind the Gap. Mind the Gap. Mind the Gap'," *The Letter: Lacanian Perspectives on Psychoanalysis* 6 (Spring 1996): 50.

20..Dany Nobus, "Not Enough and Never Too Much," *The Letter: Lacanian Perspectives on Psychoanalysis* 6 (Spring 1996): 111.

21. This view of the symbol relates, as well, to Coleridge's account that the symbol "always partakes of the reality which it renders intelligible; and while it enunciates the whole, abides itself as a living part in that unity of which it is the representative." Coleridge, *The Statesman's Manual,* ed. W. G. T. Shedd (New York, 1875), cited by Angus Fletcher in *Allegory: The Theory of a Symbolic Mode* (Ithaca: Cornell University Press, 1964), 16.

22. I have discussed this further in relation to a contemporary documentary film, *War Neuroses: Netley, 1917, Seale Hayne Military Hospital, 1918* (Pathé, U.K., 1918), which is a record of such disorders and certain forms of treatment of them, in "The Spectacle of Actuality," in *Collecting Visible Evidence,* ed. Jane Gaines and Michael Renov (Minnesota: University of Minnesota Press, 1999), 19–45.

23. As a result of the need to treat these men, psychiatric medicine in Britain and elsewhere was fundamentally challenged and transformed. Freud's view of the unconscious came to have enormous significance for understanding the war neuroses of soldiers in the First World War, largely, historian Martin Stone has argued, the result of the article by the psychologist and anthropologist, W. H. Rivers, "Freud's Psychology of the Unconscious," which appeared in the *Lancet,* the main British journal of medicine, in 1917. See Stone's excellent re-evaluation of British psychiatry and the development of modern psychiatric practices as a result of the unprecedented medical requirements of the war neuroses of soldiers, "Shellshock and the Psychologists," in *The Anatomy of Madness: Essays in the History of Psychiatry* (Cambridge: Cambridge University Press, 1985), 242–71.

24. Freud, *Beyond the Pleasure Principle, SE* vol. 18, 14–17.

25. Jean Laplanche, "Interpretation between Determinism and Hermeneutics" in *Essays on Otherness* (London: Routledge, 1999), 165.

26. *Ibid.*

27. Lacan, *The Ethics of Psychoanalysis,* 12.

28. The subject is thus what Julia Kristeva terms *abject.* As explored in her book *Powers of Horror,* in its literary and metaphorical appearances, the abject has been a compelling concept and account for discussions of the horror film, articulating the fascination as well as the horror of the abject. The abject, or·abjection, refers to two distinct phenomena. The first is the act of abjection in which the subject separates itself from the object and thereby designates it as abject, the "horrible," thus also instituting a distinction of inside/outside but

where what is put outside is abjured, evicted, and effaced. Yet in this process of abjecting, the abject retains a dreadful fascination. The second is the state of abjection, of being the lost, abjected, reviled object. Lacan's concept of the *objet a* makes clear its role as cause or support of desire, avoiding (Kleinian) implications of the object abjected as bad. It is our terrors of the real, the taint of which always remains attached to the *objet*, not the projections of the abject, which are central for understanding the unpleasures and pleasures of horror. See Julia Kristeva, *The Powers of Horror*, trans. Leon Roudiez (New York: Columbia University Press, 1982).

29. Lacan, *The Ethics of Psychoanalysis*, 12.

30. Quoted in Durgnat, 83.

31. Jacques Lacan, *The Four Fundamental Concepts of Psycho-Analysis*, trans. Alan Sheridan (Harmondsworth, U.K.: Penguin Books, 1979), 41.

32. My view of the role of "small doses" here thus develops a different emphasis from that discussed by Lowenstein, *op. cit.*, who draws on Eric Santner's essay, "History Beyond the Pleasure Principle: Some Thoughts on the Representation of Trauma," in *Probing the Limits of Representation: Nazism and the "Final Solution,"* ed. Saul Friedlander (Cambridge, MA: Harvard University Press, 1992), 143–54.

33. The terror and dread of the specular and its fascinating seduction in cinema are vivdly articulated in Kristeva's essay, "Ellipsis on Dread and the Specular Seduction" (1975), trans. Dolores Burdick, *Wide Angle* 3, no. 3 (1979): 42–47. The specular seduction brings identity, meaning, and symbolization so that "The glance by which I identify an object, a face, my own, another's, delivers my identity which reassures me: for it delivers me from frayages, nameless dread, noises preceding the name . . . Intellectual speculation derives from this identifying, labelling glance" (42). The specular is the point of origin not only of signs, and of narcissistic identifications, but also for "the phantasmatic terror one speaking identity holds for another." Once that terror, which is the incursion of the other, "erupts into the seer, that seen stops being simply reassuring, trompe-l'oeil, or invitation to speculation, and becomes the fascinating specular. Cinema seizes us precisely in that place" (45). The specular for Kristeva here marks that which is beyond identification, unverbalized, unrepresented, namely, the real. It represents the unrepresented because it "includes an excess of visual traces" (42), useless for signification, but insistingly there and naming the before of symbolization.

34. Seduced to speculate, Kristeva labels terror as "to do with the dependency on the mother" while seduction lies with "an appeal addressed to the father." While she invites a dangerous homogenization in the categories "man" and "woman" here, she goes on to say, "But if they enter the game, they will both be led to cross both zones and attempt both identifications—maternal, paternal. Test of sexual difference—of homosexuality, that brush with psychosis—they never stop letting it be intimated, even when they don't let it be seen: Eisenstein, Hitchcock" ("Ellipsis on Dread," 45). I would wish to draw upon this qualification as well in relation to Barbara Creed's important

work, *The Monstrous-Feminine: Film, Feminism, Psychoanalysis* (London: Routledge, 1993).

35. Godfrey Lienhardt, *Divinity and Experience: The Religion of the Dinka* (Oxford: Oxford University Press, 1961), 149.

36. *Ibid.*, 150.

37. Durgnat, 31.

38. This is, of course, an image in E. T. A. Hoffmann's *The Sandman*, discussed by Freud in his 1919 essay "The 'Uncanny'," *SE* vol. 17.

39. *The Independent* (June 7, 2002): 6. Porton Down is the top-secret U.K. military research center, specializing in biological warfare.

40. Cosimo Urbano very usefully describes four representational strategies of the modern horror film—the uncanny, the monster, the mise-en-scene of violent physical assault, and the mise-en-scene of "all hell breaking loose," in "Projections, Suspense and Anxiety: The Modern Horror Film and Its Effects." *Psychoanalytic Review* 85 (December 1998): 909–30.

41. We are informed of this by one of the mourners, in reply to his companion's question. The term secretary in the English subtitles is given with quote marks around it, implying a query about her status that we may answer by inferring that she is, in fact, his mistress.

42. It is this feature that will be recognized by Jacques from the Policeman's account of the second victim's friend's description of the woman who had become her patron. Jacques contacts the police after recognizing Christiane's voice when she makes her second phone call to him, after Edna's death and the failure of the transplant.

43. Genessier instructs his daughter to smile, but when she does he quickly follows "but not too much."

Aristotelian Reflections on Horror and Tragedy in *An American Werewolf in London* and *The Sixth Sense*

Angela Curran

Can horror films be tragic? At first glance at least, the answer would seem to be "no." Monsters, of one sort or another, are at the center of most, if not all, horror films.[1] The monster is typically depicted as a creature that is dangerous, disgusting, and fearsome, and that ultimately meets its demise—at least, until the next sequel comes around—but not before it brings havoc to the lives of its human victims. This suggests that horror films with narratives that centrally revolve around the existence of a monster are unlikely to evoke the audience's pity and fear, which Aristotle in his *Poetics* regards as the characteristic emotions of tragic response.[2] This point also seems to hold even if we consider horror films that do no include monsters, or unnatural beings, *per se*. Norman Bates (Anthony Perkins), for example, in *Psycho* (1960), may not be a creature whose existence goes counter to science, yet he and others of his ilk are unlikely candidates for tragic protagonists.

In fact, tragedy and horror would seem to evoke conflicting emotional responses in the audience. Tragedy, in Aristotle's view, evokes a sense of sympathetic engagement between the central protagonist and the audience. The tragic character must be someone "like us" in order to evoke the audience's pity and fear. Yet horror creates its particular pleasure through a central conflict between the humans in the story and a monster or monster-like creature. The disgust and revulsion we feel toward the monster is central to evoking the pleasure of what Noël Carroll calls "art-horror," which is the emotional response in the audience brought on by the thought of the monster.[3] Yet the more the monster appears to be a sympathetic figure, the less its power to horrify, and therefore thrill the audience. From an Aristotelian perspective, then, it would appear that the only way a horror film could be tragic is if a human protagonist in the story is a tragic figure. But even in these cases, we might expect that the tragic aspect of the protagonist is secondary to the story's concerns with evoking horror in the audience as the humans in the story encounter and confront the monster.

Yet, a surprising number of horror films are also tragedies. In this essay, I examine two such films, *An American Werewolf in London* (John Landis, 1981), and *The Sixth Sense* (M. Night Shyamalan, 1999) in order to see how this intersection of horror and tragedy is possible and what end is served by such an intertwining of genres. *American Werewolf*, a brilliant, dark comic retelling of George Waggner's *The Wolf Man* (1941), and *The Sixth Sense*, a ghost story with a surprise ending, are examples of two different subgroups of films that intersect horror and tragedy. In the first group are films that are tragic because, somewhat surprisingly, the monster figure is pitiable and tragic in the way Aristotle describes. I discuss *American Werewolf* as an example of this kind of film. In the second group are films that have a tragic dimension because they feature human protagonists who are tragic characters. I discuss *The Sixth Sense* as an example of this kind of film. In the first section, I explore in more detail what is unusual, from an Aristotelian perspective, about combining horror and tragedy. I then give an overview of the features that characterize horror films that are also tragedies. In sections two and three I illustrate these ideas with reference to *American Werewolf* and *The Sixth Sense*. In my conclusion, I consider what purpose is served by intertwining horror and tragedy in these films and also discuss how it is possible to retain an Aristotelian framework to explain why these horror films are tragic in spite of the initial difficulties to the contrary.

Horror and Tragedy: A Thematic Overview

From some theoretical perspectives, it is not hard to see how a horror film could also be a tragedy. As noted, a monster or a monster-like creature is at the center of most, if not all, horror films. Robin Wood argues from a Freudian perspective that the monster in a horror film has the potential to be a sympathetic or pitiable, yet horrifying, figure because it represents that aspect of society that has been "repressed," due to the violation of either sexual or social and political norms.[4] Drawing on Nietzsche, Daniel Shaw argues that the monster can evoke a dual response in which viewers admire the monster's wielding of power even as they are repulsed by the evil the monster represents.[5] While both accounts stress the ambivalent nature of the audience's identification with the monster, they also leave room for the possibility that it can be a tragic figure.

From an Aristotelian perspective, however, it is harder to understand how the audience can sympathize with the monster. This difficulty is related to Aristotle's view of what it is that makes it possible to feel pity and fear, which is the proper emotional response to a tragic character's misfortune. Aristotle holds that the tragic emotions are properly felt for someone whom we feel is "like us."[6] In Aristotle's view, the morally admirable character is at the basis of the audience's sympathetic engagement with the tragic protagonist. If a character is a morally decent person—a person "intermediate in virtue"—who suffers in greater proportion to any mistake he may have made, his suffering will be tragic and the audience will feel pity and fear for him as he goes from good fortune to bad.[7]

These requirements make it difficult for an Aristotelian to see how the monster of a horror film could be a tragic figure. In order to attain such lofty status, the plot would have to facilitate a sense of sympathetic identification between the monster and the audience on the basis of the monster's possession of morally admirable qualities that are recognizably human. To the extent that the monster seems more "like us," i.e., more human, it becomes less horrific and therefore less terrifying. The more the tragic appeal of the monster is heightened, in other words, the less the film offers the peculiar pleasures of horror. But the more terrifying and threatening the monster is to the humans in the story, the more outside the sphere of human morality the monster will appear. Therefore, it is less likely the audience will be able to forge a sense of sympathetic identification with the monster and see its demise or destruction as tragic.

Yet the monster is represented as a sympathetic character in a surprising number of films. At least three different sorts of plot patterns fit this representational strategy. First, some films feature a sympathetic human protagonist who turns into a monster, either through his or her own mistake, random bad luck, or because of the actions of other humans or the actions of monsters (e.g., vampires who turn innocent victims into other vampires, zombies, beasts. etc.) Because the audience's sense of pity for the human protagonist is evoked early on in the plot, and because the film establishes a sense of similarity between the monster–creature and the human protagonist it once was, the audience is able to retain a sense of emotional engagement with the monster and pity it for its suffering and demise, even though the monster's physical appearance is quite horrific. In this category, I discuss *American Werewolf.* But other examples of this plot pattern include *The Fly* (Kurt Neumann, 1958; David Cronenberg, 1986), *Night of the Living Dead* (George Romero, 1968), *Interview with the Vampire* (Neil Jordan, 1994), The *Exorcist* (William Friedkin, 1973), and *Invasion of the Body Snatchers* (Don Siegel, 1956; Philip Kaufman, 1978).

Second, some films represent the monster as a creature that comes into existence due to human "over-reaching"[8] and suffers at the hands of human mistreatment. The original *Frankenstein* (1931) and *Mary Shelley's Frankenstein* (1994) are examples of this sort of depiction of the monster. While the monster in these films is a horrific creature, it also evokes considerable sympathy because of the mistreatment it suffers at the hands of Dr. Frankenstein and the people with whom it comes into contact.[9] Kenneth Branagh's 1994 version, in particular, follows Shelley's treatment of the monster more closely in suggesting that the creature resorts to violence only after it has been mistreated by, and cast out from, human society. Though the monster eventually takes revenge on its creator by bringing harm to him and his kin, Dr. Frankenstein's creation regrets his actions at the end of the movie; in Shelley's and Branagh's version, it even mourns the passing of Dr. Frankenstein as the loss of his father. Although the monster is frightening and destructive, these story elements make his demise tragic by linking the physical destruction he brings about to the moral mistreatment he suffers at the hands of humans, who themselves refuse to recognize his "humanity."[10] This strategy of representation makes the monster a sympathetic figure through a role reversal of the monster—human relationship found in more typical monster movies (I will explore this notion in more detail in connection with *American Werewolf*). Other examples in this category include *Blacula* (William Crain, 1972), in which an African prince gets "cursed" and turned into a vampire by a white racist aristocrat, and *It's Alive* (Larry Cohen, 1973), which features a monster baby born to human parents.

Third, films can create sympathy for the monster through a characterization that makes it more "like us" in virtue of the possession of admirable features that are recognizably human. The depiction of Frankenstein in both the James Whale and Branagh versions follows this pattern. Dr. Frankenstein's monster is appreciative of nature, has aesthetic sensibilities—in his love of music and beauty—and has a moral regard for others (e.g., when he becomes the "angel of the forest" to the family he encounters in the countryside). Francis Ford Coppola's *Bram Stoker's Dracula* (1992) follows this pattern as well by making the character of Count Dracula a sympathetic aristocrat by linking his transformation into a vampire to the loss he experienced, centuries earlier, when his wife, thinking him dead, committed suicide. Other vampire films follow this kind of sympathetic representation of the vampire (e.g., *The Hunger* [1983]).[11] *The Mummy* (1932) depicts the monster as a tragic creature unjustly murdered for religious sacrilege in his human life as an Egyptian prince, who returns from the dead with the quest to reincarnate his lover.

The representational strategies used in these films narrow the gap between the human and the inhuman by depicting the monster-figure as more sympathetic relative to (most of) the humans in the story. When the humans are portrayed as cold, unfeeling, heartless, or cruel, then there is more chance for the monster to be depicted sympathetically. Other examples include *Blacula*, previously mentioned, where the vampire-figure suffers at the hands of white racism; *Carrie* (Brian De Palma, 1976), in which the title character uses telekinesis to unleash monstrous rage only after she is tormented incessantly by her classmates; and *King Kong* (Merian Cooper and Ernest Schoedsack, 1933), where the monster, Kong, is represented as the victim of a cruel manhunt.[12]

Horror films can also be tragic because they depict the human protagonists in a sympathetic light as well. Films that fit this representational strategy frequently refer back to Aristotle's formula in the *Poetics* for evoking the proper tragic response of pity and fear. Classical tragedy featured characters that go from good fortune to bad owing to a causal nexus that is beyond the tragic protagonist's control (e.g., war, fate, and the actions of the Gods, societal factors, and simple bad luck). At the same time, Aristotle stresses in *Poetics* 13 that in the ideal tragic plot, the protagonist is not simply an innocent victim of circumstances beyond his control, but is causally implicated through an unwitting error (*hamartia*) that brings about his own misfortune. The conditions for voluntary action are met, according to Aristotle, insofar as the agent is not compelled by an external source to commit the action that contributes to his misfortune, but the source of the action "rests with the agent himself."[13] But the error of the protagonist that leads to tragic misfortune also has an element of the *involuntary* in that the agent acts in ignorance of the particular circumstances of his actions, especially their consequences.[14]

In this way, ideal Aristotelian tragedy, such as Sophocles's *Oedipus the King*, shows the situation of a character caught between the moral and the immoral. The ideal tragic protagonist is a morally decent person who does not intend to bring about unhappiness for himself and his loved ones; yet through his mistake he is implicated in a causal nexus that brings about this very situation. The protagonist's role in bringing about the tragedy means that he must reflect on and reassess who he is and what he has done. Yet because there is no evil intent on the protagonist's part, his suffering—which is greater than any mistake he has made—evokes the audience's pity and fear. This is even truer if the character evinces regret for what he has done.[15]

A number of examples of human protagonists in horror films fit—to varying degrees—these Aristotelian requirements for tragic characters. In *American Werewolf*, David Kessler's (David Naughton) idea to backpack in Northern England leads to an attack on him and his friend Jack (Griffin Dunne) by a large and powerful animal, resulting in Jack's death and David's transformation into a werewolf. The two film versions of *Frankenstein* discussed earlier show that Dr. Frankenstein's unbridled desire to "play God" and master the secrets of life and death leads to his own destruction and those of all his loved ones. A misdiagnosis by child psychologist Malcolm Crowe (Bruce Willis) in *The Sixth Sense* (1999) leads one of his former patients to seek revenge ten years later and kill him in his home, leaving Malcolm's wife grief-stricken and distraught over his death. In *The Blair Witch Project* (1999), the young woman director's insistence that the project must go on at all costs brings about her own demise and those of the two film crewmen who join her in the woods. As I will discuss further, the horror film is a perfect popular genre within which to examine the depth and scope of human responsibility typically raised within the context of classical tragedy.

While this overview goes some way towards explaining how both human and nonhuman characters in horror cinema can be tragic figures, we will need to consider one additional question in relation to films that fall within the intersection of the two genres. Can the tragic effect be achieved by the depictions of the horrific and terrifying creatures in these films? That is, can these films successfully balance the character and plot requirements for sympathy and pity against the genre's demand for horror and disgust? We will need to consider whether these two emotions—horror and sympathy—are separate aspects of the audience's response or directly integrated and related to one another via the film's narrative. I will return to this issue in the last section of the essay. Now I turn to an analysis of *An American Werewolf in London*.

An American Werewolf in London

American Werewolf combines horror, tragedy, and black comedy to give a new spin on the classic film *The Wolf Man*, a horror story of a man who is attacked by a werewolf and then turns into one himself whenever the moon is full. This film, like David Cronenberg's 1986 version of *The Fly*, is a narrative of transformation in which a sympathetic human protagonist turns into a monster and meets a tragic death at the end of the story. The tragic protagonist of *American Werewolf* is more centrally David Kessler than the werewolf into which he transforms. Yet the film's ending affects a role reversal of sorts, suggesting that it is the werewolf that is the victim of human aggression, and not the other way around. Rather than depicting the werewolf as an alien and unnatural creature, the film points to some underlying similarities between human culture and animal nature, closing the divide between human and monster. This narrative strategy enables the film to expand the domain of horror—the confrontation between the human and the inhuman—to include themes central to Greek tragedy: the confrontation between the best and the worst aspects of human nature and culture.

David and Jack are two American college students backpacking one summer in Northern England. They come across a strangely named pub ("The Slaughtered Lamb") where the clientele are even stranger. The pair is given an odd and even menacing response when they inquire about a pentangle ("Lon Chaney Jr. in Universal Studios, 1941, maintained that it was the sign of the wolf-man," Jack says to David) on the pub's wall. Feeling unwelcome, the young men announce their intention to depart into the night. The pub owner—who happens to be the only woman present—urges the others to advise the visitors to stay, but in the end they encourage David and Jack to go, with the advice that they should stick to the road, stay off the moors, and beware the full moon. The audience's suspicion that all is not well is confirmed by the discussion in the pub that ensues after David and Jack depart. As the cry of some creature is heard off in the night, a debate ensues between the pub's patrons as to whether they should go out and find the young men before it is too late; but in the end, no action is taken. In the darkness Jack and David stray off the road onto the moor. They hear the howling of some creature, which soon attacks Jack, and then David, who, after regretting leaving Jack alone, runs back to help him. Jack dies almost instantly, but David is saved by the late intervention of the very folk in the pub whose menacing behavior made Jack and David depart. They shoot the animal, which turns into a human being as it dies, confirming what was already apparent to the audience: David was attacked by a werewolf and now he, too, will become such a creature with the return of the full moon.

The film has a considerable amount of blood and gore, including horrific scenes in which the werewolf attacks his human victims and leaves them to die, half-eaten. The people whom the werewolf has attacked, including Jack, return and speak to David as decomposing corpses, saying that they will walk the earth as the "living undead" until the last of the werewolf's blood line is severed, meaning until David, the new reincarnation of the werewolf, is dead. The scenes in which David transforms into a werewolf are also terrifying. Unlike *The Wolf Man*, *American Werewolf* does not just take the transformation of human into wolf halfway; instead, the film depicts this physical change in its entirety, showing how unnatural it is for a human being to turn into a wolf through the excruciating pain David undergoes during his transformations.

This "physical horror"—the transformation from a human being into a mere beast—is causally linked via the narrative with "moral horror": the sense of revulsion the film evokes at the unethical decision of the group in the pub to let the young Americans depart into the night when they believe that the werewolf is on the prowl.[16] For example, as Jack and David enter the pub, Jack comments that it is odd that the pub's sign "The Slaughtered Lamb" does not show a lamb, but a wolf. While the sign signals to the audience that the young men will soon encounter the werewolf, it is also refers to the idea that David, who will become the werewolf, is like an innocent lamb being sent to the slaughter by the pub folk.

A patron of the pub, a dart player whose menacing stance made Jack and David feel unwelcome, admits as much to the kindly Dr. Hirsch (John Woodvine), David's attending physician in London, when he investigates David's claim that they were attacked by a large animal, and not by a deranged man as the local authorities had reported. "It was a mistake," the dart player tells Dr. Hirsh, warning him that other people will die when the moon becomes full, before another patron, a chess player and "leader of the pack" in the pub the night of Jack and David's visit, cuts him off from further conversation. In this way the moral horror evoked by the behavior of the patrons of the pub is causally linked to the physical horror evoked by the werewolf. This makes the werewolf's death and the deaths of those it kills not simply sad, but also tragic, as they are victims of the collective moral mistakes of the pub's patrons.

David's own feeling that he is somehow responsible for Jack's death also heightens the sense of tragedy. As the film begins, Jack tells David that he would have preferred that they were in Italy, rather than shivering from the cold and fog of the British countryside. The "Slaughtered Lamb" sign is foreboding, and as they step into the pub, somewhat reluctantly, Jack again tells David to remember that "It is your fault" if anything goes wrong. When Jack is attacked by the werewolf, David runs away, despite Jack's appeals for help; then, feeling guilty, David runs back only to find that Jack is dead and that he will be the werewolf's next victim. Given the beast's strength and ferocity, it is not reasonable to think that David could have saved Jack from the werewolf. In fact, to even attempt to do so would be morally supererogatory. David's regret and subsequent attempt to save Jack makes him morally admirable. But this sequence of events leaves the impression in David's subconscious, and perhaps also in the audience's, that David's actions have somehow brought about Jack's death and his own attack by the werewolf.

David's error of judgment and his initial lack of courage make his suffering as he turns into the werewolf even more tragic, for he is not simply a victim of bad luck, but causally implicated in bringing about his own misfortune. David is a morally decent person who regrets not helping his friend in the first instance, and this heightens the tragic effect of his death as the werewolf at the end of the story.

The film's ending is also quite sad. David has turned into a werewolf and has gone on a killing spree. The werewolf is cornered in an alley, with the police aiming to shoot it, when Alex Price (Jenny Agutter), the nurse with whom David is romantically involved, arrives to intervene. She pleads with the police to let her help "David" and says that she loves him. For a moment, the creature seems to recognize her, but then snarls ferociously before it is shot dead by the policemen. The creature's body then transforms back into that of David. The ending is very downbeat, even though, in keeping with its black humor, the film quickly cuts to the credits and a 1950s rendition of "Blue Moon." In an odd sort of reversal, the conclusion directly evokes our sympathy for the werewolf. For it is represented as a victim, hunted and cornered, with Alex being the only thing standing between it and the policemen's fire.

The suggestion here is that it is the werewolf, and not just David, who is the tragic protagonist of the story. This is not surprising, for the film presents the idea that there is an underlying similarity between the life of the werewolf and aspects of human culture. When the humans confront the werewolf, they are not so much confronting a monster that is alien and unknown to them as a being with which they share moral and biological affinities. This reconfiguring of the monster as in some way "like us" moves the narrative from the realm of horror into the domain of Aristotelian tragedy, within which we are forced to confront aspects of our humanity that go unacknowledged or unrecognized until misfortune ensues.[17]

This theme is first introduced in a sequence of dreams that reflect David's worries that he will change into a werewolf with the arrival of the full moon. In the first and second dreams, David runs naked through the forest, hunting deer and then eating their flesh, just as a wolf might. In the third dream, David walks quickly through the forest, the way he did when the werewolf was chasing him and Jack. He sees a scene off in the distance in which he lies in his hospital bed, approached by the smiling Nurse Price, whom in real life he finds very attractive. The David in the hospital bed suddenly changes into a monster with fangs bared at Alex. On one level, these dreams reflect David's worry that he cannot "get away" from the werewolf's curse and that he will do harm to Nurse Price should they continue to get involved. Yet on another level, they suggest that the attraction David feels for Alex is like the base animal desire of the wolf to eat the deer's flesh.[18]

The nature of sex and sexual attraction is, in fact, a theme that is touched on throughout the story. At the beginning of *American Werewolf*, Jack and David talk about Jack's desire to sleep with Debbie Klein, a young woman whom Jack has lusted after since meeting her in the eight grade. Jack's fascination with this woman resides in her "great body," but David chides his friend for desiring a woman who is "a mediocre person with a good body." When David and Alex have sex, their lovemaking is tender and erotic, in sharp contrast with the anonymous sex we see in the porno movie, "See You Next

Wednesday," which is playing in the porn theater where David and Jack take refuge to talk. All this makes the relationship between David and Alex seem more than one just based on sexual attraction, but also one that is expressive of their feelings of mutual regard and affection. However, the fact remains that they sleep together without really knowing one another. This raises the question about whether their attraction is essentially "just physical," and if so, how this makes humans any different than animals.

This connection between animal nature and human culture is continued in the fourth dream sequence, which includes what is perhaps the film's most terrifying scene. David is back home with his family in the United States. His little brother and sister watch *Sesame Street* while David is studying at the dining room table. When David's father answers the door, zombies dressed like Nazi storm troopers rush in and brutally murder David's family while he is forced to stand by, unable to help. David wakes up in the hospital, greeted by Nurse Price. He is relieved to find that the previous incidents were all just part of a bad dream. Yet he is mistaken, as a zombie storm trooper appears and kills Alex.

Though the narrative purpose of these dream sequences is to explore David's growing anxiety over becoming a werewolf, they also depict an underlying connection between human culture and animal nature. While the creatures in David's dream that kill his loved ones are zombies, their dress and tactics call to mind the horror of the Nazi brown-shirts in World War II. The dreams, in other words, start with the attacks of the werewolf that David is concerned he will become, and end with a reference to one of the most violent and immoral acts committed by human beings in the 20th century.

This connection between werewolf and human aggression is also subtly brought out through cultural references that reveal the "animal-like" side of human society. The *Sesame Street* episode that is on TV as the Nazi zombies rush in shows Miss Piggy discussing the merits of the popular British puppet show, "Punch and Judy." Miss Piggy refers to the show's use of violence, explaining that letting out one's aggressive feelings, as Punch does with his "knockabout" sadistic behavior and violence, is a good thing. We are reminded that violence is so much an accepted part of society that it permeates even a children's television program.

Other human recreations that are prominently featured in the film also point to the link between human and animals. Sex, as noted, permeates society, from the daytime news shows to porn theaters like the one in Piccadilly Circus, where David converses with the "living dead" who urge him, in a scene of gallows humor, to take his life before the moon becomes full. Even the games of darts and chess played in the pub, and seen again on the British television, are recreational pastimes with origins that trace back to archery, hunting, and the strategies of war and self-defense. These features of modern life enable us to fill in the gap between human and werewolf, and in so doing to draw the connections, in our imaginations at least, between human culture and animal nature.

It is, therefore, fitting that after David suspects he is a werewolf, he sits in a porn house with the living dead thinking that he is no longer fit for the company of Nurse Price and the compassionate Dr. Hirsch. David's desire to protect Alex and Dr. Hirsch from harm is admirable, enhancing our sense of pity and fear for his inevitable destruction when he next turns into the werewolf. The film ends with a depiction of car crashes, mass hysteria, and general mayhem, stressing once again the parallels between the violence and chaos of human culture and animal nature. With its positioning of Alex between the werewolf and the mob of onlookers, the film also suggests that romantic love may be the only barrier between human culture and a more primitive, animal-like existence.

The film ends, as noted, with a final shot in which the werewolf is represented as a tragic victim, cornered in an alley, with policemen ready to fire and a throng of bystanders clamoring to get a thrill from a look at the werewolf. This role reversal of the monster and the humans and the reference to the worst side of human nature reminds us of the theme of "moral horror"—the ethics of humans in their worst moments—that is *American Werewolf*'s underlying subject.

The Sixth Sense

The Sixth Sense is an example of another subcategory of film that combines horror and tragedy—a horror film that features an (ostensibly) human protagonist that is a tragic character. On the narrative level, the film is a classic ghost story: Malcolm Crowe (Bruce Willis), a child psychologist in Philadelphia, has a young patient, nine-year-old Cole Sear (Haley Joel Osment), who is anxious and not communicating well with his mother Lynn (Toni Collette), a working-class single mother. More specifically, Cole has a "secret": he possesses a "sixth sense" that enables him to see and communicate with the ghosts of dead people, especially those who have suffered a violent death through the injustice of others.

Malcolm is, in the end, able to help Cole learn the reason for the ghosts' visits: they want him to listen to their stories. In order to assist Cole, Malcolm must go outside the area of his expertise—the scientific study of the mind—in order to, first, believe in the existence of these otherworldly visitors and, second, find a way to rid Cole of his problem, if not by making the visits of the ghosts cease, then by figuring out how to make Cole's encounters with them less frightening.

Although the scenes that show Cole's encounters with the ghosts are startling, the evocation of horror at the ghosts is not, as Margaret LaCaze observes, the film's central focus.[19] Instead, *The Sixth Sense* uses the story of the ghosts and their visitations in order to examine a theme that is central to Greek tragedy—the confrontation between humans and their own limitations, specifically their mortality. In order for Malcolm to help Cole, he must in some basic sense be able to recognize his limitations. These include the limits of his own discipline, which cannot countenance the existence of anything not known by the five senses, and personal limitations, including his misdiagnosis of a patient, Vincent Grey (Donnie Wahlberg), who suffered some ten years earlier from the same problem that afflicts his current patient, Cole.

Through a surprise ending, the film also reveals that Malcolm must come to terms with another constraint—his own mortality. For unbeknownst to Malcolm—and most of the audience—he *too* is a ghost, having died from the shot inflicted by his angry former patient, Vincent, depicted at the start of the film. In this way, *The Sixth Sense* unfolds like the ancient Greek tragedy, *Oedipus the King*, which also features a central protagonist who is morally admirable, makes an innocent "mistake," and in a moment of recognition at the end of the story, learns a surprising fact about his identity that brings about a reversal of fortune entailing his need to reexamine who he is in light of his newly acquired self-knowledge.

This moment of recognition occurs at the very end of film, when Malcolm sees his wedding ring roll off of his sleeping wife's hand, revealing that she has been mourning his death rather than his preoccupation with his work, as Malcolm had previously thought. Malcolm flashes back to the night he was shot, and realizes (as do those members of the audience who did already guess it) that the wound inflicted by Vincent Grey was in fact fatal. The knowledge that Malcolm acquires about the existence of the ghost world, therefore, turns out to be a kind of self-knowledge, for he is one of them.

This identity of Malcolm as a ghost also serves the purpose of showing that the ghosts are not too different from ordinary people, in spite of their frightening appearances. In representing Malcolm as a sympathetic figure, the film also evokes our sympathy for the ghosts, many of whom are, like Malcolm, trying to come to terms with the manner in which they died.

In this way, *The Sixth Sense* uses the narrative of the ghost story to raise issues central to Greek tragedy: self-knowledge, the nature of responsibility, and human mortality. The film evokes our sympathy and fear for the two central characters, Malcolm and Cole, in order to explore our own fears and terrors. The object of these fears is not, most centrally, the ghosts, but relates to concerns about our own personal lives: failures in our careers and in our relationships, the loss of communication between ourselves and those we are closest to, and the ultimate separation from them—death.[20]

Horror and Tragedy Reconsidered

With these readings of *An American Werewolf in London* and *The Sixth Sense* in place, we can now return to some of the questions raised in the opening section of this essay. In particular, how do horror and sympathy work together in films that intertwine the genres of horror and tragedy? Does the representation of the monster-figures in films such as *American Werewolf* and *The Sixth Sense* enhance or detract from the tragic effect? And what is the point of intertwining horror and tragedy in this manner?

It is not surprising that a work can belong to both horror and tragedy, for there are similarities between the two genres. Both genres, for example, have their own associated "paradoxes." As Aristotle recognized, tragedy is paradoxical, for its representations of suffering evoke pity and fear, which are uncomfortable emotions to experience. Yet the audience takes pleasure from experiencing them in response to a mimetic representation. Why exactly Aristotle thinks this is so is a matter of scholarly contention. On the most plausible readings of Aristotle, this is because the audience is able to move from a response of pity and fear to a certain kind of pleasurable learning via the narrative and mimetic framing of suffering.[21] The point, in fact, of evoking pity and fear via tragedy is to induce this pleasure through contemplation of the universal generalizations concerning human action, happiness, and suffering that tragic narratives offer.

As scholars have noted, the appeal of horror is also puzzling. For how can horror, which evokes the audience's fear and revulsion, induce the pleasure that it obviously does in many viewers? Several solutions have been offered to this paradox. Carroll argues that horror induces a dichotomous response: on the hand, the emotional pain from the fear and disgust evoked by the monster, and on the other, the cognitive pleasure which results from following out the narrative.[22] In itself, the representation of the monster is disgusting, for it is a creature that crosses species boundaries. Yet the entire narrative structure in which the presentation of the monster is embedded evinces pleasure in the viewer, for it provides the satisfactions of discovering and confirming the existence of the monster.[23] The disgust the audience feels toward the monster is, Carroll says, the price we must pay for the cognitive pleasures offered by the narrative. Robert C. Solomon and Murray Smith suggest, in contrast, that it is precisely the revolting and the disgusting depicted in horror films that is the object of our fascination and interest in these pictures.[24] This is so, on Solomon's view, because horror "reminds us of something essential about ourselves . . . our most basic vulnerabilities"[25]; while Smith argues that "the horrific phenomenon is the object of our interest and attention."[26]

My Aristotelian framework for looking at the intersection of horror and tragedy is indebted to both of these approaches. An Aristotelian would side with Carroll in maintaining that our response to films such as *American Werewolf* and *The Sixth Sense* does not suggest that it is disgust in the form of the monster that pleases or fascinates. Instead, it is the learning and reflection that accompanies our emotional responses to the characters in these films that induces pleasure. In this sense, an Aristotelian would say that Carroll is correct that it is the narrative *representation* of the monster that pleases, not disgust itself. But films that intertwine horror and tragedy do what Solomon suggests all horror has the power to do—redirect our attention to the underside of human culture that for the most part goes unrecognized and is in need of critical examination.

We have seen this illustrated in both films. In *American Werewolf*, the disgust evoked by the werewolf is linked via the narrative to another kind of horror—the "ethical horror" we feel in response to the disregard shown for David by the patrons of the pub. In this way, the evocation of horror and sympathy are integrated through the connections the film makes between human culture and a terrifying animal nature. In *The Sixth Sense*, meanwhile, the pity and fear we feel for Malcolm Crowe in response to his situation is most centrally a fear of the unknown aspects of our own lives. We derive pleasure from the film's narrative framing of the monsters, for it enables us to consider the other side of human existence.

In conclusion, let us return to our original question: Can horror films be tragic? My initial response, from an Aristotelian point of view, was "No," for it is difficult to see how a film where the plot centers on the existence of a monster could evoke pity and fear in the audience. Yet films like *An American Werewolf in London* and *The Sixth Sense* work as a popular form of film tragedy by framing the essential conflict in the story not as human versus inhuman but as a confrontation between human protagonists and their own lives and natures. By positioning the characters—both human and nonhuman—as figures surprisingly "like us," the horror film moves away from the terrain of mere "spectacle" and into the domain of Aristotelian tragedy.

Notes

1. Noël Carroll, *The Philosophy of Horror; or, Paradoxes of the Heart* (New York and London: Routledge, 1990), 14–17.

2. Aristotle, *Poetics*, ed. and trans. Stephen Halliwell (Cambridge, MA and London: Harvard University Press, 1995), 1449b22–28. All references to the *Poetics* are to this edition.

3. Carroll, 27–35.

4. Robin Wood, "An Introduction to the American Horror Film," in *Movies and Methods, Volume II: An Anthology*, ed. Bill Nichols (Berkeley: University of California Press, 1985).

5. Daniel Shaw, "Power, Horror, and Ambivalence," *Film and Philosophy*, Special Edition 2001: 1–12.

6. Pity is directed toward the underserved suffering of another person, "which the person himself might expect to suffer, either himself or one of his loved ones" (Aristotle, *On Rhetoric*, trans. George A. Kennedy (New York and Oxford: Oxford University Press, 1991), 1385b14–15). Fear is a pain or disturbance due to imagining some harm that occurs or will occur to a person "like us" (*Poetics* 1453a5).

7. Unfortunately, Aristotle seems to be guilty of sexist bias in favoring male over female characters as the ideal tragic protagonists. See Cynthia A. Freeland, "Plot Imitates Action: Aesthetic Evaluation and Moral Realism in Aristotle's *Poetics*," in *Essays on Aristotle's Poetics*, ed. Amélie Oskenberg Rorty (Princeton: Princeton University Press, 1992).

8. For plots that features human protagonist who overstep natural boundaries and unleash a monster, see Carroll, 118–24.

9. See the reading of Cynthia A. Freeland, *The Naked and the Undead: Evil and the Appeal of Horror* (Boulder: Westview Press, 2002), 25–54.

10. Robin Wood (*op. cit.*) suggests this treatment of the monster figure as downtrodden and cast out from human fellowship makes him a metaphor for the poor and working-class members of society. He argues that this representational strategy enables the monster in these films to serve as a critique of social hierarchies.

11. See Freeland's discussion of vampire films in *The Naked and Undead*, Chapter Four. Freeland argues that the vampire story permits a kind of "shifting identification with or critique of the monstrous vampire figure and his victims".

12. I thank Steven Schneider for suggesting some additional films to consider as illustrations in this section.

13. Aristotle, *Nichomachean Ethics* III.1. 1110a5, trans. Martin Ostwald (Bobbs-Merrill: Indianapolis and New York, 1962).

14. *Ibid.*, III.1.111a5.

15. *Ibid.*, 1110b20.

16. Murray Smith evokes this contrast between "physical horror" and "moral horror" in his analysis of *The Fly* in "(A)moral Monstrosity," in *The Modern Fantastic: The Films of David Cronenberg*, ed. Michael Grant (Westport: Praeger, 2000), 69–83. My use of these terms owes much to Smith's illustration of these concepts in this essay.

17. For the suggestion that horror, as a genre, resembles tragedy in its concern with examining human values and vulnerabilities, see Robert C. Solomon, "Review of Noël Carroll, *The Philosophy of Horror*," *Philosophy of Literature* 16 (1992): 163–73. See especially pages 168 and 173.

18. See Steven Jay Schneider, "'Suck . . . don't suck': Framing ideology in Kathryn Bigelow's *Near Dark*," for a discussion of the human/inhuman contrast in relation to this film. In *The Cinema of Kathryn Bigelow: Hollywood Transgressor*, ed. Deborah Jermyn and Sean Redmond (London: Wallflower Press, 2003), 72-90.

19. Marguerite LaCaze, "The Mourning of Loss in *The Sixth Sense*," *Post Script: Essays in Film and the Humanities* 21, no. 3 (Summer 2002): 111-21.

20. Cf. La Caze, *op. cit.*

21. The controversy centers around what Aristotle means in saying that tragedy induces a "catharsis" of pity and fear (*Poetics* VI, 1449b22–28). One reading suggests that "catharsis" is the expunction of the emotions of pity and fear for the purpose of "getting rid" of these uncomfortable emotions in one's everyday life. See Jacob Bernay, "Aristotle on the Effect of Tragedy," *Articles on Aristotle*, Vol. 4, ed. Jonathan Barnes, Malcolm Schofield, and Richard Sorabji (London: Duckworth, 1979). The leading interpretations of "catharsis" suggests that "catharsis" evokes a certain kind of pleasurable emotional reinforcement of truths previously held (Jonathan Lear, "Katharsis," in Rorty, *op. cit.*); or that "catharsis" induces pleasure through a "clarification" of who

we are and what we value (Martha C. Nussbaum, "Tragedy and Self-Sufficiency: Plato and Aristotle on Pity and Fear," in Rorty, *op. cit.*).

22. Carroll, 186–87.

23. Carroll, 184.

24. Solomon, *op. cit.*; and Smith, *op. cit.*

25. Solomon, 173.

26. Smith, 81.

27. I thanks the editors, Steven Jay Schneider and Daniel Shaw, for their very helpful comments, and Cynthia Freeland for her suggestions on films to consider for the writing of this essay.

Heidegger, the Uncanny, and Jacques Tourneur's Horror Films

Curtis Bowman

Most horror films are not very horrifying, and many of them are not especially frightening. This is true, of course, of the bad or mediocre productions that populate the genre. Since the failure rate among horror films is very high, it should come as no surprise that we frequently remain unmoved by what we see on the screen. But if we are honest about our reactions, then we must admit that even some of the classics neither horrify nor frighten us. They must have acquired their classic status by moving us in some significant way, but how they managed to do so is not always obvious. We need an explanation of the fact that some of the most successful horror films fail to move us as the genre seems to dictate they should. After all, we typically think that horror films are supposed to horrify and, by implication, to frighten us.[1]

Excessive familiarity with some films tends to deaden our response. However much we might admire the original *Frankenstein* (1931), it is difficult for us to be horrified or frightened by it any longer. We respond favorably to the production values, director James Whale's magnificent visual sense, Boris Karloff's performance as the monster, and so forth. The film no longer horrifies or frightens us, yet we still consider it a successful horror movie, and thus not merely of historical interest for fans and admirers of the genre. We can still be moved by it in ways that depend on its possessing the features that we expect to find in a horror film.

Some successful horror movies were not especially horrifying or frightening when they first appeared, yet we consider them worthy additions to the genre. Therefore, unlike the case of *Frankenstein*, here we are not dealing with something where the capacity to produce its intended effect has deteriorated over time. Instead, we are reacting to them more or less as we are supposed to do. Arguments about artistic intention and its role in the audience's reception of the work of art aside, we commonly recognize that a particular horror movie is attempting something besides trying to horrify and frighten us. Naturally, horror and fear are often present in us. But it is frequently the case that neither is our most powerful response to the film; nor is it always the case that these feelings are the most important ones that the film is trying to elicit in us. In fact, horror and fear may be entirely absent in us—and rightly so, since the film was not striving to produce them in us in the first place.

It is not always easy to describe this type of reaction that stands apart from horror and fear. We might resort to calling a film "spooky," "creepy," or "disturbing" in our efforts to tell others how it moved us. These terms are far from exact, but others agree with us and say that they have felt the same way. Furthermore, they recognize that we are praising the film with such language. It is doubtful that we are dealing with only one response, since films work on us in many ways. The purpose of this chapter is to look at the experience of the uncanny, which is sometimes aroused in us independently of feelings of horror or fear.

The most famous discussion of the uncanny is Freud's 1919 essay "The 'Uncanny'."[2] Despite the usefulness of Freud's account, I intend to extend the notion of the uncanny beyond psychoanalysis into the realm of ontology. The source of my discussion will perhaps surprise most readers, since I shall draw on §40 of Heidegger's *Being and Time*. His discussion of angst and the related notion of the uncanny, so I claim, will prove helpful in understanding one type of response to horror films.

To readers who hesitate to deploy the heavy artillery of Heidegger's fundamental ontology against the battered redoubts of the horror film genre, let me say the following: Given that monsters play a significant role in horror films, it is appropriate to investigate a genre populated by ontological misfits in terms that take their peculiar ontologies seriously. Noël Carroll has done this superbly. Carroll, though, concentrates on the emotion of horror engendered by thoughts of monsters with cross-category natures that are regarded as impure and hence as disgusting and threatening. My recommendation is that we also look at the philosophical responses that works containing such creatures can produce in us. Heidegger can help us to understand these reactions, as well as the experience of uncanniness that can arise in the complete absence of monsters.

In order to illustrate the Heideggerian view on these matters, I shall apply it to Jacques Tourneur's horror films of the 1940s and 1950s. I shall also very briefly touch on how we might use my reading of Heidegger as a justification of the horror genre as a whole, that is, as one way of possibly understanding its value to us. Contrary to those who might mutter that Heidegger is to horror as cause is to effect, I shall suggest that Heidegger is to horror as Aristotle is to tragedy.

Concepts of the Uncanny in Freud and Heidegger

Freud's concept of the uncanny is often employed in horror film criticism.[3] Because of the sexual nature of many horror films, it pays to interpret them in light of a theory disposed to take their sexual elements seriously. As a result, Freud's essay has been employed to explain how horror films are often manifestations of repressed sexuality (or not-so-repressed sexuality, as is frequently the case nowadays). But there is more to the uncanny, he says, than repressed sexuality.

Freud claims that the feeling of uncanniness is not to be identified with horror and fear; however, he also claims that it is related to such feelings, especially to fear. He initially formulates the concept of the uncanny as "that class of the frightening which leads back to what is known of old and long familiar."[4] Freud never defends the assertion that the uncanny includes some element drawn from our past mental life; he simply takes this as part of his starting point. We might quarrel with this assumption, but any exposition of Freud's account must begin with it. As Freud's analysis progresses, we learn that the two main sources of the uncanny are repressed infantile beliefs and desires (e.g., the Oedipus complex and all that accompanies it), and surmounted beliefs (e.g., the omnipotence of thought and the idea that the dead can return as spirits). In general, surmounted beliefs are outmoded ways of thinking that are reactivated and confirmed in the experience of the uncanny.

That we once accepted these notions, says Freud, accounts for the feeling of familiarity in the experience of the uncanny: their reappearance in consciousness reminds us of our former beliefs. Furthermore, the reappearance of repressed beliefs and desires is not simply a matter of recognizing some part of one's past mental life, but also a source of disturbance, given that repressed material is always accompanied by anxiety as it returns to consciousness.[5] Surmounted beliefs do not seem to be subject to repression, and thus their confirmation is not accompanied by anxiety. When we confirm a surmounted belief, it is as if, Freud writes, we say to ourselves that "the dead *do* live on" and the like.[6] But is this also painful? Freud does not say. Perhaps the reemergence of surmounted beliefs signifies a painful loss of intellectual mastery. Such a dynamic—we might call it "the confirmation of the disavowed"—could account for any disturbance that might be found in the case of surmounted beliefs. This type of disturbance, regardless of whether or not it is implicit in Freud's essay, will reappear in our discussion of Heidegger.

Freud regards E. T. A. Hoffmann's "The Sandman" as an especially effective uncanny tale. The eponymous figure of the Sandman, a mythical being who tears out children's eyes, he argues, is the primary source of the feeling of uncanniness aroused in the reader. Freud interprets the fear of losing one's eyes as an expression of castration anxiety. Nathaniel, the story's protagonist, identifies the lawyer Coppelius, a figure from his childhood whom he holds responsible for his father's death, with the Sandman, since Coppelius used to appear every night before the child's bedtime to visit his father. Several years later, while at the university, Nathaniel encounters a barometer-seller named Coppola; he is immediately convinced that Coppola is in fact Coppelius, and that Coppelius has come back into his life once more to harm him. Nathaniel's obsession with Coppelius/Coppola alienates him from his sweetheart Clara, as well as from the other people who care about him. Freud significantly points out that the Sandman always appears in the story as a disturber of love.[7] Eventually, Nathaniel commits suicide.

Another uncanny element in the story, says Freud, is the figure of Olympia, a mechanical doll created by Spalanzani, who is one of Nathaniel's professors, along with Coppelius/Coppola. She seems to have been created so that Nathaniel will fall in love with her, and thus, it seems, as a test of how convincing of a human simulacrum the two men can devise. Olympia, Freud says, is a living doll, and as such she confirms a surmounted belief that is common among children, namely, that their dolls can come to life. Such a belief, he says, is an expression of an animistic conception of the world that we outgrow as we mature.

Freud's reading of the story satisfies his criteria for the uncanny: the Oedipus complex is expressed in symbolic form in the figure of the Sandman, and the figure of Olympia confirms a surmounted belief in animism (at least, Freud would add, in those readers who still possess some vestige of the belief). According to Freud's reading of Hoffmann's story, these are its uncanny elements. Strangely enough, though, Freud never mentions the story's most uncanny aspect: the conspiracy against Nathaniel extending at least from his days at the university to the end of his life (but perhaps all the way back to his early childhood and the death of his father).

Since neither the narrator of the story nor any of the characters openly declare that there is a conspiracy against Nathaniel, the reader is left to infer its existence. Many incidents in Nathaniel's life are best explained as elements of a plot designed to manipulate him for unknown reasons and purposes. Nathaniel himself has an intuitive grasp of his situation: he frequently refers to malevolent forces when he gives expression to what sound like the paranoid delusions of a deranged mind. He believes that these forces control his life and have some terrible fate in store for him; his friends and loved ones, especially Clara, tell him that they are merely figments of his imagination. Nathaniel considers them supernatural forces. Ultimately, though, we see that they are mundane in origin, consisting principally of Coppelius/Coppola, Spalanzani, and some students at the university. Perhaps his father was part of the conspiracy; even Clara might be a part of it, as the final moments before Nathaniel's suicide might be taken to intimate. It is unlikely, though not completely impossible, that Olympia is of supernatural origin; she really seems to be nothing more than a cleverly constructed mechanical doll. One of Nathaniel's childhood memories, which is probably best interpreted as a fantasy expressing his adult feelings of paranoia and persecution, suggests that he too is a mechanical doll (or at least that he saw himself as such at one point in his life, and thus that his thoughts about dark forces controlling his life go all the way back to his childhood).

Many of the details are open to interpretation, but by the end of the story the reader realizes that Nathaniel was right all along. He really was in the grip of forces beyond his control, contrary to what everyone told him all his life. We cannot be sure of exactly when the conspiracy began and ended. Nor can we precisely determine all of its participants. But the inescapable conclusion is that there was a plot against Nathaniel. If we read many of the most significant events of "The Sandman" as manifestations of a conspiracy, then it affects us differently than Freud would have it. Freud looks to the uncanny as the reappearance of that which was once familiar to us. He begins his analysis with this claim and then proceeds to explain its possibility through an appeal to psychoanalysis.

We rightly wonder how Freud's reading can aid us in interpreting the conspiracy against Nathaniel. The apparatus of psychoanalysis does not seem too helpful here. Freud actually mentions "secret injurious powers" as a possible source of the feeling of uncanniness (in its second form as the confirmation of a surmounted belief), although the essay nowhere reveals why he thinks that we possess a surmounted belief in such powers.[8] But he never lets on that he considers such powers relevant for interpreting Hoffmann's story. Instead of speculating about how we might apply Freud's account to the conspiracy against Nathaniel, I shall now turn to Heidegger. Once I have set out Heidegger's view of the uncanny, I shall briefly return to "The Sandman."

Some knowledge of Heidegger's project is required for understanding his views about the uncanny.[9] What follows is necessarily a simplified picture. Heidegger says that *Being and Time* deals with the question of being, and is thus a work in ontology. Past difficulties in answering the question—which stretch all the way back to the ancient Greeks, he claims—lead him to raise it again. He argues, though, that these persistent difficulties are a sign that we do not know how to formulate the question properly, much less how to answer it. We have one hope, he says. Since human beings possess some understanding of their own being prior to any philosophical investigation of their being, Heidegger believes that we can study what it is to be a human being in order to learn how to ask and answer the question of being in general. As a result, the focus of *Being and Time* shifts from the question of being to a study of the being of human beings (i.e., to employ Heidegger's terms, the focus shifts to an analytic of Da-sein).

Da-sein in its very being, says Heidegger, is concerned about its being. In other words, Da-sein is essentially caught up in some sort of interpretation of what it is to be a human being, even if its self-understanding is inchoate and incorrect. Regardless of the truth or falsity of this interpretation, he argues, Da-sein has some pre-reflective understanding of its being. Once this pre-reflective understanding is subjected to philosophical scrutiny, it can be articulated into an ontology of Da-sein that will serve as the model for raising and answering the question of being in general.

Heidegger never completed *Being and Time*, and thus he never returned to answer the question of being. Nonetheless, the analytic of Da-sein is quite impressive. As it unfolds, Heidegger argues that Da-sein's fundamental mode of existence is being-in-the-world. The world includes "innerworldly beings" (i.e., the instruments and tools of the surrounding environment that draw their being from Da-sein's purposes). Heidegger famously provides the example of a hammer in §15. Such things are said to be "handy," i.e., useful. When things fail to be handy, we then see them in terms of "objective presence" (i.e., the type of being captured by mathematics and the theories of the natural sciences). Handiness and objective presence make up the realms of being of the beings that are not Da-sein. How Da-sein understands its relationship to these beings, and to the world in general (which also includes other beings that are Da-sein), is of great importance for Heidegger.

Typically, Heidegger claims, we have tended to see the world in terms of objective presence, and, as a result, Da-sein has tended to interpret itself in the same terms. For Heidegger, this is the cause of many mistakes and distortions. In particular, it is one source of the inauthenticity that characterizes Da-sein in its "average everydayness" (i.e., the manner in which it relates to the world and to itself prior to any explicit philosophical reflection on its being). Da-sein, without even realizing it, is in the grip of some self-understanding that it has failed to make its own. In other words, regardless of whether or not that self-understanding is true or false, Da-sein has never made it an explicit object of reflection and hence of critical evaluation. Instead, Da-sein exists in accordance with the unexamined beliefs, values, and choices of "the they"; it possesses a "they-self" with a view of the world (and thus, according to Heidegger, of itself) acquired uncritically from its surroundings—hence its inauthenticity.

Da-sein refuses to understand itself as potentiality of being (i.e., as a being for which there are many possible ways to live, act, and understand itself); and this refusal stems in part from seeing itself in terms of objective presence. For Heidegger, this is a lamentable ontological failure. Furthermore, this refusal is not accidental; in fact, it is highly motivated. Da-sein is said to escape into the they-self for the same reason that it flees from some frightening object: that is, it finds itself threatened. I might flee in fear from a bear in the woods. Da-sein does something similar, says Heidegger, in that it flees in angst from a threat which it poses to itself. Angst, for Heidegger, is not primarily an emotion like fear, although it may appear in the more familiar psychological guise of anxiety from time to time. Instead, it is a mode of insight into Da-sein's very nature.

The threat that angst reveals to us, says Heidegger, is posed by our very nature; as a result, we have a perpetual motive to flee from ourselves. The threat lies in the fact that Da-sein is a scene of possibility that burdens it with responsibility and uncertainty. The easiest thing to do is to flee into the comforting arms of the they-self and to surrender to its cheap bromides and flattering self-deceptions. Sometimes, though, we face up to ourselves and to the world around us. In moments like these, says Heidegger, we enter into the uncanny.

The main element of the uncanny is not-being-at-home in the world. We lose, so to speak, our ontological balance and become unsure of ourselves and of our understanding of the world around us. The main form that this can take is the realization that more possibilities exist for action and understanding than we ever thought. Perhaps we revise our ideas in light of experiencing the uncanny; perhaps our ideas remain the same. The point is that the experience of uncanniness forces us to appropriate or reject accustomed ways of thinking and acting. In this way, we make some small step towards authenticity.

Heidegger's style of writing attempts to elicit the uncanny in us. In §7 he says that we lack both the words and the grammar for the project that he envisions. His esoteric language is supposed to jolt us out of the philosophical complacency we have inherited from our predecessors. Part of the intent of *Being and Time* is to effect the very transformation in the reader that Heidegger advocates throughout the book, namely, the movement from inauthenticity to authenticity. His writing style has probably revolted as many readers as it has attracted, but it is always motivated by an important element of the project.

Heidegger never explicitly associates the style of *Being and Time* with the goal of provoking uncanniness in us. Furthermore, he gives no concrete examples of uncanniness, nor does he provide criteria for recognizing it. He leaves it to us to experience and explain it for ourselves. My contention is that works of art can arouse Heideggerian uncanniness in us. If we interpret "The Sandman" in a Heideggerian spirit, especially the conspiracy that Freud overlooked, we can see why this is so.

Hoffmann draws us into a vividly rendered life that is destroyed by mysterious forces for no apparent reason. The conspiracy is so vast that it undoes our ordinary notions of the world around us. It hardly seems possible, yet by the end of the story we must entertain the thought of its reality in order to make sense of Hoffmann's tale; otherwise, too much goes unexplained. But such a thought is greatly disturbing. This is not merely because Nathaniel is a sympathetic character who comes to harm, but also because the very context of his life resists comprehension. Who could do such terrible things to him? And why? We hesitate to think that there can be such people, yet we must imagine that they exist in the world that Nathaniel inhabits, if not in our own. To think this, though, is to entertain the revision of some of our fundamental notions about our fellow human beings and about how to live our lives. The world slips from our grasp. Furthermore, this is so even if the story contains no supernatural elements at all. In fact, the shock caused by the thought of a vast conspiracy against Nathaniel might be lessened if we imagined that supernatural agency was also involved in his undoing.

But, of course, Hoffmann's story is only a story. We know this, and so it is unlikely to cause us to revise our actual thinking. Nonetheless, we entertain various thoughts long enough to disturb ourselves, which might lead to actual revisions in our thoughts about the world. However briefly, we are no longer at home in the world, even if only in our imagination. Perhaps we are also horrified and frightened, but neither emotion is required for experiencing uncanniness. All that is required is that we lose our ontological equilibrium. We right ourselves as we leave Hoffmann's fictional world, but perhaps we return to our world slightly changed.

Freud recognizes the role played by esoteric ontologies in many stories involving the uncanny, as his discussion of surmounted beliefs shows. Some of these beliefs (e.g., those involving the omnipotence of thought) commit those who hold them to supernatural views of the world. For Freud, however, the important point is not so much the metaphysical content of the beliefs, but rather their confirmation as they return to consciousness. Heidegger's concept of the uncanny essentially relies on the overthrow of our ontology, even if it lasts for only for a moment. This loss of intellectual mastery is almost certain to disturb us—hence the uneasiness that we usually feel in uncanny circumstances. Sometimes we also feel fear, perhaps even horror, but neither emotion is a necessary condition for feeling uncanniness. In fact, their presence often inhibits the experience of uncanniness, which is more subtle than either horror or fear and is thus easily crowded out by powerful emotions.

Tourneur and the Heideggerian Uncanny

Tourneur directed four horror films during his long career: *Cat People* (1942), *I Walked with a Zombie* (1943), *The Leopard Man* (1943), and *Curse of the Demon* (1957).[10] The first three were made by Val

Lewton's production unit at RKO.[11] Lewton's films typically imply more than they show, relying on viewers to supply a great deal for themselves in their imagination. *Cat People* contains a monster, Irena Dubrovna (Simone Simon), but her monstrous nature is unambiguously revealed only at the end of the film. *I Walked with a Zombie* may or may not contain a zombie; the audience can never be certain that Jessica Holland (Christine Gordon) is anything more than a mental case. Since *The Leopard Man* appeared shortly after Universal's *The Wolf Man* (1941), the original audience was primed to expect some leopard-like monster akin to a werewolf. No such creature appears, however. We do not directly witness the killings of the three women, yet we never really have any reason to think that the first victim is killed by anything but a leopard. By the end of the film we discover that Dr. Galbraith (James Bell) is a sexual psychopath who has disguised his two murders as leopard attacks.

Unlike the Lewton productions, a monster appears in spectacular fashion only minutes into *Curse of the Demon*. The demon employed by Julian Karswell (Niall MacGinnis) to kill Professor Henry Harrington (Maurice Denham) is unmistakably supernatural. It is a creature from some nether region summoned by means of black magic to do Karswell's bidding; this is unambiguously clear to the audience from beginning to end. In this respect, therefore, *Curse of the Demon* is strikingly different from Tourneur's other horror films.

These four films contain moments that are frightening, if not especially horrifying. The first killing in *The Leopard Man* is quite disturbing, even though we only hear Teresa Delgado's (Margaret Landry) screams for help as she is mauled to death by the leopard in front of her house. The effect is heightened by the blood that seeps under the front door, indicating how savage the attack was. Since we experience Teresa's death from within the house, we can only imagine how the leopard kills her. A scene in *Curse of the Demon* convincingly depicts Rand Hobart's (Brian Wilde) terror at the thought of being passed the parchment that summons the demon. We sympathize with his terror and understand why he jumps from a window to his death.

These are isolated moments that do not accurately reflect the overall tone of these films. The dominant mood, I submit, is one of uncanniness. In what follows, I propose no criteria for producing or experiencing the Heideggerian uncanny, but we will see that these films give rise to precisely the feeling of uncanniness that concerned Heidegger. They might also produce feelings of horror and fear, but this is a secondary concern for us.

Cat People slowly reveals that Irena Dubrovna's fears about her ancestry are fully justified. Initially, it seems that she has heard too many tales about the history of her village, which is said to have fallen into Satanism after being captured by the Mamelukes long ago. Years later, so it is said, the village was liberated by King John of Serbia; some of the village's witches were executed, while others escaped into the mountains. She relates this legend to Oliver Reed (Kent Smith), her new American friend. As their relationship develops, it becomes clear not only that she believes these stories, but also that they govern her life. After Irena and Oliver declare their love for each other, she shies away from kissing him, hinting darkly at some evil that he cannot understand. On their wedding night, Irena is too afraid of this unnamed evil to consummate their marriage.

Irena seems to be nothing more than a neurotic with an overactive imagination—except for the fact that the animals from the local pet store are afraid of her. This oddity is revealed during the couple's courtship. Its significance seems slight, though, given that the store owner herself says that some people simply cannot come into her store because of the animals' reaction to them. Since Irena's problems continue to come between them, Oliver arranges for her to see a psychiatrist. Dr. Judd (Tom Conway) learns the secret of her sexual anxiety: Irena believes that if aroused by jealousy, anger, or passion she will turn into a panther and kill her lover. Under hypnosis, she revealed a childhood trauma: Her father died in "some mysterious accident in the forest" before her birth, and the children of her village called her mother a cat woman. (The viewer is left to infer that her father was killed by her mother when she was conceived.) Oliver obtusely tells Alice (Jane Randolph), a friend from work, that Irena is seeing Dr. Judd, thereby marking the beginning of Irena's jealousy toward Alice.

The thought that Irena is in fact a cat woman is now slowly forced on the viewer. Irena stalks Alice through the park one night. Tourneur uses sound to suggest Irena's transformation into a panther. Her clicking heels suddenly stop echoing, and we no longer see her following Alice. Alice comprehends the menace behind the sudden silence and runs to a bus stop. A growling sound grows louder and comes closer, but is nothing more than a bus suddenly coming into the frame from the right side as Alice looks to the left. We see moving branches above a wall, several dead sheep in the zoo, paw prints that turn into tracks made by a woman's high heels, and then Irena herself. She arrives home looking disheveled. She spends a restless night dreaming of cats, King John of Serbia (who appears as Dr. Judd wearing armor and wielding a sword), and the key to the panther's cage. The next day she steals the key while the animal's keeper is preoccupied.

In another scene, Irena follows Alice to the swimming pool of Alice's building. Frightened by growling and a shadow on the staircase, Alice dives into the water. More growling is heard, and more shadows appear around the pool. One shadow looks suspiciously like that of a large cat. The lights come on to reveal Irena as we had seen her earlier. After she leaves, Alice discovers that her robe has been shredded.

Alice tells Dr. Judd that she has been pursued by Irena in her cat form; he is reluctant to believe her, but the torn robe puts him on guard. He interviews Irena again, and she seems to him to be more psychologically disturbed than before. Yet he seems to have helped her, since she tells Oliver later that day that she is no longer afraid. Oliver spoils her breakthrough, saying that he is now in love with Alice. The new couple becomes the target of Irena's rage.

Alice and Oliver are at the office when a panther enters their studio—after the door has been mysteriously locked. As the panther approaches, Oliver picks up a T-square, which casts a cross-like shadow on the wall. The panther is heard once more, but no longer seen; the locked door is now open. Alice and Oliver see the open elevator and head downstairs. We see the elevator door close; a revolving door to the outside stops spinning. Finally, Alice notices Irena's perfume. Dr. Judd has contrived to be in Irena's apartment when she returns home. He takes Irena in his arms and kisses her; the screen darkens a bit as her eyes take on a malevolent glow; she moves forward out of the frame. Dr. Judd steps back in horror and draws the sword hidden in his cane. A struggle erupts. Shadows of a man and a large cat fighting each other are cast on the wall, and at the final moment, a panther leaps on a man on the floor. Alice and Oliver arrive to hear Dr. Judd's screams. They rush upstairs, passing Irena, who has hidden herself. She walks to the zoo, nursing her shoulder. She opens the panther's cage. The frightened creature draws back, like the animals in the pet shop; it then leaps out, striking Irena in the head. She falls to the ground, with part of Dr. Judd's cane protruding from her left shoulder, and dies.

Because Irena had stolen the key to the panther's cage, it is remotely possible that the creature that appeared in Oliver and Alice's studio was the panther from the zoo. How Irena could have managed to lead it there is unclear, given her effect on animals. But since the panther seems to leave the room in response to the cross-like shadow on the wall, we are meant to infer that it was Irena, and that she was driven away by the power of the cross. In the climactic struggle with Dr. Judd, we clearly see a panther, and we have no reason to think that it is not Irena. Thus, the legend about Irena's village is unambiguously confirmed. Irena says on several occasions that she has always told the truth about herself; no one, of course, was willing to believe her until the truth became obvious to everyone.

Cat People forces its viewers to entertain an ontology involving ancient curses, shapeshifters, and evil fraught with sexuality. Hardly the stuff of everyday life, in other words. Tourneur's direction does much to heighten the uncanny feelings evoked by the action of the tale. Darkness and sound contribute to the otherworldly atmosphere that follows Irena; shadows and clicking heels intimate danger of an esoteric sort. None of this is especially horrifying or frightening, but it is disquieting and eerie.

I Walked with a Zombie conjures up a similar atmosphere, but never unambiguously reveals that Jessica Holland is a zombie. Betsy Connell (Frances Dee), her nurse, looks for a scientific cure for her condition, which Dr. Maxwell (James Bell) says resulted from a fever that burned out her mind. Insulin shock treatment fails. Alma (Theresa Harris), a family servant, tells Betsy of voodoo cures. Since Betsy has fallen in love with Paul Holland (Tom Conway), Jessica's husband, she will try anything to make him happy, even if it involves voodoo magic.

Betsy and Jessica make an atmospheric journey to the Houmfort, the site of the voodoo rituals. They pass Carrefour (Darby Jones), a watchman who looks like a zombie. Betsy speaks to Hungan, a voodoo deity, only to learn that Mrs. Rand (Edith Barrett), Jessica's mother-in-law, impersonates him (from behind a closed door) in order to deceive supplicants into practicing ordinary health measures like boiling water. The scientific worldview remains in place.

Meanwhile, however, the cult members have been watching Jessica. The saber man cuts her hand to discover that she does not bleed. (We must take everyone's word for this, since we do not see the cut.) In the ensuing uproar, Betsy leads Jessica home. Carrefour is sent to retrieve her, but Mrs. Rand intervenes and orders him back. (A slightly out of focus close-up of Carrefour efficiently conveys the thought that he is not human.) To avoid an investigation, Mrs. Rand confesses that she had asked Hungan to turn Jessica into a zombie because Jessica was planning to run away with her son Wesley Rand (James Ellison), who is Paul Holland's half-brother. She sincerely believes that she is responsible for Jessica's condition. Dr. Maxwell points out that Jessica had not died or gone into a coma, that is, had not met a necessary condition in voodoo lore for being turned into a zombie. Once again, the scientific worldview seems to triumph.

The cult members attempt to draw Jessica back to complete their tests. We see them pulling a doll resembling Jessica on a string. It is revealed that Jessica did in fact lapse into a coma on the night when her mind burned out. Jessica no longer obeys commands and attempts to leave the plantation. Wesley, who believes that she is a zombie, opens the gate and follows her. The voodoo summoning suddenly stops, and we see Wesley standing over Jessica's corpse. He has stabbed her with an arrow. He wades into the ocean with her body, as Carrefour approaches, and drowns himself.

The mere recitation of significant incidents from *Cat People* and *I Walked with a Zombie* is enough to put us in mind of ontologies different from our own. Both films force us to think of supernatural forces and creatures in order to make sense of what we see. Tourneur presents normal realities out of which the uncanny arises. As the weirdness sets in, our sense of the ordinary slips away; our expectations are flouted as the supernatural (or perhaps only the thought of it) invades the everyday world.

The Leopard Man and *Curse of the Demon* apply different means to the same end of arousing the uncanny. In many respects, the former film is just a murder mystery presented under the guise of a horror film. An escaped leopard kills the first girl because it is scared and too tame to hunt its natural prey any longer. Jerry Manning (Dennis O'Keefe), who suggested using the leopard in a publicity stunt for his client and girlfriend Kiki Walker (Jean Brooks), understandably feels guilty about Teresa Delgado's death. After the second attack—this time on Consuelo Contreras (Tuulikki Paananen), who was inadvertently locked inside the cemetery while waiting to meet her lover—Jerry begins to suspect that the leopard was not involved this time. No one pays attention to him, reasoning that he is trying to excuse his complicity in the second death. Signs of a leopard attack are discovered at the scene, but it seems improbable to Jerry that a leopard would deliberately climb over a cemetery wall to attack a young woman, especially when it would make more sense for it to flee to open country away from people. Clo-Clo (Margo), the dancer, is killed on a dark street in the middle of town. She was putting on lipstick right before the attack because she thought that her lover was coming toward her. Jerry becomes even more convinced that the attacker is human. As events unfold, Dr. Galbraith, a former college professor who is now the curator of the local museum, becomes the prime suspect, and Jerry and Kiki try to prove his guilt. They manage to do so (quite improbably, unfortunately), and after he confesses to killing Consuelo and Clo-Clo, Raoul (Richard Martin), Consuelo's lover, shoots him dead.

Joel Siegel calls the film "a thin, nasty-minded story," which fails to do it justice.[12] It subtly depicts the theme announced in a conversation between Jerry and Galbraith. (This scene occurs between the first and second killings.) Galbraith points to the fountain on the nightclub floor and says: "I've learned one thing about life. We're a good deal like that ball dancing on the fountain. We know as little about the forces that move us, and move the world around us, as that empty ball does about the water that pushes it into the air and lets it fall and catches it again." Nathaniel, as he went through life in terror of the Sandman, could have said the same thing. Like the ball in the fountain, Galbraith is in the grip of forces that he does not understand. A similar thought is aroused in us by the scenes of the fortune teller who constantly reads Clo-Clo's impending death in her cards. Clo-Clo's rising panic strikes a chord with us. Perhaps some supernatural force is driving her into an encounter with the thoroughly human killer. None is ever confirmed for us, but the thought remains.

Curse of the Demon announces its alternative ontology at the outset, and so viewers are not slowly drawn into it. An unabashedly supernatural film tends not to produce the feeling of Heidegerrian uncanniness, since we usually accept its ontology as the operative one without reservation (just as we accept the world of fairy tales in order to understand them properly). Horror and fear might be aroused in us, but our initial commitment to one ontology is not overturned by subsequent events, and thus we ordinarily do not experience the uncanny in viewing such a film. Instead, *Curse of the Demon* depicts an American psychologist named John Holden (Dana Andrews) whose world becomes uncanny.

Holden, a complete skeptic about the supernatural, has come to England to attend a conference devoted to investigating Karswell's cult. (This is Karswell's motive for killing Harrington, since he too was part of the investigation.) Too many inadequately explained things or incidents accumulate to be dismissed as superstition: the disappearing writing on Karswell's calling card, the windstorm at Karswell's estate, a repeated melody associated with witchcraft that Holden hears on several occasions, the strange behavior of the parchment that Karswell passed to Holden, the smoky shape that pursues Holden through the woods next to Karswell's house, and so forth. They slowly prove to Holden what the audience has known from the beginning.

Karswell accurately predicts the psychic collapse that will undo Holden's faith in science:

> I'm sorry that you remain so skeptical. But as the time gets closer, mental disintegration will set in. First, weakness and unsureness, and then horror as the fear of what is behind you grips your heart. Because it's there, Dr. Holden, it's there! It has been from the moment we met in the museum.

Holden realizes that Karswell was speaking the truth: The parchment passed to him during their first meeting in the British Museum is his death warrant. His only hope, he learns, is to pass it back to Karswell. He manages to do this at the film's climax, but this is hardly the sort of thing that the brash psychologist who came to England to expose superstition would ever have considered doing. He saves himself, but at the cost of his worldview. He was the close-minded one, given over to prejudice parading in the guise of science. We sympathize with his mental plight, besides fearing for his safety. The effect of having one's world rendered uncanny is convincingly portrayed for us, so much so that we cannot avoid entertaining the uncanny thoughts ourselves. Holden's comeuppance might inspire a moment of schadenfreude, but we understand all too well what he is experiencing.

Conclusion

The ability of Tourneur's horror films to make the world uncanny in our imagination—which is, after all, where we would prefer that this happen—depends on typical features of the genre. His four horror films either contain monsters and supernatural powers or intimate that they contain them, and thus all produce thoughts of ontologies different from our own. Each film contains at least one representative of the scientific worldview who is at odds with the ontology confirmed or suggested by the unfolding action.

The representatives of scientific rationality in *Cat People* and *Curse of the Demon*, Dr. Judd and Dr. Holden, respectively, experience total refutations of their views about the supernatural. Betsy Connell and Dr. Maxwell, the nurse and doctor of *I Walked with a Zombie*, are unable to cure Jessica Holland. This failure leads Betsy to consider voodoo as an alternative, which she would never have done in her native Canada. We are drawn in as well, and begin to wonder whether or not Jessica really is a zombie. Galbraith, the college professor turned museum curator in *The Leopard Man*, explains all three killings in familiar terms. He does so before we suspect that he is trying to deflect attention away from himself. But even when we learn that he is the killer, we realize that he was right in what he said about the ball in the fountain, at least as it applied to himself. He was, in fact, in the grip of forces that he did not understand. True, the explanation would be a piece of abnormal psychology, but thoughts of less mundane forces arise in us. Clo-Clo certainly had such thoughts before her death.

Heidegger claims in §40 of *Being and Time* that the uncanny leads us to no longer feel at home in the world. I have sketched out ways in which Tourneur's horror films provoke the feeling of uncanniness in viewers. They produce occasional feelings of horror and fear. (This viewer has never felt them too strongly, but was obviously sufficiently drawn to the films to write about them in this chapter.) But they also produce the discomfort of the uncanny. The quiet uneasiness provoked in us reflects the subtlety of Tourneur's direction. The effects are muted largely because the means to them are also muted.

The loss of intellectual mastery present in the Heideggerian uncanny is bound to be unpleasant. Yet, as is the case with horror and fear produced in artistic contexts, we find ourselves drawn to the uncanny. Why does it appeal to us? Heidegger's account of the uncanny and its role in angst suggests a compelling reason for why we are drawn to certain horror films that neither horrify nor frighten us. Uncanny horror films act as aids to self-understanding. They slowly turn us toward different ways of looking at the world; they confront us with characters in situations progressively shown to be far different from our own. The characters are always faced with mystery; frequently, with the supernatural and genuine evil; sometimes, only with their own imaginations.

Their struggles are artistic expressions in dramatic form of a more ordinary activity, which, according to Heidegger, we are engaged in all the time. Da-sein, he says, is always ontological. Although the uncanny thoughts might be ones that we ultimately reject (for good or bad reasons), it is the entertaining of them that is of greatest importance for the Heideggerian account of the uncanny. By engaging in a rudimentary form of ontological reflection, we prepare ourselves for reflection of a more sustained sort. As we watch uncanny films, we must revise or abandon the ontology that we initially used to understand what we see on the screen, and by doing so we become more explicitly aware of our own ontological commitments. We might, of course, also be horrified and frightened, but the feeling of uncanniness is paramount. If some horror films are capable of arousing feelings associated with Heidegger's concept of the uncanny, then we have at least one good reason to take the genre seriously, just as Aristotle gave us reason to esteem tragedy. We no more live the lives of the characters in Tourneur's horror films than we live the lives of Achilles or Oedipus. But being confronted with the lives of such people can not only be moving, but can also be revelatory in unexpected ways.[13]

Notes

1. I agree with many of the views that Noël Carroll puts forward in *The Philosophy of Horror; or, Paradoxes of the Heart* (New York: Routledge, 1990). In particular, I accept his claim that an emotion exists, which he calls art-horror, that combines disgust and fear. This is why horror implies fright. I think, though, that the legitimate boundaries of the horror genre extend beyond works that produce, or merely attempt to produce, art-horror (as Carroll understands it) in us. In this chapter I concentrate on articulating one understanding of the uncanny response that is elicited by some films that are acknowledged instances of the horror genre. The larger question of the boundaries of the genre will have to be deferred.

2. Sigmund Freud, "The 'Uncanny'," in *The Standard Edition of the Complete Psychological Works of Sigmund Freud, Vol. 17*, ed. James Strachey (London: The Hogarth Press, 1953), 217–56.

3. For a recent example, see Steven Schneider, "Monsters as (Uncanny) Metaphors: Freud, Lakoff, and the Representation of Monstrosity in Cinematic Horror," in *Horror Film Reader*, ed. Alain Silver and James Ursini (New York: Limelight Editions, 2000), 167–91.

4. Freud, 220.

5. *Ibid.*, 241.

6. *Ibid.*, 248.

7. *Ibid.*, 231.

8. *Ibid.*, 247.

9. I employ the terminology of Joan Stambaugh's translation of *Being and Time* (Albany, N.Y.: State University of New York Press, 1996), although I speak of "angst" without capitalizing and italicizing the term as she does.

10. For studies of Tourneur's films, see Chris Fujiwara, *Jacques Tourneur: The Cinema of Nightfall* (Jefferson, NC: McFarland, 1998); and Kim Newman, *Cat People* (London: BFI Publishing, 1999).

11. For studies of Lewton's films, see Edmund Bansak, *Fearing the Dark: The Val Lewton Career* (Jefferson, NC: McFarland, Inc., 1995); Joel Siegel, *Val Lewton: The Reality of Terror* (New York: The Viking Press, 1973); and J. P. Telotte, *Dreams of Darkness: Fantasy and the Films of Val Lewton* (Urbana and Chicago: University of Illinois Press, 1985).

12. Siegel, 116.

13. Thanks to Sarah Norman and Steven Schneider for their comments on earlier versions of this chapter.

Hitchcock Made Only One Horror Film: Matters of Time, Space, Causality, and the Schopenhauerian Will

Ken Mogg

I

> It was a novel [*À Rebours*] without a plot, and with only one character, being, indeed, simply a psychological study of a certain young Parisian, who spent his life trying to . . . sum up, as it were, in himself the various moods through which the world-spirit had ever passed, loving for their mere artificiality those renunciations that men have unwisely called virtue, as much as those natural rebellions that wise men still call sin.
>
> —Oscar Wilde[1]

> Central to the effect and fascination of horror films is their fulfillment of our nightmare wish to smash the norms that oppress us and which our moral conditioning teaches us to revere.
>
> —Robin Wood[2]

In *Psycho* (1960), at the point where we finally learn the truth about Mrs. Bates, at least two notable horror films are invoked by its eclectic-as-ever director, Alfred Hitchcock. One is Rupert Julian's *The Phantom of the Opera* (1925), in which the unmasking of the disfigured Erik (Lon Chaney) terrifies young Christine (Mary

Philbin).[3] The other is Albert Lewin's *The Picture of Dorian Gray* (1945). In this film, and in Hitchcock's, a light bulb is set swinging, casting ghastly shadows that appear to animate the inanimate— respectively, the dead Dorian Gray (Hurd Hatfield), now suddenly aged and wrinkled, and the hideous grinning skull of Mrs. Bates. The effect is literally uncanny. Is this shocking object dead or alive?[4]

But the climax of *Psycho* seems equally indebted to a stage play, Luigi Pirandello's *Right You Are! (If You Think So)*, whose first London performance, under the title *And That's the Truth*, took place in 1925, when it starred Claude Rains.[5] Pirandello arouses the curiosity of the audience to breaking point about the appearance and exact identity of old Mrs. Ponza, whose face is hidden by a thick, impenetrable black veil. Finally, she addresses her inquisitive neighbors, claiming that she has no identity except the one(s) given her by relatives—who both accuse the other of being mad. "As far as I am concerned," she adds, "I am just whoever you think I am." Whereupon the play's narrator exults, "And that, ladies and gentlemen, is the voice of truth! Are you happy now?" The play ends to the sound of his derisive laughter. Four years later, Hitchcock borrowed this effect to end his sound version of *Blackmail* (1929), where laughter accompanies the image of a jester pointing mockingly at the audience.

In fact, subjective truth was always Hitchcock's stock-in-trade. His films knowingly depict what Immanuel Kant and then Arthur Schopenhauer called the phenomenal realm, our accustomed world of appearances, in which something like self-deception is both universal and inevitable. As a corollary, the films are actually very cinematic. They are mood pieces. Typically, they also touch on larger, noumenal issues, or, at any rate, raise questions—both philosophical and moral—about the *limits* of subjectivity. In *Rope* (1948), Professor Rupert Cadell (James Stewart) accuses the two young killers, "Did you think you were *God*?" In *Psycho*, Norman Bates (Anthony Perkins) speaks for everyone in the film, to varying degree, when he observes, "We're all in our private traps." But then, he also *acts* for everyone in the film. In a moment worthy of Pirandello, the psychiatrist Doctor Richman (Simon Oakland) says of Norman that "when reality came too close," he resorted to masquerade, to "dressing up." In a 1960s interview, Hitchcock opined that "reality is something that none of us can stand, at any time."[6]

Now, the contents of several Hitchcock projects might easily have made outright horror films. In *Shadow of a Doubt* (1943), about a serial murderer (Joseph Cotten) who comes to an unsuspecting California town, the dialogue invokes "the story of Dracula." *Rope*, on examination, offers a variant of the Frankenstein story. Its screenplay calls Rupert "distinguished in appearance, manner and thought," and makes him something of a dandy: "He is completely self-possessed and elegantly detached. His manners are beautiful, his speech is eloquent and his tongue can be sharp." But he also has a sinister aspect: "[Y]ou cannot really be sure whether he means the extreme ideas he propounds or whether he is joking. Just as you cannot be sure whether Rupert is essentially good or essentially evil."[7] In sum, in a film about two gay killers and their mentor, the latter resembles an Oscar Wilde-figure whose ideas and teachings get out of hand, and who ends up playing Lord Henry Wooton to these incipient Dorian Grays. In real life, Wilde had been at the height of his fame when he wrote for an Oxford undergraduate magazine an egregious piece titled "Phrases and Philosophies for the Use of the Young" (1894). Among its maxims: "Wickedness is a myth invented by good people to account for the curious attractiveness of others," and "Nothing that actually occurs is of the smallest importance." The tone is a mixture of Baudelaire ("Il faut épater le bourgeois")[8] and Nietzsche. And it is by teaching just such ideas to his students, without regard to the subjective license they might provide, that Rupert in *Rope* shows his own irresponsibility. It takes a particularly heinous murder to sober his outlook—though too late to save the life of promising undergraduate David Kentley.[9]

So here is what I propose. According to Donald Spoto, two works that the young Hitchcock read "several times" were Wilde's *Dorian Gray* (1891) and Robert Louis Stevenson's *The Strange Case of Dr. Jekyll and Mr. Hyde* (1886), the latter itself an influence on Wilde's novel.[10] (Other influences included Goethe's *Faust* and Huysman's *À Rebours* [1884].[11]) Spoto adds that "the resurgent Gothicism in late Victorian literature and the suddenly abundant stories of dual personality were the modes for exploring the dark underside of human nature . . . ."[12] In this chapter, I want to trace some of the implications of Spoto's insight for Hitchcock's art and suggest why only one Hitchcock film, *Psycho*, is a true horror film. I will use as my main analytical tool the work of Arthur Schopenhauer who, a colleague of Goethe, grew up in the Romantic Era but whose writings were never

more influential than in the late 19th century, of which Spoto writes
above.[13] Distinguished 20th-century Schopenhauerians included
Pirandello, Joseph Conrad, W. Somerset Maugham, Giorgio de
Chirico, Charles Chaplin, and Samuel Beckett—all of whose work
touched Hitchcock's at some point or other.[14]

II

The self that becomes the star performer in modern European
philosophy [from 1750] is the transcendental self, or transcendental
ego, whose nature and ambitions were unprecedentedly arrogant,
presumptuously cosmic, and consequently mysterious.
                                                —Robert C. Solomon[15]

Carrie's horrific aspect enables the fruition of a deeper pleasure,
viz., the manifestation of the infantile delusion of the omnipotence
of the [individual] will.
                                                —Noël Carroll[16]

What Robert C. Solomon calls the "transcendental pretence"—because
those who affect it presume to treat the human mind as a microcosm of
the cosmos at large—is critiqued in such Hitchcock films as *Rope*,
Vertigo (1958), and *The Birds* (1963). Hitchcock's typical method of
critiquing subjectivity *in general* is to first indulge the whims and
fantasies of characters and audience, even to the extent of encouraging
us to side with law-breakers and criminals, and then to call in question
the basis of such fantasizing. For example, in *Rope* it turns out that
Brandon (John Dall) and Phillip (Farley Granger) have given Rupert's
words "a meaning [he] never dreamed of." Even then, positions are
relative. After the murder, which they intended as a demonstration of
their "superiority," Brandon and Phillip visibly feel fear, and the film
emphasizes Brandon's stammer when talking to Rupert at the party.
Likewise, in *Lifeboat* (1944), set on the open sea, what betrays the
would-be *Übermensch*-figure Willi (Walter Slezak), who has failed to
share his secret water supply, are the drops of salt water, sweat, on his
forehead. (As I will want to note further later in the chapter, such
scenes show that beyond the individual's will is a universal "Will," to
which all individuals are finally subject.[17]) By the same token,
Rupert's teachings on "superiority" cannot exactly be disproved. With
cogent irony, *Rope* refers to the recently ended World War II, and

gives Rupert a limp—suggestive not just of his own frailty, and
perhaps impotence and/or homosexuality, but his victimization by a
society that sent him and millions of others to possible death.[18]
Hitchcock makes a similar point about relative values in *Strangers on
a Train* (1951), where he has the gay psychopath Bruno Anthony
(Robert Walker) echo Rupert by asking, "What's a life or two, Guy?"[19]

No doubt, there was a bit of Rupert in Hitchcock himself. As
fellow director George Cukor saw fit to observe: "He'd never tell you
what he really thinks—never, never!" [20] Nonetheless, in the matter of
Hitchcock's clearly ambivalent attitude to the *Übermensch,* I judge
that he took it from John Buchan, his favorite author of all. Before
Buchan wrote *The Thirty-Nine Steps* (1915), he created a
"Nietzschean" villain, one Julius Pavia, in *The Power-House* (1912), a
novel with a title that is as pointed as Willi's name in *Lifeboat.*
Eventually the hero, Edward Leithen, confronts Pavia thus: "You love
power, hidden power. You flatter your vanity by despising mankind
and making them your tools. You scorn the smattering of inaccuracies
which passes for human knowledge, and I will not venture to say that
you are wrong . . . Unhappily, the life of millions is built on that
smattering, so you are a foe to society."[21] Leithen's words anticipate
both the bravely anti-fascist speech Hitchcock gives Barry Kane
(Robert Cummings) in *Saboteur* (1942) and Rupert's eventual shrill
denunciation—a little *too* shrill and self-serving—of his two protégés
at the end of *Rope*. In watching the latter film, or *The Wrong Man*
(1956), one is reminded that "society" is indeed the arbiter of worldly
justice, but that it is a tribunal grievously flawed. Not surprisingly, in
several of Hitchcock's films, you find a higher court of appeal being
mooted. But the next minute, the director's "Schopenhauerian"
pessimism shows through.

Take *Vertigo*. The power-hungry Scottie (James Stewart), who
had once hoped to be Chief of Police, soon becomes a virtual Faust-
figure to Gavin Elster (Tom Helmore), the film's Mephistopheles,
after the latter induces Madeleine (Kim Novak) to tempt the ex-
detective with "color, excitement, power, freedom." In effect, Scottie is
being offered the unfettered life of the *Übermensch.*[22] Furthermore, as
Scottie trails Madeleine around San Francisco, with its missions, forts,
shops, and art galleries, the city is portrayed, as it were, *sub specie
aeternitatis,* and Madeleine becomes an alluring "eternal feminine"
figure. Now, Arthur Schopenhauer distinguishes between flawed

"temporal justice" and ideal "eternal justice." The latter is surely mooted by *Vertigo*, perhaps in Madeleine's very person. But the film is not only Hitchcock's *Faust*, it is also his *Dorian Gray* and his *À Rebours*. Of the latter, scholars report that it was "hailed by many as the literary incarnation of Schopenhauer's metaphysics."[23] Its symbolist/decadent hero, Des Esseintes, speaks these words: "Schopenhauer . . . pretended to heal nothing, offered the sufferer . . . not the slightest hope; but his theory of Pessimism was . . . the great consoler of higher souls."[24] That ambivalence is precisely how I read the endings of both *Vertigo* and *Psycho*.

What Schopenhauer says about the blind striving of the cosmic Will, and the suffering it inflicts, is everywhere illustrated in *Vertigo*. The world's cruelty is represented by Elster's fiendish murder plot, by the film's backstory about "the mad Carlotta, the sad Carlotta," by Scottie's failed relationship with Midge (Barbara Bel Geddes), by artful allusions (notably, to the aptly-named Mission Dolores), and by the general ambience of San Francisco, including the city's history of earthquake and fire as well as its proximity to the dark and turbulent waters of the Bay—that superb symbol of omnipresent Will. And still you may come away from the film convinced that what Schopenhauer says about the capacity of great art to somehow free us, albeit momentarily, from the phenomenal world is true. For you will have glimpsed, if not the noumenal, then perhaps the very Idea of how the world goes. Following Schopenhauer, I am invoking Plato here, while being mindful, with the Catholic Hitchcock almost certainly, of the transcendental pretence involved. Vertiginous indeed!

III

Only from the fact that this attachment or clinging to a life so little worthy of it is entirely *a priori* and not *a posteriori*, can we explain the excessive fear of death inherent in every living thing . . . On it ultimately rests the effectiveness of all tragedies and heroic deeds. . . [T]he fear of death may also be due partly to the fact that the individual will is so reluctant to separate itself from the intellect . . . without which it knows that it is helpless and blind.

—Arthur Schopenhauer[25]

[W]e glimpse in [*The Creature From the Black Lagoon*] the central evasion of energy, the central fear of the life-force itself which underlay the witch-hunts and HUAC purges.

—Frank D. McConnell[26]

Every image and remark in *Vertigo* is telling. The felon being chased across rooftops at the start, and who escapes into the twilight, might symbolize Elster, who, from the perspective of what Schopenhauer calls "eternal justice," hardly matters.[27] In effect, the film is saying: Leave him to God. The film's last line, spoken by the nun, "I heard voices," is equally evocative. To me, it suggests the very Idea of humanity that Schopenhauer says tragedy can give.[28] Notice that he carefully distinguishes between the folly of trying to know the noumenal realm (in only one respect does he differ from Kant's rigid position on this) and the gaining of real knowledge of Platonic Ideas or Forms that he describes as "grades of the Will's objectification."[29]

A succinct formulation of what became Schopenhauer's worked-out viewpoint on the value of art and a resigned detachment from life is given in one of his early notebooks: "As soon as we *objectively consider, i.e., contemplate* the things of the world, then for the moment *subjectivity* and thus the source of all misery has vanished."[30] It is a position that has more than a tinge of Hinduism and Buddhism about it, and which goes to the heart of a paradox that beset many Romantic artists (e.g., Keats), not to mention much of humanity in general at various times—a conflict between active and contemplative lifestyles. It is something that I will try and show is fundamental to *Psycho*. As for Schopenhauer's distinction between the world as Will (the One) and Representation (the Many), or reality versus appearance, that theme propels *Vertigo* almost as inexorably as Will itself, as Scottie seeks desperately to find "the key."

However, Scottie is no doctrinal Buddhist. From the outset, we see him quite literally clinging to life. With this in mind, I am almost ready to turn to Hitchcock's masterful design for *Psycho*. But there is another film to consider first. As a critique of the sheer mechanics of subjectivity, *The Wrong Man* is exemplary, and Schopenhauer can tell us why. His "principle of sufficient reason" explains that though the unknowable *Ding-an-sich*, the Will, is one and indivisible, the individual subject perceives objects as separate because the mind applies to them a priori categories of time, space, and causality.[31] For Schopenhauer, as for Kant, time and space are less physical entities

than they are products of mind. And what Hitchcock does brilliantly in
The Wrong Man is draw on those concepts to portray Manny (Henry
Fonda) and Rose (Vera Miles) as literally very human. When we turn
to consider *Psycho*, Freudian explanations of behavior may appear
inadequate. We shall see that Hitchcock has a more poetic vision.

The Wrong Man has been called "the film which perhaps best
conveys the underlying unease of 50s America."[32] It starts with a
prologue featuring the director. A shadowy figure, he addresses us
across an empty soundstage ("This is Alfred Hitchcock speaking").
Paradoxically, while he appears far off, his voice seems close at hand
and confiding. The effect is suggestive: it is as if we were being given
privileged "interior" information that transcends the circumscribed
space of its telling, which, of course, having been recorded on film, it
does. There is little attempt to make the prologue "naturalistic."
Instead, everything about it—including the bare and deserted studio,
and a musical motif consisting of a few menacing notes plucked on a
double bass—contrives to suggest one of the ingredients of literary or
visual expressionism: a man forced to bring himself to judgment in his
own mind.[33] Yet that is not the end of the matter. The double bass is
not only, as it were, Hitchcock's instrument (his "double" in every
sense, which he struggled to load aboard a train in *Strangers on a
Train*), it is also the instrument of the film's main character, whom we
are about to meet. Furthermore, the same expressionist stylization that
accompanies the prologue will pretty well envelop everything that
follows. In effect, we are being told that all the world's a soundstage,
and that Hitchcock is both master of ceremonies and, like us, just one
more participant.[34]

Now comes the credits sequence. A cut introduces New York's
famous Stork Club, where "Manny" Balestrero plays in the Latin
band. Another master of ceremonies presides here: on the right of
screen hovers the maître d'hotel. Likewise, there is another double-
bass, which we both hear and see being played by Manny. But, too,
there is again a sense of dislocation. Under bunches of balloons,
patrons dine and dance to the band's rumba accompaniment, yet these
festive notes are undercut—for what the sequence proceeds to show,
via a series of near-invisible dissolves, are people seemingly being
spirited away. This "ghostly" effect, and memento mori, gives a
foretaste of what is to come. Equally, because the dissolves condense
an evening's festivities into a few seconds, the sequence complements

the prologue; only now, instead of space being primarily what is transcended, it is time.

IV

The bourgeois mind is really the inability to rise above the absolute reality of time and space, and as such is therefore able to devote itself to the highest objects, e.g., prayer, [only] at certain times and with certain words.

—Sören Kierkegaard[35]

Janet Leigh [in *Psycho*] is playing the role of a perfectly ordinary bourgeoise.

—Alfred Hitchcock[36]

Here is a brief aside. When in interviews Hitchcock was asked to state the theme of his film *The Birds*, his typical reply was "complacency" and the "catastrophe [that] surrounds us all." [37] This is both pure Schopenhauer[38] and a concept scarcely less applicable to Hitchcock's earlier film about a besieged family, *The Wrong Man*. But I do not count either film as horror, exactly. Perhaps the main reason is simply that Goethe's fine phrase "the dignity of significance" gets in the way. *The Birds* I see as apocalyptic fantasy, *The Wrong Man* similarly—it might as well be called *The Last Man*, with a suitably Nietzschean resonance.[39] Both films treat Will largely in negative fashion and in the abstract.[40]

Repeatedly, the camera in *The Wrong Man* asserts its power over time, space, and causality; meanwhile, the Balestreros are shown to be utterly subject to those factors. Rose finally speaks of locking the doors and turning people away, but she is being willful, and by now a bit mad. Pointedly, in an early scene, after Manny gets home from work to a darkened house, the camera "miraculously" penetrates the front door in order to follow him inside. In the main bedroom, Rose is lying awake. She has been suffering from impacted wisdom teeth, something that her dentist had explained in "a little lecture on evolution." As Rose tells it: "Seems the human race is growing smaller jaws and having fewer teeth, but the teeth are ahead of the jaws . . . " Against the scale of time evoked here, that of the Balestreros' lives is modest: they have enough problems making monthly installment payments.[41] The scene ends when Rose mentions how she sometimes feels frightened at night while waiting for Manny to return, and a small bedside *clock* chimes the hour—a puny enough sound. Yet Manny, the musician and patriarch, trusts to his time-honored rules. When, next afternoon, he joins his two sons beside the piano, on top of which is a *metronome*, he gives them this homespun advice: "You mustn't let anything throw you off the beat."

The fact that Manny has a look-alike who commits the robberies for which he is arrested is patently the case. However, coincidences continue to pile up against him: for example, he makes the same spelling error as the original holdup note. Not only does he lack rules of time and space to adequately explain what is happening, but he and the police have only the normal person's grasp of the principle of causation, and that is not helpful to Manny here. But the masterful Hitchcock gives us hints of what could or might be. Arrested and detained overnight, then released on bail, Manny glances at his front porch where the arrest had occurred. "It feels like a million years ago," he notes, bemusedly.[42] At the end of the film, Manny hopes for "a miracle" to quickly restore Rose's sanity and win her release from the sanatorium where she is being held. A nurse assures him, "Miracles happen, but they take time." But maybe, just maybe, one "miracle" has already happened—what Hitchcock called the "ironic coincidence" of the arrest of the right man, and which the film introduces (contrary to the earlier, nearly invisible dissolves) with a long, emphatic lap-dissolve from Manny at prayer.

Vera Miles, who plays Rose in *The Wrong Man*, returns in *Psycho* as Lila, sister of the murdered Marion (Janet Leigh). A couple of seeming throwaway lines may be this film's key. In the Loomis hardware store, Lila and Sam (John Gavin) have been waiting for the private investigator Arbogast (Martin Balsam) to report. But Lila wants them to drive straight away to the Bates Motel to snoop around for themselves. "Patience doesn't run in my family," she notes. Sam is sympathetic, but tells her that one of them must stay behind. "Well," asks Lila, "what am I supposed to do? Just sit here and wait?" In answer, the scene dissolves out. We see the darkening store and Lila alone, while, behind her, a stand of garden rakes creates an "effulgence" about her head.

Now, according to the famous last line of John Milton's sonnet known as "On His Blindness" (1652): "They also serve who only stand and wait." Milton is specifically referring here to the highest orders of angels, those who serve God not by "post[ing] o'er land and ocean without rest,"[43] but simply by contemplation and by "waiting" in the two senses of "stay expectant" and "attend."[44] The line is evoked in *Psycho* as early as the first scene, when Marion tells boyfriend Sam that he is not alone in working for others who "aren't there." "I pay, too," she tells him. "They also pay who meet in hotel rooms." (It may not be irrelevant to note that Arbogast's Christian name in both the novel and the film of *Psycho* is "Milton.")

Hitchcock commented to François Truffaut that in this first scene he "wanted to give a visual impression of despair and solitude" and to reflect "the younger viewers . . . the way they themselves [are]."[45] One implication of Sam's and Marion's complaint about working for those who "aren't there" (including Sam's dead father) may be their feeling that "God is dead!" Nietzsche's phrase would feature on the cover of *Time* in 1966, just six years later, but of course the theme of a loss of religious faith had been a recurring one in art and literature since the latter half of the 19th century. In a scene where Lila and Sam go looking for local sheriff Al Chambers (John McIntire), they find him and his wife coming away from morning service at the Fairvale Church. On the steps in the background, most of the congregation are middle-aged or elderly, including one particularly myopic-looking man. The previously mentioned scene in Sam's hardware store offers a further irony or *frisson*. It begins with Sam's remark, "Sometimes Saturday night has a lonely sound. Ever notice that, Lila?" Did Hitchcock intend us to hear the voice of a lost generation?

V

When I consider how my light is spent / Ere half my days in this dark world and wide, / And that one talent which is death to hide/ Lodged with me useless, though my soul more bent / To serve therewith my Maker, and present / My true account . . .
—John Milton[46]

Genius is its own reward; for the best that one is, one must necessarily be for oneself. "Whoever is born *with* a talent, *to* a talent, finds his fairest existence therein," says Goethe.
—Arthur Schopenhauer[47]

The actual techniques by which Hitchcock evokes horror, whether in elaborate fashion, in *Psycho*, or largely in passing, as in *Sabotage* (1936), where a boy is blown apart by an anarchists' bomb, require more discussion than I can give them here.[48] My comments ultimately concern Hitchcock's mind-set.[49] *Sabotage*, of course, was based on a novel, *The Secret Agent* (1907), by a Schopenhauerian, Joseph Conrad. And when Rose in *The Wrong Man* speaks of her nightly fears, I hear Hitchcock and Schopenhauer agreeing that a deep-seated "blind terror" is what horror films—playfully or not—threaten to expose us to. Furthermore, I think both men would agree that our *intellect* offers our only defense against such exposure, so again it seems evident that we are playing a game when we attend a horror movie. To Hitchcock's credit, he offers us real rewards for our participation. When the film is over, we are typically left with much to consider. We may call our resulting post-film discussion mere "icebox talk," which is how Hitchcock himself referred to it, but its underlying subject amounts to nothing less than an entire Romantic *Weltanschauung*. Such, I'm certain, is the case with *Psycho*.

If *Psycho*'s Lila is ironically compared via the mise-en-scene to an angel, albeit of a lesser (i.e., common or garden) order, so too is her sister. The shower scene is fittingly crucial in this respect. Far from detracting from the horror of the occasion, the subliminal connotations of sound and image here only enhance the effect. For a start, *both* of the film's murders (Marion's, Arbogast's) are virtual blindings. According to art director Robert Clatworthy, Hitchcock insisted on the bathroom having "blinding white tiles."[50] Further, when Marion is stabbed, her eyes close and her mouth opens in a succession of gasps and screams. But her screaming mouth is echoed visually just moments later by a shot of the bath's plughole, which in turn dissolves to a close-up of one of Marion's now *staring but un-seeing eyes*. As for the second murder, Arbogast dies after being slashed by a knife that traverses the length of his face, *passing directly across his left eye*.[51]

Another result of the use of blinding white tiles is to suggest a certain kind of "innocence." As in the Freudian *Spellbound* (1945), this is akin to what a famous poem by Milton's contemporary Henry Vaughan calls "Angell-infancy."[52] When Marion steps into the shower, she is given a halo or nimbus by the shower cone above her head. The difficult subjective shot from Marion's point of view of the water spray—evoking baptism or a benediction—is something else that Hitchcock insisted on.[53] It puts us right inside the scene as we sense Marion's desire to "come clean." Moments earlier, this entire visual conceit had been foreshadowed in the parlor scene with Norman. Next to a picture in an oval frame of ascending angels hovers one of his stuffed birds, a black crow. The shadow of its knife-like beak poised above the picture is ominous.

The conceit can be given a specific reading. The flight of angels represents both Marion Crane and the flight of Hitchcock's imagination; and *Psycho* at one level is about nothing so much as an imagination that has been struck down prematurely. This, of course, is also the subject of "On His Blindness." However, the difference between Marion and Hitchcock—and Milton—is that Marion belongs to an altogether lesser order of beings. If, as I'm about to argue, she and Lila and Sam represent different degrees of a bourgeois *gravitas*, or practical seriousness, Hitchcock by contrast represents a mastermind or genius—thus says the conceit.[54]

Again, I find Schopenhauer to be an excellent guide to all of this. Like other Romantic thinkers, he sees a close resemblance between genius and madness. As he puts it, there is something *impractical* and perhaps childish about both.[55] It is all a question of the intellect and how it is used. "The normal person, even the extremely intelligent and rational man, whom we might almost call wise, is very different from the genius" because his intellect "is concerned with the choice of the best of all ends and means; it therefore remains in the service of the [individual] will . . . "[56] On the other hand, genius consists in an *excess* of intellect, "such as is not required for the service of any will."[57] The formula that Schopenhauer gives is this: The person of genius has two-thirds intellect and one-third will, while the "normal person" is the other way round.[58]

Of course, as Norman Bates remarks, "We all go a little mad sometimes." By the same token, some of us may have at least occasional flashes of genius. Marion shows signs of both tendencies. On the other hand, Sam is *gravitas* personified,[59] and suitably located in the hardware trade. As for Norman, in the melancholy attic scene set amidst his boyhood playthings, which include a 78-rpm record of Beethoven's "Eroica" Symphony, we are told that he, in his own *mad* way, is no genius either. The equivalent scene in *The Wrong Man* is the one at the piano with Manny's two boys, who compare themselves to Mozart. For Schopenhauer, the essential ingredient of genius is a form of imagination.[60] It is this that lets the intellect free itself for periods of will-less contemplation, to see with "the clear eye of the world,"[61] and to "complete, arrange, amplify, fix, retain, and repeat at pleasure all the significant pictures of life" given it by its capacity for recognizing the universal in the particular.[62]

It makes sense, then, for Milton's "On His Blindness" to mock any idea of the blind poet's descending to workaday tasks ("'Doth God exact day-labour, light denied?'/ I fondly ask.").[63] Told by a personified Patience that "'Who best / Bear His [i.e., God's] mild yoke, they serve him best',"[64] the poet resolves to emulate the highest orders of angels and to simply "wait" on God. It is as if he knew that he would one day write "Paradise Lost" and "Paradise Regained." Composing the sonnet was itself an act of genius on Milton's part. In making *Psycho*, Hitchcock was happy to identify himself with fellow Cockney, Milton—and ultimately against the "wrong 'un," Marion[65]—and to construct his film accordingly. After all, he had himself in the past often sought to "justify the ways of God to men." In *Vertigo*, for instance, there is a sense in which the forbidding nun is like the Puritan Milton, and hence she, rather than Elster, appears as Scottie's nemesis-figure, though she may yet be his, and our, savior. Equally, *Psycho* depicts a "dark world and wide" in which forms of blindness are commonplace and mortality constantly looms. All too soon, Marion's "one talent"[66]—her capacity for motherhood[67]—which the film artfully links to the stolen money, will be "lodged with [her] useless." And why? Because she has *blindly* and *madly* followed her will, instead of "waiting." Ignoring warnings and portents, like the cop with dark glasses, she drives dazzled to her fate. Unlike Manny Balestrero, Marion is never seen by us praying, nor do we (have opportunity to) see her "present [her] true account"—though both of those things are parodied in the scene where she sits down to reckon how much of the $40,000 she has spent and will need to make up.

"The intellect," said Schopenhauer, "like the claws and teeth, is nothing but a tool for the service of the will."[68] Of course, *Psycho* is about many things besides the monstrous Will itself. For example, it is about "Momism," and the infantilism of American life. Norman is "society" writ large. Most of the film's characters have their secrets: Lowery (Vaughn Taylor) with his bottle hidden in his desk, or Cassidy (Frank Albertson), the millionaire, with his undeclared earnings, or

Mrs. Chambers (Laureen Tuttle), the sheriff's wife, whispering "In bed!" to Lila. Sam's line about turning (Marion's) mother's picture to the wall is resonant in such a context. But Hitchcock's take on all of this is mature, pitched somewhere between the witty pessimism of Oscar Wilde and the compassion of Luigi Pirandello. In a word, his attitude is Schopenhauerian. Schopenhauer advocates escape from the destructive urgings of the individual will through a process of encouraging it to turn against itself and be still—which is what we see parodied at the *end* of *Psycho*. Norman in his cell, wrapped in a blanket and intoning, "I'm not even going to swat that fly," has finally become a Buddhist monk! Schopenhauer knew that what he advocated was paradoxical and not for everyone.[69] Shades of *Vertigo*'s nun again! In the case of Norman, Hitchcock gives us a worst-case scenario. *Beyond* the film, however, and defying normal rules of time and space (as well as psychology), the example of Milton presents imaginative self-overcoming as a glorious possibility.

So why didn't Hitchcock make other horror films? Obviously, it was always going to be hard to top *Psycho*. During his English period, Hitchcock decided that crude horror was not for him. In 1936, he spoke of his distaste for "films which, to supply the desired emotional jolt, exploit sadism, perversion, bestiality, and deformity."[70] He was determined to stick to picaresque romantic thrillers.[71] There would still be plenty of opportunity to exercise his Romantic bent, his German training, and a certain traditional English predilection for the eccentric and the macabre—in sum, what might pass for "total experience"[72]—even if certain content would need to be understated or merely hinted at. Above all, there would still be room for humor and the license it gives. But then came America and, almost immediately, World War II. Hitchcock and countless others were jolted into a much deeper awareness of what human beings are capable of, for both good and evil. You can see him attempting, in films like *Foreign Correspondent* (1940), *Suspicion* (1941), and *Saboteur*, to make the English models still work. But the rest of the 1940s and then the 1950s were a period of experimentation for him. Without forsaking either his popular image or his personal preferences and expertise, he progressively broadened and darkened the types of films he made. *Notorious* (1946), in which the fallen Alicia (Ingrid Bergman) epitomizes would-be self-overcoming, and *Rope*, in which something like depravity is glimpsed, are typical of this period.

There was also a new emphasis on subjectivity. I am inclined to think that *I Confess* (1953) represents a turning-point in this respect: Quebec City is a city of churches, if not exactly the City of God, and at the expressionist heart of it is a sorely-tried priest, one of Hitchcock's unlikely everyman-figures—in the world and yet apart from it (very much like Norman Bates, in fact). Hitchcock was eventually stung into making *Psycho*, both by the artistic success of Henry-Georges Clouzot's *Les Diaboliques* (1954) and by the box office success with young audiences of low-budget horror films from studios such as Universal-International and Hammer.[73] *Psycho* is the ultimate in Hitchcock's experiments with subjectivity, taking us beyond the individual will to a metaphoric "Heart of Darkness."[74] "The horror! The horror!" indeed.[75] But now his natural impulse was to broaden things out again.[76]

Notes

1. Oscar Wilde, *The Picture of Dorian Gray* (London: Penguin Classics, 1985), 156.

2. Robin Wood, *Hollywood from Vietnam to Reagan* (New York: Columbia University Press, 1986), 80.

3. In making *Psycho*, Hitchcock even used parts of the old *Phantom of the Opera* set. See Stephen Rebello, *Alfred Hitchcock and the Making of Psycho* (New York: Harper Perennial, 1991), 70. Note that when in *Phantom* the soprano Christine is first seen, as Marguerite in *Faust*, she is being carried heavenward by an angel.

4. The borrowing from *Dorian Gray* for the *Psycho* climax was Saul Bass's idea. See Rebello, 126.

5. Luigi Pirandello, *Right You Are! (If You Think So), All for the Best, Henry IV* (Harmondsworth, U. K.: Penguin Plays, 1962), 13.

6. "Alfred Hitchcock on his films," a discussion with Huw Wheldon, *The Listener* (August 6, 1964): 190.

7. My copy of the studio screenplay of *Rope* is missing its title page but carries the date 1/13/48. The notes on the characters, at the front, are on un-numbered pages; they were presumably written by Arthur Laurents.

8. Charles Baudelaire (1821–67), attributed.

9. Arthur Laurents thinks that once James Stewart was cast as Rupert in *Rope*, audiences were denied a full understanding of the Professor's true sexuality and his relationship to Brandon in particular. See Paul Alan Fahey,

"'Alfred Hitchcock's *Rope*': a director and his cast uncover Rupert's true sexual identity," *The MacGuffin* 28 (May 2002): 8.

10. Donald Spoto, *The Life of Alfred Hitchcock: The Dark Side of Genius* (London: Collins, 1983), 264.

11. Further literary influences on Wilde's novel are listed in Lelia Loban and Richard Valley, "The Pictures of Dorian Gray," *Scarlet Street* 41 (n.d.): 42.

12. Spoto, 264.

13. Cf. Christopher Janaway, *Schopenhauer* (Oxford: Oxford University Press, 1994), 10.

14. Janaway has a useful chapter on Schopenhauer's influence: see pages 100-107. Re: Beckett and Hitchcock, I suspect that *Waiting for Godot* (1952) influenced the prairie scene in *North by Northwest* (1959). See Ken Mogg, *The Alfred Hitchcock Story* (London: Titan, 1999), 154.

15. Robert C. Solomon, *Continental Philosophy Since 1750: The Rise and Fall of the Self* (Oxford: Oxford University Press, 1988), 4.

16. Noël Carroll, *The Philosophy of Horror; or, Paradoxes of the Heart* (New York: Routledge, 1990), 172.

17. Beginning with *The Manxman* (1929), Hitchcock's films often effectively symbolized the ever-present "Will" via moody images of the sea. Another 1944 film, Lewis Allen's ghost story *The Uninvited*, conveys this idea perfectly in a line worthy of *Vertigo*, describing the sea as "a place of life and death and eternity, too."

18. A similar irony of scale informs Chaplin's *Monsieur Verdoux* (1947), which had just come out. As for Rupert's limp, symbolizing impotence and/or (repressed) homosexuality, it finds variants in two other James Stewart films for Hitchcock: *Rear Window* (1954) and *Vertigo*.

19. A possible influence here is Carol Reed's *The Third Man* (1949): the scene with Harry Lime (Orson Welles) on the Ferris wheel.

20. Quoted in Leonard J. Leff, *Hitchcock and Selznick: The Rich and Strange Collaboration of Alfred Hitchcock and David O. Selznick in Hollywood* (London: Weidenfeld & Nicolson, 1987), 243.

21. John Buchan, *The Power-House* (London: Great Pan, 1961), 104–105.

22. I pursue the *Vertigo-Faust* correspondences in Mogg, 146-49.

23. Shehira Doss-Davezac, "Schopenhauer according to the Symbolists," in *Schopenhauer, Philosophy, and the Arts*, ed. Dale Jacquette (New York: Cambridge University Press, 1996), 251.

24. *Ibid.*

25. Arthur Schopenhauer, *The World as Will and Representation*, trans. E. F. J. Payne (New York: Dover, 1966), Volume II, 240; 500.

26. Frank D. McConnell, *The Spoken Seen: Film & the Romantic*

Imagination (Baltimore: Johns Hopkins University Press, 1975), 144.

27. See the beautiful passage in Schopenhauer, Vol. I, 353–54, beginning, "Eternal justice is withdrawn from the view that is involved in knowledge following the principle of sufficient reason . . . "

28. See Janaway, 69. Janaway notes that tragedy is especially important to Schopenhauer because it can show life in its true colors, including the Will's antagonism with itself, and the world's suffering.

29. Schopenhauer, Vol. I, 129-30.

30. Quoted in Janaway, 14.

31. Cf. Janaway, 17.

32. Colin McArthur, quoted in Patrick Humphries, *The Films of Alfred Hitchcock* (London: Bison Books, 1986), 139.

33. I owe this insight to a memorable lecture on German Expressionism given by Dr. Margery Morgan at Monash University, Melbourne, many years ago. Critic Philip Kemp has suggested to me that G. W. Pabst's *Secrets of a Soul* (1926) also treats this theme.

34. Several Hitchcock films, as part of their subjectivity theme, show characters living in the world and yet cut off from it. *The Trouble with Harry* (1955) is typical in implying how these people hope to one day be admitted back to their former "home." And Hitchcock sometimes seems to number himself among them. Cf. V. F. Perkins on *I Confess* (1953): "[Hitchcock] was making an avowal of his riven nature, his inability to find a point of rest between the desire for recognition and the terror of being known. So he was one of us, after all." Perkins, "*I Confess*: Photographs of People Speaking," *CineAction* 52 (2000): 39.

35. Sören Kierkegaard, *The Living Thoughts of Kierkegaard*, presented by W. H. Auden (Bloomington: Indiana University Press, 1963), 37.

36. Quoted in François Truffaut, *Hitchcock*, updated edition (Frogmore, U. K. : Paladin Books, 1978), 349.

37. The latter phrase ("catastrophe surrounds us all") is quoted in Kyle B. Counts, "The Making of Alfred Hitchcock's *The Birds*," *Cinefantastique* (Fall 1980): 26.

38. See another beautiful passage in Schopenhauer, just before the one cited in *n.*27, beginning, "Just as the boatman sits in his small boat, trusting his frail craft in a stormy sea . . . " (Schopenhauer, Vol. I, 352-53.)

39. The "last man" is Nietzsche's term for the opposite of the "overman," the *Übermensch*, meaning someone who is weak-willed and tired of life. Nietzsche contends that Western civilization is moving in the direction of the "last man." Hitchcock's attitude to such a figure is, I think, ambivalent. Cf. what I say in the text about John Buchan.

40. I see *The Birds* as being quite literally about trying to turn the Will back on itself. See Mogg, 162–65.

41. Cf. the scene in *Vertigo* where Scottie and Madeleine pause beneath the 2,000-year-old sequoias.

42. In Pierre Boileau and Thomas Narcejac's novel *D' entre les Morts*, on which *Vertigo* was based, we are told that the Scottie character "would have had to pour out far more vitality than he possessed to keep [Madeleine] in the world." It does seem to me that the Romantic notion of "genius" (cf. in this context William Blake's line "Energy is Eternal Delight," and Poe's *Ligeia*) attends *The Wrong Man, Vertigo*—and *Psycho*.

43. John Milton, "On His Blindness," 1.13. Milton became totally blind in the year he composed this sonnet.

44. Cf. *Milton*, 2nd edition, ed. Maynard Mack (Englewood Cliffs, N. J. : Prentice Hall, 1961), 77.

45. Truffaut, 338.

46. Milton, ll. 1-6.

47. Schopenhauer, Vol. II, 386.

48. There is a stimulating discussion of Hitchcock's techniques apropos the horror film, by Steven Schneider, "Manufacturing Horror in Hitchcock's *Psycho*," in *CineAction* 50 (1999): 70–75.

49. My discussions with Bill Krohn have been especially formative in this respect. Besides Bill's superb book, *Hitchcock at Work* (London: Phaidon, 2000), I would recommend his article, "Le musée secret de monsieur Hitchcock," in *Cahiers du Cinéma* (juillet-août 2001): 66–71.

50. Rebello, 102. In the film's script, it specifically states: "The white brightness . . . is almost blinding" (Rebello, 70).

51. This of course anticipates the death of farmer Dan Fawcett (actor's name not known—he is only a dead man in the film) in *The Birds*, both of whose eyes are pecked out.

52. Henry Vaughan, "The Retreate." It begins: "Happy those early dayes! when I/ Shin' d in my Angell-infancy./ Before I understood this place/ Appointed for my second race,/ Or taught my soul to fancy ought/ But a white, Celestiall thought . . . "

53. Stephen Rebello, *"Psycho," Cinefantastique*, special double issue (October 1986): 69. When designing the shower scene, Hitchcock may also have remembered the "sacrificial" death of the asylum inmate named Miss Archer in the Francis Beeding novel *The House of Dr. Edwardes* (1927), which the director filmed as *Spellbound* (1945). Miss Archer, who suffers from religious mania, is killed by fellow inmates in a flurry of imagery representing her ecstatic consciousness, angels, a burning white radiance, and the cleansing "water of life." "And at that moment the knife fell, and the blood spurted, and her spirit passed to prove the truth of her vision" (Chapter Ten).

54. Cf. William Rothman, *Hitchcock—The Murderous Gaze* (Cambridge,

MA: Harvard University Press, 1982). Rothman's thesis puts a God-like Hitchcock at the center of all of his films, waiting for our "acknowledgment." Call this a form of the transcendental pretence. (Note that V. F. Perkins seems to be referring to Rothman's idea in the passage quoted in *n*.34)

55. Schopenhauer, Vol. II, 386–98.

56. *Ibid.*, 386.

57. *Ibid.*, 388.

58. Janaway, 63.

59. In the same year as *Psycho*, John Gavin played a Roman Senator in Stanley Kubrick's *Spartacus*. Very gravitas indeed.

60. Cf. Janaway, 64.

61. *Ibid.*, 63.

62. *Ibid.*, 63.

63. Milton, ll. 7–8.

64. *Ibid.*, ll. 10–11.

65. The term "wrong 'un" is (though not exclusively) Cockney slang for a dishonest person or rogue. In *Psycho*, it is the car salesman, California Charlie (John Anderson), of all people, who applies the term to Marion ("She look like a wrong one to you?").

66. "On His Blindness," ll. 3–6, alludes to the parable of the talents in St. Matthew's Gospel (25:14 ff). There, the good servants put to use what their Lord has entrusted to them, while the bad servant merely hides it. A "talent" was originally a monetary unit, of course.

67. Ever since Hitchcock's first film, *The Pleasure Garden* (1925), his heroines had often been shown yearning for a baby. It is therefore no coincidence that the money Marion steals to give to Sam, so that they can get married, is called by Cassidy a present for his "baby" daughter. The maternal instinct, even when travestied, is everywhere present in *Psycho*.

68. Schopenhauer, Vol. II, 397–98.

69. I have heard philosophers ask skeptically, "How can you unwillfully change the direction of the individual will?" Presumably, they haven't practiced Zen or yoga.

70. Alfred Hitchcock, "Why Thrillers Thrive," in *Hitchcock on Hitchcock: Selected Writings and Interviews*, ed. Sidney Gottlieb (Berkeley: U.C. Press, 1995), 111. This essay was originally published in *Picturegoer* (January 18, 1936).

71. Cf. Alfred Hitchcock, "Let 'Em Play God," in Gottlieb, 115. This essay was originally published in *Hollywood Reporter* 100.47 (October 11, 1948, 18th Anniversary issue).

72. Cf. Jacques Barzun: "It is clear why the Romantic artists took *Faust* as their bible: it depicts the quest for total experience." Jacques Barzun, "Romanticism," *The Penguin Encyclopedia of Horror and the Supernatural*,

ed. Jack Sullivan (New York: Penguin, 1986), 357.

73. Rebello, *Alfred Hitchcock and the Making of* Psycho, 21–22. According to Rebello, Hitchcock came to *Psycho* in the first place because he had instructed assistant Peggy Robertson to look out for material that might make a "typically un-Hitchcock picture" (19).

74. It was of course Robin Wood who, in the original *Hitchcock's Films* (South Brunswick, NJ: A. S. Barnes, 1965), insisted that *Psycho*'s themes were hardly new: "obvious forerunners include *Macbeth* and Conrad's *Heart of Darkness.*" See Robin Wood, *Hitchcock's Films Revisited*, Revised Edition (New York: Columbia University Press, 2002), 150.

75. For the sort of passage in Schopenhauer that may well have inspired Conrad's, see Schopenhauer, Vol. II, 354–56. Schopenhauer's passage describes, inter alia, "an immense field [in Java] entirely covered with skeletons," which prove to belong to giant turtles driven ashore to lay their eggs and in the process become prey to dogs that, in turn, are preyed on by tigers.

76. This chapter is for Sarah Nichols.

What You Can't See *Can* Hurt You: Of Invisible and Hollow Men

J. P. Telotte

> Just as weapons and armor developed in unison throughout history,
> so visibility and invisibility now began to evolve together, eventually
> producing *invisible weapons that make things visible.*
> —Paul Virilio, *War and Cinema*[1]

> He's invisible, that's what's wrong with him.
> —*The Invisible Man* (1933)

In the course of discussing the relationship of war and cinema, Paul
Virilio describes a troubling principle that he sees at work throughout
modern Western culture: an opposition between the visible and the
invisible that he identifies as a kind of cultural conflict akin to warfare
itself. He sees our visibility as linked to our sense of vulnerability in the
contemporary, thoroughly mediated, and fully surveilled world. As our
various smart bombs and cruise missiles have so effectively
demonstrated, whatever we can see, we can kill; whatever our
technology can render visible can be destroyed. Analogously, whatever
we reduce to the status of spectacle, see as essentially an object of
passing visual interest or pleasure without any real claims on our
humanity, we can ultimately drain of any strength, standing, or power.
This "fateful confusion of eye and weapon," as Virilio terms it,[2] has
significant implications for the movies, not only because of the ways
that cameras have been joined to military technology—as both
surveillance and guidance devices—but also for the ways in which we
have come to equate spectacle with value. We also insert the cinematic

experience, a particular way of seeing the world, into everyday culture, turning our world and even ourselves into spectacles that can all too easily be dismissed, devalued, or destroyed.

Paul Verhoeven has pursued this same examination, a dissection of what Virilio terms "the vision machine" of contemporary mediated culture, through a series of fantasy films that sound a similar warning about our relationship to the spectacle. *Robocop* (1987), his first American film, describes the creation of a cyborg policeman whose actions are regulated by a series of "prime directives" programmed by the company that created him from an officer shot in the line of duty. The film underscores the controlling effect of those directives by repeatedly showing them in subjective shot, projected on Robocop's face-shielding visor, thereby representing to him his own monitored status and suggesting how his very vision has been suborned by his corporate programming. *Total Recall* (1990) examines the corporate government power to seduce us into *wanting* such control, specifically by desiring dreams that can be implanted into our subconscious. The effect is so powerful that, at film's end, the protagonist stands wondering if all of his seemingly heroic efforts on behalf of Mars' exploited population, if all the stuff of this exciting action-adventure, this personal movie that *is* his life, is nothing but a dream.

Starship Troopers (1998) follows the same pattern, describing how the powerful mediated environment we inhabit easily manipulates and controls the larger *human* perspective. In this case, a fascist world government deploys its media control in a cinematic style reminiscent of World War II propaganda films,[3] to build support for a war against the insect planet Klendathu, in the process demonstrating how readily we can be reduced to the level of unthinking and reactive insects. All these works consistently explore how various powers in contemporary culture insinuate a control over our vision, manage the visible world, either on an individual or a global basis, yet render their own powerful force, much like that of the movies themselves, quite invisible.

With his latest foray in the genre, *Hollow Man* (2000), Verhoeven offers a new take on these issues of the visible and the invisible, one that emphasizes both the "spectacular" role of the individual and our complicity in that control of vision. To do so, he has mined a classic fictional touchstone, H. G. Wells' invisible man tale, as the basis for his story about a secret government program to discover an invisibility serum. The result is a film that was generally panned by critics for its overreliance on special effects and for its failure to explore the implications of invisibility. Roger Ebert, for example, dismissed it as "just a slasher film with a science gimmick."[4] Far more than simply a gimmick, though, the elaborate treatment of invisibility here effectively illustrates the problem Virilio describes. By linking invisibility to the military and showing, through state-of-the-art computer-generated imagery, the horrific potential of such a development, the film graphically warns of how we might literally be turned into "invisible weapons," while it also tries to "make things visible" for us: to help us understand the dangerous spectacle-viewer relationship on which much of postmodern culture—and, ironically, much of our cinematic pleasure—hinges.

The classic formulation of this relationship is Guy Debord's account of "the society of the spectacle." As Debord offers, for modern culture "the spectacle is both the outcome and the goal of the dominant mode of production. It is not something *added* to the real world," but rather "the very heart of society's real unreality," such that our world is typically "apprehended in a partial way . . . as a pseudo-world."[5] In that way, of course, our world can be manipulated as a series of "representations" or "illusions,"[6] much like a movie, and our place in that world can be more easily regulated, as we become the consumers of those illusions or for a brief time spectacles ourselves. Advancing this formulation, Virilio emphasizes how seeing itself has been altered and manipulated by this sort of environment. Paying special attention to the cinema, perhaps the preeminent symptom of a "society of the spectacle," he describes how photography, since the time of Muybridge and his sequential image studies of human and animal motion, has both usurped the place of representational art and become a dictatorial source of "truth." The "totalitarianism" of our "communication technologies," he suggests, has produced a kind of "eugenics of sight, a preemptive abortion of the diversity of mental images."[7] In short, those technologies today, while allowing us a seemingly enhanced field of vision, letting us "see" in ways we have never seen before—via x-rays, magnetic resonance imaging, ultrasound, etc.—also limit what we *can* see, construct a limited range of vision. Simply put, the machinery of vision—a *Robocop* visor of sorts—lets us view some things and renders others quite invisible.

Of course, film has always to some extent followed this principle: constructing an apparently seamless on-screen world by rendering the far larger space of the off-screen invisible. Georges Méliès demonstrated early on how cinematic technology could create a fantastic world out of the everyday by allowing for amazing and sudden disappearances. And our horror films have long capitalized on this potential by mining the power of the shadows: suggesting unseen presences and suddenly drawing hardly imaginable creatures into our field of vision. As I have elsewhere argued,[8] the horror film thereby trades in a kind of morality of seeing, challenging our relationship to the world and to others by confronting us with certain images that, we might hope, are not part of our normal image contents—disturbing images that we are thus urged to banish from the normal visual register. And in the new reign of digital technology, as a film like *Star Wars: Episode One—The Phantom Menace* (1999) exemplifies, figures that do not even exist, virtual actors—or "veractors," as they have been termed—take narrative prominence, while we digitally erase—or render invisible—actors who do not quite fit a narrative's needs. Generally then, film, and especially film fantasy, has always played at the margins of the visible and the invisible, and in the process struck a bargain with us: offering certain entertaining images at the cost of others, and providing us with the sort of dreams we relish, as *Total Recall* shows, while covering up whatever might interfere with those dreams, and any "messy" cultural concerns, such as racial discrimination, gender typing, or class consciousness, that might dampen our cinematic pleasure.

Certainly, Verhoeven recognizes both the power of the spectacle and the "eugenic" capacity of cinematic technology. As evidence, we need only recall his examination of how the individual becomes a show in *Showgirls* (1996), or the ease with which Quaid/Hauser (Arnold Schwarzenegger) is sold a technological "dream" in *Total Recall*. To better understand his development of this spectacle context, though, we might compare *Hollow Man* with the 1933 James Whale adaptation of *The Invisible Man* and what that earlier film found "wrong" with invisibility. For while the earlier work focuses on the spectacle itself, the later emphasizes our *complicity* in such a "society of the spectacle" and the effects that such a spectacular context is increasingly having on us.

In a seeming paradox, invisibility and spectacle are fundamentally intertwined at various levels in Whale's *The Invisible Man*. The film is, after all, the first made by Claude Rains, who plays the title character, and indeed the one credited with establishing him as a Hollywood star. Yet, save for the film's final scene, we never really see Rains. We hear his voice, observe his clothed body, view a bandage-wrapped head, but we do not view his face until the film's end when, on his deathbed, he rematerializes.[9] Death defeats his invisibility serum as no one in the film could, and as he too could not, even as he struggled to find an antidote, a way of coming back from the invisible realm. However, through his very invisibility, an effect that maximized the power of his stage-trained voice, Rains, like the character he plays, apparently became quite visible—a "star" in the Hollywood firmament, a spectacle in a spectacular world.

More significantly, though, the narrative emphasizes a desire for another sort of visibility on the part of its central character, Jack Griffin. Prior to his spectacular discovery, he had been, as he styles himself, just "a poor struggling chemist," culturally unimportant and in that way invisible. However, he is driven by a desire "to do something no other man in the world had done" and thereby become "somebody." When his self-experimentation makes him *physically* invisible, he thus becomes obsessed with claiming another kind of visibility: "Don't you see what it means?" he says, "Power! Power to rule, to make the world grovel at my feet." He is simply willing to trade his physical visibility for an outward sign of his power, for stature in the world, or what Debord, with his modernist vantage, might term "commodification." As a result, he becomes angry when the police dismiss reports of an invisible man as "a hoax." Instead of using that skepticism to his benefit, to remain unknown and elusive, he assaults an officer, taunting him with the word "hoax" as he beats him to death, leaving his body as a vivid measure of his violent presence. Yet more than just a marker of how far Jack has gone, of the madness caused by the drug he has concocted, this scene points up what is so "wrong" with invisibility in this context: it could enable him to bypass normal social controls, to rise in the world, and thus become a key player in the society of the spectacle—one to be feared by those in power.

And the response, played largely for comic effect, is to seek out ways to make him *physically* visible—and hence powerless—once again a culturally insignificant and in that way truly invisible figure. A montage of locks, bars, and barriers being put in place (all standing in for Griffin's threatening presence) announces that a reward is being posted, followed by another montage of citizens and police considering how his presence might be noted and traced. What these schemes, no less than Griffin's own meditation on the dangers of such natural phenomena as fog, rain, smoke, and snow, accomplish is to remind us how both the natural world and the human order conspire to maintain visibility and thus a kind of cultural control over the individual. In fact, with the resulting pattern of montages, the film articulates a most fundamental conflict between the individual's uneasiness about being a spectacle and the culture's panopticon priority. The various shots of the frantic police efforts to find Griffin and to solve the problem he poses remind us just how strong that imperative for cultural control is, even as the invisible man's own felt danger suggests the anxiety implicit in defying that control. It is an ongoing conflict, the film reminds us, using this dynamic of visibility/invisibility to illustrate the play of power and its frustrations, and to suggest how much our culture invests in a kind of formal visibility, that is, in all the mechanisms that place the self in a readily recognizable cultural position—as spectacle—and thereby help to maintain a cultural control over the individual.

Verhoeven's version of the "invisible man" tale, *Hollow Man*, offers a postmodern take on this cultural paradox by exploring our role in that relationship, particularly how the individual can embody the controlling power over vision that our cultural institutions exercise. Certainly, this film follows the broad outlines of the earlier one and of Wells' novel: an overreacher, Sebastian Caine (Kevin Bacon); a girl who has been in love with him, Linn McKay (Elisabeth Shue); self-experimentation producing invisibility; a fascination with the power granted by this invisible condition; repeated attempts to render Caine visible; his own ultimately murderous efforts to maintain his condition; and a painful end to that struggle, as death once more restores some level of normalcy to the world. Most pointedly, what these films share is a sense of the force behind that invisible status, as both suggest that this power is quite seductive—hence the voyeuristic rape scene with Caine's neighbor, as well as the tag line with which the movie was advertised: "It's amazing what you can do when you don't have to look at yourself in the mirror any more."

Yet, as I have suggested, these films ultimately approach the invisible in strikingly different ways. For while the earlier film trades in invisibility itself, and in the abnormal state that its protagonist achieves—abnormal in the context of the society of the spectacle—the latter is more concerned with *how* we see, or fail to see, and how that seeing is controlled. If the former focuses on a paradoxical spectacle, on the amazing figure who vanishes in hopes of becoming something substantial, and a spectacle in a world that values such things, the latter offers a figure who is already, in his own way, "spectacular," one who *already embodies* this world's values and wields its powers. As Caine the young genius assures us, in the lab he is "god," and as such he commands a level of "grandeur and spectacle." He has, we gather, always been praised and deferred to: by his teachers, fellow scientists, and even the military funders of his research. His work on invisibility—and his own persona—foregrounds the absent spectacle as a way of interrogating our own relationship to a world of spectacle. If the earlier *Invisible Man* seems firmly grounded in Debord's vision of modernist culture, then, *Hollow Man* points to Virilio's more recent assessment of postmodern culture as a realm defined by our struggle to renegotiate visibility, and to take charge of our place in a world where the spectacular nature, we now believe, is largely a technologically produced and manipulated effect of the "vision machine" of culture.

In *Showgirls*, Verhoeven's protagonist Nomi Malone (Elizabeth Berkley), a Las Vegas chorus girl who has become a star, walks away from her position, from her spectacular status. She simply refuses to pay the human price required to be "the show," as one character styles her, instead opting for the cultural invisibility of being, as her name might suggest, no one ("No me")—albeit one who has in the process come to know herself ("Know me"). While Nomi's rejection of the spectacle is a positive, self-affirming act, a return to her true self, and a reminder of our complicity in fashioning those spectacles, Sebastian Caine's interest in leaving the visible spectrum signals a different attitude: a desire for greater power, a greater distance from the self, and an even greater danger to others—all effects that further establish his lineage to Jack Griffin of *The Invisible Man*. Caine has simply put his genius at the service of the military, as he works on a Pentagon-funded project "to phase shift a human being out of quantum sync with the visible universe." In making himself part of the experiment and a stand-in for the military's weaponry, Caine thus links himself not to the victimized and controlled subjects of Verhoeven's earlier films—as *Robocop* terms them, "poor schmucks"—but to the sort of cultural controls those films examine, to the deadly power in those controls, and a new kind of threat to his fellow humans, one already suggested by *his* name and its allusion to the story of Cain and Abel.

Underlying this vision of the new sort of brotherly danger that our culture has fostered are two central issues at the heart of this film, which we might see as twin outgrowths of the society of the spectacle and twin sources of control: the industrialization of vision (with its necessary attendant commentary on film itself) and, as the film's title implies, a consequent hollowing out of the human. *Hollow Man*'s primary setting immediately establishes the context for this first issue, as Caine and his fellow researchers can only enter their underground lab through a run-down industrial sector and old factory—one that recalls the abandoned factory setting for much of *Robocop*, or the machinery that provides air for the Martian colonists of *Total Recall*. And indeed, the lab itself, thanks to its animal cages, exposed pipes, and dark corridors, more closely resembles an industrial world than a high-tech research facility. This is, very simply, a secret, created, and quite unnatural world that enables these researchers to defy what would seem to be the very laws of nature—or for Debord, the laws of culture.

As part of the research in this industrial setting, everything is filmed, every subject monitored, every physiological response carefully measured. In short, every sort of "seeing" here is technological. Consequently, every research subject, and eventually Caine himself once he becomes invisible, seems to exist primarily as a set of digital readings, sensor measures, or thermal images. In different parts of the narrative, both Isabel, the gorilla subject, and Caine appear to be no more than electrodes and wires seemingly floating in space. And as both Isabel and Caine linger in their invisible states, unable to be brought back, they are represented as strands of DNA in a computer program, as chemical and mathematical problems to be worked out, and as models to be manipulated in three dimensions on the computer screen. This emphasis on abstraction and technological representation, on the products of an industrialized vision, neatly corresponds to Virilio's suggestion that the current age is characterized by "the ascendancy of the 'reality effect' over a reality principle."[10] We have simply become enamored with and dependent upon our ability to displace the real—or "phase shift" our very selves.

Another consequence is that, in order to work in this context, the researchers must become complicit with this "reality effect"— much as they all become complicit with Caine's research, with doing what Sarah reminds them is "bad science." In order to deal with their invisible subjects, they must all wear special thermal goggles, which are cumbersome devices that effectively tunnel and even block out normal vision.[11] And when their thermal vision devices—both goggles and special cameras—prove inadequate for tracking a marauding Caine through this industrial environment, they resort to motion detectors installed at an earlier time to help locate escaped lab mice. What *Hollow Man* thus sketches is an environment in which vision itself has become unnatural, one more product of the industrial world that constrains how we interact with others and with our world, and one that, consequently, bears distinct dangers for the lab mice we are all in the process of becoming. Foremost among these dangers is the relative ease with which all seeing can then be manipulated or rendered ineffective in this industrial climate. Of course, this effect is a primary reason for the military's interest in invisibility—its application as another sort of "stealth" technology to render normal perceptions and protections useless.

But a more general consequence quickly becomes apparent when Caine tires of being a lab subject, and an absent spectacle for his colleagues to monitor. Being a master of the technology—uniquely, both experimenting scientist and "lab rat"—he simply steps out of the limited view of the thermal camera pointed at his bed (the constructed range of vision here) and then roams through the complex, even fondles his sleeping colleague Sarah. While he agrees to don a latex "skin" that allows the others to see him and him to move around in the visible world—to pass by the garage guard, for example—he also realizes he can remove that industrial interface, literally shedding his skin and thus his humanity for greater freedom and power—a power that is identified as dangerous when he rapes his neighbor and later murders his boss Dr. Kramer (William Devane). In order to avoid any detection, he also creates a computer-generated loop of thermal images, showing him asleep in his lab bed. When the others try to hunt him down using their thermal goggles, he simply raises the heat in the lab, thereby manipulating and rendering ineffective that industrialized vision, just as he does the motion sensors embedded in the floor when he retreats to the exposed pipes and beams through the corridors to prey on his former colleagues. And to complete the effect, he erases their passwords from the computer security system, so that it no longer recognizes their voices or thumbprints, effectively depriving them of their technological or social identities. It is a most effective bit of irony, since this move means that, to this industrial system, they have become essentially invisible, even nonexistent, while the physically invisible Caine, thanks to his technical prowess, retains a powerful technological and social presence or visibility. Striking in a rather different direction than Whales' invisible man, then, Caine has not only escaped from his lingering status as a spectacle, but has also gained a kind of ascendancy over the contemporary situation because of his ability to "live" within a thoroughly technologized environment. In his own radical and dangerous way, he has mastered the "vision machine" of this world, in the process revealing how much of what often passes for vision—the "blips" air traffic controllers see on their radar screens, the storm intensity indicators on television weather maps, and radio-telescope views of the universe—is simply a technical "effect," and thus how much we have come to rely on such "reality effects."

Yet such mastery comes at a great cost—a cost measured not just in the number of lives Caine takes in order to maintain his invisibility and power, but in the draining away of the self that was already underway in, and even a natural function of, the world of the spectacle. We might note that the very first word encountered in the film is "unstable," seen in close-up as a readout on Caine's computer monitor, as he tries to solve the "reversion" problem of invisibility. While the word initially suggests the difficulties and frustrations that attend this work, it also warns us about Caine himself, the unstable genius—or mad scientist—at the center of this narrative. In this respect, it recalls the earlier *Invisible Man* film and its emphasis on the maddening effects of the chemical that produces invisibility. However, *Hollow Man* admits of no such simple explanation; its causality is not drawn from the horror film's generic storehouse of mad scientists and monsters. Caine is, we note from the start, prone to wander mentally, to quickly shift his focus and fascinations: hence the sign he puts on his ceiling, reminding him to keep working, and the relish with which he turns his attention to his beautiful neighbor, whom he watches undress through the open window.

More to the point, we learn that he is someone who is never quite all there for others. As Linn, his former lover notes, she always found "the concept of Sebastian . . . much more appealing than Sebastian himself," who was always distracted and self-obsessed. The repeated shots of him looking at himself in the mirror—whether visible, invisible, or wearing his latex skin—emphasize not only that self-fascination, but also the very insubstantiality, the absence or hollowness that lies behind this attitude. Those shots thus remind us of a fundamental irony of the film, since the invisibility effect that they denote here (with its implications of no outer surface but with physical insides) underscores Caine's truly hollow character (that he is ultimately little more than an outer surface of humanity with nothing inside).

That word "unstable," though, also suggests a larger problem of cultural stability for which Caine is only symptomatic. For if we inhabit not just a world of spectacle, but one of "reality effects," such as latex skin, then we are prone to act in a fittingly superficial way. Hence, this "crack" research team seems to take a strangely "larkish" approach to their work, as if they were simply playing at science and scientific research. Caine and Matt, for example, like teenagers setting out on a game of paintball and in a way that comments on our common tendency to transform violence into play, turn the recapture of Isabel into a contest of marksmanship with tranquilizer darts. A similar attitude surfaces when Linn shortly after walks up to the pair, swinging her arms and clapping her hands, and, as if she were inviting the others to play, announces they are ready for the big experiment on Isabel. And in the same vein, their assistant Carter (Greg Grunberg) repeatedly comments on how "neat" it must be to walk around invisible and "to mess with" people; thus, he prods Caine to tell him what "secret" things he did while invisible. It is an attitude that the film itself evokes and towards which it, to some extent, caters with its voyeuristic scenes, particularly when Sebastian fondles the sleeping Sarah or rapes his neighbor. For in both instances, similar to a style with which we have become familiar from various slasher horror films, the narrative seems to invite us to participate or "mess with" these people through subjective shots that link our point of view and Sebastian's—only to then pull back and effectively indict that voyeuristic perspective, which is a vantage that, we should understand, is precisely what the movies, in their own spectacular fashion, frequently offer up for our unthinking pleasure.

If we think of this "invisible man" as a kind of weapon that can "make things visible," as Virilio offers, then what are those "things"? How does he help us see what is so "wrong" with being invisible? As we have noted, Verhoeven's other fantasy films repeatedly confront us with our readiness to become the unstable extensions of the very technology created to serve us. In *Robocop*, for example, officer Alex Murphy (Peter Weller), a "good cop," becomes robocop, a "product" and possession of Omni Consumer Products, but one whose personality is unstable, torn between human and machine, and prone to unexpected "somatic response" or dreaming. *Total Recall*'s Quaid/Hauser tries to explore his strange fascination with Mars only to discover he has two identities, and his digital dream of Mars, his technological implant, leaves him unsure if *he* is real or just the product of a very pleasing set of store-bought recollections. And the soldiers of *Starship Troopers* become little more than the unwitting products of a fascistic ruling government that can read their thoughts and even shape them through its planetary propaganda machine. In every case, the inhabitants of these futuristic societies live carefully controlled lives, designed to serve the ruling economic and political powers, but lives that are ultimately unstable, lacking in any *self*-control or direction, or even any certainty about their identities.

More specifically, the people of Verhoeven's films typically live in a dream-like world, the world dreamed up by their culture—by corporate/political alliances, the media, and the lurid dream factories of Las Vegas and Hollywood. It is very much the postmodern dream described by Virilio when he talks about how the "new man-machine" illustrates our "cutting loose . . . from reality," and a "disturbance in self-perception that will have lasting effects on man's rapport with the real."[12] I would read this "disturbance" in the self as a kind of hollowing out, an effect experienced to some degree by all of Verhoeven's characters, and one brought on by that very violent and mediated culture they inhabit. This effect helps explain why Verhoeven cast *Starship Troopers* with stars drawn from American prime-time television—the prettiest of faces and most perfect of bodies. The resulting characters seem to be little more than those *visible* attributes with nothing inside—hollow people. *Hollow Man* simply pushes this dimension of his ongoing cultural examination to the foregound with its latex-skinned, hollowed-out researcher, all too ready to "cut loose from reality." Thus, in commenting on the play of mirrors in the film, Jonathan Rosenbaum notes that this sort of looking "is precisely what his movies get us to do, regardless of how ugly and distorted, or how grotesque and accurate, the reflected image turns out to be be."[13] Verhoeven simply wants us to look, and wants us to see the beastly or insect-like reflection we too often cast, for the alternative is finally most frightening; to recall Caine's remark, "it's amazing what you can do when you don't have to look at yourself in the mirror anymore."

However, getting us to see in this way is a difficult task when we are all too ready to settle into—and for—the "reality effect" of postmodern life, and when our register of vision is normally so carefully calculated. Verhoeven's films have often been attacked for their horrific violence: the bloody murder of Murphy in *Robocop*, the impailings of several characters in *Total Recall*, and the beheadings and dismemberings of *Starship Troopers*. But as Verhoeven explains, he does not believe "that people are violent because they see a movie," but rather that "people are violent in the first place," and he wants us to see in his movies "a reflection of what society is about."[14] In *Hollow Man*, Sarah rushes to get blood for Carter who is bleeding to death, only to find herself endangered as Sebastian traps her in the lab. In a desperate effort to make him visible and perhaps save herself, she opens the blood containers, splashes it all about, and through that bloody display traces Caine's menacing outline. On the one hand, this scene further illustrates the sort of irony we have noted throughout this film (an irony typical of Verhoeven's method): what we usually cannot see, those inner, invisible fluids, are turned to visual effect, becoming external signifiers of Caine's presence. On the other hand, it speaks to Verhoeven's often violent and bloody technique, suggesting that in order to see in ways we are not supposed to—and thus to render those new technological threats visible—we might require a most visceral shock. In short, the bloody violence serves to reflect our own cultural tendencies, showing us a different and more disturbing sort of spectacle than our culture typically reveals. The hope is that the tracings of something tangible, of something undeniably real and of our own blood might cast in relief the immediate dangers of this "reality effect."

Of course, Verhoeven's films imply that, culturally, we would prefer not to gaze in that mirror "anymore." In *Total Recall*, when Quaid/Hauser inquires about the sort of implanted memories the Rekall company can provide, a salesman offers: "Let me suggest that you take a vacation from yourself." Taking a vacation is easy and usually pleasant, but the sort of vacating of the self bound up in this Faustian invitation has a troubling prospect.[15] For what these films describe is the way in which we would take a holiday from ourselves and our human responsibilities—a most fundamental hollowing out of the self. Once we vacate the ego—or as *Total Recall* explains, replace it with an "ego program"—we simply become something quite other. This "other" is qualitatively not much different from the apes and dogs on which Caine and his fellow researchers initially experimented, or more frighteningly, is something monstrous, like Caine when he only partially reappears, inside-out and with the veneer of humanity—the skin—stripped away. Yet perhaps the worst scenario is that we might simply disappear from all consideration, like those disembodied presences of *Hollow Man*, traceable only by the various pieces of technology to which we have been/become attached—or by the sheet that Caine, in what seems a vestigial human act, throws over his head and shoulders to keep warm. The hope, though, is that by forcing us to look through the movie screen into another sort of mirror, and to glimpse the sort of "unstable" or even horrific image that we seem to be increasingly crafting for ourselves through the "reality effect" we inhabit, we might avoid the fall that the monstrous Caine quite literally experiences at the film's conclusion. By glimpsing this new sort of invisible weapon, that is, seeing ourselves within a realm of "cinematic derealization,"[16] we might come to recognize our spectacular complicity, one that the movies themselves too often encourage, and perhaps halt our own trajectory toward an invisible and indeed hollow destiny.

Notes

1. Paul Virilio, *War and Cinema: The Logistics of Perception*, trans. Patrick Camiller (London: Verso, 1989).

2. Virilio, *War and Cinema*, 88.

3. For a discussion of Verhoeven's adaptation of World War II propaganda films, particularly the Frank Capra-produced "Why We Fight" series, see J. P. Telotte, "Verhoeven, Virilio, and 'Cinematic Derealization'," *Film Quarterly* 53, no. 2 (2000): 30–38.

4. Roger Ebert, "Hollow Man," *Chicago Sun-Times*, August 4 2000, www.suntimes.com/ebert/ebert_reviews/2000/08/080403.html (June 3, 2003).

5. Guy Debord, *The Society of the Spectacle*, trans. Donald Nicholson-Smith (New York: Zone Books, 1995), 13; 120.

6. Debord, *The Society of the Spectacle*, 32.

7. Paul Virilio, *The Vision Machine*, trans. Julie Rose (London: British Film Institute, 1994), 12.

8. J. P. Telotte, "Faith and Idolatry in the Horror Film," *Literature/Film Quarterly* 8, no. 3 (1980): 143–55.

9. The way the film alters the original novel's conclusion seems noteworthy in this context. For Wells' book ends with the admonition to cover up the face of the no-longer invisible man, since it is apparently too horrible to view. In fact, adults hurry several children out of the room to spare them the gruesome spectacle. In this way, the novel seems a clear retreat from the power of the spectacle and a rather ambivalent indication of the fascination that the spectacle would hold for a dawning modernist era.

10. Virilio, *The Vision Machine*, 60.

11. We might compare the use of thermal goggles in *Hollow Man* with the visored helmet imposed on Robocop or the face shields worn by the soldiers of *Starship Troopers*. As a mark of his rejection of corporate control, Robocop removes his visor—that on which we have seen his computerized controls displayed—and asks his human partner, Anne Lewis (Nancy Allen), to help him adjust his "sighting," implicitly to help him *see straight*, like a true human might. In *Starship Troopers* a soldier takes off his helmet during live fire training because he cannot see clearly, and when he does, he is immediately shot in the head and killed. What these films point to is the importance our culture attaches to control over vision and the potentially deadly consequences that can attend any rejection of that cultural control.

12. Paul Virilio, *The Art of the Motor*, trans. Julie Rose (Minneapolis: University of Minnesota Press, 1995), 147.

13. Jonathan Rosenbaum, "Seeing Right Through Us," *Chicago Reader*, August 11, 2000, www.chireader.com/movies/archives/2000/0800/000811.html (June 3, 2003).

14. Chris Shea and Wade Jennings, "Paul Verhoeven: An Interview," *Post Script* 12, no. 3 (1993): 15.

15. Verhoeven's films are full of such Faustian bargains, typically linked to the media's technological eye. The opening of *Robocop* offers a most obvious one, as the evening news announces, "Give us three minutes and we'll give you the world." That note quickly frames the sort of easy bargain that has been struck between contemporary techno-culture and the media—a bargain that suggests the world is the media's to give, and our role is passively to receive it.

16. Virilio, *War and Cinema*, 79.

On the Question
of the Horror Film

Michael Grant

The temptation to seek for a systematic explanation of how it is that horror films affect their viewers seems irresistible. Not only does *Psycho* (1960), for example, combine to enduring effect the visceral destruction of the human body with a comedy of errors, it also succeeds in producing a sense of enigma such that the film may be found endlessly elusive and yet almost within reach. The paradoxical condition that is Norman's self—Norman is the son of a mother he has both destroyed and become, a self created anew out of an origin he has himself engendered—seems to embody the dynamics of artistic creation as such. It is as though Hitchcock had found in him a figure through whom he could elaborate a dialectics of conflict which so shapes time that we can live—can participate in—the passage of the film's elapsing, its duration, with unusual attention to the elaborate interweaving of its end and its beginning.

Earl Wasserman has noted how, since the end of the 18th century, "the poet has been required to conceive his own structure of order, his own more-than-linguistic syntax, and so to engage that structure that the poetic act is creative both of a cosmic system and of the poems made possible by that system."[1] On this view, poetry is addressed to the construction of the syntax that makes it possible, a process seen at its extreme in Mallarmé and T. S. Eliot. One might say that, whatever else may appear to engage the poem's interest, its fundamental concern is with its own processes of coming into being. The crucial analogy is, of course, with music, a condition to which *Psycho* unquestionably aspires, an aspiration driven home by Herrmann's score. In other words, *Psycho* invites overdetermination. Both its openness to a complex of literary traditions, and the obvious invitation posed by its title, encourage the search for some more abstract and unifying act of interpretation; such an act of interpretation is incorporated within the film itself, only to be dismissed in our encounter with the reality of what Mrs. Bates actually is—an impossible being, whose mode of existence is that, not of a human psychology, but of cinema. It is as though Hitchcock is reminding us that the meaning of what takes place in *Psycho* is inherent within the totality of the film, and is not separable from it. It is the film itself that is constitutive of the myth that gives rise to it, and not an externally given system or a set of explanatory paradigms.

Given this order of subtlety, it is hardly surprising that *Psycho* should have drawn so forcibly to it writers whose conceptual structures were built on Freudian and Lacanian psychoanalysis. The complex of attraction and repulsion embodied in Norman can be mapped onto the dialectic arising out of the nightmare's expression of incestuous desire. Similarly, Norman's mode of being, that of the "neuter," his being neither woman "nor man," can be redescribed in terms of the *objet petit a* and the algorithms of fantasy, or the function of lack engendering desire. Norman, one might say, is *différance* incarnate. Or, in another idiom, he just *is* the divided subject.

A recent example of the assimilation of *Psycho* to psychoanalysis is Laura Mulvey's attempt to locate it in relation to the death drive.[2] She speaks of how the film moves towards death, as it "reaches towards stillness and then towards the dead: Mother's skull appears superimposed briefly on Norman's features and they merge"[3] There is, according to Mulvey, a homology connecting terms like "stillness," "death," and "ending," as applied to cinematic narrative, which takes the cinema back to its own secret stillness and the death inherent within it. She would seem to be saying that the achievement of *Psycho* is to have made this "homology" explicit, inasmuch as it has found for it what Eliot called "an objective correlative"—the Bates' mansion, reverberating with archaic and gothic echoes of the House of Usher and other *unheimlich* dwellings of the Romantic imagination.

However, if one responds in this way to the aesthetic achievement of the film, the claims of the psychoanalytic reading to explain that achievement dissolve. This emerges in relation to the Freudian account of the uncanny. Here, the persuasiveness of the notion, as Freud describes it, derives, not from his analysis of incestuous desires or the theory of castration, but from the power invested in the tearing out of eyes and sexual ambivalence (in his account of Hoffmann's story, "The Sandman."). If conviction *does* result from Freud's analysis, it arises out of the effective and compelling realization of the horror of the Sandman in the story *itself*, a power Freud appropriates as evidence for his explanation of it. In other words, it is Hoffmann's story that constitutes the aesthetic potency of the notion of the uncanny, and so the meaning of its psychic reality, not the Freudian exegesis. So with Mulvey's essay: the theoretical body of her reading is parasitic upon the film, and it is *Psycho* itself that gives life and illumination to her concepts. It would seem, then, that so far as aesthetic appreciation is concerned, psychoanalytic explanation cannot give us what we are looking for—and what we need. This is not only a matter of reductionism or of confusing a causal explanation with giving reasons for responding as one does. The point is that only for someone who has responded to the aesthetic life of the work do the psychoanalytic explanations of that life have pertinence. Psychoanalytic readings presuppose what it is they seek to explain, and they do so by projecting their methods of explanation onto the objects of their address. Just as Freud projects onto "The Sandman" a reading whose plausibility the story has already established (a maneuver he achieves by redescribing the actions of the Sandman as those of the "castrating father"), so Mulvey projects onto *Psycho* a sense of a drive towards death which the film has already constructed as the inherent dynamic of its development. If her reading seems illuminating, it is because she uses a Freudian idiom to give *a further description* of this dynamic.

An approach I find exemplary for a critical appreciation of art understood in this way is Wittgenstein's response to the account in James Frazer's *The Golden Bough* of the Beltane fire festivals in 18th-century Scotland. His comments come in the latter part of his *Remarks on Frazer's Golden Bough*, and were probably written around 1948. The *Remarks* were not intended for publication, and they should not be read as though they made up a systematically revised body of work. Nonetheless, they are of great interest, especially for their treatment of a theme that is also crucial to Frazer, that of religion's deep roots in human nature.

The pagan Celtic year was divided into two periods, with the new year celebrated at the beginning of November, at the festival of Samhain, or Hallowe'en. The second festival took place six months later, on May Day, or *Là Beltane*. They signal seasonal changes in the weather, with Samhain preceding winter and Beltane heralding the return of summer. Frazer was interested in the Beltane festivals in

Scotland, particularly the lighting of huge fires that took place on this day. He cited a description given by John Ramsey, laird of Ochtertyre, near Crieff, the patron of Burns and friend of Sir Walter Scott:

> Towards the close of the entertainment, the person who officiated as master of the feast produced a large cake baked with eggs and scalloped round the edge, called *am bonnach beal-tine*—that is, the Beltane cake. It was divided into a number of pieces, and distributed in great form to the company. There was one particular piece which whoever got was called *cailleach beal-tine*—that is, the Beltane *carline*, a term of great reproach. Upon his being known, part of the company laid hold of him and made a show of putting him into the fire; but the majority interposing, he was rescued. And in some places they laid him flat on the ground, making as if they would quarter him. Afterwards, he was pelted with egg-shells, and retained the odious appellation during the whole year. And while the feast was fresh in people's memory, they affected to speak of the *cailleach beal-tine* as dead.[4]

Frazer sees the festivals as rituals of purification: the fires, he believes, were thought to burn up and destroy all malign influences, the chief evil being that of witches. "Again and again we are told that the fires are intended to burn up or repel the witches; and the intention is sometimes graphically expressed by the burning of an effigy of a witch in the fire."[5] Thus, the pretence of throwing someone into the fire, or the burning of an effigy, are traces of something darker. As Brian Clack puts it, "previously human beings thought to be witches, or else representing evil forces, were *really* burned in the flames."[6] For Frazer, what remained of the Beltane festival in the 18th century was a survival of an earlier practice of sacrificing human beings regarded as witches in the fires.

Wittgenstein does not dismiss Frazer's views, nor does he dismiss the worth of historical enquiry. As he says: "It is now clear that what gives this practice depth is its *connection* with the burning of a man."[7] Were it the custom at some festival for men to ride one another, we might see nothing in this but a harmless game reminding us of men riding horses. But if we were to be told that in the past it had been the custom to use slaves in this way, we should then see in the harmless practice of our own times something deeper and more sinister. In other words, historical investigation may reveal sinister antecedents for what survive as apparently simple and homely customs. These antecedents may, in turn, color our sense of the customs and make them appear darker and more sinister in the present. However, while this is so, it is nonetheless the case that, as Clack points out, "What is crucial for Wittgenstein is that no historical research is required to show that the Beltane festival is sinister".[8] For Wittgenstein, what is at stake is the impression made by one specific festival—the Beltane festival—and beyond that impression no further justification for seeing it as sinister is required:

> The question is: does the sinister, as we may call it, attach to the practice of the Beltane Fire Festival in itself, as it was carried out one hundred years ago, or is the Festival sinister only if the hypothesis of its origin turns out to be true? I believe it is clearly the inner nature of the modern practice which seems sinister to us, and the familiar facts of human sacrifice only indicate the lines along which we should view the practice.[9]

The Beltane Festival is a practice exhibiting what Frank Cioffi has called "a physiognomy of terror,"[10] and its meaning is revealed through that same physiognomy. Its "inner nature" is such that the festival simply strikes us as having to do with human sacrifice, whether or not it actually originated there. Clack remarks: "The Highland custom strikes us as being *like* human sacrifice, and it is this which imbues it with its sinister atmosphere."[11] The aspect under which we see it just *is* that of human sacrifice. And this of itself impresses us, because what I see impresses me directly, without the intervention of a hypothesis: "If I see someone being killed, is what makes an impression on me simply what I see, or is it only the hypothesis that here a man is being killed?"[12]

Wittgenstein compares the enactment of the festival with a play, since the Beltane rituals appear to have much in common with aspects of the theater. Yet, despite the similarities, the events of the festivals are infused with a mood or state of mind that differs from that of a theatrical performance. Even were the festival performed in the manner of a play, we would still want to ask: What is the *meaning* of this performance? And irrespective of any interpretation we might give of it, our unease would not be wholly assuaged. The impact of the Beltane festival is not expressible solely in terms of an aesthetic appreciation. There remains inherent in the proceedings a strange meaninglessness (*sinnlosigkeit*)—a queer absurdity. The festival seems to embody an excess or expenditure that eludes conceptual grasp, and to this extent it strikes us as being in some way uncanny (*unheimlich*) or weird. Cioffi seems to have this in mind when he speaks of how the festival brings about an "eruption of the demonic into the quotidian."[13] Clack elucidates Cioffi's point by reference to two facets of the Beltane rite: the use of a cake to select a victim, and the carnival atmosphere that pervades the event. Wittgenstein finds the manner of drawing lots especially chilling: "The fact that the lots are drawn by the use of a cake is particularly horrible (almost like betrayal by a kiss), and that it strikes us this way is again of fundamental importance for the investigation of such practices."[14] Something that has homely and convivial characteristics is being used in a new and threatening context, so it is not surprising that the familiar takes on a sinister aspect. Similarly, as Clack suggests, "The uneasy balance between violence and merriment" is also what "impresses us here, and it comes to the fore in certain accounts of actual human sacrifice."[15] He notes, in this connection, accounts of the gaiety of the crowds attending the sacrifice of human beings in Mesopotamia and Mexico, a point reinforced by Wittgenstein: "The concept of a 'festivity.' We connect it with merrymaking; in another age it may have been connected with fear and dread."[16]

There was a further chilling aspect to the Highland festivals, having to do with the nature of those who participate in them. To get a sense of the horror of human sacrifice, one has to recognise the kind of creatures human beings are. Wittgenstein asserts that "what I see in these stories is nevertheless acquired through the evidence, including such evidence as does not appear to be directly connected with them—through the thoughts of man and his past, through all the strange things I see, and have seen and heard about, in myself and others."[17] The rites of Beltane are not isolated or idiosyncratic actions of a remote group of people in a distant age. Those who performed them reveal tendencies within ourselves, and their propensities are ones we also share. Clack compares Wittgenstein's perception here with that found in Conrad's *Heart of Darkness*, a novel in which men experience the awakening of brutal and forgotten instincts.

To give a more general characterization of Wittgenstein's discussion of Frazer and the fire festivals, one might say that what he is considering is the seeing or dawning of *aspects*. At one point, Frazer describes how the participants in the Beltane festival divide a cake into as many portions as there are people present. One of these portions is daubed in black, and all the bits of cake are placed in a bonnet. Everyone is blindfolded and draws out a portion; whoever draws out the black piece is the one to be sacrificed to Baal. Wittgenstein remarks that there is "something here that looks like the last vestige of drawing lots. And, through this aspect, it suddenly gains depth."[18] Again, after comparing the drawing of lots in this fashion to betrayal by a kiss, he says:

> When I see such a practice, or hear of it, it is like seeing a man speaking harshly to someone else over a trivial matter, and noticing from his tone of voice and facial expression that this man can on occasion be terrible. The impression I receive here can be very deep and extraordinarily serious.[19]

Rush Rhees has noted a connection between remarks of this kind and Wittgenstein's discussion of the notion of "aspects" in *Philosophical Investigations*, II, xi, where he speaks of ways in which "thought" and "seeing" run together, "not as components of a complex have to be thought of together, but as concepts may 'run together,' and what we should *mean* by 'seeing' is also what we should mean by 'thinking' here."[20] The further significance of Wittgenstein's position on aspects dawning upon us has been drawn out by Avner Baz:

> The most important thing about the aspect is that there is a sense in which it isn't really there and a sense in which it is very much there; a sense in which to speak about "truth" and "falsity" with respect to it is to miss its point and yet another sense in which in seeing it and in giving it expression you are truer to the object than if you stick to objective terms—the terms, that is, of what Wittgenstein calls "the language-game of reporting," or "the language-game of information."[21]

The seeing involved in recognizing an aspect is not simply seeing in general, but *seeing* (the emphasis is one Wittgenstein employs throughout his discussion). The ordinary sense of "seeing" goes hand in hand with "knowing" and is to be distinguished from aspect seeing. This is clear from the fact that aspects do not teach us anything about the external world, if "teaching about the external world" is understood on the model of giving objective information. To *see* an aspect is not to see a property of an object, and so the expression of a change of aspect (as in what is perhaps an over-worked example, from duck to rabbit or back again), while it may have the form of a report of a new perception, is not quite such a report. As Baz indicates, Wittgenstein also says that the criterion for what you see, when "seeing" in the sense of seeing aspects is involved, is your representation of what is seen. Thus, when Wittgenstein tells us that he sees a resemblance between the drawing of lots by using pieces of cake and a harsh manner of speech he could be lying, but he could not be mistaken. In this respect, then, the expression of the *seeing* of an aspect is not a report on objective fact: it is an *Äusserung*, an avowal.

As Baz notes, there are connections with the Kantian account of aesthetic judgment and, more specifically, with Cavell's reworking of that account: "Aspects, like beauty, hang somewhere between the object and the subject, and that position is constituted by the expectation, the demand, from our partner to see what we see, in spite of the fact that we have no way of making him realize that he should."[22] Though the expression we give to the seeing or dawning of aspects may look like giving a report, it is not used for that purpose. Instead, its aim is the seeking of intimacy. This is not the intimacy in which one reveals something about one's heart or inner feelings; in giving expression to the seeing of aspects, we seek intimacy with someone else by trying to reveal, to bring out, something about the *object*.[23] When we say "It's running!" in front of a painting of a running horse we are not doing so in order to inform other people: it is a reaction in which people are in touch with one another. It is intimacy in this sense that characterises the predominant tone of Wittgenstein's remarks on Frazer, many of which are cast in the form of avowals.

The idea of intimacy hangs together with two further points, both of which have relevance to Wittgenstein's discussion. The first is that aspects are subject to the will. The second is that an aspect is something that *strikes us*. Dependency on the will means that it makes sense to say: "Now see the figure like *this*." In real-life situations, it makes sense for me to ask you to see, or at least try to see, the resemblance between two faces that has struck me, and it makes sense for Wittgenstein to ask his readers to see the resemblance between the drawing of lots and a manner of speaking. Thus, if there is an air of paradox attaching to the dawning of an aspect, it derives from the fact that the aspect "appears over *there*, in the object, and *yet* we know we must have had something to do with that appearance."[24] We know that what has so radically changed, now that we have *seen* or been struck by the aspect, has in another sense not changed at all. It is as though we were bringing a concept to bear on the object, which is why, as Baz points out, "The aspect *cannot be* our (or the) usual, obvious way of seeing the object, but rather has to be new to us."[25] The aspect is not obviously there, as a property might be, but neither have we placed it there by a pure act of the imagination.

It is this peculiarity of the aspect—its being something that *fits* the object, and at the same time something that *we bring* to the object; its being a way of seeing something anew while remaining faithful to it— that gives expressing it its point in ordinary contexts.[26] It is precisely this dynamic that Wittgenstein respects in his account of how he stands toward the fire festivals. His consideration of them is subtly balanced, between the "inner nature" or physiognomy of the rites themselves, and the character of the people who celebrated them. It is for this reason that the festivals can only be understood in a certain spirit, one which we impute to those who performed them from an experience in ourselves.

The pertinence of the preceding discussion to the manner in which we respond to horror cinema may, I think, be established by reference to the work of Jean Louis Schefer. Schefer writes:

> It's true that we—all of us—go to the cinema to see simulations that are terrible to one degree or another, and we don't go to partake of a dream. Rather for a share of terror, for a share of the unknown, things like that . . . Which is to say that, at bottom, the cinema is an abattoir. People go to the abattoir, not to see images coming one after the other. Something else happens inside them: a structure that is otherwise acquired, otherwise possible, painful in other ways, and which is perhaps tied inside us to the necessity of producing meaning and language.[27]

Cinema appears, for Schefer, to be less an art form than a kind of public spectacle of death and deformation—an abattoir, a freak show, or even an execution. A salient instance of his approach is his discussion of Tod Browning's *Freaks* (1932), a film that puts before us the tantrums, pain, and anger of dwarfs. Their emotions are expressed in high pitched voices, and reduced, as Schefer puts it, to tiny clenched fists and minuscule tears. And because of the reduction in scale of the persons who suffer, there is invoked in us a sense of revulsion. Our bodies are not like theirs, and the pain of their unrequited love "is for us nothing more than the fate of painfully small dolls."[28] This he condemns as frightening—the worst kind of butchery. In the cruelty of our sarcasm, we look down upon them, and it seems that there is no way for the small protagonist, a being in the process of discovering the world's bitterness, to escape his fate when he can't even reach the door handle. The meaning of the scene dawns on us only later, "in the wake of the emotional instability of such tiny bodies. It arrives when we begin to ask, 'Why is our hell so small?'"[29]

These comments are reminiscent of a remark Schefer makes elsewhere: "The image can only be seen by way of what it lacks,"[30] in which he seems to be giving voice to an idea not unlike Wittgenstein's, concerning what it is to be struck by an image. For Wittgenstein, there is a kind of double movement whereby we bring a concept to what we see, so that seeing an aspect might be likened to an echo of a thought in sight or a palpable reverberation of such a thought. And so it is in the case of *Freaks*, where, according to Schefer, we come to *see* the film later, as though our thoughts were echoing from it back toward us. In a subtle and intricate passage, Schefer develops this idea, suggesting that there is a mystery attaching to the meaning we add to an image, which is linked to something we can never be sure about: what we are adding to the image may simply be "ourselves." There is meaning in what is projected, a meaning that is not simply an extension of ourselves, and yet we recognize ourselves in it. Schefer wants to say that words like "guilty," "criminal," and "sin" attach themselves to our involvement in this spectacle:

> Crime isn't the act of extortion in the world. It designates a man tied by signs to the limits of his universe, and this man, guilty even before infringing any laws, is guilty because he reveals himself as a subject in this universe, and because within him there is the consciousness of this world without freedom to which he himself is the link.[31]

The guilt here is that of an "original sin," arising from the primordial separation that makes meaning possible: guilt is inherent in the very fact of signification. It is this truth that the monsters and freaks of cinema embody. They exist frequently as impossible figures outside conventional meaning, who return us to what Schefer calls "the interior body." By this he means to refer to an enigmatic uniqueness to the our individual existences that is essentially paradoxical, a grounding of our being outside the law in what is ungraspable. It is this, the being of my being, that the freaks Schefer discusses make me aware of. Dudley Andrew has aptly observed that Schefer "lodges the dialectic at the very heart of this primary fact of viewing: at the cinema we are both ourselves and the representation built for us."[32] We are, so to speak, subject to the representation and yet at the same time have dominion over it. Hence, the viewing experience is, as Schefer presents it, an interminable repetition of the dawning of aspects, inasmuch as it involves a developing interplay between the confined and the excessive, the doxical and the paradoxical. It is to explore this that he turns to concrete instances, in the manner of the later Barthes, eschewing the systematic structures of explanation to be found in Metz and other film theorists of a similar psychoanalytic persuasion. Again, like Barthes, he is prepared to give himself over to the fascination of the image, a memorable example of which is the section entitled "The Sausage," another consideration of a moment from *Freaks*.

A white man, in medium shot on the right of the frame, stands casually, addressing a black man lying on a table. His right hand is extended, having just placed a cigarette in the black man's mouth. The figure on the table lacks arms and legs, and is dressed in a white woollen sweater, with a darker woollen strip like a cummerbund around his waist. The sausage man has just lit the cigarette, using only his mouth to strike a match from a box placed on a small plinth in front of him. Schefer asks: "Is this still a man, or a monster? Is it a man other than in the face, where he can seem indifferently sublime or horrible?"[33] Then something strikes him. The figure, reduced to a single swaddled member, suddenly evokes the idea of the Husserlian reduction, or bracketing, of phenomena that allows us to get at essences. This avowal is then developed further, into a series of more disquieting questions. "What does such a sausage do, not about his desires or about sleeping, but what does he do with his excrement?"[34] Do we not feel our own arms stuck to our sides as his are? Could it be that we too are that larva, without arms or legs? Could it be that what we see here in this primordial form is a being that is also profoundly our own? Perhaps the cigarette stuck in his mouth is meant to prevent him speaking to that part of ourselves that is indeed *that*. Did this man ever know the pangs of love? It may be, says Schefer, that a monster is nothing other than a perpetual suffering of love and its animal lament.

This account of The Sausage corresponds very precisely to Dudley Andrew's description of how Schefer's writing "answers to the call expressed by the text in the aspirations and gutturals of its voice. To utter an expression is more than to designate a meaning; it is to respond to a situation with a certain cry."[35] Evident in Schefer's avowals is an expressive and unhesitating response which is inseparable from being struck by an aspect of something, and it is equally clear that his basic response is one of horror. According to the tradition within which Schefer situates himself, a tradition deriving from Hegel, and whose literary exemplars include Mallarmé, Valéry, and Ponge, the act of writing is inseparable from death—the death of things as things. The act of naming, of substituting a word for a thing or sensation, delivers things to us, but only at the cost of subordinating them to concepts and so depriving them of their being. To write is therefore to murder, and every poem is—as T. S. Eliot has it—an epitaph.[36] Maurice Blanchot has made the position clear:

> For me to be able to say, "This woman" I must somehow take her flesh and blood reality away from her, cause her to be absent, annihilate her. The word gives me the being, but it gives it to me deprived of being. The word is the absence of that being, its nothingness, what is left of it when it has lost its being— the very fact that it does not exist.[37]

Tzvetan Todorov takes a similar view. He argues that literature cannot be simply a tracing or image of the reality of what is not itself. Words do not have their life in relation to the things to which they refer; for writing to be possible it must be born out of the death of what it is speaking about. And yet this death makes writing impossible, since there is no longer anything for writing to engage with:

> Literature can become possible only insofar as it makes itself impossible. Either what we say is actually here, in which case there is no room for literature; or else there is room for literature, in which case there is no longer anything to say.[38]

The conclusion is inescapable: For writing to be literature, it must be literature, and, at the same time and in the same sense, *not* literature.

It seems obvious enough that a statement of this kind amounts to a violation of the law of noncontradiction, that is, that a proposition and its negation cannot both be true. Todorov would thus seem to have committed himself to a genuine contradiction, saying of the same thing that it exists and does not exist. It is, however, a contradiction that is more apparent than real. The position derives from an identification of a Kantian concern for the possibility of meaning with the "transcendence" of meaning, with that which is taken to lie *beyond* meaning. It is an identification—or slippage—that serves to locate the possibility of meaning in its impossibility, and the resulting equivocation, while important for Todorov's critical endeavour concerning the modern fantastic, is no less fundamental to Blanchot. Especially in relation to the latter's exploration of romantic, symbolist, and post-symbolist poetry, a poetry he encounters crucially in the work of Hölderlin, Mallarmé, and Rilke. What "contradiction" amounts to here is the proposal that within the actual practice of specific poets a set of conflicting assertions is put into play, and the resulting self-conscious juxtaposition of different perspectives on what is represented calls the status of literature into question. Hence the modern fantastic does not induce hesitation concerning what it represents; it stands in a hesitant relation *to itself*. It is an art based upon equivocation and ambivalence, and like the poetry of symbolism it attends above all to the process of its own coming into being. In this sense, it may be said to articulate its own impossibility.

As Rosemary Jackson has noted, the fantastic understood in this way is based on a split between things that have no names ("It," "The Thing," etc.) and empty signs that are devoid of meaning (names such as Lovecraft's Cthulhu or Nyarlathotep, or Poe's "bobok"), and whose only reality derives from their own palpability as words.[39] Jackson quotes Sartre, who considers the modern fantastic (as exemplified by Blanchot's Kafka-like *récit*, *Aminadab*) to be a language of non-signifying signs leading nowhere. They are means without ends, which appear full and yet are capable of achieving only a terrible emptiness.

> The law of the fantastic condemns it to encounter instruments only. These instruments are not . . . meant to serve men, but rather to manifest unremittingly an evasive, preposterous finality. This accounts for the labyrinth of corridors, doors and staircases that lead to nothing, the innumerable signs that line the road and that mean nothing. In the "topsy-turvy" world, the means is isolated and is posed for its own sake.[40]

As with the Beltane Fire Festivals, we experience a mode of uncanny meaninglessness, an experience part of whose horror lies in its lack of purpose.

I will seek to bring the themes of this essay together by reference to two films, Tobe Hooper's *The Texas Chain Saw Massacre* (1974), and Carl-Theodor Dreyer's masterpiece of 1943, *Day of Wrath*. Hooper's film contains in its last reel a scene of extraordinary ferocity and madness, in which Sally Hardesty (Marilyn Burns), the one person left alive after the depredations of Leatherface (Gunnar Hansen), is subjected to a horrifying ordeal by the crazed family whose captive she is. The living members of the family would seem made up of a grandfather and three grandsons, the old man having worked in his younger days killing cattle in the slaughterhouses of Texas. The grandsons urge him on to repeat his exploits by killing Sally in the same fashion, by hitting her on the head so hard that she drops dead. The old man is too feeble, however, and the hammer falls nervelessly from his withered hand, clattering into a tin bucket, above which Sally is held by the brothers. Her screams are piercing and interminable, driven as she is to unmitigated dementia by fear and horror. The power of the scene derives in part from its combination of the domestic—the brothers are sitting down to a dinner of meat cooked by Leatherface, who takes on the role of mother—and utter derangement.

It is fruitful to see the film against the background of the Western, and to contrast the heroics of Fenimore Cooper's Leatherstocking with the abject degeneration of Leatherface.[41] One might also contrast the themes of wilderness and civilization, in order to suggest how the degeneracy of the family involves a confusion of that opposition. Degenerate descendants of the pioneers though they may be, they also represent the values of business (the older brother complains bitterly about the power of big government and the burdens of taxation) that have destroyed the wilderness the pioneers opened up.

Nonetheless, the film reaches beyond these possibilities of interpretation and meaning, into a weird carnival of human destruction. The scene is protracted beyond the needs of the narrative, until the exuberance and jubilation of the family and the monotonous screaming of the girl combine to create an effect of suspension. The film seems to fold back on itself, as its kinetic energy slows down in response to the repeated actions of the family and the unvarying agony of the girl. An uncanny meaninglessness attaches to what takes place, and the viewer is brought—as in Schefer's tableau of the abattoir—not to see images following one after the other, in narrative order, but to share in the unknown, and to sense something of what exists there. *The Texas Chain Saw Massacre* creates a parodic vision of tribal transgression, in which, for the duration of the festivities, the forbidden becomes the norm and the appeasement of the divine urge to ruin and destroy becomes the ground of action. The sublimity of so outrageous a pretension is acknowledged in the film's final image, as Leatherface swings his chainsaw in great sweeping arcs above his head in salutation to the rising sun.

Dreyer's *Day of Wrath*, made during the Nazi occupation of Denmark, is set in 1623. Witchcraft and the burning of witches are central to it, an issue that ultimately focuses on the figure of Anne (Lisbeth Movin). She is the young wife of an elderly priest, Absalon Pedersson (Thorkild Roose), living in his house with him and his mother, Meret (Sigrid Neiiendam). The first part of the film lays out the indictment for witchcraft of an old woman, Herlofs Marte (Anna Svierkier), and her subsequent capture, trial by torture, and burning. Absalon plays a crucial role in this, authorizing the indictment, overseeing her trial and signing her death warrant. Following the old woman's death, the second section of the film centers on the love between Anne and Martin (Preben Lerdorff), Absalon's son, concluding with Absalon's death. In the final sequence of the film, Anne, Martin, Meret, and the elders of the church are gathered around Absalon's coffin. It is here that Anne is accused of the murder of her husband by witchcraft and the bewitchment of Martin. The accuser is Meret, the priest's mother. On hearing the denunciation, Martin abandons Anne, moving around his father's coffin to stand alongside his grandmother. Anne herself has been a figure of ambivalence throughout the film: there has been a consistent hesitation in the manner of her presentation, and we are never certain as to whether or not she is possessed of demonic powers.

In effect, *Day of Wrath* offers in Anne a clear focus for what Todorov defines as the classic dynamic of the fantastic—we hesitate between a natural explanation for her actions and a supernatural one. This same hesitation continues now as she confesses to the crime, a confession that must send her to the stake. The motivation for the confession remains unclear, and Dreyer does nothing to establish it more certainly. At the very end, Anne raises her eyes from her dead husband, lying before her, and looks off-screen, an act David Bordwell reads as follows: "The look, *at nothing*, breaking once and for all from the gazes of the social and natural worlds, defines her entry into a new realm."[42] Bordwell takes this view to be supported by the film's transition at this point to the Dies Irae scroll, which intervenes finally to break off the narrative in a moment of abrupt intervention, as the words of the scroll move up the screen accompanied by images and music. Bordwell contends that the image supplementing the first verse, showing souls being transported to heaven, and that supplementing the second verse, of men and women kneeling at the foot of the cross, is an implicit act of absolution. Anne is absolved in this way of whatever she has done, and the film's hesitations about her motives are negated by fiat.[43] The final image of the film, however, is of the black cross superimposed over the scroll. The cross remains after the scroll has left the screen, placed on a white ground (in a manner reminiscent of the ending of Bresson's *Diary of a Country Priest* [1950]). As we watch this final image, two diagonal pieces appear at its top, pointing downward: a witch emblem, evoking the cross present at the immolation of Herlofs Marte. The cross signals to us that Anne has similarly been burnt alive in the name of the cross. The question of absolution remains as uncertain as the question of Anne's spiritual powers, and the juxtaposition of these images in no way resolves it.

Day of Wrath points in exactly the same direction as do the descriptions of the Beltane Fire Festivals. What is deep and sinister in Dreyer's film arises from the eruption of the demonic into a world that is recognizable in its stability or order, while in the people themselves there is something that induces an impression of terror and sense of dread. The awfulness of the solemnity with which the torture of an old woman is conducted; the fact that when she is burnt her immolation is accompanied by a choir of young boys; the grave hypocrisy of Absalon's piety; the implacable hatred visible in Meret's face whenever she sees or speaks to Anne; the failure of Martin to support the woman whom he has assured of his love when confronted by Meret's denunciation—these confirm one's sense of how human beings are, "of what I have seen and heard about, in myself and others."

The meaninglessness of what we see, and the lack of redemptive significance in it, return us to the darkness within ourselves. In other words, *Day of Wrath* betrays itself to its own undoing. The film is split from itself, in a movement of double negation that turns it towards the outside, the exterior, beyond language and concept, where there is no intimacy, and no place to rest. The work *says* the nothing that is the condition of its simultaneous possibility and impossibility. And this nothing is made palpable in the final image of the cross. Here, too, we may be struck by the pertinence of Freud's discussion of the uncanny: *das unheimliche*, in art as in life, is the occurrence of a consciousness that is attenuated, incapable of mastery over its own negativity. Like the narrator of Poe's *The Premature Burial* (1850), or the protagonist of Dreyer's *Vampyr* (1932), it is as though in certain horror films we are solicited by images from which we cannot escape, and which condemn us to the ultimate horror—that of the impossibility of dying.

Notes

1. Earl Wasserman, *The Subtler Language* (Baltimore: The Johns Hopkins University Press, 1968), 172.

2. Laura Mulvey, "Death Drives: Hitchcock's *Psycho*," *Film Studies* 2 (Spring 2000): 5–14.

3. *Ibid*, 8.

4. James Frazer, *The Golden Bough* (London: Macmillan, 1992), 618.

5. Fraser, *The Golden Bough*, 648.

6. Brian Clack, *Wittgenstein, Frazer and Religion* (London: Macmillan, 1999), 139.

7. Ludwig Wittgenstein, *Philosophical Occasions 1912–1951*, ed. James Klagge and Alfred Nordmann (Indianapolis: Hackett, 1993), 143.

8. Clack, *Wittgenstein on Freud and Frazer*, 142.

9. Wittgenstein, *Philosophical Questions*, 143–45.

10. Frank Cioffi, *Wittgenstein on Freud and Frazer* (Cambridge: Cambridge University Press, 1998), 87.

11. Clack, *Wittgenstein, Frazer and Religion*, 144.

12. Wittgenstein, *Philosophical Questions*, 149.

13. Cioffi, *Wittgenstein on Freud and Frazer*, 92.

14. Wittgenstein, *Philosophical Questions*, 147.

15 Clack, *Wittgenstein on Freud and Frazer*, 146.

16 Wittgenstein, *Philosophical Questions*, 147. Cited from Ludwig Wittgenstein, *Culture and Value* (Oxford: Blackwell, 1980), 78.

17. Wittgenstein, *Philosophical Questions*, 151.

18. Wittgenstein, *Philosophical Questions*, 145.

19. Wittgenstein, *Philosophical Questions*, 147.

20. Rush Rhees, "Wittgenstein on Language and Ritual," in *Wittgenstein and His Times*, ed. Brian McGuinness (Oxford: Blackwell, 1982), 101–102.

21. Avner Baz, "What's the Point of Seeing Aspects?" *Philosophical Investigations* 23, no. 2 (2000): 106.

22. Cited by Baz, "What's the Point of Seeing Aspects?" 107. The reference to Cavell is Stanley Cavell, "Aesthetic Problems in Modern Philosophy," in *Must We Mean What We Say?* (New York: Charles Scribner's Sons, 1969), 89, footnote.

23. See Baz, "What's the Point of Seeing Aspects?" 108.

24. Baz, "What's the Point of Seeing Aspects?" 110.

25. Baz, "What's the Point of Seeing Aspects?" 111.

26. See Baz, "What's the Point of Seeing Aspects?" 111.

27. Jean Louis Schefer, *The Enigmatic Body* (Cambridge: Cambridge University Press, 1995), 120.

28. Schefer, *The Enigmatic Body*, 121.

29. Schefer, *The Enigmatic Body*, 121.

30. Schefer, *The Enigmatic Body*, 120.

31. Schefer, *The Enigmatic Body*, 130.

32. Dudley Andrew, *Concepts in Film Theory* (Oxford: Oxford University Press, 1984), 189.

33. Schefer, *The Enigmatic Body*, 123.

34. Schefer, *The Enigmatic Body*, 123.

35. Andrew, *Concepts in Film Theory*, 190.

36. "Every phrase and every sentence is an end and a beginning, / Every poem an epitaph." From "Little Gidding," in T. S. Eliot, *The Complete Poems and Plays of T.S. Eliot* (London: Faber and Faber, 1975), 197.

37. Maurice Blanchot, *The Gaze of Orpheus*, trans. Lydia Davis (New York: Station Hill, 1981), 2.

38. Tzvetan Todorov, *The Fantastic: A Structural Approach to a Literary Genre* (Ithaca: Cornell University Press, 1975), 175.

39. Rosemary Jackson, *Fantasy: The Literature of Subversion* (London: Methuen, 1981), 38–40.

40. Jean-Paul Sartre, *Situations 1* (Paris: Gallimard, 1947), 131. Cited in Jackson, *Fantasy: The Literature of Subversion*, 41.

41. An account of this kind is briefly sketched in Phil Hardy, *Horror* (London: Aurum Press, 1985), 298.

42. David Bordwell, *The Films of Carl-Theodor Dreyer* (Berkeley: University of California Press, 1981), 139.

43. See Bordwell, *The Films of Carl-Theodor Dreyer*, 140.

An Event-Based Definition
of Art-Horror

Matt Hills

Revisiting *The Philosophy of Horror*

Recent philosophical reflections on the horror film have frequently taken Noël Carroll's *The Philosophy of Horror* (1990) as a point of departure.[1] The strengths and weaknesses of Carroll's approach have been much discussed, and the debate has often focused on Carroll's major presupposition: that the horror genre is distinctively characterized by its monsters. Moving on from this point, later critics have contested Carroll's definition of "the monster," arguing that serial killers and "realistic" monsters must be admitted into Carroll's theory of horror.[2] Meanwhile, dissenting voices have suggested that Carroll's emphasis on the entity of the monster as horror's distinguishing feature gives rise to an incomplete or, worse, a radically flawed definition and analysis of the horror film.[3]

In this essay I want to consider the latter argument, suggesting that cinematic horror can be more effectively defined and philosophically addressed not through an analysis of fictional entities, but rather through an "event-based" definition (one that nevertheless takes in "monstrous" horror). It is only by altering our approach and shifting emphasis in this way that we can take in the widest possible range of texts that have been discussed as "horror" by audiences and labeled as such by filmmakers and marketers.

Carroll begins his survey of the horror film by observing that any philosophical definition of the genre's distinctiveness should involve "an attempt to rationally reconstruct the latent criteria for identifying horror . . . that are already operative in ordinary language . . . This genre . . . is recognized in common speech and my theory of it must ultimately be assessed in terms of the way in which it tracks ordinary usage."[4] This is indeed an admirable yardstick for any philosophy of horror, and it is one that I accept. Instead of assuming that the theorist is free to reconstruct lines of generic affiliation to suit his or her particular purposes, the theorist should aim to reflect upon the judgments and experiences that determine audience definitions of horror.[5]

This basic standard is surrendered by Carroll on a number of occasions, however, typically at moments where his theorized definition of horror can be seen not to fit a substantial series of films that have been discussed as "horror" in a variety of "ordinary languages" (the most obvious example being the already alluded to problem of whether serial killer fictions count as "art-horror" on Carroll's definition). Carroll's tendency to jettison horror films that fail to correspond with his model of art-horror has already been noted by prior critics; as Russell alleges, "Carroll resolves the contradictions in his system by throwing out the contrary portions" of horror's cultural history.[6]

One such "portion" of horror that Carroll rules out of his system is what he terms "art-dread." Carroll's "emphasis on monsters," he comments, "should make it clear that my theory of art-horror is what might be called entity-based. . . . Notice . . . that I have not taken *events* to be among the primary objects of art-horror."[7] Art-horror—that is, fictional horror across different media, and its corresponding audience emotion—is Carroll's object of study. He opposes this to a second group of differently emotive fictions that

> are frequently grouped together with the type of fictions from which my theory has been derived. Nevertheless, I do think that there is an important distinction between this type of story . . . *tales of dread* . . . and horror stories. . . . The uncanny event which tops off such stories causes a sense of unease and awe, perhaps of momentary anxiety and foreboding. These events are constructed to move the audience rhetorically to the point that one entertains the idea that unavowed, unknown, and perhaps concealed and inexplicable forces rule the universe. Where art-horror involves disgust as a central feature, what might be called art-dread does not.[8]

Art-horror involves disgust, but it also involves entities that are not currently scientifically believed to exist, and that are interstitial by virtue of violating cultural categories.[9] Art-horror is therefore part of an "entity-based" theory, and involves eliciting what are assumed to be characteristic audience emotions, one of which is disgust or revulsion (at the "impure" monster[10]). Despite his initial concern to track "ordinary usage," Carroll diverts from that aim by separating "art-horror" from "art-dread," despite noting that these fictions are "frequently grouped together." And while he remains happy to concede that "art-dread will bear some affinities with art-horror since both traffic in the preternatural—with both supernatural and sci-fi variations," Carroll's conclusion remains that "the two emotions [and thus bodies of films—MH], though related, are still discriminable."[11]

Although Carroll acknowledges that "some fictions may traffic in both art-horror and art-dread; the admixture may take a range of forms in different stories,"[12] he nevertheless proceeds *as if* "art-dread" had been definitively removed from the scene of his philosophical investigations. The relationship between "art-horror" and "art-dread" is therefore less than clear in Carroll's discussion: it moves swiftly from being concerned with distinct "groupings" of texts to discriminable emotions, and from there to textual "admixtures" that, one can only suppose, might evoke differently weighted combinations of disgust and dread, or indeed, some emotional hybrid or compound such as "dread-disgust."

This shifting relationship is, I would suggest, evidence of Carroll's uncertainty in the face of what he wants to term "art-dread." The question for Carroll is seemingly how best to expel the unwanted portion of what is identified as "horror" by non-philosophical audiences (fans/industry) in order to bring theoretical and philosophical order to "art-horror." Positing two clear types of fiction, or two types of emotion, are his first expulsive strategies. Admixtures are then admitted but immediately marginalized (and, strikingly, they are subsequently forgotten about in his argument). By suggesting that "art-dread probably deserves a theory of its own, though I do not have one ready-to-hand,"[13] Carroll reifies his own categories, implying that the theory of art-horror is secure since another theory altogether must be developed to account for the distinctiveness of "art-dread." But this neglects the horror-dread "admixture" as well as ignoring audience "ordinary language" that does not distinguish between "art-horror" and "art-dread."

"Subtlety of horror"[14] was valued in one survey of female horror fans who placed Robert Wise's *The Haunting* (1963) in their "top twenty horror films,"[15] despite the fact that it (arguably) either withholds or lacks a monster and more closely resembles Carroll's definition of art-dread rather than art-horror (see the following section for more discussion of this film). Likewise, films that would need to be classified as "art-dread" given Carroll's approach, where evil is "a disembodied, vague state of cosmic affairs" and where "like the very best stories by...Lovecraft...complex and intriguing visions of an evil cosmos"[16] are put forward, have been among the canonical "horror" movies of the past quarter century; for example, Freeland's commentary here refers to *The Shining* (1980).

Carroll's final attempt at resolving the question of art-horror versus art-dread, contained in a footnote, demonstrates what else is at stake here. He suggests that discussions of horror as "imagined" (rather than as focused on a clearly defined fictional monster) imply that the best horror works by suggestion, by getting the reader to imagine what is the case. The presumption is that the reader can scare himself—can imagine what horrifies himself most—better than any author:

> Lovecraft...works this aesthetics of suggestion into a definition of horror in terms of cosmic fear, a kind of secular awe. *But I don't think that this line of thought is useful in thinking about the definition of horror. For it really indicates an aesthetic preference for one type of horror...* Moreover, this standard is explicitly rejected by a number of horror writers... One cannot...use suggested or imagined fear to define horror without begging the issue between a Lovecraft and a Barker.[17]

Carroll astutely identifies different approaches to what should count as "authentic" horror across the cultural history of the form. Horror can be "suggestive" and "creepy" or it can be "gross" and "gore-splattered" (these aesthetics are, of course, variously ideologically loaded and contested). However, what Carroll's problematic separation between "art-horror" and "art-dread" achieves is nothing less than *the elevation to theoretical status of the very aesthetic preferences that he suggests his work must transcend.* Rather than "begging the issue between a Lovecraft and a Barker," or indeed between Lovecraft and Guy N. Smith, author of *Crabs on the Rampage*,[18] Carroll positions "art-horror" firmly in line with a Barkeresque/Smithian stance (where horror must "show" rather than withhold the monster). Lovecraftian "cosmic fear"—where the monster is either absent or has to be "imagined" by the audience—is expelled as belonging to the terrain of "art-dread." Therefore, Carroll's art-horror/art-dread theoretical distinction does not at all surmount or transcend the "aesthetic preference for one type of horror." Quite the reverse: it cements in place the "preference for one type" by defining this type alone as "art-horror." By doing so, Carroll's philosophy of horror rules out, as non-art-horror, types of Lovecraftian "horror" described as such by "ordinary" audiences in their "ordinary language" of generic classifications.

The challenge this poses for any account of horror is how to deal with the Lovecraftian *and* Barkeresque ends of the horror spectrum *without* enacting a theoretical split that fails to correspond to ordinary-language discussions of "horror." One must also avoid reinforcing fan disputes over "authentic" versus "inauthentic" horror by sustaining a specific aesthetic agenda over and above its other serious competitors (favoring a "Barkeresque" stance on "horror" over a "Lovecraftian" aesthetic, which would then be ruled out as non-art-horror).

My suggestion is that these quandaries can be immediately done away with by altering our philosophical perspective on horror from an entity-based model to a primarily event-based one. This will offer a means of defining and analyzing horror as concerned primarily with events which may or may not, secondarily, give rise to and define "monstrous"/evil entities. And it will encapsulate what Carroll unhelpfully opposes as "art-dread" and "art-horror," thus more accurately reflecting "ordinary language" usage in descriptions of "horror." Note that contrary to my own previous rhetoric in this piece, and to Carroll's own binary opposition, I am not, in fact, contrasting "event-based" theories of horror to "entity-based" theories, and then choosing one over the other. Rather, I am arguing that *events take logical precedence over entities where we are dealing with art-horror as it is embodied in fictional horror narratives.* Entities that 1) violate cultural categories, 2) inspire revulsion and disgust, and 3) cue a sense of threat can, after all, only do so via the representation of narrative events such as the victim shrinking away from the monster, an *event* that is central to Carroll's supposedly entity-based approach.[19]

Carroll's model distinguishes between threatening and impure horror monsters and *non-horrific* monsters appearing in fantasies and fairytales—which can conceivably share the same monstrous, fantastic, and impure biologies—by virtue of specific narrative events that cue and define the horrific monster's "threatening" nature. By way of further explication, Carroll's discussion of David Cronenberg's *The Fly* (1986) can be usefully referred to here. Carroll notes that

This film has all the trappings of a horror film, including a monster.
But classifying it as a horror film as such, without qualification,
seems not quite right. It fails to capture an essential difference
between this film and the rest of the genre. . . . The fly figure in this
film is undeniably impure. . . . He would appear to be the very
paradigm of the horrific object and yet he is not. Why? The horrific
object is a compound of threat and impurity. However, for much of
the film, *the fly monster is not threatening.* He has a girlfriend, who,
as we have argued, cues our response to the fly, and until the end of
the film, at least, she does not feel threatened by the fly.[20]

As this "special case" makes clear, the *horrific* monster—the figure that
defines and supports art-horror for Carroll—cannot be defined solely or
sufficiently via reference to physical/biological properties of the
monster-as-entity. While fantastic biology is necessary for monsters to
violate cultural categories, as does the hybrid monster of *The Fly*, it is
not sufficient to predict whether or not a particular monster is
threatening and thus "horrific" and a proper object of art-horror. This is
dependent on "the attitude of characters in the story to the monster they
encounter," and is what distinguishes horror from "mere stories with
monsters, such as myths."[21] In other words, despite explicitly ruling out
an "event-based" approach, Carroll's definition of art-horror hinges on
a narrative event (or series of events) without which his postulated
entity cannot function as a marker of art-horror.

Now, it could be argued philosophically that actions require
entities (in the sense of causal agents) given that the "happening . . . is a
necessary, but not a sufficient, condition of the action,"[22] whereas
happenings do not imply causal agency. However, this distinction
makes less sense when applied to narrative fictions, since here we
require the representation of an event before we can decide whether or
not it is a fictional "happening" that requires no agency ("the gun has
fired") or a fictional action that implies, or occurs as a result of, agency
("X has fired the gun"). In this case, then, the existence of a fictional
entity (read here "a fictional agent") remains secondary to the
representation of an event through which this entity and its properties
can be known by the reader/viewer.

I am suggesting that *art-horror's events are in fact the only*
necessary and sufficient conditions of art-horror. Monsters are not a
sufficient condition in Carroll's account, and I would argue further that
they are actually unnecessary, since "horror" can be evoked—
according to audience "ordinary language" and generic attribution—by
films that do not contain clearly defined monsters, but which are

predicated instead on diegetic evil, transcendent forces that the audience must imagine (e.g., *The Blair Witch Project* [1999], discussed later; Do we really want to conclude that this is not an example of "horror"/"art-horror"?). Regardless of this latter, stronger argument, monsters become art-horrifying for Carroll by virtue of the way in which a monstrous entity is framed narratively as threatening within specific events. And if we accept the primacy of events here, then the threat of a monster can arise, at the same time, *through the aesthetic representations of horror cinema's narrative events*. A monster may be threatening because we see characters shrink from it, because we see it kill/attack other ("good") characters, but its threat may also be represented by virtue of camera angles and framings used to represent this attack, or thanks to devices of lighting that precede characters' shrinking away, and so on.

This latter aspect of art-horror has been explored by Derek Matravers. Arguing for an extension of cognitive approaches, Matravers suggests, somewhat controversially, that: "representational works of art act upon an observer's emotions in two ways. First, by causing the observer to imagine a proposition in such a way that it arouses a feeling, thereby causing an emotion; second, by arousing a feeling directly, without a cognitive intermediary."[23] Of course, Carroll concedes the latter point, but only in relation to what has been called the "startle reflex," which is provoked by horror's characteristic "shock edits" and the use of abrupt sound or sudden movements into frame.[24] Matravers's argument goes beyond any such concession, noting that horror movie representations of Count Dracula are not only concerned with propositional contents:

> properties of the representation—the setting, the lighting, the menacing music, the Count's appearance, the way he moves, and so on—might strengthen the effect of such propositions by acting directly on the observer's feelings. The total effect is more than could be achieved by the propositions alone; two films telling the same story need not (as a matter of fact) have the same effect.[25]

Propositional content is therefore only ever half of the story, as it were. Such content, which is absolutely central to Carroll's cognitive account of "art-horror," can be supplemented/reinforced/contradicted by "the way that the content is represented,"[26] given that this acts affectively rather than emotively on the spectator.[27] This noncognitive affect can account for the fact that the same propositional content, "Count Dracula" in this case, might be art-horrifying (i.e., Dracula is perceived as threatening and impure) to an audience when represented in a contemporary horror film but amusing to that same audience when viewed in "horror films from the early days of cinema."[28] In the latter case, anecdotally but nevertheless empirically supported by my own experiences screening 1930s Universal horror films to undergraduate students, Dracula's aesthetics are such that his narratively enframed threat is rendered unconvincing.

Carroll's approach—which we should recall aims to explain art-horror across different media rather than focusing specifically on the horror film—appears to have no way of distinguishing between these very different empirical, systematic audience reactions to the same propositional content. To an extent, then, the medium specificity of horror cinema goes missing in Carroll's philosophy, given that film aesthetics can work in the service of narrative events to sustain the monster as art-horrifying, or that (in an "unsuccessful" horror film) the mise-en-scene involved may be such as to affectively neutralize or even overpower the monster's narrative, eventful representation of threat. This difficulty has been alluded to by Malcolm Turvey, who argues that it "is almost as if the prototypical spectator of these theories [he is discussing the work of Noël Carroll and Murray Smith—MH] is blind to the film itself."[29]

In the next section I want to apply the approach that I have been developing to the analysis of a trio of horror films: *The Haunting*, *Event Horizon* (1997), and *The Blair Witch Project*. This will allow me to:

(1) consider "art-horror" as a more inclusive category than it has been to date; by refocusing on a primarily event-based model, it is possible to see as art-horror films that either withhold monstrous entities or else lack them altogether (*contra* Carroll's definition of "art-horror"), but which have nevertheless been discussed as "horror" by general/fan audiences; and

(2) discuss the specific ways in which art-horror's propositional contents are aesthetically—that is, filmically—represented, in affectively variable ways that Carroll's philosophy of horror has not, to date, dealt with convincingly.

Art-Horror's Haunting Events: Actions or Happenings?

A surprising range of horror films fail to present us with definite "monsters" as entities that drive a narrative of disclosure. Indefiniteness persists either a) when the issue of whether a monstrous agency is at work remains open, since narrative events indicating this may be imagined or coincidental, and/or b) where a monstrous agency cannot be reduced to any given "entity" (i.e., where it is represented as a transcendent force not defined by limits of embodiment, spatiality, temporality, or by recognizably "theological" explanation).

This is a tendency that has persisted across the genre's cultural history, and it is evident across films as otherwise diverse as *The Haunting* and *The Blair Witch Project*. The latter has been positioned as part of a trend away from gore-filled and special effects laden horror,[30] recapping the "aesthetic preferences" argument addressed by Carroll. Other recent films, such as *Event Horizon*, have been more neutrally considered as part of a move to overcome problems of audience overfamiliarity with classic horror monsters. This generic shift has involved "the introduction of ever more bizarre, alien, and/or inchoate monsters."[31]

Whether monsters are absent or increasingly "inchoate" (and not merely "formless" or represented via "horrific metonymy" in Carroll's terms[32]), they can be quite difficult to address as distinct or definite "entities." We are thus faced with a situation where films commonly described as "horror" by their audiences cannot be accounted for via such cognitive approaches to monstrosity.

The writings of Christian Norberg-Schulz, as drawn on and adapted by C. S. Tashiro, offer a way to think about the materiality and the precise aesthetics of these types of horror *film*: "Norberg-Schulz . . . describes architecture and space as a series of ever-widening affective circles extending from the human subject,"[33] ranging from the "graspable object" through to "cosmic space" in Tashiro's filmic reworking.[34] It could be suggested that films such as *The Haunting*, *Event Horizon*, and *The Blair Witch Project* all fail to conform to a "standard cinematic form . . . built on middle distances, the cutting patterns of spaces calculated to human scale."[35] Instead, these films—in varying ways—either focus on the materiality of "graspable objects" or shift dizzyingly between extreme affective circles, moving from the "graspable" to the "cosmic" and back again.

Thinking about how "standard cinematic form" is distorted and reworked in these films is significant because it allows us to analyze their affective power as horror films not simply as a matter of narrative threat, but also via their specific mise-en-scenes (following Matravers's argument set out previously). The way that these films focus on the materiality of extreme detail—*Event Horizon*'s emphasis on detritus and different objects floating weightlessly, *The Blair Witch Project*'s repeated close-ups of "texture," and *The Haunting*'s framing of door frames, statues, and mirrors—works to intensify and complicate their narrative representations of threat (representations that do *not* resolve into present art-horrifying "monsters" in line with Carroll's model). The question I want to consider here is why a nonstandard cinematic form is adopted in these types of horror film, given that each film also shares a non-definite, absent, or withheld "monster" and thus fails to tally as Carrollian "art-horror."

Consider the mise-en-scene of *Event Horizon*. This film repeatedly shifts dramatically between "graspable objects" and "cosmic space" in extreme camera "zooms" from spacecraft windows to panoramic (and literally cosmic) vistas of space. We spin and pull back from Dr. Weir (Sam Neill) aboard the Low Earth Orbit Daylight Station, moving smoothly from a person-centered shot to a view of the Earth; later this camera "action" is repeated as we swoop in to see Mr. Smith (Sean Pertwee) working on the hull of the "Lewis and Clark" space vessel. The film also cuts rhythmically in on Captain Miller (Laurence Fishburne) standing at a cruciform window of the Event Horizon's bridge. In contrast with cosmic space, the affective circle of "graspable objects" is repeatedly emphasized through a series of special effects shots where objects such as bottles and a watch, as well as globules of fluid, "float" past the camera. These camera shots and effects are not central to any narrative analysis of the film, nor to an emphasis on the "inchoate monster" or entity-based definitions of horror, but they are affectively important in terms of the film's form. They represent formal and nonnarrative events that are repeated across the picture, generating a sense of unease and vague threat.

The Blair Witch Project also achieves some of its intensely unsettling nature by emphasizing "graspable objects" through its extreme, blurred close-ups of sleeping bags, torch-lit tree trunks, and, of course, the rough, primitive textures of the archetypal "house in the woods" encountered at the film's conclusion. Those following Carroll would want to highlight the way that Heather (Heather Donahue), Mike (Michael Williams), and Josh's (Joshua Leonard) represented faces and voices convey their mounting fear. A similar reading of *The Haunting* has been made by Alex Neill, who focuses on the responses of Eleanor (Julie Harris) and Theodora (Claire Bloom) to a sound coming from outside their bedroom door, suggesting that this is truly a terrifying scene; indeed, perhaps one of the most terrifying scenes in fiction film. In Carroll's terms, their responses "are the 'cues' for our responses . . .

[W]e respond as we do because in this scene we see the situation that the two women are in *from their point of view*. *We* find it terrifying because *they* find it terrifying."[36]

Such audience—character emotional mirroring is also seemingly true in the case of Heather in *The Blair Witch Project* (no radical shift in the gendering of fear here). We see her cry in close-up, and she croons "it's OK, it's OK, it's OK" to herself on a number of occasions, following fits of screaming. But, although we are given emotional cues by both Heather in *The Blair Witch Project*, and Eleanor and Theo in *The Haunting*, these cues occur in the absence of any defined entity or monster. Of course, it could be argued that *The Blair Witch Project* has a very obvious monster, the Blair Witch, but my argument is that this "monster" is withheld or implied in such a way that we, as viewers, are not cognitively able to conclude that "the Blair Witch" is diegetically responsible for those narrative events that are attributed to "her" across time. In effect, both this film and *The Haunting* dramatize the "action/happening" philosophical distinction, where the crucial question for characters and audiences alike becomes one of whether, and to what extent, narrative events can be attributed to the agency of a monstrous entity.

There is a specific hesitation here that is not quite Todorov's event-based model of the "pure fantastic" (where we hesitate between supernatural and natural/psychologistic explanations of an event).[37] Instead, the hesitation in this case runs as follows: As viewers of a horror film where the title cues the expectation of a monstrous entity (a haunting or a witch), we accept the narrative existence of a ghost or witch—these being precisely the cultural categories that we associate with horror movies. But we remain unable to determine whether the various events of the narrative are "actions" attributable to the ghost's/witch's agency or whether they (or some of them) are "happenings" that do not imply diegetic supernatural agency. There is thus an epistemological deficit here, one that constantly makes narrative *events* the focus of audience and character hesitation rather than the "discovery" of a clearly defined monstrous entity. Events in the film are not only threatening (being lost in the woods, being in a "haunted" house); their threat is also that of a malignant disembodied/transcendent agency that may or may not be implicated indexically and causally in these narrative signs and events. By contrast, in what Carroll terms art-horror, there is never any doubt on the part of the ideal or implied spectator that a threatening and impure monstrous entity is responsible for the negative fates befalling the victims. In fact, this doubt must be removed by definition, since it is only via narrative representation of the monster's evil that its threat can be established and its horrific nature fixed.

In light of the fact that there is an absence of any defined object for Heather's fear in *The Blair Witch Project*, and for Theo and Eleanor's terror in *The Haunting*, audience reactions must be accounted for in affective, rather than strictly cognitive-emotional, terms. An ultimately objectless affect or anxiety that permeates the *events* of these films is thereby generated; it is an anxiety that is provoked by keeping open a semiotic space between narrative events characterized as "actions" or as "happenings."[38] Naming *The Blair Witch Project* in part after an entity was, I would argue, an attempt to convince us as viewers that we would (in line with the traditions of horror monsters and their eponymous films) be treated to the witch-as-monster. The qualifying "Project" detracts in part from this possibility, but so strong are the conventions surrounding monster-named horror films that such a title could be held to invoke expectations of entity-based horror that the film's events then work to disorient and undermine. As an audience, we are therefore seemingly promised a monster that the film posits but withholds, meaning that the film's events and its form become affectively saturated with expectation, and with the anxious tension called up by hesitation between action and happening. And if we, as viewers, are cognitively unable to resolve the action/happening puzzle (as a result of our identification with the fear *and confusion* of onscreen characters), then a premium is placed on decoding the smallest signs of the diegetic world before us.

This emphasis on signs and portents, on what we might term "the semiotics of the action," take us back to Tashiro's use of Norberg-Schulz. Tashiro notes that "[g]raspable objects form Norberg-Schulz's first category. Objects close to us in space contribute toward the construction of a sense of a center and personal territory. For this reason, apprehensible objects, overlooked in order to privilege narrative, ground the viewer in a set of details."[39] Much of *The Blair Witch Project* deals with exactly this attempted grounding, in contrast to the historical scope and thus potential supernatural narrative threat of "the Blair Witch." The film's narrative quest to find out about the witch, or to escape from the woods, is periodically disrupted not by an eruption of filmic "spectacle," but rather by the eruption of non-classical "detail." Close-ups of brick walls or trees are hardly spectacular, but they do disrupt the narrative, which is noncognitively unsettling for the audience.

The "startle reflex," which lacks a cognitive component, can be stimulated by shock edits and sudden movements within or into frame, and *The Blair Witch Project*'s focus on close-up detail—to the point of a loss of camera focus—achieves something similar to this. However, where the startle reflex is best suited to monster-driven horror narratives (since its sudden movement could indicate the appearance of the threatening, impure monster), *The Blair Witch Project*'s close-up camera pans and wobbles are best suited to its event-driven type of horror narrative, one focused on action/happening indeterminacy and withheld/absent monstrosity. For here, the key threat is not whether a monstrous entity might be about to enter the frame, but whether the details within the frame can be read so as to indicate supernatural actions in place of happenings with no clear agent. By moving in on close details, and deliberately emphasizing framings rather than motion in and out of frame, the mise-en-scene seeks to center/ground characters and audiences in a narrative world of "graspable objects," while simultaneously stressing that these objects are possible signs or sites of monstrous agency. The ambiguity and hesitation presented via narrative events is thus amplified and replayed at the level of mise-en-scene, since here the narrative world is mediated in such a way as to suggest that it is pregnant with meaningful detail, implying that the quotidian might not only ground and reassure the self, but might also erupt into, or indexically code, a source of threat.

Alongside these formal "special affects," *The Blair Witch Project* trades on a series of cognitive, narrational links (e.g., introducing seven rock piles to parallel serial killer Rustin Parr's seven victims), and three additional piles to insinuate the deaths of the three explorers. The film's conclusion also deliberately recaps Parr's 1940s modus operandi. However, these cognitive links or symbolic repetitions are focused on events that evoke a pandeterministic affect rather than an entity-based emotion. The fact that there are three "manifestations" of the Witch introduced early in the film—namely Rustin Parr's crimes, the legend of Coffin Rock, and the earliest incidence of the witch—also forms part of this emphasis on symbolic repetition. It introduces the possibility that the Witch is more than an "entity" per se, being a sequence of events that is reiterated or a force that can be manifested in different ways. A single, defined entity or object does not emerge out of these events; instead the accumulation of reported events implies that they cannot be coincidental: "What is truly spectral is the *apparitional event*, which, like an analogue tape loop or stuck vinyl recording, replays itself."[40] As Julian Wolfreys has recently argued, it is not the appearance of a ghost as an entity that is necessarily haunting; it is rather the apparitional event, the replaying of an event, that has the power to affectively disturb audiences.[41] The narrated events of *The Haunting*, *Event Horizon*, and *The Blair Witch*, through their very repetition, indicate a cosmic force or power that transcends any given embodiment or entity. Narrative repetitions work to indicate diegetic "actions" rather than "happenings," and supernatural agency rather than contingency.

Intriguingly (given that Carroll distinguishes between Barkeresque and Lovecraftian aesthetics of horror), in her commentary on *Event Horizon*, Tanya Krzywinska cites both horror writers:

> [*Event Horizon*] takes us into the realms of H. P. Lovecraft's cosmic evil and the bodily tortures of [Clive Barker's—MH] *Hellraiser* . . . Dr. Weir is a scientist who becomes possessed by an evil force . . . As Weir's brain-child we could infer that the gateway technology carries with it his unconscious desires . . . [A]t first this force is not embodied.[42]

However, Krzywinska does not develop a discussion of the aesthetic clash that is implied here; instead, she resolves the film's contradictions by reading it as entity-based horror where "[a]fter a series of uncanny happenings chaos takes up residence in the mind and body of Weir."[43] As the previous quote indicates, even when the chaotic force posited in the film is disembodied, Krzywinska nevertheless interprets it as somehow belonging to the character of Dr. Weir. This entity-directed reading, in which Weir is the "primal father"-as-monster, marginalizes the significance of the monster's "inchoate" nature, as well as the "uncanny happenings" that take up most of the film's running time. I would suggest that we need to view *Event Horizon* as cognitively interesting in relation to Weir's eventual monstrosity, but also as noncognitively and affectively compelling in relation to its apparitional events and formal devices.

In contrast to Krzywinska, David Sanjek does not refer to *Event Horizon*'s "monster," indicating that, as with *The Blair Witch Project* and *The Haunting*, the very nature and definition of the "monster" remain open questions rather than being clearly delimited diegetically. For Sanjek, the film is concerned with a cosmic, chaotic force, and the "attempt to delineate that force . . . lacks sufficient imagination to engage one on other than the most visceral level."[44] Engaging the audience viscerally and noncognitively is, however, one of the film's strengths. Although it does indeed offer up Weir as a monster at its conclusion, complete with dream sequence and startle-reflex-edit (and as I have already suggested that this editing technique makes most sense where we have a clearly defined monster, it is perhaps no accident that the film uses this device here), *Event Horizon* also repeatedly suggests diegetically that the Event Horizon spacecraft is itself alive as a result of its travels. The spacecraft's "aliveness" is never literally developed (i.e., the ship does not directly manifest a sentient or animate nature in the diegesis; it doesn't wave electrical cables around as if they were tentacles), but it remains in excess of Weir-as-monster, providing an instance of entity-based horror being supplemented by event-based horror. The spacecraft's sentience or animation are implied rather than narratively shown, typically remaining at the level of character's attributions. This is a highly significant point because, if we were shown obviously sentient actions on the part of the craft as an agent then there would be no action/happening hesitation. However, since we know, as viewers, that some supernatural, cosmic force is at work, we are likely to accept the notion that the craft may have been "infected" or transformed in some way. But as this is never clearly confirmed, instead being suggested by characters who may well be mistaken, the action/happening hesitation remains, and the Event Horizon does not conclusively become a monstrous entity.

There is a metaphorical space preserved here: We can read the "actions" of the spacecraft "as if" it were a monstrous entity, but we are not finally able to conclude that it actually "is" such an entity. Further diegetic evidence is needed to move from the "as if" attribution of monstrosity to the "is" definition of monstrosity. Freeland's comments on *The Shining* and *Eraserhead* (1976) are apt here: "Though at times in these films the evil is localized in . . . a murderous agent . . . I would contend that neither man is a true horror-film monster. Rather, they are signs and perhaps even victims of the vague yet powerful cosmic evil that the movie posits".[45]

Weir is, as much as the Event Horizon spacecraft itself, both a sign and a victim. Since "the horror here goes beyond, or lies behind, the . . . monster . . . [and here this term is meant to apply only to Weir—MH], we cannot invoke Noël Carroll's views to explain" the appeal of a film like *Event Horizon*.[46] However, despite challenging Carroll's approach, it should be noted that Freeland's otherwise excellent account of "uncanny horror" finally collapses back into Carroll's art-horror/art-dread distinction: "*Dread . . . is different from fear because it is looser and less focused on an object . . .* Uncanny films . . . are not enjoyable for their presentation of interesting monsters, as some other horror movies are."[47] The difficulty with restoring the art-horror/art-dread distinction is that it suggests that films such as *Event Horizon*, *The Haunting*, *The Blair Witch Project*, and *The Shining* (Freeland's major example) should in fact not be classed as "horror," given that "art-horror" is meant to define all that has been generically marked as "horror" in ordinary language. And if the term "horror" is not denied to these films, a theoretical distinction is nevertheless introduced where none is made in ordinary language, defeating the object of the philosophical exercise, which (lest we forget) was initially intended to track ordinary languages of genre attribution.

Like *Event Horizon*'s eponymous vessel, *The Haunting* also suggests that an inanimate object, this time Hill House, may have become eerily animate. In fact, Carroll has argued that the haunted house (and by extension, we could add "the haunted spacecraft") fits perfectly well into his entity-based theory of horror. Responding to the criticisms of Alex Neill,[48] he comments that: "My theory is directed at beings not objects . . . and, where objects like haunted houses come into play, they are animate."[49] So, although haunted houses and spacecraft might be thought of as inanimate objects rather than animate entities, by virtue of their haunting they become honorary entities, while also presumably becoming monstrous by violating the very cultural categories of animate/inanimate.

However, to describe the Event Horizon or Hill House as a monstrous entity rather misses the point. Both spaces are marked out as ghostly by their repeated apparitional events, and thus by loops of replayed events, whether these are the relived personal tragedies of Captain Miller and Dr. Weir, or the multiple tragic deaths at Hill House. Neither space diegetically or definitively displays sentience or animatedness: the description of haunted houses as "alive" is more of a metaphor or a pandeterminist threat than Carroll seems to allow. Neither haunted space is actually represented as coming alive; instead this remains an associative leap, a possibility that hangs over and affectively saturates these fictions without being clearly realized, just as the historical endurance of the Blair Witch is suggested rather than explicitly indicated in the diegesis of *The Blair Witch Project*. Both films share an approach that withholds the "objective" confirmation of the monster within a realist diegesis in favor of mediating monstrosity through the viewpoints and reports of characters, via the close-up ambiguities and framings of "portentous" mise-en-scenes, and through indexical signs (hence the importance of bundles of sticks in *The Blair*

Witch Project and the mysterious written message "HELP ELEANOR COME HOME" in *The Haunting*).

The fact that we are driven to treat haunted houses (and spacecraft) *as if* they were monsters is crucial; were Hill House actually represented as a monster (in line with Carroll's claims), then the film would lack its affective power—and arguably, this is exactly what occurs in the remake, where the House's demonization/personification is carried far enough that any ambiguity concerning this issue is destroyed. On the other hand, in the 1963 version, although the house is personified through a variety of devices, both in character dialogue and mise-en-scene,[50] it is never fully diegetically defined as a monstrous entity, and thus the action/happening hesitation remains, along with its anxious, affective saturation of details rendered as portents (this is rendered beautifully, for example, in the "face in the wallpaper" sequence). Pam Keesey's strategic inability to pinpoint *The Haunting*'s monster, and her focus on the film's aesthetics, therefore seem more persuasive than Carroll's recuperation of the haunted-house-as-monster:

> The monster of Hill House—is it the house? Hugh Craine? Abigail? Theo? Eleanor herself?—is never brought to light. The complex interplay of personality and experience, of light and sound, of circumstance and setting—these are the monsters of Hill House.[51]

To conclude: I have argued that Carroll's philosophy of horror is weakened by its attempt to favor one aesthetic of horror, separating out broadly "Barkeresque" and "Lovecraftian" aesthetics into the spurious theoretical categories of "art-horror" and "art-dread." I have argued for a critical response to cinematic horror that does not split apart "art-dread" and "art-horror," and which thereby remains closer to "ordinary language" attributions of horror, covering a wider range of texts than Carroll allows for. Although my readings of *The Blair Witch Project*, *Event Horizon*, and *The Haunting* have been somewhat cursory or programmatic, I hope to have indicated the need for philosophies of horror to reflect more carefully on the events of art-horror that underpin and give rise to its horrific entities, as well as exceeding the need for horror to be defined through "monsters" per se.

With regard to horror *film*, this also means considering how art-horrifying narrative and mise-en-scene may not necessarily work in harmony, given that a narrative threat might be amplified or itself threatened and undermined by the affective workings of mise-en-scene.

In the case of the "successful" horror films that I have considered here, mise-en-scene consistently works to amplify the narrative threat of disembodied/transcendent forces, recapitulating the action/happening hesitation surrounding narrative events by focusing on the ground of "graspable" close-up details until these become estranged, portentous, and shrouded in "cosmic" indexicality.

Notes

1. See, e.g., Alex Neill, "On a Paradox of the Heart," *Philosophical Studies* 65, nos. 1-2 (1992): 53–65; Noël Carroll, "A Paradox of the Heart: A Response to Alex Neill," *Philosophical Studies* 65, nos. 1–2 (1992): 67–74; Susan L. Feagin, "Monsters, Disgust and Fascination," *Philosophical Studies* 65, nos. 1–2 (1992): 75-84; Noël Carroll, "Disgust or Fascination: A Response to Susan Feagin," *Philosophical Studies* 65, nos. 1–2 (1992): 85–90; Robert C. Solomon, "The Philosophy of Horror, or, Why Did Godzilla Cross the Road?" in *Entertaining Ideas—Popular Philosophical Essays: 1970–1990* (New York: Prometheus Books, 1992); Berys Gaut, "The Paradox of Horror," *The British Journal of Aesthetics* 33, no. 4 (1993): 333–45: Noël Carroll, "Enjoying Horror Fictions: A Reply to Gaut," *The British Journal of Aesthetics* 35, no. 1 (1995): 67-72; Berys Gaut, "The Enjoyment Theory of Horror: A Reply to Carroll," *The British Journal of Aesthetics* 35, no. 3 (1995): 284–89; Mark Vorobej, "Monsters and the Paradox of Horror," *Dialogue: Canadian Philosophical Review* 36, no. 2 (Spring 1997): 219–46; and Matt Hills, *The Pleasures of Horror* (London: Continuum, forthcoming 2003).

2. See David Russell, "Monster Roundup: Reintegrating the Horror Genre," in *Refiguring American Film Genres*, ed. Nick Browne (Berkeley: University of California Press, 1998), 233–54; and Steven Jay Schneider, "Monsters as (Uncanny) Metaphors: Freud, Lakoff, and the Representation of Monstrosity in Cinematic Horror," in *Horror Film Reader*, ed. Alain Silver and James Ursini (New York: Limelight Editions, 2000), 167–91, for very different extensions of Carroll's definition of "art-horror."

3. See, e.g., Mark Jancovich, *Horror* (London: Batsford, 1992) and Cynthia A. Freeland, *The Naked and the Undead: Evil and the Appeal of Horror* (Boulder: Westview Press, 2000).

4. Noël Carroll, *The Philosophy of Horror; or, Paradoxes of the Heart* (New York: Routledge, 1990), 13.

5. Although see Carroll, "Enjoying Horror Fictions," 70 and Gaut, "The Enjoyment Theory of Horror," 285–86 for an extension of this debate in which Carroll argues that *both* theorists and "ordinary speakers" may be "equally confused" over "the sources of our attraction to horror."

6. Russell, 238.

7. Carroll, *The Philosophy of Horror*, 41.

8. *Ibid.*, 42.

9. *Ibid.*, 27, 32.

10. See Carroll, *The Philosophy of Horror*, 28.

11. *Ibid.*, 42.

12. *Ibid.*

13. *Ibid.*

14. Brigid Cherry, "Refusing to Refuse to Look: Female viewers of the horror film," in *Identifying Hollywood's Audiences: Cultural Identity and the Movies*, ed. Richard Maltby and Melvyn Stokes (London: BFI Publishing, 1999), 195.

15. *Ibid.*

16. Freeland, 215; 239.

17. Carroll, *The Philosophy of Horror*, 219, *n.*27; emphasis added.

18. See Carroll, *The Philosophy of Horror*, 163.

19. *Ibid.*, 30–31.

20. *Ibid.*, 39–40; emphasis added.

21. *Ibid.*

22. Carlos J. Moya, *The Philosophy of Action: An Introduction* (Cambridge: Polity Press, 1990), 12.

23. Derek Matravers, *Art and Emotion* (Oxford: Oxford University Press, 2001), 90.

24. See Carroll, *The Philosophy of Horror*, 36.

25. Matravers, 91.

26. *Ibid.*

27. See also Will H. Rockett, *Devouring Whirlwind: Terror and Transcendence in the Cinema of Cruelty* (New York: Greenwood Press, 1998), 91-92, on the "transcendental style" of many horror films.

28. See Matravers, 91.

29. Malcolm Turvey, "Seeing Theory: On Perception and Emotional Response in Current Film Theory," in *Film Theory and Philosophy*, ed. Richard Allen and Murray Smith (Oxford: Oxford University Press, 1999), 433.

30. See Pam Keesey, "*The Haunting* and the Power of Suggestion: Why Robert Wise's Film Continues to 'Deliver the Goods' to Modern Audiences," in *Horror Film Reader*, ed. Alain Silver and James Ursini (New York: Limelight Editions, 2000), 315.

31. Schneider, 176.

32. Carroll, *The Philosophy of Horror*, 32; 51.

33. C. S. Tashiro, *Pretty Pictures* (Austin: University of Texas Press, 1998), 18.

34. *Ibid.*, 36.

35. *Ibid.*, 38.

36. Alex Neill, "Empathy and (Film) Fiction," in *Post-Theory: Reconstructing Film Studies*, ed. David Bordwell and Noël Carroll (Wisconsin: University of Wisconsin Press, 1996), 180–81.

37. See Tzvetan Todorov, *The Fantastic: A Structural Approach to a Literary Genre* (Ithaca, NY: Cornell University Press, 1975).

38. Although Carroll's typical art-horror clearly sets up its narrative events as "actions," it could be argued that disaster movies often present art-horrifying narrative "happenings."

39. Tashiro, 19.

40. Julian Wolfreys, *Victorian Hauntings: Spectrality, Gothic, the Uncanny and Literature* (London: Palgrave, 2002), 5; emphasis added.

41. *Ibid.*

42. Tanya Krzywinska, "Demon Daddies: Gender, Ecstasy and Terror in the Possession Film," in *Horror Film Reader*, ed. Alain Silver and James Ursini (New York: Limelight Editions, 2000), 261.

43. *Ibid.*, 262.

44. David Sanjek, "Same as It Ever Was: Innovation and Exhaustion in the Horror and Science Fiction Films of the 1990s," in *Film Genre 2000*, ed. Wheeler Winston Dixon (Albany NY: State University of New York Press, 2000), 121.

45. Freeland, 216.

46. *Ibid.*, 238.

47. *Ibid.*; emphasis added.

48. Neill, "On a Paradox of the Heart."

49. Carroll, "A Paradox of the Heart," 69.

50. See Steven Jay Schneider, "Thrice-Told Tales: *The Haunting*, from Novel to Film . . . to Film," *The Journal of Popular Film & Television* (Summer 2002): 166–76.

51. Keesey, 314–15.

Haunting the House from Within: Disbelief Mitigation and Spatial Experience

Aaron Smuts

In this chapter I attempt to explain the lasting effectiveness and critical success of Robert Wise's *The Haunting* (1963) by roughly sketching the role that spectator belief might play in a revised version of the so-called "Thought Theory" of emotional response to fiction. I argue that *The Haunting* engages viewers in a process of "disbelief mitigation"—the sheltering of nontrivial, tenuously held beliefs required for optimal viewer response—that helps make the film work as horror, and prevents it from sliding into comedy. Haunted house films do not have to extend much effort to keep us from walking away, since most viewers come to the theater ready to entertain the idea that haunted houses exist. Using the experiential philosophy of John Dewey, I propose that this willingness has to do with a fundamental aspect of our relationship with space. It is common to speak of places as "charged" or "tense," to get feelings of dread or nostalgia from certain spots. Some haunted house films leverage this experiential characteristic to fuel the horror, and without it, the subgenre would probably not exist.

Should We Believe the "Thought Theory"?

Noël Carroll's "Thought Theory" is a compelling resolution to the "paradox of emotional response to fiction": the problem of why we respond emotionally to fictional characters and events even though we know that the characters and events portrayed are not real. Carroll develops his Thought Theory in reaction to both Illusion and Pretend theories.[1] Unlike the Pretend theorist, he argues that there is no reason to suppose that the emotions we feel in reaction to fictions are any less genuine than other real-life emotions. And contrary to the Illusion theorists who argue that a measure of belief in the reality of the fiction is necessary for emotional response, Carroll presents his Thought Theory, which states that "thought contents we entertain without believing them can genuinely move us emotionally."[2] A useful test of this theory might be to ask why we are willing to entertain certain ideas and not others—why haunted houses, in particular, are not dismissed as absurd.

Steven Schneider criticizes Carroll's description of the imagination[3] as untethered by belief, arguing that the "mere entertaining in one's mind of a horror film monster is insufficient to generate fear; at the very least, it renders the production of such an emotional response either mysterious or irrational."[4] Instead, Schneider differentiates between beliefs in the *possibility* of something and in its *actual* existence, arguing that at least a belief in the possibility of the monster must be present for there to be fear.[5] Carroll might respond that belief in the possibility of something *just is* to "entertain the proposition nonassertively," or a thought, and is not, properly considered, a belief. However, the belief in possible existence is just as easily entertained assertively, for example, "I believe that there may be ghosts." If this were merely a thought, then we would have to explain why some thoughts are more plausible (or better candidates to be entertained assertively) than others, which would involve some measure of belief. What we lack is a criterion for what counts as assertively entertaining a thought.

Carroll's strong definition of belief—meaning "to entertain a proposition assertively"[6]—undergirds the conclusions of his Thought Theory, but the casting of belief and thought in such sharp contrast is unnecessary and confuses the issue. To merely assume the definition that proves the Thought Theory is to beg the question; the distinction could alternatively be described as one of degree, and not of kind. Schneider's distinction between "belief in actual existence" and "belief in possible existence" meshes with Carroll's talk of "existence beliefs" and may provide a start for developing a belief/thought continuum compatible with the major arguments of the Thought Theory. To simplify, if we consider the difference between belief and thought as a gradation, then we might be able to determine the location of any given statement by, for instance, the willingness of the person to bet on its truthfulness, as in

Rational Choice theory. Beliefs in possibility might fall somewhere between the two extremes.

We can accept two parts of the Thought Theory—viewers 1) need not confuse film and reality, and 2) need not believe in the *actual* existence of the referent of the fiction—and still attribute an important role to belief in the production of an emotional response. There are obvious limits on the efficacy of the thoughts viewers are willing to entertain; and within the range of acceptable fictional situations, there are those that viewers will less readily consider and ones that effectively provoke strong responses. Carroll gives an example of a person standing stably near the edge of a cliff, in no danger of falling, but able to become frightened by thinking about dropping off. He argues that it is not the belief that we are about to fall that makes us scared, since we are not, but the mere thought of falling that provokes the fear response.[7] However, one could argue, and the thought theorist would agree, that the reaction to this thought scenario is highly influenced by various beliefs. We do not hold the one particular belief that Carroll mentions; however, we do believe (in the strong sense of the term) a great number of trivial things such as: things fall; I can fall; I could get hurt if I fall from high up; or my grandfather broke both of his wrists by falling from a roof. If we believe that we are in danger of falling, or that someone fell recently, then imagining the plummet would certainly produce a greater amount of fear. Thoughts about flying upward uncontrollably and hitting your head on the ceiling are less likely to scare you than they are to make you laugh, since the supporting beliefs are not available.

At a minimum, emotional response is both primed and partially constrained by our web of potentially acceptable beliefs, however minor they may seem. The notion of "possibility beliefs" is too easily confused with "probability" and too monster-specific, hence I find it clearer to speak of the various types of "supporting beliefs." Some of these are 1) explicit "occurrent" beliefs; others may be 2) low-level unexamined beliefs, better described as "dispositional beliefs"; and many more might be 3) variations on previously surmounted beliefs that still linger in our minds with a sense of possibility and may or may not be candidates for assertive entertainment. Though viewers do not have to confuse fiction and reality, the imagination cannot run wild and still pull the emotions, but serves best when fed by acceptable scenarios backed by supporting beliefs.[8] It is common to hear people criticize a film by saying "It just wasn't believable. I couldn't get into it." The Thought Theory does not need to dismiss the role of such beliefs in the process of rejecting the role of the Illusion theorist's existence beliefs.

One could reply that this discussion of belief takes place at an unnecessarily high level and that my "flying up" example shows that there are constraints on the emotion-provoking abilities of thoughts, but this has nothing to do with belief. Recent work in cognitive neuroscience suggests that the physiological states of individuals imagining the performance of some bodily movements like tapping a finger are very similar to those of the actual performance of the action.[9] If emotional response is correctly described as a feedback pattern, where physiological states and awareness of those states heightens emotion that, in turn, increases bodily response, then the physiological effects of visualization could be key to explaining emotional response in a manner consistent with the "Thought Theory." This is even more compelling if we consider recent studies on rats that demonstrate that observation of movements performed by others, imagination of actions, and actual execution of motor performances share common neural substrates.[10] The thought theorist could argue that the lack of response to thoughts of flying up and hitting the ceiling is not the result of missing supporting beliefs; instead, it is the result of a lack of some sort of brain and bodily memory.

In an interview about the making of his films, Italian horror auteur Dario Argento described how he tries to confine displays of pain to common experiences in order to evoke visceral reactions. Rarely will he have a character shot by a gun, since few of us know what it is the like to be shot; instead, his victims are either stabbed or, more likely, cut by a broken window. We all know what it is like to bump our heads against a sharp table-edge or to hit our teeth on a drinking-glass, so Argento will couple these two common experiences and show people getting their teeth rammed against a table corner. One could argue that belief has nothing to do with Argento's strategy. It is not that we don't believe it hurts to get shot, but that we *know* what it is like to get cut by broken glass. Instead of belief, it is some sort of "physical memory" akin to what Antonio Damasio describes as "dispensational representations,"[11] sparked by visualization, which makes these actions more emotionally provocative.[12]

One might try to characterize these established brain routines that fuel the visualization response as some sort of low-level proto-"embodied" beliefs; however, this would require a more complete description of the underlying phenomena and may require stretching the concept of belief to meaningless proportions. At a high level, the "beliefs" in question can be considered unconscious (or barely conscious) cognitive contributing factors in higher-order consciousness. They seem to affect the plausibility of emotion-provoking scenarios by somehow lessening higher-order, error-detecting filters.[13] The liberalization of various higher-order filters could be a result of multiple factors. One such factor could be a belief system of sorts whereby bodily memory and filter relaxation patterns that develop from experience partially account for why certain more common thought scenarios are more effective than others.

In dealing with examples like Carroll's "thoughts of falling" and my "thoughts of flying" scenario, we may be oversimplifying the phenomena with which we are dealing. It is difficult to decouple the roles played by fear of the monster and fear of the mechanism of the threat. Perhaps confusing the issue, most discussion has centered around thoughts of the mechanics of danger—the specific devices, often resulting from the powers or weapons of the monster, that threaten the characters—rather than thoughts of the monsters themselves. To exacerbate the problem, in *The Haunting*, as in most equivocal, supernatural horror, the monster and the psychological (if not physical) threat are ambiguous and difficult to disentangle.

The Haunting employs higher-order, belief-oriented rhetorical strategies that must be accounted for in order to explain the film's effectiveness, and that cannot be casually dismissed as idle work. Disbelief mitigation, understood as a technique for maintaining inroads to emotional response by protecting higher-order filter liberalization from conscious, rational conservativism, may provide a gross cognitive explanation for the rhetorical strategies evident in films like *The Haunting*.

Spatial Experience and Haunted Houses

Since haunted house movies build on a readily acceptable belief—that spaces are emotionally charged—they have an easier job of overcoming skeptical blockage to their premise than many other types of horror fiction. Instead of having to reconfirm a previously "surmounted" belief, *The Haunting* is in a special position relative to most horror films, since it can capitalize on an actual belief: a real-world phenomenon that provides a foundation—at the intersection of imagination, experience, and belief—upon which the narrative can be built. In what follows, I will argue that if we accept the idea that space is experienced as "funded," or rich with meaning, then everyone is primed to (or might already) believe that spaces in general are, in and of themselves, intelligent or alive in some way. The phenomenological importance of spatial experience may provide the basis upon which to offer a solution to the particular paradox of emotional response to haunted house fictions. We might ask: Why are tales of haunted houses so often frightening if most of us do not (purport to) believe in them?

Psychologists refer to our personification, or funding, of space as "projection," according to which feelings associated with our memories of things and spaces are attributed to the things themselves. An excellent account of the phenomenological significance of the matter is found in the writings of the pragmatist philosopher John Dewey, who considers the sustaining environment that one encounters in experience by emphasizing the importance of embodiment and activity. In his essay "The Live Creature and Ethereal Things," Dewey argues that in experience space "becomes something more than a void in which to roam about, dotted here and there with dangerous things and things that satisfy the appetite. It becomes a comprehensive and enclosed scene within which are ordered the multiplicity of doings and undergoing which man engages."[14] He might agree with Foucault that space "is fundamental in any form of communal life; space is fundamental in any exercise of power."[15] But in some ways, Dewey's account of space is more interesting and complete than this. It is not only a form of power and control, it is a source of meaning.[16] For Dewey, space becomes a source of meaning as the environment becomes deeply ingrained with memories and desires—a unifying element of experience.

In "The Common Substance of the Arts," Dewey briefly discusses the importance of space in structuring and controlling experience. He argues that movement in space is qualitative, so that "[n]ear and far, close and distant, are qualities of pregnant, often tragic import—that is, they are stated not just measured by science."[17] It is not the "homogeneous space"[18] described by Newton or a scientific account of a spatial grid[19] that Dewey is concerned with here, but rather lived, qualitative space. Experienced space is "infinitely diversified in qualities."[20] Qualitatively, space can be roomy or cramped, stifling or emancipatory. Though it offers room to live, it is not experienced as a container; instead "space and time are also occupancy, filling."[21] A different spatial environment has a substantially different feel as our relations with it vary.

Perhaps the fundamental element of Dewey's account of space is *place*, or particular spaces. Dewey explains how "places, despite physical limitation and narrow localization, are charged with accumulations of long-gathering energy."[22] Lived space is not encountered as a homogeneous "container"[23] in which one can move about as if it were nothing but a life-sized map, but as a living site with locales of personality. Places are experienced as qualitative—as fearful, depressing, nostalgic, alienating, and lonely—because they are invested with accumulated meanings. Novelist Toni Morrison captures this element of lived place with her animistic rendering of the house in *Beloved:* "Shivering, Denver approached the house, regarding it, as she always did, as a person rather than a structure. A person that wept, sighed, trembled and fell into fits."[24] This perfectly captures Dewey's insight into how places are experienced.[25] They are often encountered as having a temperament of their own; sometimes a temperament so terrible that all one can do is flee, if one can.

Most important for haunted house narratives, Dewey explores the relationships we have with the spaces of experience, and how they fund our future interactions, adding to their meaningfulness. It is not just the investment of familiar lived space with which Dewey is concerned, but with how present experience is "funded" in our relations with new space when the "past is carried into the present so as to expand and deepen the content of the latter."[26] Haunted house films often try hard to "fund" the space of the house in an effort to control our response to the idea that a particular place might be haunted, and they offer evidence so viewers will be willing to accept this premise. As we shall see, one of the primary strategies of disbelief mitigation employed in *The Haunting* is to predispose us by providing a historical background for the house, so that we will understand how the characters must feel when approaching it.

Our willingness to accept the presence of a haunted house in a film can be partially explained as the result of a process of associational aversion that produces barely cognitive beliefs, resulting in higher-order filter liberalization. The animistic belief in cursed spaces may not be pronounced, and if it does present itself to examination we will most likely deny a rational belief in the matter. Many beliefs of this kind sit in an unexamined state, until something calls them forth and they are cast out in a rational exorcism. The belief in cursed or haunted places holds a special position among the unexamined, since it is often seen as acceptable even when made explicit. For example, the preternaturally popular Oprah Winfrey once held a show on the power of place, and recounted her experiences of a house that emanated the pain of its past inhabitants. She explicitly expressed a belief in the space's supernaturally charged quality. No one in the audience seemed to find this the slightest bit ridiculous, and the belief remained "unsurmounted."

Lingering unexamined beliefs play a crucial role in the course of an emotional response. Greg M. Smith has provided an account of the emotions as an "associational network,"[27] whereby signals triggering emotional responses come from various sources, often prior to cognitive evaluation:

> Emotional evaluation takes place in parallel to the conscious assessment of stimuli. If the emotion system's signals become strong enough to reach consciousness, emotional experience results. Once both conscious thought and the emotion system are initiated they tend to interact through a highly interconnected linkage, allowing thought to influence the course of an emotion and vice versa.

If we accept something like Smith's account of cognitive reassessment of emotional response as leading to intervention, reduction, or amplification, the importance of mitigating disbelief is crucial. Interference with the fear produced by disbelief is harmful to the film's success, and building associations that provoke the fear reaction is vital for maintaining higher-order filter liberalization. Instead of stopping at a purely low-level associational emotional response, the unexamined belief in cursed spaces provides a semi-cognitive amplifier for the viewer's response, or, in Schneider's terms, something "for the fear to latch on to."[28]

Disbelief Mitigation in *The Haunting*

In fictional worlds, we are less likely to fight supporting beliefs, and rational examination is less likely to diminish the emotional response since we are not asked directly to believe, but only to hold the belief for the sake of the story. However, when a fanciful fictional truth engages with a nonfiction belief, the two domains interfere and real-world disbelief mitigation becomes necessary. One side of disbelief mitigation involves holding criticism at bay. This "defensive" work is achieved in two ways: (1) a character will present a refutation of the belief only to suffer from its denial or eventually be converted; and (2) often the required belief will not be made explicit within the diegesis.

In *The Haunting*, characters unreceptive to the film's premise are put in extreme danger and punished for their doubt. Dr. Markway's (Richard Johnson) wife is skeptical about the possibility of a house being haunted and finds her husband's work a waste of time. She arrives at Hill House late in the film and, ignoring protest, decides to stay the night in the haunted hot seat: the old nursery. The house grows angry at her arrogance and, working as an agent of Nell's (Julie Harris) jealousy, puts

Mrs. Markway (Lois Maxwell) through an inquisition. The pounding and thumping grows to an unprecedented intensity, the passage to the nursery is blocked, and the entire group of characters is threatened by the mistake of her skepticism. When finally discovered running through the grounds, she recalls trying to escape from the house, explaining that when fleeing from the evil place she somehow fell from a trap door in the library and then ended up outside in the woods and badly shaken. The house puts her through hell as a punishment for her sinful heresy.

Luke Sanderson (Russ Tamblyn), the skeptical nephew of the current owners who is sent to Hill House to keep an eye on things, is slightly traumatized by the house and is eventually converted; he avoids extreme punishment only because his disbelief was not as firm as Mrs. Markway's. When he arrives, the doctor warns him that the doors of his closed mind could be "ripped from their hinges" in a traumatic episode if he does not at least consider the possibility of a haunting. Early in the film, Luke strongly doubts the legend surrounding Hill House, and can only think of how much he stands to gain when he succeeds in selling it; however, after the torment of the doctor's wife, he too becomes a believer in the haunting and suggests burning the evil place down, partly so that skeptics like him do not endanger the lives of anyone else. *The Haunting* presents a world in which heretics who threaten the film's premise with disbelief are punished or converted. This serves as a suggestive example to deter any viewer who might be entertaining similar doubts, letting them see the error of their ways.

To be effective, a haunted house film needs to do more than offer rebuffed skeptics as examples. The mitigation of disbelief is not only a reaction against raising critical questions, as the film can also try to encourage the belief, or else draw upon the source of an unexamined belief that we may hold. This "offensive" work is performed by 1) personifying the house; 2) personalizing the haunting experience; and 3) funding the space through a history of the location. In the process, the film keeps any statement of the belief in haunted houses unnecessary and implicit by making the source of the events ambiguous, serving the second defensive function.

Haunted house films are in a curious bind concerning the presentation of visual evidence, since it is not exactly clear what a manifestation of the haunting would/should look like. There seem to be two basic types of hauntings: those in which the house is inhabited by ghosts that do the haunting (e.g., in *The Others* [2001]); and those in which the house itself is the source of the haunting, as in *The Haunting*. Films featuring the second type of haunting have both hands tied behind their backs, since they are unable to throw a ghost at the audience; however, this can work to their advantage, as Jan De Bont's criminally bad remake of *The Haunting* (1999) demonstrates with its goofy computer generated monsters. In Wise's original version, some puzzling visual evidence is presented (mainly the closing of doors when no one is looking), but the film refrains from other, more obvious means of visually presenting the threat. Furniture never moves around the house and plates never fly off tables. Instead, the film builds a mood of confusion and looming danger by portraying the house as a living maze of doors and a trap of loose staircases. Schneider points out that the director frequently animates the house by giving it a perspective through point-of-view shots, distortion, and pans that take the view of neither character nor objective camera.[29] In the staircase sequence, for example, the camera shifts views from Nell's perspective of her feet on the stairs to the house's view of her climb. Pam Keesey finds that the house, "described in the novel as 'diseased' and 'not sane,' remains essentially the same [in the film]. Hill House, we are told, is not merely haunted. It is the haunt."[30] Instead of localizing the horror to a supernatural inhabitant, as many haunted house films do, the source of the haunting here (and of the numerous point-of-view shots) is Hill House itself. Again, it is not ghosts who do the haunting in Wise's film, but lived place that is the mechanism of fear.

Like taste aversion, people seem to have a "place aversion" response to the locales of traumatic events. *The Haunting* draws on our understanding of the obvious associational aversion Nell would have to Hill House. Knowing that her coincidental relation to the house primes the space as one she should not be in is a first step in setting up the haunting. Nell's particular relationship with Hill House is emphasized both cinematically and situationally. Keesey provides an excellent description of how Wise's camerawork portrays the house as watching Nell. When she first arrives, Wise establishes a shot-reverse-shot pattern between the house and Nell, as if they were looking at each other. Once inside, Nell's image is reflected in the floors and mirrors throughout the house, as if her image is reflecting off the house's eyes. When Nell enters her room, the camera sweeps down from the ceiling around and under Nell, as if the omniscient house has swallowed her whole.[31] One of the house's many direct calls to Nell comes when an inscription shows up on the foyer wall, telling her to "go home." It is Nell's history that makes the house, in popular horror slang, "shine." We expect space so charged with individual meaning to be experienced as such. It is thus no surprise that Hill House seeks out Nell throughout the film. In the end, her relationship with the house makes her unable to leave, and Theodora (Claire Bloom) suggests that Nell has been absorbed by or joined the house since she was so much a part of it to begin with.

The shared history of Nell and Hill House's previous residents allows the horror to be experientially located and presented through the perspective of a character, which opens the possibility for doubting the veracity of evidence. This is especially effective when the sanity of the character is constantly being questioned.[32] A fundamental means of mitigating the rational absurdity of a haunted house is to present a view of the house through the experience of a particular character. The house is rarely portrayed as terrifying unto itself, without the verification of a character's fear. Though this is a common horror device, it is especially pronounced in *The Haunting*, where we are shown more than just screams and reaction shots: throughout the film, we are allowed to hear Nell's unspoken thoughts and reactions to events. For much of the narrative, we actually experience events through her perspective. Theodora's ESP gives her at least partial access to Nell's thoughts, such as her desire to change into her new clothes and her feelings for Dr. Markway. When exploring the house, Theo shares in Nell's feeling that the house wants her. The initial haunting episode on the first night is mainly filtered through Nell and her psychic channel, and only later do the episodes questionably involve others outside her experience as the evidence mounts and the premise becomes easier to accept.

Our spatial experiences are largely governed by our historical understanding of particular locales, especially our personal relationship and role within that history. *The Haunting* gives a careful recounting of the sordid history of Hill House, which is marked by successive female deaths resulting from mysterious causes. Charging the space by providing it a history is the primary means by which viewers are brought into a ready state where they will be willing to accept the haunting. The place must "shine" for the audience as well as the characters in the story, and it is often necessary to build a historical understanding of the site for the film in question to succeed. Preconception formation is crucial for audience acceptance and understanding when dealing with haunted houses.

The Haunting presents evidence for the house's haunting and punishes those who do not believe, but it never actually *forces* viewers to accept the reality of the supernatural. The film is careful never to show us too much, never to push our belief to the limit where it would have to be accepted for a scene to work. In Montague Summers's classificatory scheme, this is an "equivocal gothic"[33] narrative—a fiction that casts the supernatural origins of events in doubt. Keeping the source of the horror ambiguous is a central strategy for disbelief mitigation, since it prevents skeptical thoughts from interfering with emotional responses that rely on unexamined beliefs. This is done by primarily relying on nonvisual evidence of the haunting, never visually presenting a monster, questioning evidence, and continually disputing whether the haunting is in Nell or the house.

While the film relies primarily on sound to present the source of terror, we are also given temperature evidence of the evil. Employing what is now a common trope in horror films, when the thumping noise comes for Nell, her room grows cold and we can see her breath. The house also has a cold spot in front of the nursery door that all the characters feel but for which they have no explanation. The source is never directly presented as the house itself, but this is a conclusion arrived at by the characters and the viewers through suggestion. We are never beaten over the head with causes, since that strategy can backfire; instead, viewers are asked to come up with their own answers supporting the premise prior to (or without) their presentation in the diegesis. Providing a history of the house is crucial to funding our imaginative experience of the place, so we will actively come to the conclusion that it is indeed haunted.

The Haunting is careful to avoid showing the source of the horror even when characters are being attacked by something in the house. On the second night of their stay, Nell goes to sleep next to Theodora in an adjacent bed. When she wakes up she does not realize she is now alone on that side of the room and assumes it is Theo's hand that she is holding in the dark. The grip becomes tighter until it is almost crushing, but Nell never looks over. Wise never reveals what is on the other end of the grasp; it is only suggested to us through Nell's comments and reaction. This keeps the source of the haunting ambiguous and allows us to question whether it is the house or Nell that is mad. After allying us with Nell, Wise employs Hitchcock's suspense technique of giving the viewer more information than the characters. This is achieved by shifting the perspective from Nell to Hill House in order to provoke a protective reaction. We know it is the house squeezing her hand and want her to get out of the room. Instead of confining our knowledge to what the characters know and sharing in their skepticism, the film puts us in a superior but helpless position where we are incapable of applying our knowledge. To reiterate: the film is careful not to present the source of the horror, which might serve to provoke reactions of disbelief; instead, we are asked to imagine the source and take the bait. By providing superior situational knowledge, we are encouraged to apply our belief in a protective emotional response. Provoking the application of an encouraged belief—one that might be questioned in other contexts—is a clever strategy of disbelief mitigation.[34]

Until the end, the film leaves the possibility of doubt an option. Emotional response is rather short-lived, a few minutes at the most, and our belief is both highest and most needed during peak sequences. In less heightened moments, because we are less sure about the source of the horror, critical examination of any loosely held beliefs is not prompted. At the conclusion of *The Haunting*, Nell attempts to leave, but her car seems to be chauffeured by the house. She winds up driving through the woods, blinded by darkness and branches, until she swerves to avoid the doctor's wife and crashes headlong into a tree. However, the true cause of the crash is indeterminate. The other characters question whether it was the house or Nell that brought about the accident. Since she died by hitting the same tree that the original founder's wife crashed into, we are encouraged to believe that the house is responsible, but the source is left open. Keeping the cause ambiguous further mitigates our disbelief in what we are encouraged to believe. Keesey argues that "the key to supernatural storytelling—whether on-screen or on the page—is the power of suggestion,"[35] but this only describes one component of a fundamental three-part structure. The pattern of disbelief mitigation goes from 1) belief encouragement, to 2) suggested application, to 3) reflective options. Such a pattern allows the film to successfully navigate our skepticism, minimize higher-order conservative responses, and leave behind a sense of uncertainty and a mood of horror.

Conclusion

Disbelief mitigation is a battle engaged in on two fronts: films relying on unexamined beliefs to effectively fuel the imagination must try to both counter criticism and encourage belief. Techniques for countering criticism may well be generic across horror films, and a frequently employed strategy is to prevent the required belief from being made explicit, often by keeping the source of the horror ambiguous. Another common technique for countering criticism is to present and punish heretics who challenge the required belief. On the other front, belief encouragement may be more specific to the type of horror and the particular belief we are dealing with. In a film like *The Haunting*, a belief in the possibility of haunted places is helpful for optimal response. The film funds the source of this belief by personalizing the house and providing it with a history, thereby making the events understandable, even if not expected. It draws upon the belief by presenting situations and examples that encourage us to decide that Hill House is indeed the source of the horror. Haunted house films often use our interactive experience of space, and an accidental and unexamined animistic belief resulting from this interaction, as their foundation. Often, before we even see the house, we have a foot in the door.[36]

Notes

1. Space does not permit an elaboration of the two rival theories and Carroll's convincing arguments against both in *The Philosophy of Horror; or, Paradoxes of the Heart* (New York: Routledge, 1990).

2. *Ibid.*, 81.

3. Carroll highlights two uses of the term "imagination": 1) "entertaining a thought non-assertively," and 2) where we "are the creative and primarily voluntary source of the contents of our thoughts" (88). Carroll finds that the second notion of the term is misleading since viewers need not add anything via the imagination to what the fiction presents.

4. Steven Schneider, "Monsters as (Uncanny) Metaphors: Freud, Lakoff, and the Representation of Monstrosity in Cinematic Horror," in *Horror Film Reader*, eds. Alain Silver and James Ursini (New York: Limelight Editions, 2000), 177.

5. Offering an account of how horror might plug in to our imagination, Schneider presents an explanation of our response to monsters as the metaphorical presentation of suppressed beliefs. He argues that: "All horror film monsters metaphorically embody surmounted beliefs, but not all of them manage to reconfirm those beliefs by their very presence." (184). Regardless of whether horror functions by presenting metaphorical examples supporting surmounted beliefs, Schneider's argument emphasizes the necessity of a conceptual foothold to prevent horror films from becoming pure camp.

6. Carroll, 80.

7. *Ibid.*

8. The other side of the coin might be how fear of a new technology or nuclear war or something poorly understood can broaden the acceptable range of beliefs by putting beliefs in limits in question.

9. "Studies of cerebral metabolic activity have demonstrated that most of the regions that are active during overt movement execution such as the parietal and premotor cortices, the basal ganglia, and the cerebellum are active during mental simulation as well." A. Sirigu, et al., "The Mental Representation of Hand Movements after Parietal Cortex Damage," *Science* 273 (1996): 5281. Recent work on "mirror neurons" may provide a neurological basis for the effectiveness of graphic displays of bodily harm.

10. See Maria B. Leggio, et al., "Representation of Actions in Rats: The Role of Cerebellum in Learning Spatial Performances by Observation," *Proceedings of the National Academy of Sciences, USA* 97, no. 5 (2000).

11. Antonio Damasio, *Descartes' Error: Emotion, Reason, and the Human Brain* (New York: Quill, 2000), 94–105.

12. I discuss Argento's "visceral technique" in more detail in "The Principles of Association: Dario Argento's *Profondo Rosso* (*Deep Red*, 1975)," *Kinoeye: A Fortnightly Journal of Film in the New Europe* 2, no. 11 (June 10, 2002): www.kinoeye.org/02/11/smuts11.html. (June 12, 2002)

13. Building upon the work of Joseph LeDoux, Daniel H. Barratt presents something akin to a mediated shock-response explanation for emotional reaction to visual horror, where visual stimuli take a fast track to emotion pre-evaluating brain regions only to be later refereed by higher-order consciousness: "our biological makeup and our evolutionary history . . . crosses, say, a 'fast-acting' thalamus-amygdala circuit (an 'early-warning system' which effectively sacrifices accuracy for speed) with higher-order consciousness (a late 'error-detection system' which effectively sacrifices speed for accuracy)." Barratt, "The Paradox of Emotion Revisited: Uncovering the Emotional Foundations of Pictorial Representations" (unpublished manuscript): 20. See also Joseph LeDoux, *The Emotional Brain: The Mysterious Underpinnings of Emotional Life* (New York: Touchstone, 1998).

14. John Dewey, "The Live Creature and Ethereal Things," in *The Philosophy of John Dewey*, ed. John J. McDermott (Chicago: University of Chicago Press, 1981), 544.

15. Michel Foucault, "Space, Knowledge, Power," in *The Foucault Reader*, ed. Paul Rabinow (New York: Pantheon Books, 1984), 253.

16. My approach to Dewey has been influenced by John McDermott, especially his book *The Culture of Experience: Philosophical Essays in the American Grain* (New York: New York, 1976), where he develops similar themes in his discussions of Dewey. In the introduction to his edited collection, *The Philosophy of John Dewey*, McDermott points out several of Dewey's major concerns: the lived body, the primacy of growth, nonsexual repression, and the affective dimension of human activity (xxvii). Since these are central themes in Dewey's writings, it is not surprising that some of my concerns overlap with McDermott's. However, in this essay and elsewhere I develop similar themes (especially that of space) in distinct ways, through the intersection of philosophy, literature, and film, in order to argue that Dewey has developed (or else I am distilling out of his analyses) a significant social-critical tool that to date has been unfortunately ignored.

17. John Dewey, *Art as Experience* (New York: Capricorn, 1958), 207.

18. In *The Quest for Certainty*, ed. Jo Ann Boydston (Carbondale: Southern Illinois University Press, 1990), Dewey describes the scientific view of space as "homogeneous space" (75; 78).

19. In *Art as Experience*, Dewey contrasts the different treatments of space by science and art: "As science takes qualitative space and time and reduces them to relations that enter into equations, so art makes them abound in their own sense as significant values of the very substance of all things" (207).

20. *Ibid.*, 210.

21. *Ibid.*, 209.

22. Dewey, "The Live Creature and Ethereal Things," 544.

23. Dewey describes Newtonian space as "container space" in the *The Quest for Certainty*, 113.

24. Toni Morrison, *Beloved* (New York: Plume, 1998), 29.

25. Another passage in *Beloved* is relevant and rewarding for thinking about Dewey: "I was talking about time. It's so hard for me to believe in it. Some things go. Pass on. Some things just stay. I used to think it was my rememory. You know. Some things you forget. Other things you never do. But it's not. Places, places are still there. If a house burns down, it's gone, but the place—the picture of it—stays, and not just in my rememory, but out there, in the world" (36). This passage highlights the locatedness of experience and the indelibility of this attribute.

26. Dewey, "The Live Creature and Ethereal Things," 545.

27. Greg M. Smith, "Local Emotions, Global Moods," in *Passionate Views: Film, Cognition, and Emotions*, ed. Carl Plantinga and Greg M. Smith (Baltimore: Johns Hopkins University Press, 1999), 111.

28. Schneider, 177.

29. Steven Jay Schneider, "Thrice-Told Tales: *The Haunting*, from Novel to Film . . . to Film," *Journal of Popular Film and Television*" (Summer 2002): 166–76.

30. Pam Keesey, "*The Haunting* and the Power of Suggestion: Why Robert Wise's Film Continues to 'Deliver the Goods' to Modern Audiences," in *Horror Film Reader*, ed. Alain Silver and James Ursini (New York: Limelight Editions, 2000), 308.

31. See Keesey, 310.

32. See Steven Jay Schneider, "Barbara, Julia, Carol, Myra, and Nell: Diagnosing Female Madness in British Horror Cinema," in *British Horror Cinema*, ed. Stephen Chibnall and Julian Petley (London: Routledge, 2001), 117–30, for a discussion of the ambiguity of the source of horror in *The Haunting*.

33. Montague Summers, *The Gothic Quest: A History of the Gothic Novel* (London: Fortune, 1938).

34. Carroll identifies a larger technique he calls "fantastic hesitation," found frequently in "equivocal gothic," where explanations are disputed and the viewer is asked to puzzle an explanation with a few pointers (156–57).

35. Keesey, 306.

36. My thanks go out to Daniel Barratt, Heidi Bollich, Jeanne Deslandes, Cynthia Freeland, Anne Jaap Jacobson, Paul Molnoski, and Steven Jay Schneider for reading and commenting on earlier versions of this chapter.

Murder as Art/The Art of Murder: Aestheticizing Violence in Modern Cinematic Horror

Steven Jay Schneider

A man who robs would always be an object to be rejected by the poet who wishes to present serious pictures. But suppose this man is at the same time a murderer, he is even more to be condemned than before by the moral law. *But in the aesthetic judgement he is raised one degree higher and made better adapted to figure in a work of art.* Continuing to judge him from an aesthetic point of view, it may be added that he who abased himself by a vile action can to a certain extent be raised by a crime, and can be thus reinstated in our *aesthetic* estimation.

—Friedrich Schiller[1]

Violent acts compel an aesthetic response in the beholder of awe, admiration, or bafflement. If an action evokes an aesthetic response, then it is logical to assume that this action—even if it is murder— must have been the work of an artist.

—Joel Black[2]

I

To the extent that aesthetic metaphors found a place in horror films of the classic era, they served to equate monstrousness with a flawed, degraded, or corrupt work of art. As often as not, it was a work of literature that provided the inspiration here, but celluloid would prove a uniquely effective medium for bringing such metaphors to life. In

James Whale's *Frankenstein* (1931), for instance, Henry (Colin Clive) rejects his unholy creation not because of any real scientific failing—after all, "It's alive!"—but because of his perceived inability to produce a work of sufficient beauty. In Rupert Julian's *The Phantom of the Opera* (1925), the prodigious talents of silent film star Lon Chaney were exploited to the fullest, as the actor's trademark combination of gruesome makeup and facial contortion resulted in a Phantom so hideous that viewers could not help but contrast him with his ultra-ornate surroundings. Eight years later, director Michael Curtiz would similarly explore/expose disfigurement anxiety in *Mystery of the Wax Museum*: a gifted sculptor named Ivan Igor (Lionel Atwill), his face horribly burnt in a fire, goes about murdering attractive young women so as to embalm them in wax. Here, as in *House of Wax* (the 1953 remake starring Vincent Price), the monster kills with his art, but what *makes* him a monster is first and foremost his gruesome visage. In the various film versions of Oscar Wilde's *The Picture Of Dorian Gray* (1913, 1916, 1945), the eponymous anti-hero's moral depravity receives embodiment in the physical deterioration of his own self-portrait. And Max Schreck's Count Orlok in *Nosferatu: A Symphony of Horror* (1922) is by any measure a ghastly creature in his physical appearance, what with his gaunt body, bald, pointy head, and rat-like features, especially when contrasted with the film's dreamlike cinematography and mise-en-scene. As Angela Dalle Vacche argues, Murnau's picture in its totality can be viewed as "an Expressionist work of art [that] . . . stands up to the comparison with Freidrich's Romantic canvases."[3]

As a major stylistic influence on early (notably German) horror cinema, Expressionism itself warrants further mention here. For one of the defining features of such classics as *The Cabinet of Dr. Caligari* (1919) and *M* (1931), as well as of many subsequent productions—from Roger Corman's 1960s cycle of Edgar Allen Poe adaptations up through Tarsem Singh's neo-Expressionist serial killer film *The Cell* (2000)—is a warped reflection of the antagonist's psychological instability in highly artificial and often hyper-aestheticized costumes, set designs, atmospherics, and even acting styles.[4] Despite the fact that the crazy, compulsive killers in such movies usually do not suffer from any striking physical abnormalities, the distorted quality of these external elements serves to "make apparent the internal workings of an anguished self."[5] And though the monsters of Expressionist-influenced horror cinema may not *themselves* be equated with flawed, degraded, or corrupt works of art, they still qualify as derivative versions of this metaphor, since the audience's focus tends to be not so much on these creatures' abnormal psychologies as on the remote manifestations of such perverse and dangerous minds.

Simply stated, in each of the previously named films—and in many others of this era—monstrousness is conceived of primarily in *aesthetic* (rather than moral, spiritual, or philosophical) terms. What makes Frankenstein's creature, Erik the Phantom, Ivan Igor, Dorian Gray, Count Orlok, and Price's aristocrats so disturbing is less a function of their malicious motives or bad behavior than of their physical or externally reflected "ugliness." This claim is attested to by the fact that these beings are not so much *evil* as they are hyperbolically confused, frustrated, compelled, misunderstood, or mistaken, as well as by the fact that they always fare miserably when compared, either explicitly (via dialogue, voice-over narration, etc.) or through contextual cues (usually the result of mise-en-scene or montage editing), with more "legitimate" works of art.

From these initial observations it is tempting to conclude that classic-era horror's operative aesthetic metaphor—the monster as corrupt or degraded artwork—depends in large part on a culturally enforced equation between inner and outer beauty and goodness, along with its converse, according to which outer ugliness and wickedness visibly testifies to the state of one's inner life or "soul." But such a conclusion would be mistaken. Many classic horror film monsters are sympathetic to a greater or lesser (but nearly always conspicuous) degree; besides those listed above, consider King Kong, the Wolf Man, and the Mummy. This holds especially true in relation to the humans who misunderstand them, hate them, and hunt them down due to an often irrational fear and loathing. Despite being sympathetic, however, sometimes even quite beautiful or virtuous on the inside, the creatures in question are nevertheless depicted as undeniably *monstrous* within their respective diegesis. This, I assert, is due primarily to the widespread cultural influence of a "legitimate" art that positioned artworks as a matter of beauty rather than, say, hermeneutic difficulty or incongruity.[6]

Though Alfred Hitchcock's *Psycho* (1960) has received most of the glory, Michael Powell's *Peeping Tom* (released earlier the same year) deserves just as much credit for heralding a new era of cinematic horror. In both of these films the monster is human, all too human, and besides that, all too real. Real in the sense that no obvious or Expressionistically rendered signifiers of physical deformity— simplistically (and sometimes misleadingly) signifying moral corruption—are made available to the audience/protagonist/victim for the purpose of immediate identification. In fact, as I will seek to show, one distinguishing mark of the modern horror film is a shift in the genre's dominant aesthetic metaphor: what used to be the monster as corrupt or degraded work of art has become (evolved into? We shall see . . .) the *monster as corrupt or degraded artist*. In the following section, the nature of this shift will be elucidated with a closer look at *Peeping Tom* and *Psycho*. That will pave the way for a rudimentary typology that seeks to carve up the monster-as-corrupt-artist trope into more specific thematic categories. After elaborating on the various examples in this typology, the following questions will be addressed: What cultural and sociohistorical conditions might be cited to explain this profound transformation in the horror genre? And just how much should we be concerned with the increasing trend toward cinematically depicting murderers as artists, and murder as an art form, considering that such romanticized portrayals can be seen—at least according to one line of thinking about media effects—as giving license to, perhaps even inspiring, real-life (though usually not nearly so creative) acts of violence?[7] With respect to the former question, and in line with what has been said thus far, my contention is that our popular/public understanding of "art" has culturally mutated, and that this shift has been paralleled and drawn upon in horror cinema's reconfiguration of its dominant aesthetic metaphors.

II

In *Peeping Tom*, an otherwise unremarkable young man by the name of Mark Lewis (Karlheinz Böhm) murders young women with a retractable spike attached to a movie camera. Also affixed to the camera is a small mirror that enables him to record the terrified expressions on his victim's faces as they watch themselves getting killed.[8] Mark's psychotic tendencies are inextricably tied up with a perverse aesthetic sensibility, and to the extent that we as viewers find ourselves interested in his homemade snuff films, to that extent are we implicated in the murders he commits to obtain them. If one compares this movie with *Mystery of the Wax Museum*, it becomes apparent that, although in both films the murderer is a kind of artist who, so to speak, kills with the tools of his trade, it is only in *Peeping Tom* that the murderer is primarily coded as monstrous *not* because of some physical or mental deformity (despite his deep-rooted insanity, Mark happens to be a pretty nice, pretty normal-looking bloke), but because he puts his artistic talent to such malevolent use. It is true that Mark, via his social isolation coupled with his ostensible normality, fits to the tee the burgeoning stereotype of the "invisible/average killer" or the "killer among us." And although this prototypical characterization can itself be understood as a coding of monstrosity (one that to some extent prefigures and predicts Mark's pathology), it seems more accurate to hold that, absent the killer's eventual manifestation as a corrupt and murderous artist figure, such a coding instead supports the overly rational view that "realistic" sociopaths are a species wholly distinct from the fantastic monsters of lore.

   Psycho's Norman Bates (Anthony Perkins) may not be as creative a killer as Mark Lewis, but he is just as nondescript, just as sweet (when he's not dressed up as his mother), and just as artistic—that is, if one considers taxidermy an art. William Rothman goes so far as to connect Norman/Mother's murder of Marion Crane (Janet Leigh) with her aesthetic disinterest in the young man's collection of stuffed birds: "Marion . . . is totally unable to appreciate Norman's creations. His disdain for her, at one level, is that of an artist for a contemptible critic."[9] Rothman proceeds to argue that "Norman Bates stands in for every artist whose life is circumscribed by acts singularly composed of murder and creation," where the murderous component in question is to be understood as a product of every artist's desire "to avenge himself on those who, beholding his creations, draw sustenance from them."[10] But one need not subscribe to such an extreme view of artistic creativity, nor to such a loose interpretation of Norman's character. For present purposes, it is sufficient to note that in going to such dramatic lengths to keep his mother "alive"—by maintaining her corpse, but more important, by dressing like her, by mimicking her voice, and by identifying with her so completely—Norman provides ample evidence of not only a psychotic but also an artistic temperament. Whereas Ivan embalms, and Mark shoots film, Norman effectively *method acts* in order to fulfill what André Bazin calls "the primordial function of statuary, namely, the preservation of life by a representation of life."[11] Of course, the only lives any of these artist-murderers are interested in preserving after death are those they have taken themselves.

   If, in the "modern" horror film—by which I have in mind here less a genre-specific modification of particular formal and stylistic conventions than a large-scale, cross-media transition to a period where the meaning of "art" became open to cultural challenge and reconfiguration—monsters are predominantly typed as depraved or corrupt artists rather than as flawed, degraded, or corrupt works of art, how are we to understand the murders these monsters commit in pursuit of their aesthetic calling? An admittedly selective survey of the genre, with some attention paid to international examples in addition to those from the United States and Britain, reveals two major trends in the artistic (re-)presentation of murder: on the one hand are those horror films that showcase murder as an artistic *product*, and on the other are those that showcase it as an artistic *performance*. With respect to the former trend, what matters most from an aesthetic point of view is the scene of the crime and/or whatever remains of the victim(s), rather than the motive, the *modus operandi*, or even the presence of the murderer. With respect to the latter trend, what matters most aesthetically-speaking is precisely the contrary of this, namely the way in which the murderer goes about committing (i.e., "performing") his crime. It is important to keep in mind, however, that these two trends are by no means mutually exclusive; many horror films play around with both of them, often in interesting and complementary ways. I will now turn to some examples so as to fill in the picture sketched above.

A. Murder as Artistic Product

In one group of films employing this theme, dead bodies are literally reused for practical purposes. Examples here include *Motel Hell* (1980), in which an organic farmer earns a huge profit by turning his victims into human jerky (tagline: "It takes all kind of critters to make Farmer Vincent's fritters!"); *The Texas Chainsaw Massacre 2* (1986), in which a family of ex-slaughterhouse workers wins the Texas-Oklahoma Chilli Contest two years running because of their "prime meat"; and the infamous Hong Kong "Category 3" horror film, *The Untold Story* (1993), in which sadistic murderer Wong Chi-hang (Anthony Wong) feeds the remains of his victims to the police investigating his case by disguising them as pork buns.[12] In each of these movies, it is the recognition and admiration accorded the respective killer-chefs by a satiated, albeit ignorant, public—a public that is exposed as hypocritical (and, at a deeper level, culturally repressed) for its simultaneous taste for and repudiation of cannibalism—which codes them as artists. What makes them *monsters*, of course, is the horrifying nature of their art.

Though neither the mask of human skin worn by Leatherface (Gunnar Hansen) nor the various pieces of "bone furniture" that appear in *The Texas Chainsaw Massacre* (1974) are ever subject to aesthetic appraisal from people *within* the diegesis, these objects are made with enough care and exhibit a sufficient degree of craftsmanship to elicit a reaction more complex than mere shock from most viewers. The very fact that this reaction characteristically involves a measure of disgust or revulsion on the part of both victim and viewer lends support to the distinctly modern notion that art need not command admiration to "count" as art (a point to which I shall return), as well as to Noël Carroll's identification of disgust as one of the two essential evaluative criteria of fictional horror (the other being perceived threat).[13] A more recent example along these lines occurs in Jonathan Demme's *The Silence of the Lambs* (1991), in which the high-culture cannibal Hannibal Lecter (Anthony Hopkins) escapes captivity by wearing the sliced-off facial epidermis of a dead prison guard over his own, and in which an on-the-loose serial killer (Ted Levine) skins his female victims only to sew together their hides like some demonic dressmaker in order to fashion himself a new sexual identity. That we should find thematic overlap between this film and *The Texas Chainsaw Massacre* is not surprising, considering that both were inspired in part by the real-life story of Wisconsin-based serial killer Ed Gein (as was the novel upon which *Psycho* is based). Of course, no monster recycles human body parts more proficiently than Dr. Frankenstein's, since the creature could hardly exist without them. But the fact that it is *Henry* who puts these parts together, who somehow brings them back to life, means that his monstrous progeny is at best a work of art, not an artist in his own right. And since most film versions of Mary Shelley's novel downplay the reality of Victor's *own* monstrousness, the monster-as-corrupt-artist metaphor has been left for others to explore.

In the second group of films to employ the theme in question, dead bodies are carefully positioned and manipulated, often symbolically arranged, so as to make more or less comprehensible "statements." Alternatively (though these are by no means mutually exclusive options), the blood of victims is literally used as paint by struggling artists who, in campier productions such as Herschell Gordon Lewis's 1965 gorefest *Color Me Blood Red*, are in desperate need of a brighter, more "vibrant" shade of red; or else who, in more pretentious fare like William Gove's *The Apostate* (1998) and Hideshi Hino's *Guinea Pig 4: Mermaid in the Manhole* (Japan, 1991), seek inspiration and greater "authenticity" in their macabre works of art. As in the "consumer cannibalism" films discussed above, special fun is poked at members of the unsuspecting public, who are here exposed as dilettantish and hypocritical insofar as the high esteem—measured primarily in terms of monetary value—they confer upon the artworks in question depends precisely upon their *not knowing* what raw materials were used to create them. This holds especially true for *Color Me Blood Red* and *A Bucket of Blood* (1959), Roger Corman's horror-comedy in which a would-be sculptor uses the corpses of those he kills—or parts thereof— as the underlying substance of his supposedly clay statues.[14]

Similarly, in Curtis Harrington's *Games* (1967), Paul Montgomery (James Caan) plasters over the corpse of a young man he and his wife have accidentally killed, keeping it in the house right next to the statue of a human form made by a well-known artist. Not only does Harrington play off the fact that the expensive, aesthetically pleasing statue and the grotesque, hastily disguised corpse are equally regarded as works of art by those in the diegesis; he doubly confuses the matter by revealing in the end that the latter was just a trick on Paul's part to drive his rich wife crazy: sandbags, and not a corpse, were used to give the makeshift statue "more body." Thus, viewers of *Games*— encouraged by earlier events to feel secure in the knowledge that they, at least, can tell the difference between a work of "real art" and one of "mere murder"—are shown (up) to be equally incapable of making such a distinction on the basis of surface appearance. *The Apostate* turns this same joke-*cum*-critique on its head by having a potential buyer admire the canvases painted by serial killer Lewis Garou (Dennis Hopper) precisely *because* they are rumored to have been made with human blood. In this respect, Gove's film offers an interesting twist on a real-life and somewhat disturbing trend in American consumer culture: the serious collecting, for posterity or financial gain, of artwork—sketches, drawings, wood carvings, and the like—made by serial murderers, often while they are behind bars serving life-sentences for their crimes.[15]

When it comes to movies that feature the symbolic positioning of dead bodies, there are an abundance of examples to choose from. Here, I will restrict myself to just a few. In each case, great emphasis is placed upon control and composition of the mise-en-scene, responsibility for which effectively shifts from the director (as behind-the-scenes narrator) to the murderer (as diegetic set-designer). At times, and as film scholar Linda Badley's recent work endeavors to theorize, these authorial positions threaten to collapse into one another, the boundary between auteurist horror director and fictional murderer-*artiste* blurring to the point where the latter appears to be nothing less than a sublimated alter-ego of the former.[16]

- *Halloween* (1979): After killing off a number of her chums, superhuman psychopath Michael Myers plans a distinctly unpleasant surprise for Laurie Strode (Jamie Lee Curtis). Upon entering the upstairs bedroom of her friend Annie's (Nancy Kyes) house, Laurie is confronted by the following sight: next to a lit Jack-o-lantern, Annie's corpse lies face-up on a bed with her arms spread wide. In back of her head is a tombstone, upon which is engraved the name of Michael's dead sister Judith. Besides all of the questions it raises—Why the tombstone? What is the connection between Annie and Judith? Why is Laurie the intended audience?—this horrifying tableau practically cries out for aesthetic acknowledgment; were the meticulously arranged display not sufficient to make this point, director John Carpenter's camera subtly reframes and slowly zooms in, approximating Laurie's point-of-view as she edges closer to the bed. Instead of running away immediately, she clearly wants another, closer look. And even if Laurie—who despite her fascination is understandably beside herself with fright—is incapable of giving due credit to the artist responsible for this mise-en-scene of death, viewers of *Halloween* are in a far less precarious position than she, and so are far more likely to respond to Michael's/Carpenter's handiwork with a terror tinged with pleasure. It seems that here, and in numerous other examples [see the following paragraph], we encounter a situation which runs counter to Carroll's observation that (as Marguerite LaCaze summarizes his position) "horror appears to be one of those genres in which the emotive responses of the audience, ideally, run parallel to the emotions of characters."[17] Precisely because of our safe vantage point—the "aesthetic distance" we are given to contemplate the killer in question's creative crime scenes, and, conversely, our imagined closeness to the camera's gaze—our feelings as spectators are systematically distinct from the feelings of the protagonist.

Similar moments occur in *The Texas Chainsaw Massacre*, when Sally Hardesty (Marilyn Burns) suddenly finds herself in a room littered—but excessively, and self-consciously so—with the feathers and bones of dozens, possibly hundreds, of animals, and in which human skeletal remains dangle precariously from the ceiling on thin bits of string; and in Brett Leonard's *Hideaway* (1995), where a back-from-the-grave serial killer artistically arranges his victims' corpses within a massive skull-like structure, to the horror of a teenage girl temporarily trapped inside it. (An obvious question to ask here, albeit one I am unable to pursue in this essay, is why so often it is a young *woman* who is first confronted with these spectacles of death within the diegesis. Is it because femininity is traditionally assumed to respond "better," at least more viscerally, to works of art and murder?)

• *Manhunter* (1986): Five minutes into the film, we find ourselves alone in a house with former FBI agent Will Graham (William Petersen), who is trying to make some sense of the horrible crime scene before him. It seems that an unknown intruder, after murdering a couple in their bedroom and splattering the walls with their blood, placed shards of mirror in their eyes. Detective Graham speaks into a tape recorder: he describes the room down to the smallest detail, then enters into a mock dialogue with the killer. He praises him as "skillful," asks him questions, and wants to know why he acted *this* way rather than some other—all of which serves to highlight the comparisons effected in this picture between detective and art critic, serial killer and artist. Graham's conclusion, which he reaches only near the end of the film, is telling: "You rearranged the family into an audience so they could watch what you do." What we have here is a paradigmatic case of the "murder as artistic product" theme dovetailing with that of "murder as artistic performance." Badley usefully elaborates on the sense in which *Manhunter*'s monster, Francis Dolarhyde (Tom Noonan), can be understood as a sort of serial-killing performance artist:

> Dollarhyde turns killing into a theatrical, cinematic performance whose purpose is to (literally) transform himself into the Red Dragon, which is in his mind a composite of Blake the visionary artist (who believed that the imagination could change reality) and the Red Dragon. This becomes obvious in the complementary ritual by which he works out in front of a full-length mirror, literally reconstructing his body into a semblance of Blake's Michelangelesque figures. Dollarhyde is attempting to remake reality/himself through his performance of murder.[18]

As will become apparent in the next section, Dolarhyde's narcissism—manifest in the fixation he exhibits with his own mirror image—is less a feature of the performance-art murders of other cinematic serial killers than is their concern with putting on a good show, and with giving both victims and viewers their money's worth (quite literally in the case of the films' paying audiences).

• *White of the Eye* (1988): A door opens to reveal the living room of a trashed flat. Amidst all the chaos, a goldfish bowl and one high-heeled shoe have been carefully positioned atop a white blouse that is resting on a smashed microwave sitting on a table in the middle of the room. This collection of items looks rather like a piece of cinematic sculpture or pop-art; as such, it forces Detective Mendoza (Art Evans) into the role of art interpreter and critic. In much the same fashion as *The Apostate*, *Manhunter*, and *Se7en* (1995), the detective/viewer is forced to determine the meaning of, or message in, the murder scene; to share aesthetic sensibilities with the killer and thereby distance himself (only occasionally herself) from the moral repugnance of the crime. Next we cut to a PoV shot of Detective Mendoza's hands reaching down to pull a plastic covering off of something quite strange: a pot with something unidentifiable in it (an internal organ?) is surrounded by four kitchen knives, their blades turned outwards. The pot is sitting on a white table that acts as a virtual canvas, and what appears to be the victim's blood is smeared to the left. It is in reference to this bizarre constellation of objects that Mendoza remarks to his partner, in all seriousness, "I know a goddamn work of art when I see one." "Picasso, my ass" is the cynical, naïve reply. But Mendoza is not to be deterred: "We're talking post-Cubist Picasso . . . or maybe even later." Some viewers may be inclined to laugh at this exchange, thinking it pretentious at best, totally inappropriate at worst. But in defense of *White of the Eye*'s director and co-writer, Donald Cammell, it is clear that was here less interested in comparing the work of serial killer Paul White (David Keith) with that of post-Cubist Picasso at the level of technical skill than of visceral impact. (Along these lines, it may be worth recalling *Guernica*, Picasso's 1937 testimony to the horrors of the Spanish Civil War—a painting of terrible beauty filled with symbolic archetypes and encoded meaning. In terms of the shifting meanings of "art" and "aesthetics" invoked by the film, it can hardly be an accident that Picasso is invoked here.)[19]

• *Se7en*: Probably the most ambitious (certainly the most transparent) murder-as-artistic-statement since *The Abominable Dr. Phibes* (1971), in which a revenge-seeking scientist/organist/religious scholar played by Vincent Price murders the doctors who failed to save his beloved, using the ten Biblical plagues as inspiration. Here, a nameless serial killer (Kevin Spacey) justifies his crimes as absolution for the world's ignorance of the Seven Deadly Sins.[20] The film takes us from the tortured remains of one murder victim to the next as the sociopathic John Doe sermonizes to Detectives Somerset (Morgan Freeman) and Mills (Brad Pitt). Among the most creative and disturbing crime scenes are those thematizing Gluttony, where we view the remains of an obese man, his hands and feet bound together, who was apparently forced to eat himself to death; and Sloth, where we see a severely emaciated young man who was tied to a bed, starved, and kept barely alive for over a year. At one point, John Doe explains himself as follows: "Wanting people to listen, you can't just tap them on the shoulder anymore. You have to hit them with a sledgehammer, and then you'll notice you've got their strict attention." Similar words have been spoken by many a modern artist. As Stephen Mulhall elegantly writes, "Doe's murderous activity can be mistaken for the work of a performance artist because human culture as such embodies the results of the labours of the best thinkers and artists of the race to build significance into and out of the most savage, brutal and base aspects of human existence, to make the meaningless meaningful."[21] I would only qualify Mulhall's assertion that Doe counts as a "performance artist" rather than as an artist in the traditional sense, since what seems to matter most to him is not the actual committing of murder but rather the reception and interpretation of his crime scenes.

Along the same lines, it is crucial to note that in each of the scenes described previously, violent death is presented *not* as a hyperkinetic spectacle, but instead as a gruesome tableau. Jeffrey Sconce rightly points out (with specific reference to John McNaughton's *Henry: Portrait of a Serial Killer* [1990]) that it is in virtue of their self-conscious constructedness that such tableaux "ask to be read as an artistic decision in the representation of violence."[22] The weakness of Sconce's analysis is that he fails to distinguish between those horror films in which we can safely attribute the artistry in question to the murderer—again, to be understood as "diegetic set-designer"—and those in which we must reserve our aesthetic praise for those working behind the (murder) scenes. The former attribution can be made "safely" because of the emphasis these films place on the in/ability of particular characters (detectives, "final girls," future victims, etc.) to fully appreciate and grasp the meaning of the killer's disturbing artworks. Attributions of the latter sort, meanwhile, are inevitably less secure—at least upon first viewings—given that a seemingly senseless and indiscriminate murderer can always be provided an artistic agenda in the end (consider, for example, *Jeepers Creepers* [2001]).

Dario Argento's *Suspiria* (1977) provides a case in point here. The series of gruesome, bloody tableaux in the double-murder scene that opens the film, which resemble "nothing more than an expressionist painter's messy, colourful pallet,"[23] forcefully convey the director's disturbed imagination much better than that of the ephemeral supernatural killer, whose primary role is to carry out his master's murderous plans. (Although I have intentionally left it ambiguous here as to whether the killer's "master" is Helene Marcos, the film's "Black Queen" of witchcraft, or Argento himself, the answer is obviously "both." The crucial point is that neither of these masters/artists are coextensive with the diegetic murderer.) *Henry: Portrait of a Serial Killer* presents a quite different but equally suitable example. In the film's opening scene, we are treated to a montage revealing the corpses of some of Henry's (Michael Rooker) victims before they were discovered by the police. This montage is as visually expressive—one might even say as poetic—as it is emotionally distressing. Scenes such as this are what lead Sconce to label *Henry* "a film with an artistic agenda."[24] He is right, of course. But he never qualifies this claim by pointing out that the artistic agenda in question is McNaughton's, and McNaughton's alone; it certainly doesn't belong to Henry, who kills pretty much at random and makes little if any effort to aestheticize his murderous acts. As Matt Hills points out, nothing less than the horror genre's perceived or attributed cultural value is at issue here: "the diegetic killer stands in for a critically valued type of social realism: he isn't 'arty,' pretentious or 'unreal' in any conventional or contrived sense, but the director's vision works transformatively to aestheticize the film's 'real' killing . . . *Henry* thus combines a certain traditional notion of the auteur with a valued sense of sober realism rather than a sensationalist generic tat."[25] Even the spontaneous snuff movie Henry makes with his partner in crime Otis (Tom Towles)—the pair start videotaping themselves while sexually assaulting a suburban housewife and slaughtering her family—arguably strikes viewers less as a work of art than a work of trash (at least trash cinema); as Cynthia Freeland notes, "the amateur camera[work] . . . makes the murders seem more real: things happen unexpectedly, everything seems unplanned and awkward. The viewpoint is not standard, and the murders are not cleanly centered for our observation."[26] The bottom line is that cinematic murder can be presented artistically to a greater or less degree depending on the talents and inclination of the director, but this fact alone does not give us sufficient reason to view the monster-murderer portrayed in the film as an artist in his own right.

Going in the other direction, Amy Taubin, in a 1996 *Sight and Sound* review of *Se7en*, writes that "There's almost no violence enacted on the screen. All we see is [*sic*] the end products of violence—butchered bodies, rotting flesh. Its director is an aesthetician of rot and entropy."[27] Here, Taubin is guilty of an oversight opposite to that of Sconce: instead of failing to distinguish, at the level of artistic intention, between the director of the film and the killer, she makes too *firm* a distinction, labeling director David Fincher an "aesthetician"—albeit one of a perverse sort—while ignoring the crucial fact that John Doe *himself* is given full credit for the artistic mise-en-murder-scenes within *Se7en*'s narrative.

B. Murder as Artistic Performance

If murder in the modern horror film is frequently coded as an artistic product of one kind or another, it is nearly as often coded as a kind of artistic *performance*. In one group of films featuring this strategy—mainly consisting of entries in the so-called "slasher" subgenre and its Italian cousin, the *giallo*[28]—the surprisingly resourceful killer dispatches his victims in ever-more-creative, and ever-more-bloody, fashion. In *Friday the 13th* (1980), Mrs. Voorhees (Betsy Palmer) hides under a bed and kills a young man with a spear that pierces the mattress and goes straight through his throat. In *Halloween 2* (1981), a nurse gets a hypodermic needle in the neck; the blood is then drained from her body via a transfusion tube. More recently, in *Urban Legend* (1998), a revenge-seeking psychopath turns to society's grislier folktales (e.g., The Backseat Axe Murderer, The Fraternity House Massacre, The Microwaved Pet) for murderous inspiration. In each of these cases, and in dozens of other ones, what makes the acts of violence *artistic* in nature is not so much the creative use or display of the victims' bodies as the sheer ingenuity and showmanship exhibited by the murderers in committing their crimes—an ingenuity and showmanship that is clearly intended to elicit a complex and at least partially aesthetic response from viewers. Beyond this, and especially for fans of body horror, gore, and "splatter" movies (who discuss scenes such as those cited above as instances of profilmic special-effects wizardry), the auteurist position discussed previously is occupied not so much by the director-linked-to-the-camera's-gaze as by the celebrated make up artists and f/x designers and technicians—Tom Savini, Rick Baker, Rob Bottin, Bob Keen, and others—who continually devise and employ new tools in order "to picture grievous physical wounds and mutilations in greater, more lurid and convincing detail than ever before."[29]

It is worth noting that in a number of slasher films (though less so in the *gialli*), the spectacle of violent death crosses over from "serious" artistic performance into the realm of satire or black comedy. In *Friday the 13th, Part V: A New Beginning* (1985), Freddy dispatches one of his teenage victims by stuffing a lit flare into his mouth. In the sixth installment of *A Nightmare on Elm Street*, misleadingly titled *Freddy's Dead: The Final Nightmare* (1991), a videogame addict becomes a character in one of his own games; Freddy, joystick in hand, beats the kid's "high score" by killing him. Five years later, in Wes Craven's slasher send-up *Scream* (1996), the killer plays a game of "horror movie trivia" with one of his female victims, disemboweling her boyfriend when she fails to answer a particularly tricky question. This satirical spin on the murder-as-artistic-performance trope is characteristic of the postmodern treatment of cinematic horror generally, whereby audience overfamiliarity with character types and narrative conventions is offset (in theory, if not always in practice) by the knowing laughter generated from self-referential dialogue and plot devices.[30] In the neo-slasher film in particular, the largely interchangeable bad guys and gals—along with their directors—seem to be engaged in some sort of intertextual killing competition, in which top prize goes to the most creative or well-conceived murder and the results are determined by comparing box-office take and the total number of sequels generated. Regardless of whether the artistic performance in question is serious or satirical, however, the rule of thumb here is that it is never enough *just* to kill—that is way too easy, and apparently way too boring.

Perhaps the most interesting take on the monster-as-corrupt-artist metaphor is to be found in the other group of films analogizing murder with artistic performance. For here, the act of murder takes on the aura of a performance-art piece. *Peeping Tom* and *Manhunter* belong in this group, if one considers the *manner* in which Mark Lewis and Francis Dolarhyde kill as interesting and self-consciously stylized as the actual recordings they make of those killings. Three additional examples appear below:

- *A Clockwork Orange* (1971): Though Stanley Kubrick's adaptation of the 1962 Anthony Burgess novel may occupy a position on the fringes of the horror genre, the scene in which Alex DeLarge (Michael McDowell) stomps on the body of a helpless old man while performing "Singin' in the Rain"—complete with cane and phallic-nosed mask—is as disturbing and perversely/sadistically enjoyable as anything to be found in a hard-core slasher. By combining the conventions of the musical (a song-and-dance number) with those of the horror movie (a home invasion and the protracted beating of a defenseless victim), uniting the jubilant lyrics of a familiar song with images of brutality and ultra-violence, this scene effectively challenges the idea that traditional aesthetic opposites such as culture and nature, civility and wildness, need occupy wholly different experiential spheres.

• *Theatre of Blood* (1973): Well-known thespian Edward Lionheart (Vincent Price) fakes his own death after being snubbed by a group of London theater critics for the Actor-of-the-Year award. Some years later, he embarks on a bloody mission of revenge. With the help of his devoted daughter and a group of social outcasts, Lionheart stages performances of a number of Shakespeare's plays, using the unsuspecting critics as real-life victims in the Bard's dramatic murder scenes. Just as critics have the power to "kill" with their unsympathetic reviews, *Theatre of Blood* argues that actors can kill (quite literally) through their art. And so we watch Lionheart cut the head off of one critic and place it in his own wife's bed, as per *Cymbeline*. In another scene, taken from *Richard III*, Lionheart's cast drowns a critic in a drum of wine. Despite its campy, ironic sensibility, Douglas Hickox's film deserves credit for returning Shakespeare to his low-art roots and exposing him as one of our greatest horror playwrights.

• *The Silence of the Lambs*: Lecter's escape from prison two-thirds of the way through this film stands as the high watermark of performance-art murder. After putting on a cassette tape of Bach's *Goldberg Variations*, Lecter manages to escape from the handcuffs his guards place upon him when they enter his cell during dinner. Just as the diegetic music reaches a crescendo, he jumps up, cuffs one of the guards to the door, and tears a chunk of flesh from the other's cheek. He then begins hitting the first guard in the head over and over again with a police club, looking every bit like a conductor directing his orchestra on stage (all we see at this point is Lecter swinging the baton, a look of rapture on his face). Finally, with fresh blood on his mouth and two inert bodies behind him, Lecter stands in front of the tape player and waves his hand to the music. Cynthia Freeland calls Lecter a "great master of spectacle," one who "operates with a Nietzschean aesthetic all his own."[31] And the solemn grandeur of this scene provides ample support for Joel Black's thesis that "if any human act evokes the aesthetic experience of the sublime, certainly it is the act of murder. . . . [I]f murder can be experienced aesthetically, the murderer can in turn be regarded as a kind of artist—a performance artist or anti-artist whose speciality is not creation but destruction."[32]

III

What lies behind this profound shift in the horror genre's dominant aesthetic metaphor? And what, if anything, are we justified in asserting about the impact or influence of the monster-as-corrupt-artist metaphor on the genre's young and impressionable fan base? It is apparent that the previous era's naïve, misguided, and politically incorrect equation of monstrousness with artistic failure has been largely outmoded (though one suspects it will never be completely eliminated). The question remains, however, as to whether modern horror cinema's fascination with portraying monsters as artists, murder as an art form, is a change in sensibility for the better, socially speaking. Here, the preceding discussion dovetails with larger ongoing, often acrimonious debates concerning the aestheticization of violence in contemporary filmmaking practice, spanning a number of different genres (e.g., action, comedy, war) and national traditions (e.g., Hollywood, Hong Kong, and Latin America).[33]

In 1948, W. H. Auden wrote that "murder is the act of disruption by which innocence is lost" and "the aesthetic and the ethical are put in opposition."[34] We have here an insight that can be traced as far back as Friedrich Schiller in the early 19th Century, and which receives its most eloquent defence in the writings of Thomas De Quincey. In his 1827 essay, "On Murder Considered as One of the Fine Arts," De Quincey argues that "everything in this world has two handles. Murder, for instance, may be laid hold of by its moral handle . . . , and *that*, I confess, is its weak side; or it may also be treated *aesthetically*, as the Germans call it—that is, in relation to good taste."[35] Since that time, authors and poets as historically and culturally diverse as André Gide, Oscar Wilde, Jack Abbott, Alain Robbe-Grillet, Yukio Mishima, Marcel Schwob, and Gregor von Rezzori have sought to follow De Quincey's advice. And when the human or near-human monsters populating such films as *Halloween*, *Manhunter*, *Se7en*, *Theatre of Blood*, *The Abominable Dr. Phibes*, *The Texas Chainsaw Massacre*, and *The Silence of the Lambs* (to name just a few) turn murder into an artistic product, an artistic performance, or some bizarre combination of the two, consumers of these fictions are once again encouraged, occasionally forced, to acknowledge a side of themselves they normally keep hidden, even from themselves—a side that enjoys, appreciates, and admires the display of creative killings.

It is crucial to note that the transformation which took place within the horror genre around the time of *Psycho* and *Peeping Tom*'s release in 1960 was only one small event in a much broader social, cultural, and artistic movement. To return to the scene in *White of the Eye* discussed above: What makes Detective Mendoza so sure that what he is looking at is a work of art? After all, it is certainly not something most of us would be inclined to call beautiful. Mendoza's likely response to such a question would be, first, to point out that beauty is in the eye of the beholder—monsters and serial killers may well possess an aesthetic "sense," even when they lack any semblance of a moral code; and second, that an artwork need not be "beautiful," according to any traditional understanding of the word, to be considered art. Aesthetic experience comes in a wide variety of forms, after all, and some are a great deal less pleasurable than others. The work of such modern and postmodern artists as Jackson Pollock, Willem De Kooning, and Andy Warhol, and more recently, of Douglas Gordon, Zoe Leonard, and Cindy Sherman, all testifies in various ways and degrees to this claim. (It is worth mentioning here that Sherman's 1997 film *Office Killer* centers on a female serial killer who keeps the corpses of her victims in her basement, where she manipulates them, positions them, and plays with them as if they were human dolls.[36] Rarely in horror cinema are women depicted as artistic murderers rater than as diegetic audiences for the grisly murder-as-art exhibits put on by men; more typically, female killers in the genre are portrayed as hysterical, messy, and out-of-control in their violent activity.[37]) The radical shift I have been tracing in the horror genre's dominant aesthetic metaphor could thus be held to stem not merely from sociohistorical conditions, but from virtual revolutions in the cultural discourses and meanings of "art" corresponding with the rise and popularization of modern and avant-garde artistic practice. Largely as a result of these practices, "art" itself has become more (and more) open to and associated with notions of "shock," transgression, and offensiveness, with the violation of standing cultural and conceptual categories (notably, such violations are at the heart of Carroll's theory of "art-horror" as an emotional effect generated by fictional horror narratives), and with incongruity—just think of Duchamp's "ready-mades" (e.g., the urinal in the art gallery)—rather than with traditional notions of aesthetic technique, form, and beauty.[38]

As for whether or not the monster-as-corrupt-artist metaphor is particularly liable to "corrupt" those youthful audience members most likely to consume horror fictions, this is a question that can only even be responsibly *asked* after a great deal more theoretical work has been performed, and empirical data collected and analyzed. Theoretically and methodologically speaking, the relative aestheticization of violence in modern horror cinema raises—perhaps begs—important questions concerning how we define, isolate, and study media violence.[39] And when it comes to empirical research, Stephen Prince has observed that "most studies on the viewing of media violence show an aggression-inducing, rather than a cathartic, effect" on young viewers.[40] But Prince is quick to add that a number of specific "content characteristics" are relevant to these findings. Studies suggest that post-film aggressiveness is noticeably heightened only when: (1) the aggression-evoking characteristics of film victims match those of available targets in real life; (2) when aggressive behavior within a film is rewarded; (3) when a film presents aggression as a justifiable response to some perceived insult; or (4) when little or no visible or audible signs of a victim's suffering are made available to viewers.[41] Judging from these very preliminary results, it seems reasonable to assert that what parents, politicians, and other concerned citizens should focus their attention on is not the horror genre *per se*, but those films (of *whatever* genre) that manifest specific content characteristics. In short, the prevalence of the monster-as-corrupt-artist metaphor in modern horror cinema may signify the final break of the aesthetic from the ethical, but one must always look to the specific narrative and formal context in which this metaphor appears in order to justify claims concerning its impact on young viewers.

Notes

1. Friedrich Schiller, "Reflections on the Use of the Vulgar and the Lowly in Works of Art" (1802), in *Aesthetical and Philosophical Essays*, vol. 1, ed. N. H. Dole (Boston: Aldine, 1910), 265: emphasis added.

2. Joel Black, *The Aesthetics of Murder: A Study in Romantic Literature and Contemporary Culture* (Baltimore: The Johns Hopkins University Press, 1991), 39.

3. Angela Dalle Vacche, "F. W. Murnau's *Nosferatu*: Romantic Painting as Horror and Desire in Expressionist Cinema," in *Cinema and Painting: How Art Is Used in Film* (Austin: University of Texas Press, 1996), 161–96. It is an

interesting and difficult question precisely where vampire films as a subgenre fit within this classical paradigm. As Linda Schulte-Sasse remarks, following *Nosferatu*, vampires in cinema "quickly . . . start having sex appeal and moving in high-class circles unrecognized. Already the Bela Lugosi film was released on Valentine's Day [1931] and highlighted an erotic appeal" (private correspondence with the author: May 30, 2002).

An informal survey of the vampire subgenre seems to indicate that Schreck's Count Orlok is atypical (though certainly not alone) in his hideousness. As for Lugosi's Dracula and his kin, it is not at all clear whether their eroticized qualities (the vampire-as-suave-seducer—really a Romantic/Gothic/Byronic trope) can be unproblematically aligned with what I am here calling the "monster as corrupt artist" metaphor. Linda Badley points out that "the Byronic vampire (as opposed to the revenant) has always been associated with Byron's reputed theatricalism, excess, womanizing, and artistic sensibility. . . . This reaches its most extroverted manifestation in the rock performer as vampire (Alice Cooper, Ozzie Osbourne, David Bowie as star of *The Hunger* [1983], and Gothic rock in general), and the vampire as rock performer in Anne Rice's *Lestat*" (private correspondence with the author: June 2, 2002); and she cites Ken Gelder's study, *Reading the Vampire* (New York: Routledge, 1994) as useful in this regard. But in what sense—except for a quite extended one—can the vampire-in-general be seen as creating art through his murderous acts?

It seems more promising to explore the ways in which the external, superficial beauty of the Gothicized vampire actually serve to mask a repulsive inner self; if anything, this leads us back to the idea of the monster as corrupt work of art. Along these lines, and for an essay that indicates where the classical paradigm discussed above might be seen as manifesting itself in contemporary horror cinema, see Steffen Hantke, "Monstrosity Without a Body: Representational Strategies in the Popular Serial Killer Film," *Post Script: Essays in Film and the Humanities* 22.2 (Winter/Spring 2003): 32–50.

4. It is worth noting that many popular reviews of *The Cell* considered it as the work of a director coming out of the advertising/promo and music video industry; Tarsem's uniquely expressive and dynamic visual style resulted in his being given near complete artistic control over this, his debut film, by New Line Cinema.

5. Dalle Vacche, 167.

6. I owe this formulation to Matt Hills. On sympathetic monsters, see Angela Curran, "Aristotelian Reflections on Horror and Tragedy in *An American Werewolf in London*" (this volume); and Murray Smith, "(A)moral Monstrosity," in *The Modern Fantastic: The Films of David Cronenberg*, ed. Michael Grant (Westport, CT: Praeger, 2000), 69–83.

7. As Matt Hills notes, according to another, more "literalist" line of thinking about media effects, it is the realist force of certain representations that is held to be particularly problematic. This leads one to wonder whether the diegetic and directorial "staging" of murder in recent horror films, which serves

precisely to mark it out as a stylized art object rather than a realist representation, thereby makes it *less* rather than *more* likely that such acts of violence would/could be considered as emulatable by audiences. Although I do not explore or speculate on the validity of this argument in what follows, I believe it can be taken as indirect support for my own conclusions.

8. Subsequent variations on this theme can be found in Donald Cammell's *White of the Eye* (1988), Kathryn Bigelow's *Strange Days* (1995), and Marc Caro and Jean-Pierre Jeunet's *La Cité Des Enfants Perdus* (*The City of Lost Children*, 1995).

9. William Rothman, *Hitchcock—The Murderous Gaze* (Cambridge MA: Harvard University Press, 1982), 335.

10. Rothman, 340.

11. André Bazin, "The Ontology of the Photographic Image," (1945) in *What Is Cinema?* vol. 1, ed. Hugh Gray (Berkeley: University of California Press, 1967), 9–10.

12. A variation on this theme, again courtesy of Anthony Wong, occurs in *The Ebola Syndrome* (1996). For more on Hong Kong "Category 3" horror, and these two moview in particular, see Michael Hoover and Lisa Stokes, "Enfant Terrible: The Terrorful, Wonderful World of Anthony Wong," in *Fear Without Frontiers: Horror Cinema Across the Globe*, ed. Steven Jay Schneider (Surrey, U.K.: FAB Press, 2003), 45-59; and Tony Williams, "Hong Kong Social Horror: Tragedy and Farce in Category 3," *Post Script: Essays in Film and the Humanities* 21.3 (Summer 2002): 61–71.

13. Noël Carroll, *The Philosophy of Horror; or, Paradoxes of the Heart* (New York: Routledge, 1990), 28.

14. Other films to employ this theme of corpses being displayed as works of art (which interestingly range over the whole history of the genre) include *Mystery of the Wax Museum*, *Mad Love* (1935), *Midnight at Madame Tussaud's* (1936), *Latin Quarter* (1946), *House of Wax*, *Mill of the Stone Women* (1960), *The Embalmer* (1966), *Crucible of Terror* (1971), and *The Wax Mask* (1997). It is also worth comparing/contrasting *A Bucket of Blood*— remade by Corman's production company in 1995 as *The Death Artist*—with *Génesis* (1998), a Spanish horror short by Nacho Cerdà. In this latter film, not at all a comedy, an artist attempts to work through the pain surrounding his wife's death in a car accident by creating a sculpture in her image. Slowly but surely, the sculpture begins to bleed through cracks in the clay, while the artist's own flesh mutates and crumbles into pieces. Consider too here the early German horror films *The Golem* (1920) and *Waxworks* (1924), both of which involve statues—the former made of clay, the latter of wax—which come to life and commit all manner of murder and mayhem.

15. *Collectors* (2000), a documentary by Julian Hobbs, examines this trend in great detail. See Maitland McDonagh's interview with Hobbs in the October 26–November 2, 2000 edition of *Time Out* (New York): 109.

16. According to Badley, "in exploring the relations between horror and auteurism," recent films about horror directors and the making of their

signature movies—including E. Elias Merhige's *Shadow of the Vampire* (2000, about F. W. Murnau), Bill Condon's *Gods and Monsters* (1998, about James Whale), Tim Burton's *Ed Wood* (1994), and Chris Smith's *American Movie* (1999, about Mark Borschardt)—"expose the deep structure of the auteur theory, literalizing a view of the auteur as overreaching scientist (Murnau), artist (Whale), would-be or anti-artist (Wood, Borschardt) and the making of a signature film as a transgressive act with a pathological origin and subtext." Badley, "The Darker Side of Genius: The (Horror) Auteur Meets Freud's Theory," in *The Horror Film and Psychoanalysis: Freud's Worst Nightmares*, ed. Steven Jay Schneider (Cambridge: Cambridge University Press, forthcoming 2003).

17. Marguerite LaCaze, "The Mourning of Loss in *The Sixth Sense*," *Post Script: Essays in Film and the Humanities* 21.3 (Summer 2002): 113. The quote refers to Carroll, *The Philosophy of Horror*, 17.

18. Linda Badley, private correspondence with the author: June 2, 2002. NB: In Thomas Harris's 1981 novel *Red Dragon*, from which Michael Mann's film was adapted, "Dollarhyde" is spelled "Dolarhyde." I have kept the film spelling for the sake of consistency.

19. This paragraph is excerpted in slightly revised form from my essay "Killing in Style: The Aestheticization of Violence in Donald Cammell's *White of the Eye*," *Scope: An Online Journal of Film Studies* (May 2001): www.nottingham.ac.uk/film/journal/articles/killing-in-style.htm (May 13, 2001).

20. For an extended take on the relations between these two films, see David Kalat, "*Seven* vs. *Dr. Phibes*," *Midnight Marquee Monsters* 61 (Fall 1999): 36–42. Also see Rick Worland, "Faces Behind the Mask: Vincent Price, *Dr. Phibes*, and the Horror Genre in Transition," *Post Script: Essays in Film and the Humanities* 22.2 (Winter/Spring 2003): 19–31.

21. Stephen Mulhall, *On Film* (London: Routledge, 2002), 114. For extended analysis of *Se7en*, see Richard Dyer's BFI Modern Classic devoted to the film (London: BFI Publishing, 1999).

22. Jeffrey Sconce, "Spectacles of Death: Identification, Reflexivity, and Contemporary Horror," in *Film Theory Goes to the Movies*, ed. Jim Collins, Hilary Radner, and Ava Preacher Collins (New York: Routledge, 1993), 116.

23. Linda Schulte-Sasse, "The 'Mother' of All Horror Movies: Dario Argento's *Suspiria*," *Kinoeye: A Fortnightly Journal of Film in the New Europe* 2.11 (June 10, 2002): www.kinoeye.org/02/11/schultesasse11.htm (June 12, 2002)

24. Sconce, 116.

25. Private correspondence with the author: July 19, 2002.

26. Cynthia Freeland, "Realist Horror," in *Philosophy and Film*, ed. Cynthia Freeland and Thomas Wartenberg (New York: Routledge, 1995).

27. Amy Taubin, "The Allure of Decay," *Sight and Sound* 6, no.1 (January 1996); reprinted in *Action/Spectacle Cinema: A Sight and Sound Reader*, ed. Jose Arroyo (London: BFI Publishing, 2000; 150–53), 152. It would be well worth comparing/contrasting *Henry* and *Se7en* with the Hong Kong Category 3

horror film *Dr. Lamb* (1992). Here, unlike *Henry* but like *Se7en*, the artistic agenda in question can be attributed both to the director (in some highly-stylized murder sequences) *and* to the film's serial-killing taxi driver (who takes glossy photographs of his female victims, whose bodies he carefully arranges after death; and who videotapes himself engaging in necrophilic sex acts). For more on *Dr. Lamb*, see Tony Williams, "Hong Kong Social Horror: Tragedy and Farce in Category 3," *op. cit.*

28. For a useful discussion of the *giallo* tradition, see Gary Needham, "Playing with Genre: An Introduction to the Italian *Giallo*," *Kinoeye: A Fortnightly Journal of Film in the New Europe* 2.11 (June 10, 2002): www. Kinoeye.org/02/11/needham11/htm (June 15, 2002).

29. Stephen Prince, "Violence and Psychophysiology in Horror Cinema," in *The Horror Film and Psychoanalysis, op. cit.*

30. For more on *Scream* and its ilk, see Steven Jay Schneider, "Kevin Williamson and the Rise of the Neo-Stalker," *Post Script: Essays in Film and the Humanities* 19.2 (Winter/Spring 2000): 73–87.

31. Freeland, "Realist Horror," 132.

32. Black, 14.

33. The literature here is enormous, and continues to grow. See, e.g., Martin Barker and Kate Brooks, *Judge Dredd: Its Friends, Fans and Foes* (Luton, U.K.: University of Luton Press, 1998); *Ill Effects: The Media/Violence Debate*, ed. Martin Barker and Julian Petley (London: Routledge, 1997); Stephen Prince, *Savage Cinema: Sam Peckinpah and the Rise of Ultraviolent Movies* (Austin: University of Texas Press, 1998); and *New Hollywood Violence*, ed. Steven Jay Schneider (Manchester, U.K.: Manchester University Press, forthcoming 2003).

34. W. H. Auden, "The Guilty Vicarage," in *The Dyer's Hand, and Other Essays* (New York: Vintage, 1968), 150–53. Originally published in 1948.

35. Thomas De Quincey, "On Murder Considered as One of the Fine Arts" (1827), in *The Collected Writings of Thomas De Quincey, Volume XIII* (Edinburgh: Adam & Charles Black, 1890), 13.

36. Grotesque and uncanny doll imagery is also a major theme of Sherman's still photography and sculpture.

37. See Steven Jay Schneider, "Barbara, Julia, Myra, Carol, and Nell: Diagnosing Female Madness in British Horror Cinema," in *British Horror Cinema*, ed. Steve Chibnall and Julian Petley (London: Routledge, 2002), 117–30; and Steven Jay Schneider, "The Madwomen in our Movies: Female Psycho-Killers in American Horror Cinema," in *Killing Women: The Visual Culture of Gender and Violence*, ed. Annette Burfoot and Susan Lord (Waterloo: Wilfred Laurier University Press, forthcoming 2003). Interestingly, this conventional and unequal representation of gender does not seem to hold for other genres. As Susan Felleman argues, many Hollywood films of the 1980s—including Martin Scorsese's *After Hours* (1985), Ivan Reitman's *Legal Eagles* (1986), and Dennis Hopper's *Backtrack* (1989)—effectively "conflate representations of women and contemporary art, and of women artists

particularly, with danger: ranging from explosive passion, to kidnapping, fire, sadomasochistic acts of aggression, stalking, paralysis, murder and annihilation. In all instances, the themes of art, femininity and danger are imbricated and co-implicated." Susan Felleman, "Playing with Fire: Women, Art and Danger in American Movies of the 1980s," in *New Hollywood Violence, op. cit.*

38. Thanks once again to Matt Hills for his assistance articulating this point.

39. See especially the work of Martin Barker here, e.g., "Violence Redux," in *New Hollywood Violence, op. cit.*

40. Prince, 113.

41. *Ibid.*, 114–15.

The Slasher's Blood Lust

Cynthia A. Freeland

John McNaughton's *Henry: Portrait of a Serial Killer* (produced 1986/released 1990) flouts horror-movie conventions for suspenseful narrative. Its opening scenes show an array of corpses accompanied by an eerie sound track, intercut with scenes of a young man (we infer he is the multiple murderer, Henry [Michael Rooker]) talking to a waitress in a late-night diner. The film sets up the viewer to expect him to attack her, but nothing happens. Next, Henry follows a woman home from a shopping mall. Tension rises almost unbearably, but at the last moment as she arrives home, a man greets her, and Henry drives away. Even when Henry finally does kill, the film flouts convention by withholding the spectacle of the murder. Henry picks up a hitchhiker carrying a guitar, and returns home later carrying her guitar. Then, in a long shot, we see a woman let Henry into her house with his exterminator's equipment. The audience is encouraged to expect to enter the house and witness a murder. Instead, the film cuts to a shot of a living room; a slow and impersonal pan reveals the woman, naked and dead. A third killing happens so fast and is so obscured that it barely has time to register. Henry snaps the neck of two prostitutes in his car, then goes with his friend Otis (Tom Towles) to buy a hamburger.

The plot of *Henry* seems flat and random. Certain events occur when Becky (Tracy Arnold), the sister of Henry's roommate, Otis, moves into their small Chicago apartment and disrupts their somewhat repressed homosexual partnership. Victimized by incest, Becky has sought refuge with her brother, who also proves abusive. A parole violator and drug pusher, he repeatedly kisses Becky and demands to see her breasts, as her father had. Becky tries to normalize the household by getting a regular jobs and fixing meals, but her efforts fail (at one point the film cuts from the corpse of the woman Henry has "exterminated" to a shot of a fish Becky is vigorously cleaning in the sink).

Otis and Henry had met in prison, and when Becky asks Otis what Henry was in for, he at first refuses to say. "What did he do, kill his mama?" she asks. "Yes, he killed his mama with a baseball bat.," Otis replies, as if it's a joke. Later, Becky pursues the subject with intense fascination. In the only scene in the film that tells us anything about Henry, the facts remain hazy. Henry says that he killed his mother, that he stabbed her to death. He tells Becky: "Daddy used to drive a truck before he got his legs cut off. My mama was a whore. But I don't fault her for that. She made me watch; she beat me; made me wear a dress and watch." Becky responds by confiding that she, too, was abused, by her father, then says gushingly, "I feel like I know you, have known you for a long time." Henry says, summing up, that yeah, he shot his mother on his fourteenth birthday. "Shot her?" Becky asks, "I thought you stabbed her." "Oh yeah," he says.

From this point on, the intensity of the killings in the film escalates. After a fight during a drug deal, Otis comments, "I'd like to kill somebody." Henry subsequently takes him out for sport to shoot a young man who stops to help with their car. Again, it is all over in a flash. Henry then murders a pawnshop owner after an argument over the purchase of a TV. He turns murder into a science, explaining to Otis that you must vary the method each time, switch guns so as not to be caught, and so forth. Henry remarks: "It's either you or them. Open your eyes, look at the world, Otis. It's you or them, you know what I mean."

The stage is now set for two especially gruesome final scenes of killing. First is the killing of a suburban family. In a long shot, the killers are shown approaching a house at night. Then the scene switches to a grainy, tilted home-video version of the family's murder. It will become apparent later that we are watching alongside the killers, who sit on their sofa reviewing this footage (recorded by their stolen camcorder) after the events. Point of view and real time are wrenched in a disconcerting way, with contradictory effects. On the one hand, the scene distances the viewers and makes the murders seem less awful. The effect is as though we were just watching something on TV. The people in the family are already dead, depersonalized, and not individuals. On the other hand, the amateur camera makes the murders seem more real: things happen unexpectedly; everything seems unplanned and awkward. The viewpoint is not standard, and the murders are not clearly centered for our observation.

The most graphic and bloody of the murders in *Henry* is Henry's murder of Otis, whom he has caught raping Becky. Henry blinds Otis and then stabs him while lying atop his body in an orgiastic, sexualized attack. Henry chops up Otis's body and loads it into large garbage bags, which he packs into suitcases and dumps in the river. He leaves town with Becky, who looks at him and says, "I love you Henry." "I guess I love you, too" he responds. The car radio plays the song "Loving You Was My Mistake." They stop for the night at a motel room and get ready for bed. Becky looks trustingly up at Henry, who says it is time to turn in. The next morning we see Henry shaving with a straight razor, getting dressed, and leaving the motel room—alone. He piles suitcases into the car and later stops along the road to leave a large suitcase along the roadside. In close-up, we see blood seeping through the soft-sided case. That's it—she's dead. It's inevitable. Henry drives on in his beat-up old Chevy. The movie ends.

What kind of monster is Henry in this movie? Is he an evil man? Is he a fascinating complex figure of evil like some vampires are? I would say that, yes, he is evil, but that his evil is neither fascinating nor complex. It is banal, summed up in his formulaic lesson to Otis: it is you or them. The character of Henry in this movie is unmotivated; he seeks neither intimacy in the seduction of souls nor the transvaluation of values. His only good point is that, at least temporarily, he is chivalrous to Becky. She responds by eroticizing him, and the film conspires in this as the camera lingers on the good-looking young actor, Michael Rooker, who plays Henry. He is treated throughout the movie iconographically as an angry young rebel in the Marlon Brando/James Dean mode, complete with his pout, mumbles, short curly hair, square jaw, and white T-shirt. What is most striking is that Becky begins to eroticize Henry just when she learns he is a killer—but isn't this the source of our fascination, too? Henry/Rooker's assimilation to the "angry young rebel" category is heightened by the film's promotional materials, which feature him scowling at himself in a mirror. (Indeed, when I watched the film on video, there were advertisements for Henry posters and T-shirts featuring the dark young man in a white T-shirt at the end of the tape.)

Henry provides a standard and clichéd psycho-film explanation for the behavior of its monster. When Henry was a child, his mother, who had a lot of lovers, symbolically castrated him by forcing him to wear a dress while watching her have sex. However, the fact that there are three different versions of this story marks it as a generic explanation and undermines its authenticity. The pathogenic role of the mother has become a familiar and empty formula to us, a vague sort of hand-waving in the direction of "here's why he is the way he is." We notice this and then blithely move on, ready for the next murder or scene of mayhem.[1]

Another key feature of *Henry* is its displacement of interest from plot onto spectacle. *Henry* is not a narrative of discovery like Michael Powell's *Peeping Tom* (1960) or *Frenzy* (1972). Although those two films revealed the identity of the monster to us in the audience, they kept the narrative of unveiling in the foreground by focusing on the investigations and discoveries of a key figure, either Helen (Anna Massey) in *Peeping Tom* or Inspector Oxford (Alec McCowen) in *Frenzy*. Spectacle does play a prominent role in those earlier films, but it is the very thing that structures the narrative of *Henry*. This film moves the viewer through a gradually intensifying spectacle into climax and denouement. *Henry* shocks and announces its gory nature by the opening graphic sequence of nude corpses. But it reveals its spectacle slowly, and the scenes that depict killings play with the viewer's emotions in nonstandard ways. When Henry and Otis kill the man in the pawnshop, the vicious and gruesome murder is rather comically crosscut with scenes of Becky washing the hair of a large Chicago matron who spouts racist slogans. After this murder, the spectacles begin to crescendo through the murder of the family to climax in the particularly intense, brutal, and sexualized murder of Otis. Finally, as a diminuendo or anticlimax restoring symmetry with the opening sequences, *Henry* ends after implying the off-screen murder of Becky.

"Real" Monsters and Movie Spectacle

Henry: Portrait of a Serial Killer continues the direction launched in the slasher genre by *Peeping Tom* and *Frenzy* toward new forms of realistic or naturalistic horror. Based on a real serial murderer, *Henry* features a possible, hence a realistic, monster, a psychopathic serial killer. Henry represents a kind of reversal of both *Peeping Tom* and *Frenzy*. Whereas Mark Lewis (Karlheinz Böhm) kills with the eye of a documentary filmmaker and Bob Rusk (Barry Foster) kills with frenzy, Henry kills for no particular reason, just on a whim. Like many of the more supernatural kinds of movie monsters, serial killers seem all-powerful, unpredictable, and, above all, sources of hideous violence.

Their approach to some of their fellow humans is loathsome. We do not believe, while watching the movie, that this monster threatens us; and yet monsters like him *do* threaten us—there *are* men who kill others randomly on the streets, in stores, and in their homes. A monstrous killer like Henry is a possible being—the character is based, after all, upon real Death Row killer, Henry Lee Lucas. What is monstrous about both versions of Henry, real-life and fictional, is not simply the deeds he has done but the attitudes he manifests toward them, especially the banality or the flatness of his affect. The real Henry Lee Lucas says: "It all seemed fun to start with, I should have my tail kicked for that. I just didn't have any willpower."[2] He is talking here about confessing, not about the murders themselves.

Many other horror films also feature a realistic or possible monster. As a new subgenre of horror, the slasher film would seem to be the antithesis of the vampire movie. Characters get less interesting and spectacles of violence become more graphic and pronounced. Violence in the classic vampire film is often subtle and sanitized. Bites on the neck occur after the vampire has hypnotized his victim, so there is no struggle. Instead, the victim, usually a woman, simply swoons; she may even bare her neck as she passively awaits her undead lover. Blood, if shown at all, is a delicate dribble rather than a messy flow. . . . [V]ampire movies have increasingly focused on the psychology of either vampiric seduction or undead existence. But in the slasher film, the focus is on the weapon and on scenes of attack. We see blood and damage being done. Instead of focusing on how to combat an anomalous, unknown monster like a vampire, alien creature, or mutant cockroach, we see the all too familiar "ordinary" human (a man) who commits "ordinary" (if newsworthy) violence. The films of this genre, as the name implies, highlight violent activities, often of repeated slashing, stabbing, or piercing. The primary link to the vampire genre is that this violent killing is lustful, sexualized, somehow driven by the monster's own nature. As we watch the killer deliver orgiastic thrusting motions, the knife or other weapon obviously functions as phallus. Everyone knows (like the teenagers in *Scream* [1996]) this is what such violence "means."

It is common for us to refer to contemporary serial killers and other "heroes" of realist horror films as monsters. Jeffrey Dahmer and Ed Gein, as much as "Buffalo Bill" (Ted Levine) and Hannibal Lecter (Anthony Hopkins) in *The Silence of the Lambs* (1991), are horrifying, loathsome, and disgusting creatures that skin, eat, or have sex with corpses and kill without remorse. Our interest in killers like Henry Lee

Lucas or Dahmer—the basis on which they quickly achieve a certain celebrity status—seems to amount to a direct fascination with the sheer fact of their monstrousness. Movie or TV versions of their stories may surround their vile deeds with context by supplying an alleged meaning or motivation; but the manifestation of such fundamental human evil remains baffling. Symbolic enrichment on film often lends such evil (perhaps because of its mystery) an odd erotic edge—we see this in films like *Henry* or *The Silence of the Lambs*, films that pair the monster somehow with a sympathetic young woman.

The slasher subgenre of the horror film shifts emphasis away from plot to monstrous graphic spectacle. Some might consider the movement away from evil monsters like vampires toward serial killers as a degradation of the horror genre. A theorist of evil like Fred C. Alford would see things in much the same way; the prevalence of slashers means that our culture fails to supply symbols that are sufficiently serious, complex, and interesting enough to help us face up to hard issues about evil. Alford does not even think that vampires are interestingly evil, let alone a slasher killer: Film slashers are too much like the real murderers whom Alford studied, whose conceptions of evil were shallow and bankrupt. As Alford sees it, the real-life killers enacted stories of evil in violence upon people's bodies due to their lack of richer imaginative resources to combat an inner emptiness or dread.[3]

The notable distinction between the slasher, a natural but banal human killer, and the vampire, an unnatural but interesting monster, has led Noël Carroll to deny that slasher killers should be counted as horror movie monsters. Carroll argues in *The Philosophy of Horror* that men like Norman Bates (Anthony Perkins) in *Psycho* (1960) are not monsters because they can be given a naturalistic explanation—as indeed happens at the movie's conclusion. Carroll emphasizes the *fictitious* nature of the monster in horror by defining a monster as "any being not believed to exist according to reigning scientific notions."[4] He considers this restriction essential to keeping the emphasis on narrative or plot, thus preserving the particular distanced and aesthetic response of art-horror. Carroll almost seems to see in the new monster of the slasher film, the psychotic killer, a sort of falling away from some kind of essence of horrific monstrousness. A film like *Psycho* is not horror because the monster in it, Norman Bates, is naturalized: "He is a schizophrenic, a type of being that science countenances."[5]

Movies like *Peeping Tom*, *Frenzy*, and *Henry: Portrait of a Serial Killer* are like *Psycho* in that they violate the definition of horror-film monsters laid out by Carroll. But I would insist that, even if Mark Lewis, Bob Rusk, and Henry are true-to-life rather than supernatural beings, they *are* monsters. Further, the slasher film is such a prevalent and important subgenre that it obviously deserves consideration in any discussion of the nature of evil in horror films. My examples span three decades, and countless others could be cited. The exclusion of the slasher film from the horror genre reflects a larger issue about the role of spectacle in the horror film. . . . The graphic spectacle of violence (usually directed against women) is at the forefront of the slasher genre. The killer's violence is something that might really happen, and the way it is shown on the screen sometimes makes it difficult to sustain an intellectual, aestheticized attitude towards it: the slasher gets us in the gut. But this does not fit with Carroll's deeper aims in his book. He, in effect, defends the status of the troubling genre of horror by denying that the audience's primary interest is in graphic spectacle. Instead, he argues that the enjoyment of horror is focused primarily on plot, which provides the cognitive pleasures of investigation and problem solving. These are presumably higher and more worthy than a direct interest in spectacles of gross violence.

Carroll's view falls in with opinions advanced by a long line of philosophers who have displayed suspicions about the attractions of spectacle in art. An interest in spectacles was also seen as inhuman and demeaning in classical Greek attacks on tragedy. Plato characterized our drive toward violent spectacle as lowest among his rank ordering of human desires.[6] Aristotle's *Poetics* defended tragedy by rejecting the notion that the audience responds with a direct, problematic interest in fearful violence; but even Aristotle argued that spectacle is the "least artistic"of tragedy's six parts.[7] He describes plot structures to explain that there were loftier audience interests in tragedy—that it can offer cognitive challenges leading to an emotional catharsis. Carroll similarly argues that the horror genre evokes a distinct aesthetic or distanced response, a response to fiction and not real life, which depends upon a cognitive interest in plot or artifice. Because we enjoy tracking the suspenseful narrative, we put up with the revulsion that Carroll calls "art-horror."[8] This is a distanced emotional response that refers to a representation, not a reality. Although monsters in horror are repellent and scary, they do not threaten us directly, and we are protected by knowing that they are in fact impossible. They fascinate us because they violate our conceptual categories, arousing in us a strong desire to know something unknowable.

Carroll's concerns about the role of spectacle in slasher horror mirror feminist critiques of this subgenre. All the movies I have mentioned feature graphic representations of disturbing male violence against women. One natural feminist response is to decide not to watch them—even to protest or dismiss them from serious consideration. It is easy to argue that slasher movies, mostly directed by men, are simply manifestations of patriarchy's contempt or hatred for women. But I would respond that though the films do manifest disturbing and sexist ideology, they function in ways that are more complex—perhaps even more insidious—than might be first recognized. In fact, the films I have selected actually open a path toward critical reflection because they make an issue out of particular representations of sexualized violence against women. These are not just representations of violence, but are films that ask us to reflect on the troubling messages that they present about the nature of evil—about its association with men (i.e., male humans in particular) and the possibilities of confronting it.[9]

We must go beyond the limitations of a somewhat immediate feminist condemnation of Carroll's "Aristotelian" or classical approach to horror to study violent spectacle and its role in the realist slasher horror film. Such films raise hard questions about the nature of audience interest in these new figures of monstrous evil. I would propose that even if we are interested in spectacles like those in the films we have considered, we still see the films *as* representations; and their naturalistic monsters are still the creatures of artifice. Ambivalence about the immediate spectacle of violence is the theme of these movies. They are striking not just for their depiction of the killer at their center, but for the way in which they link the monster to the horrific spectacle so as to *make an issue of* our interest in it. To look only at spectacle here and to denounce either its seeming direct appeal or its surface violence against women is to fail to respond to the complexity of these films *as* films. They foreground spectacle to evoke ambivalence, both interest and revulsion, prompting some form of moral analysis.

Let me expand on my claim that these films actually make spectacle the issue. *Peeping Tom*'s killer is a voyeur who films the murders he commits. We watch the murders through his camera, and we see his victims' faces reflected in his mirror. The movie clearly involves us in his aggressive search to get the perfect picture of fear, pointing out alternatives to Helen's intuitions and emotions. It offers a sort of moral closure when the presumed perfection can only be found as he commits suicide. *Frenzy* shows a murder where the violence against the woman's body is very graphic, reaching a new level of on-screen, horrific violence. But *Frenzy*, too, provides a moral resolution when the innocent man is finally cleared and the guilty one is caught, in the last scene. *Henry: Portrait of a Serial Killer* is more disturbing both because of its realism of style and its amoral viewpoint. It violates the usual rules of both the horror genre in general and the slasher in particular: it offers no audience identification figure, nor does its plot depict any righting of wrongs.[10] *Henry* succeeds by creating terror and unease, both promising and withholding the spectacle of violence as Henry also films and later watches his own murders—and we watch beside him. This film, like the other two, makes us contemplate our interest in the subject by forcing us to watch what the killer watches—his own crimes. A major problem I have pointed out with this film is that it takes the moral high ground in suggesting narratively that Henry is banal and uninteresting, but undercuts this message through its visual depiction of an attractive, sexy, and "interesting" rebellious killer.

If slasher killers are not interestingly evil, as Alford would say, then why do they continue to populate the screen? But if they are interestingly evil—and I am afraid that they are—what does this tell us about ourselves? I maintain, contra Carroll, that our fascination with serial killer monsters persists in the face of a basic frustration of our desire to "understand" or explain them. If the serial killer monster is given any motives at all, they are empty, formulaic sexual ones that play upon societal assumptions about aggressive male sexuality. Indeed, in a reversal of the usual relation of reality to representation, clichéd horror film "explanations" are now trotted out in news accounts of real cases and purported scientific explanations of violent sex crimes:

> In sado-sexual killings, "the payoff is erection and orgasm," said forensic psychiatrist Park Dietz of Newport Beach, Calif. The highly popular "slasher" and horror movies incessantly exploit precisely that combination. On the screen, "the baby sitter starts to take off her bra," Dietz said, "which makes the kid in the audience get sexually excited. Then Jason comes in and decapitates her."[11]

Feminists are right to complain that the particular sort of graphic violence typical of the slasher killer film—as evidenced in the three I have examined here—targets women in reprehensible ways.[12] In the three films I have discussed, the monster is a male killer who targets women. But the sexism lies at levels beyond the screen violence: it resides in the "interest" of the monster, his sexiness, and in the implied moral analysis. Although all three men are clearly evil and loathsome, the films do not exactly treat them that way—at least not consistently. The monster is at first shown as fascinating, sad, conflicted, and sympathetic (*Peeping Tom*); then as a figure of certain comic and repulsive fascination, emblematic of man's inhumanity to man and of our lives in a world that is "not the Garden of Eden" (*Frenzy*); and finally as an eroticized rebel, updated to the 1980s, and he is a man out to get others before they get him (*Henry*). It is women who cue our reactions to the killers; here, as in mad-scientist movies, men *act* and women *react*. Helen cries over Mark's dead body, Becky pities and tries to love Henry, and before she dies, Brenda Blaney (Barbara Leigh-Hunt) tries to appease Bob Rusk so as to suffer the least damage possible. But why are women forced to deal with these monstrous men in the first place? Some feminists would argue that the only way to deconstruct and undo the damaging myths of fascination of monstrous killers is to argue, persuasively and rationally, that they are not extraordinary or monstrous and deserve no particular attention.[13]

I think, perhaps cynically, that such a move is too utopian; it is impossible to undo the mechanisms that currently exist for making evil male killers sympathetic, interesting, and famous (Mark Harmon, the actor portraying Ted Bundy in the 1986 TV movie *A Deliberate Stranger*, for instance, was once dubbed "the sexiest man alive," by *People Magazine*). A less utopian, but also less cynical, alternative is to maintain, as a cognitivist might, that audiences can enjoy a filmic spectacle in ways that are not simple and transparent. We may assess and read a slasher movie by seeing it *as* a hyperbolic charade as well as by directly critiquing it. Surely we have begun to take spectacle to extreme forms that make it deconstruct itself when we find the repulsive one-eyed short and dumpy Henry Lucas recycled into the handsome Brandoesque Michael Rooker. Hitchcock's black humor maintains distanced and aesthetic responses to what is at the same time a disturbingly realistic movie. Can audiences really be duped into liking the cannibal killer Hannibal Lecter without being aware of how well this mad genius-villain is being played by the well-known and popular Anthony Hopkins (in an Oscar-winning performance)? To reflect here on a movie as a representation involves confronting real and disturbing issues along the way about our fascination with killers and with the very spectacle we are watching.

I have pointed out an insidiously troublesome feature of realist horror: the emotional burden these films bring to women. Such films often target and victimize viewers by playing on the fascination of the monster so as to eroticize him or to elicit sympathetic understanding. The killer is someone driven by blood lust like a vampire; he cannot help his nature. Male sexual desire in these films is a force easily channeled into destructive violence if its "natural" aims are blocked or thwarted. Furthermore, women often "ask for it": they place themselves knowingly into danger and behave seductively; by the films' logic, they "deserve" punishment for their sexual boldness, much like Lucy in *Dracula*. The vampire's predation and that of the slasher killer are depicted alike as the sexualized attack of a male human upon a woman, as even something that the woman longs for and enjoys. The woman fantasizes about the vampire or slasher, or she lures him from far distances; she is, then, the one "responsible" for his attack. Faced with either Lucy's bold innuendoes or Mina's purity and goodness, Dracula can scarcely resist. Like Frankenstein's monster, he is compelled by any vision of loveliness. Since slasher films typically depict an attractive woman as the killer's target, they perpetuate this sort of a view. *Psycho*, too, developed this theme and implicated the viewer, who voyeuristically watches the notorious shower scene where Norman attacks the "nude" Marion Crane (Janet Leigh).

In the slasher genre, as in some *Dracula* movies, women characters often fill in the gaps behind the inexpressive and unhappy man, making the banal killer like Henry into someone deep and interesting. This is as true in the presentation of real cases (e.g., Dahmer, Bundy, and the Menendez brothers) as it is in the fictive examples of Henry or Mark Lewis. Even Bob Rusk asks for Brenda's sympathy by wheedling: "I have my good points. I like flowers and fruit." A film like *Henry* eroticizes the killer by linking him to traditional Hollywood film heroes like James Dean or Marlon Brando. Of course, from Gary Cooper to Clint Eastwood, this hero has been strong, potentially violent, inept at communicating, independent, and the rest. Significantly, although many real-life serial killers (like Dahmer) prey on young men or boys, this sort of killer has not been made the focus of major films, presumably because he violates the clichéd association between potent maleness and heterosexuality. In other words, realist horror creates links between the "dark side" of male traits (violence, uncontrolled sexuality) and the heroic side (power, independence, and so on). This means that realist horror legitimizes patriarchal privilege through the stereotyped and naturalized representation of male violence against women. These cultural narratives treat male violence as an inevitable concomitant of normal male sexuality:

At a minimum, Deitz said, two conditions are necessary to produce a
sexual serial killer: a psychopathic personality and a highly
developed sadistic tendency. The former is in ample supply.
According to studies done for NIMH [National Institute of Mental
Health], about one in twenty urban males is psychopathic—that is,
lacking normal inhibitory feelings of guilt or remorse and operating
outside familiar social or moral constraints.[14]

In realist horror, male sexuality is a ticking time bomb, a natural force
that must be released and will seek its outlet in violence if it is
frustrated or repressed. Since women, and standardly the monster's
mother (as in *Henry*, *Frenzy*, *Psycho*, or real-life accounts of criminals
like John Hinckley Jr.), are scapegoated as sources of this repression,
they are shown somehow to "deserve" the violence they evoke. The net
effect is that we simply accept as a natural and inevitable reality that
there will be vast amounts of male violence against women.[15]

Nevertheless, I believe that the formulaic depictions of violent
male sexuality in realist horror can be seen *as* just that—formulas.
Films like *Henry*, *Frenzy*, or *Peeping Tom* may actually lead audience
members to question their own fascination with the monstrousness of
the serial killer and to query such formulas and the associated icons of
male heroism. This is a tricky point to demonstrate. Realist horror films
like *Frenzy* may toy with or parody the standard *Psycho* explanations
that scapegoat women, particularly mothers, for male violence. I have
suggested that something like this happens in *Henry*, a film that relies
upon but simultaneously empties out the formula "he did it because of
his mother." Similarly, *The Silence of the Lambs* contrasts one
stereotyped psycho-killer whom the FBI can explain ("Buffalo Bill")
with another whom they cannot begin to fathom. Although many news
accounts struggled to attribute to the Luby's restaurant (Killeen, Texas)
mass murderer George Hennard a motive stemming from his rejection
by local women, others looked beyond this to discuss the man's work
history, war record, and access to guns.[16]

The slasher horror film often involves very realistic depictions of
ordinary men who become killers. It highlights spectacle over plot, and
this means that one ideological effect of such narratives is to perpetuate
a climate of fear and random violence where anyone is a potential
victim. These films have messages that are troubling on grounds
beyond feminist objections. They often obscure the truth about factors
that produce a climate of violence: inequities in education, health care,
social and economic status, and political power; urban blight and flight;
racism; drug use; and gun laws. Thus, instead of the slasher horror film

prompting action and resistance, it works to produce passivity and conservative agenda pushing for increased censorship in campaigns by targeting films and not actual social conditions.

Notes

1. Tania Modleski finds that a similar gesture towards the direction of the pathogenic "devouring" mother is made in Alfred Hitchcock's *Frenzy* (1972), but she does not seem critical of it—that is, she takes it on face value that the devouring mother is "a familiar figure in Hitchcock." See Modleski, *The Women Who Knew Too Much: Hitchcock and Feminist Theory* (New York and London: Routledge, 1989), 106–108.

2. Michael Graczyk, "Odyssey of Henry Lee Lucas," *Houston Chronicle*, 15 August 1993: 5D. Since the movie was made, Lucas's sentence has been commuted to life imprisonment.

3. Fred C. Alford, *What Evil Means to Us* (Ithaca: Cornell University Press, 1997), 13; 89; 94.

4. Noël Carroll, *The Philosophy of Horror or Paradoxes of the Heart* (New York: Routledge, 1990), 35.

5. *Ibid.*, 38.

6. Plato, *Republic* 439e–440a.

7. Aristotle, *Poetics* 50b16–17.

8. Carroll, 179–82.

9. This is a central theme of Isabel Cristina Pinedo's *Recreational Terror: Women and the Pleasures of Horror Film Viewing* (Albany: State University of New York Press, 1997).

10. Though Carol J. Clover argues in *Men, Women, and Chain Saws: Gender in the Modern Horror Film* (Princeton: Princeton University Press, 1992) that slashers usually do obey a certain moral code.

11. See Curt Seplee, "Serial Killers May Be Closer to Normal Than We'd Like to Believe," *Washington Post*; reprinted in Houston *Chronicle* (August 7, 1991).

12. See Tania Modleski, "The Terror of Pleasure: The Contemporary Horror Film and Postmodern Theory," in *Studies in Entertainment: Critical Approaches to Mass Culture*, ed. Tania Modleski (Bloomington: University of Indiana Press, 1986), 155–66; and Linda Williams, "When the Woman Looks," in *Re-Vision: Essays in Feminist Film Criticism*, ed. Mary Ann Doane, Patricia Mellencamp, and Linda Williams (Frederick, MD: University Publications of America, 1984), 83–99.

13. See Mary Lo Dietz, "Killing Sequentially: Expanding the Parameters of the Conceptualization of Serial and Mass Killers," paper presented at the

First International Conference on "Serial and Mass Murder: Theory, Research, and Policy," April 3–5, 1992, at the University of Windsor, Windsor, Canada.

14. Seplee, *op. cit.*

15. See, e.g., R. Emerson Dobash and Russell Dobash, *Violence Against Wives: A Case Against Patriarchy* (New York: Free Press, 1979).

16. Jim Phillips, "Killeen Quiet, But Questions are Disquieting," *Austin American-Statesman* (October 18, 1991).

American Psycho: Horror, Satire, Aesthetics, and Identification

Deborah Knight and George McKnight

Mary Harron's *American Psycho* (2000) confronts us at the outset with questions about the possibilities of cinematic horror and the nature of filmic narration. It also challenges the dominant philosophical definition of the horror genre as set out in Noël Carroll's *The Philosophy of Horror; or, Paradoxes of the Heart*.[1] An unconventional horror film in a number of important ways, *American Psycho*'s remarkable use of unreliable narration, its reworking of viewer identification, and its dark satire all combine to offer a new perspective on what the horror genre can accomplish. Disturbing as it is morally to follow Patrick Bateman (Christian Bale) through the labyrinth of this film, the really unsettling questions raised by *American Psycho*'s narration are epistemic rather than moral.

The audience's prior familiarity with the conventions of classical Hollywood realist cinema, and with films that are the heirs to this tradition of fiction filmmaking, lead us to assume at least the following: 1) that ultimately what the film presents us with will turn out to be epistemically reliable as evidence on which to base our understanding of the nature of the actions represented; and 2), that "the chief dramatically significant questions do have answers that the [film] will supply."[2] The first condition tells us that whatever characters (including voice-over narrators) *say*, the primary visual narration of the film will provide us the necessary evidence to determine what is true. In other words, a film's primary visual narration is "conventionally reliable," and thus will let us discover "the true story."[3] The second condition tells us to expect that a film's narration will provide us with a resolution to the major dramatic issues it raises, usually in the form of a dramatically but also epistemically satisfying closure. In other words, the film's action will be resolved and we will know how, and why, this resolution has been achieved. *American Psycho* is a film that subverts both these conditions, a point we will return to in our conclusion. We begin with an overview of the philosophy of horror, focusing on Carroll's position and Cynthia Freeland's rejoinder to Carroll. We then turn to the film itself, emphasizing its unique use of satire, its narrative aesthetics, and its strategies of viewer engagement.

Carroll and Freeland on the Philosophy of Horror

For over a decade now, Carroll's *The Philosophy of Horror* has been the standard for the philosophical definition of horror. Cynthia Freeland has challenged Carroll's definition by defending a group of films that she claims constitute the subgenre of "realist horror."[4] Roughly, the debate between them hinges on whether "art-horror"[5] is defined by a monster whose existence cannot be explained by natural science. Carroll defends the view that horror requires a supernatural monster, while Freeland says it does not. Carroll restricts the horror genre to artworks organized around a monster that is loathsome and impure. Furthermore, because it possesses a "fantastic biology," the art-horror monster offends the categories of contemporary science. We judge the monster to be loathsome, in part, because we are unable to understand its nature or control it; but we are also revulsed by it. Art-horror narratives cue our response to the monster in a specific way: our response "mirrors" or "tracks" the reactions of the morally positive fictional characters who confront the monster. Carroll maintains that spectators value the things that the morally positive characters in art-horror narratives value and fear the things they fear. We recoil from King Kong because Fay Wray does, whereas we come to like Chewbacca in *Star Wars* (1977) because Han Solo (Harrison Ford) does. Art-horror is thus characterized both by our cognitive judgment (that the monster is loathsome) and by a specific sought-for affect (revulsion).

Contrary to our intuitions, Carroll's definition of horror cannot accommodate what many consider to be definitive examples of cinematic horror, such as Hitchcock's *Psycho* (1960), and (as we will see) this is exactly the problem upon which Freeland focuses. One might think that if *Psycho* is generally considered to be a horror film, Carroll's account ought to accommodate it, and any theory of horror that makes room for *Psycho* would, it seems, also make room for such films as *The Silence of the Lambs* (1991), *Hannibal* (2001), and *American Psycho*. Carroll has argued that his theory explains why people often want to treat *Psycho* as though it were a horror film: "even if Norman Bates is not a monster technically speaking, he does begin to approximate the central features of art-horror as I have developed them. That a madman with a butcher knife is threatening needs no comment. But, as well, Norman Bates, in virtue of his psychosis, resembles the impure beings at the core of the concept of art-horror."[6] On this explanation, we mistakenly treat *Psycho* as an example of art-horror, when in fact it only resembles art-horror in certain ways, and we should actually treat it as an example of terror.

Perhaps it is best to solve the problem posed by films such as *Psycho* and *The Silence of the Lambs* by placing them beyond the borders of art-horror, saying that they merely *resemble* art-horror in some respects. Freeland thinks not. What Carroll eventually concedes is that there is a way in which someone *could* incorporate *Psycho*, *Silence of the Lambs*, and similar films featuring serial killers and other psychotic figures under his umbrella definition of horror. Yet Carroll says emphatically: "I am not fully convinced that we should construct a theory of horror that includes these psychotics."[7] To include *Psycho* and *Silence of the Lambs* among art-horror films, Carroll believes that you would have to stipulate that Norman Bates (Anthony Perkins) and Hannibal Lecter (Anthony Hopkins) *are* in fact monsters because they take us beyond the bounds of what psychiatric texts properly describe. This move might shore up the original definition, but it is not convincing. After all, the question whether films such as *Psycho* are really examples of art-horror only arises in the first place because Carroll's definition of a monster depends on what contemporary science can and cannot explain.

That Carroll's account of art-horror excludes *Psycho* is one problem. There are (at least) two more. He does not adequately distinguish between the genres of science fiction and horror, let alone acknowledge the frequent overlaps between them. This too-hasty conflation of related but importantly different genres leads to his overemphasis on science. We might also question the starting point for Carroll's analysis of the horror genre. He begins, it will be recalled, with the idea that horror films are basically like Westerns and detective films in the sense that what marks these genres is a central and recurring figure. Carroll notes that Westerns feature cowboys and detective films feature detectives, so by parity of reasoning we ought to define the horror genre in terms of a monster. This is an overly simplistic way of dealing with genres. A more robust account of the Western genre would point out that Westerns may or may not feature cowboys in central roles, as Westerns revolving around confrontations between the U.S. Cavalry and Native Americans ought to remind us. A more general account of narrative genres would recognize that some genres are not identified by a recurring figure at all, for example, musicals. It is at least a question whether horror films might not be identified by some other feature or conjunction of features than just a recurring major figure.

But let us say that, like Carroll, you decide to define the horror genre in terms of a major recurring figure, namely the monster. Instead of defining the monster in terms of what science acknowledges, and then try to say that Norman Bates, Hannibal Lecter, and Patrick Bateman clearly outstrip any currently accepted medical account of psychosis, surely you would be better off noting that literature is replete with fantastic beings, and accepting that what marks out a monster isn't the degree to which it offends *science*, but the degree to which it offends *morality*. Carroll himself seems drawn in this direction through his argument that our affective responses are cued by morally positive characters' responses to the monster. The advantage of taking morality rather than science as our benchmark is that it allows us to talk about the peculiar status of our relation to characters such as Norman Bates, Hannibal Lecter, and Patrick Bateman. These are characters who both attract and repulse us to different degrees, not on the basis of what science says, but on the basis of what they do and how they are presented to us.

Film scholarship has long recognized the central position of *Psycho* in the horror genre's development. Steve Neale argues that "the advent of *Psycho* in 1960 is generally regarded as a turning point, as the beginning of something new: as the film which located horror firmly and influentially within the modern psyche, the modern world, modern relationships, and the modern (dysfunctional) family."[8] On this view, *Psycho* modified the genre by uniting the psychological thriller and the horror film. An alternative approach in horror scholarship sees *Psycho* not so much as a radical break in the horror tradition, but rather as the culmination of a variety of trends dating back to the 1950s.[9] Whether *Psycho* is treated as something new or as the logical continuation of previous developments, the consensus within film scholarship is that horror does not need a supernatural monster.

In her influential essay "Realist Horror," Freeland has advocated the inclusion of films such as *Psycho* among the denizens of art-horror, but while her conclusion is clearly the right one, there are reasons to be cautious about the rationale she provides. In opposition to Carroll, Freeland defends the idea of a non-supernatural monster. The subgenre she calls "realist horror" is intended to include films such as *Psycho*, *Silence of the Lambs*, *Halloween* (1978), and *Friday the 13th* (1980), whose monsters are undeniably human. Freeland's suggested subgenre poses theoretical difficulties of its own. "Realist horror" is an unfortunate category because it conflates at least two ways of understanding something fictional as "realistic," thus pulling Freeland's challenge to Carroll in opposite directions. Something fictional is realistic if we can say that it is true to life or explicable in scientific terms. Thus, Freeland argues that, since humans can act monstrously—and in fact so monstrously that we have various sciences and institutions dedicated to understanding such behavior—Carroll is wrong to say that the art-horror monster must have a fantastic biology. Frankly this criticism of Carroll seems so persuasive that it is surprising that he continues to insist on a supernatural aspect to the monster.

But there is a second sense of "realist" that has to do with the form and style that many, or perhaps most, narrative artworks take. Cinematic realism is developed around a transparent narrative form and visual style, using conventionalized editing practices, character representation, and storytelling conventions. Most horror narratives have linear-causal plots featuring characters who act in recognizably rational ways at least in terms of trying to achieve certain goals (and this includes the sort of villains you find in slasher films, vampire films, and others), whose goal-oriented behavior is enacted in easily identifiable patterns of actions, such as murdering sexually active teenagers with axes, drinking young women's blood, and so on. One problem with Freeland's proposal of "realist horror" is that many of the horror narratives that feature monsters with "fantastic biologies" are nevertheless perfectly good examples of cinematic realism. Freeland is right insofar as she argues that *Psycho* and *Silence of the Lambs* ought to count as examples of art-horror even though Norman Bates and Hannibal Lecter are only metaphorically monsters. But it is hard to see why such slasher cycles as the *Friday the 13th* and *Halloween* films ought to form part of the same subgenre that includes *Psycho* and *The Silence of the Lambs*. It may be true that, like Norman Bates and Hannibal Lecter, Jason Voorhees and Michael Myers are only metaphorically monsters, but there is reason to think that the latter two are more like the monsters Carroll favors than Bates or Lecter. It seems at least initially implausible to think that *Psycho* and *Silence of the Lambs*—both intricately plotted films interested in the psychology of psychosis—are of a piece with the sorts of teen-scream flicks where the monsters have little or no psychological depth. Freeland, who is supported by the preponderance of film scholarship, is right to reject the idea that horror must be defined, as Carroll wishes it to be, in terms of a supernatural monster. But she is wrong to think that "realist horror" properly stakes out the distinction between the sorts of films Carroll wants to include as examples of art-horror and those she wants to include.

The Monster as Protagonist in *American Psycho*

A main part of Freeland's argument is that our response to Norman Bates, Hannibal Lecter, and Patrick Bateman derives from the fact that they are more like us than not, at least as compared to Carroll's monsters with fantastic biologies. We might say that what characterizes Bates, Lecter, and Bateman is not their fantastic biologies, but their fantastic psychologies. Indeed, in films such as *Psycho*, *Silence of the Lambs*, and *American Psycho*, psychology becomes thematized in the figure of the horror villain. Hitchcock makes a bit of a game of this in *Psycho* by briefly raising the question of what happens when the human monster is the sole focus of our sympathies. After killing off Marion Crane a third of the way through the film, we are left with Norman Bates as our temporary default protagonist. Hitchcock was doubtless amused by the idea that his audience would innocently fall victim to Norman in just the way Marion herself did.

It is true that horror films have from time to time aligned us with the monster (e.g., when John Carpenter gives us shots from Michael Myers' point of view in *Halloween*).[10] Other horror films, such as *Silence of the Lambs*, offer us monsters who are strangely attractive, even fascinating, despite their horrifying deeds.[11] It is one thing to unwittingly find ourselves aligned with the monster, as in *Psycho*; it is quite another to occasionally share the perspective of the monster, as in *Halloween*, and another thing still to be confronted with a charismatic monster, as in *Silence of the Lambs*. *American Psycho* does something else again. It carries the idea of alignment with the monster to its logical limit: the monster is our central character, our primary means of access to the events of the fictional world, and in fact our narrator. The world of *American Psycho* is very much a world seen from Bateman's perspective. But can we trust what we see?

The connection between *Psycho* and *American Psycho* (both the novel and the film) has been noted before, of course. Writing before the release of the film version of *American Psycho*, Barry Keith Grant described the "yuppie horror" film as a new and distinctive cycle of horror cinema, and noted that Ellis's novel stands in relation to yuppie horror in much the same way that *Psycho* stands to the modern horror film.[12] Both *Psycho* and *American Psycho* challenge deeply entrenched cultural values. *Psycho* targets values concerning the family, motherhood, filial loyalty, and marital fidelity. *American Psycho* targets the very values that yuppie horror films typically depict positively, including "aspirations of glory, prestige, recognition, fame, social status, power, money or any and all combinations of the above."[13] What is at risk in standard examples of yuppie horror—*Fatal Attraction* (1987), *Pacific Heights* (1990), *Bad Influence* (1991), *The Temp* (1993)—is "the material success the characters so covet [which] becomes frighteningly vulnerable and fragile."[14] *American Psycho*, by contrast, reveals the ideals and values of yuppie culture to be shallow, self-serving conceits and neuroses.

Although exceptions exist, the standard configuration of characters in a horror film depends upon the clear tension between those who represent "good" and those—most notably the horror villain—who represent "evil." Anomalous cases exist, such as *Bram Stoker's Dracula* (1992), where the horror villain is far more seductive and compelling than the plodding but virtuous heroes. But even this film depends upon a reliably drawn distinction between those characters who are good and those who are not. *American Psycho* violates this convention, not by inverting the relationship between "good" characters and "evil" ones, but rather by dissolving the structural opposition between good and evil itself. This has profound consequences for the film's overall narrative. Typically, we could say that a horror narrative involves a progressively escalating series of violent incidents where evil triumphs over good, until finally good grasps victory from (what often looked to be) certain defeat and the monster is stopped. But there is no active force for good in *American Psycho*, nor, it would seem, is the monster stopped. There is even a question whether there really is a monster in the first place.

As we have seen, Carroll argues that art-horror audience members "track" the responses of the narrative's morally positive characters. But *American Psycho* has no morally positive characters whose reactions could establish the primary set of evaluative response-cues for us. By contrast, given that Bateman is our central character and that the way other characters are presented to us is thoroughly colored by Bateman's own responses to them, we wind up "tracking" the film's other characters (notably his look-alike fellow vice-presidents and Evelyn [Reese Witherspoon], his fiancée) in much the same negative terms Bateman himself uses. The opening scene establishes this point for us as Bateman, seemingly the only one to know the difference between a menorah and a draydle, criticizes the others for their anti-Semitic remarks. Although the film does not compel us to adopt Bateman's point of view uncritically, there is nevertheless the potential that audiences might begin to feel the sort of disdain for its other characters that Bateman feels.

Just how we do relate to Bateman is a complex matter, but two things are worth emphasizing. One is the motif of the mirror image or double, symbolizing a conflicted psychology. Two important examples of this trope occur at the beginning of *American Psycho.* In the film's second scene, Bateman has a coupon for a free drink refused by a nightclub bartender. She turns away to get his drink, and we see Bateman call her "a fucking ugly bitch." But then there is a cut and in the mirror behind the bar we see Bateman in reflection add that he is going to stab her to death and play around with her blood. The first remark is angry and rude, but it is the second that is figured as having been spoken by Bateman's other, darker, self.

The very next scene shows us Bateman's stark, modernist Upper West Side apartment, a space decorated primarily in black and white. Here we have the film's first use of Bateman's voice-over narration. As we hear him introduce himself ("My name is Patrick Bateman. I am 27 years old . . ."), we see him in the reflection of a framed *Les Misérables* poster, utterly expressionless. Bateman goes on to tell us in astonishing detail about his morning routine, a ritual dedicated to his body. After a complex sequence of ice packs and stomach crunches, soaps and scrubs, he applies a facial mask. Again, we watch his reflection in the mirror as he peels the facial mask off, while in voice-over he ominously informs us, "There is an idea of a Patrick Bateman, some kind of abstraction, but there is no real me." Here the trope of the double is used twice over: both the mirror reflection suggesting the doubled self, and the contrast between body (Bateman as the flesh-and-blood creature whose hand you can grasp) and soul—or more correctly, the absence of soul (as Bateman says, "I am simply not there"). Through the doubling motif, *American Psycho* signals that we should adopt a critical perspective on Bateman, even though he is our protagonist. In the meantime, the film actively discourages our identification with him. If we ordinarily tend to understand others (including fictional others) by means of such responses as empathy and sympathy, we quickly find that these responses are out of place with respect to Bateman, who does not merit our sympathy and for whom empathy is impossible. Bateman himself believes that empathy for others is impossible, and so we should not be surprised that, from the beginning to the end of the film, he is shown to be devoid of any morally charged cognitive or emotional responses. His main reaction to others is one of contempt.

The irony, of course, is that Bateman is emblematic of nearly all the qualities he despises in his friends, lovers, and colleagues. He is as shallow, as materialistic, and as attached to the yuppie ideals of "social status, power, money or any and all combinations of the above" as his fellow vice-presidents. That Bateman is regularly mistaken for one of his colleagues is a running joke in the film that culminates when his own lawyer fails to recognize him. Although some of Bateman's victims recoil from him as horror victims are supposed to do, there are no morally positive central characters in the film, thus no one with whom we are aligned as they try to vanquish the monster. In fact, only a few of Bateman's victims have any idea of the threat he (seemingly) poses to them, while Bateman's usual circle sees nothing exceptional about him at all. Bateman's lawyer describes him as, among other things, a dork and a boring, spineless lightweight. What the first-person voice-over narration makes plain is that only Bateman knows who the monster is. Nearly everyone else in the film is oblivious or misses the clues. But it remains a question whether Bateman's voice-over is reliable.

Our moral evaluation of *American Psycho*'s fictional world cannot depend on our alignment with the film's morally positive characters, because there aren't any. Moreover, there is nothing in the film itself that we could seriously take to represent a social or moral "good" against which we could judge Bateman, nor is there any figure with sufficient authority to suggest that the fictional world does, after all, have a moral center. Two candidates for the role of moral center are the police detective (Willem Dafoe) who interviews Bateman concerning the alleged disappearance of Paul Allen (Jared Leto), and Bateman's secretary, Jean (Chloë Sevigny), an ordinary, non-yuppified citizen. Jean is actually our best bet, since (at least for a while) it seems she might turn out to be the so-called "Final Girl," the conventional horror genre character who in the end must take action herself to stop or kill the monster. Detective Kimball (Dafoe), although representative of the law, is only a marginal figure, and fails to see Bateman as any sort of threat.

The police, as the film's other representatives of the law, are no more effective than the detective. The police force that seemingly attempts to hunt Bateman down near the finale fails to capture him despite their superior numbers, weapons, and sophisticated surveillance technologies. At the end of the film, Jean is shown discovering the grisly sketches in Bateman's daybook, yet there is nothing to indicate that she intends to reveal him to the authorities or try to stop him herself. Hovering in the background as a possible source of moral authority is the President of the United States, Ronald Reagan, but he is impossible to take seriously within the fictional world of the film as he attempts to justify unlawful activities during the Iran-Contra affair. Even Bateman's yuppie colleagues dismiss Reagan as a liar. The only time we find a morally positive view expressed in the film, it is expressed by Bateman himself in such evidently clichéd terms that we must understand his pronouncements early on concerning social justice and world peace as slogans that have no connection to anything he or his friends actually believe or value. However loathsome Bateman is, the culture that could have produced him is just as horrifying. The idea that the culture itself is responsible for the monsters it produces makes satire the appropriate form for the film.

Satiric Comedy and Unreliable Narration in *American Psycho*

American Psycho has been widely recognized by critics and reviewers as a satire. The target of the satire is usually said to be 1980s American capitalism, particularly its narcissistic and fetishistic overvaluation of yuppie culture. This is the "content" aspect of the film's satire. But conventions drawn from the horror genre are also targets, and these more obviously formal aspects of the film's satire have not been as generally recognized. Some of the formal satirical elements include Bateman's incarnations as axe murderer, chainsaw killer, Dracula, and so forth. They also include such iconographic elements as the quasi-Gothic night scenes of the city where Bateman appears to stalk or kill victims, the film's fondness for great quantities of blood, the pursuit of the monster by inept representatives of the law, and the final, almost hysterical crescendo of spectacle leading up to Bateman's confession of his "crimes" to his lawyer's answering machine.[15]

While it is generally acknowledged that *American Psycho* is a satire, what may be harder to see is that the film is actually a satiric *comedy*. This is partly because *American Psycho* employs the conventions of comedy in a deeply ironic way. Here, we are not referring to comedy in the sense of something whose primary purpose is to make us laugh, or even to such outrageous and darkly funny sequences in the movie as the death of Paul Allen (with its mise-en-scene of plastic raincoats, newspapers on the floor, and a bright, shiny axe). Instead, we are referring to the genre of comedy as described by Northrop Frye in *The Anatomy of Criticism*.[16] There, Frye points out that the comedy genre features a protagonist who in an important sense exists beyond the bounds of a community. Very early in the film, Bateman in voice-over warns us that he is (or at least perceives himself to be) an outsider. Another important feature of the genre is that comedies usually end "happily," with the outsider finally welcomed into the broader community. This felicitous event is a sign of the community's reinvigoration as it gathers together to mark some public celebration or social event in the final scene (e.g., a dance or marriage). As well, the broader society is made better because of its ability to overcome what was initially seen to make the outsider an outsider. It should not be a surprise that when comedy meets satire, the "felicity" of the conclusion is wholly ironic. *American Psycho* ends as it begins, with Bateman part of his co-workers' community. Their social event is nothing more dramatic than meeting for drinks after work while struggling to get a reservation at a restaurant fashionable enough in which to tolerate being seen. Bateman has been unable to get anyone, most notably his lawyer, to recognize the threat he imagines he poses. Viewed from the perspective of ironic satire, what *American Psycho*'s conclusion "celebrates" is the collapse of values and the corresponding failure of judgment on the part of those who made up the community in the first place.

In discussing *American Psycho* to this point, we have offered several reminders to the effect that what Bateman tells us, and what the film shows us, might not be reliable. To take literally the actions we see Bateman engaged in, especially the most gruesome, would mean falling for the film's two most impressive narrative conceits: first, that Bateman is a reliable narrator, one who truly and accurately describes himself, his actions, and the world around him; and second, that what we see is the true story and thus is epistemically reliable. In fact, Bateman is an unreliable narrator. In the case of prose literature, the unreliable first person narrator makes it difficult if not impossible for readers to determine what is actually happening in the fictional world of the narrative. After all, how is one to determine what counts as the truth of the fictional situation based solely upon the unreliable first-person narrator's distorted and usually self-aggrandizing or self-serving reports? Sometimes there might be systematic clues, but the trick remains how to distinguish reliable from unreliable ones. It is very much harder in narrative cinema to achieve the sort of global unreliability that one can achieve in prose literature. That is because, with prose literature, we have nothing at all to work with but the words, the descriptions, the representations, of an unreliable narrator. In most films that feature a character who also doubles as a narrator, we can compare what we are told to what the primary visual narration shows us. This allows us to see much more clearly than in the case of prose just which aspects of that character's narration are unreliable. In other words, in cinema, the visual narration provided by the camera standardly shows us the truth of the situation. Using that as our gauge, we can judge what, if anything, the unreliable narrator says is true.

American Psycho takes away our assurance of an objective world guaranteed by the film's visual narration. One plausible way of understanding the film is to conclude that everything we see is in fact a projection of Bateman's imagination. This would make it impossible for viewers to treat what *American Psycho* shows us as a standard against which to test and judge Bateman's thoughts and actions. Another plausible way to interpret the film would be to conclude that some of what we see is epistemically reliable, while other parts are projections of Bateman's imagination. But there are no clues that we can use reliably to determine which are which. Although early on we might precipitously assume that the film's cinematic narration gives us access to what is "objective" about the film's fictional world, we ought quickly to recognize that there is no easy way to distinguish between what is real and what is a figment of Bateman's imagination. A third way to interpret the film—one that subsumes the second possibility and that *we* find most plausible—is that everything we see bears the marks of the director's presence, and that what is really at issue here is not Bateman as a psychological individual with psychotic tendencies, but Bateman as a figure emblematic of a dysfunctional culture.

The film's opening credit sequence signals this deliberate and playful collapse of the ostensibly objective and the ostensibly subjective. In an homage to Hitchcock, who also used credit sequences to toy with his audience, what we see initially appear to be large drops of blood falling against a pure white background. Then, we are shown a large, shiny knife. If we respond on the basis of horror film conventions, we assume that what we see is blood and that the knife must be hacking into someone's body. But then what we see is explained to us. What we had assumed was blood is really raspberry coulis, and the knife isn't hacking into anyone but only being used to prepare an entrée of rare, roasted partridge breast. This opening warns us not to mistakenly make inferences on the basis of epistemically underdetermined images. That is, we would only have considered the knife threatening if we already believed that the raspberry sauce was blood. The lesson generalizes to everything else we think we observe in the film.

Steve Neale has argued persuasively that different "regimes of verisimilitude" characterize different film genres.[17] For instance, it is within the regime of verisimilitude of musicals that characters break into song, but such behavior would be distinctly out of place in non-musicals. What Neale means is that what counts for us as "realistic" differs from genre to genre and from film to film, and depends on the genre or genres which shape the film in question. Neale is right, but it might not be wholly obvious how his point applies to *American Psycho*. We would argue that—consistent with it being a satiric comedy—*American Psycho* plays with its own regime of verisimilitude. The scenes at the beginning of the film seem to take place in the "real world" of the fiction. Nevertheless, by the time Bateman brings his stained sheets to the Chinese laundry and abuses the staff there while waving a large cigar around in his gloved hand, we might be starting to wonder just what aspects of the film's visual narration we can actually rely on. The inference we've probably drawn is, that the sheets are stained with blood. Of course, there is nothing to show this is false, and so we interpret Bateman's story that the stains are cranapple juice as just an alibi. Yet the film offers us no conclusive explanation about the cause of the stain.

Horror narratives encourage us to construct horrible or horrific connections between seemingly distinct, yet consecutive, scenes. So when we see Bateman stalking a woman on the late-night streets of New York, we jump to the conclusion that the sheets he takes to the laundry in the very next scene must be stained with her blood. Furthermore, we assume that the scene we witness *has actually happened as we see it*. The convention of realistic cinematic narration is that, except in rare cases where the cues to the contrary are clearly recognizable, we assume that what we see is true. But we cannot assume that what the visual narration of *American Psycho* presents to us is really happening in Bateman's life. If the opening credits and the scene in the Chinese laundry have not already alerted us, we should certainly be paying attention when Batemen gleefully murders the drunken Paul Allen and then drags Allen's dead body in a Gaultieri bag past his own oblivious concierge, leaving a conspicuous trail of blood along the foyer's marble floor.

Because *American Psycho* combines irony, comedy, satire, and horror, there is the question how we should understand and respond to the film's violence. The truly graphic violence occurs in one of two quite distinct ways. One way is when the horror occurs as an unexpected shock, as for example when Bateman kills a street person and his dog in a dark alley. We might have been cued by the location and mise-en-scene to expect the worst, but the murder happens very quickly and seemingly without reason, and it is easy to imagine that audience members would not have expected the scene's brutality. More characteristic is the use of expected horror—that is, the slow anticipation of what we must be fairly confident is going to be a gruesome sequence. Paul Allen's death is an important early example. Far more time is spent acquainting us with how Bateman has set up the murder (the elaborate and preposterous newspapers duct-taped to the floor to catch the anticipated blood; the see-through plastic raincoat; the bright, shiny ax) and with the denouement (as Patrick strips off the blood-spattered raincoat), than with the grisly act itself. The focus, as always, is on Bateman. But despite the level of gruesomeness, Allen's murder has an element of artifice to it. Bateman's face appears stained with blood as he hacks away at Paul Allen, yet no blood subsequently falls onto his suit or furniture. The artifice of horror murders is also apparent when a naked Bateman chases a woman through the corridors of an apartment building wielding a chainsaw. Are we really to believe that a screaming woman pounding on apartment doors and calling for help in an upscale Manhattan condominium could possibly not alert *anyone* to her plight? As we might expect in a horror film, *American Psycho* indulges us in our fascination with things gory and repugnant, things that suggest perversity (including sexual perversity—consider the chainsaw as phallus), and with extremes of violence and aggression. Yet at the same time, the gruesome is repeatedly an object of comedy and a source of humor in *American Psycho*. Arguably, some of the moments when the film asks us to laugh at mayhem are precisely moments when we should be skeptical about what we are seeing.

The rest of *American Psycho* balances on twin paradoxes. What we see—that is, the film's visual regime—appears real, yet is presented uncompromisingly as artifice. At the same time, we have good reason to think that many of the events depicted in this fictional world are in fact imaginary. This is how Mary Harron, true to the genuinely disturbing idea behind Brett Easton Ellis's novel, creates a visual narration that is as unreliable as Bateman's own. The film's visual aesthetic complements its satire. Whether we are talking about the presentation of food at trendy restaurants, the décor of Manhattan apartments, or the couture and glasses and business cards of upscale bankers, we find that everything is surface and everything is artifice. What money buys you is a look, not a life. It is little wonder that Bateman keeps insisting that he isn't there. The moral of the story, in part, seems to be that there just isn't any there, there. This is the nihilism at the heart of Ellis's worldview.

Conclusion

The question we have been trying to answer is whether *American Psycho* should properly be thought of as a horror film. Noël Carroll's definition of horror, depending as it does on the idea that the horror monster is both dangerous and impure, would require us to say that *American Psycho* is not an example of art-horror. Cynthia Freeland's defense of "realist horror" doesn't solve our problem, although it does support the idea that horror films can feature non-supernatural monsters. Film genres are historically changeable cultural entities, and this gives us one reason to think that Carroll's definition is too wedded to a particular historical incarnation of horror. Another reason to question Carroll's definition is that it doesn't recognize the ways in which art genres rework and extend the conventions which seem to define them.

American Psycho is certainly an exemplar of art-horror. The film would make no sense apart from the thematics and iconography of both pre- and post-*Psycho* horror cinema. But director Harron's real contribution is her unrelenting problematization of our assumptions about cinematic realism and thus how she subverts our expectations concerning the epistemic reliability of what we see. The film's aesthetic strategies accomplish three things simultaneously. We are placed into an unwelcome and uncomfortable but nevertheless unavoidable relationship with Patrick Bateman. This is not a relationship of identification—not least of which because we have no reason to feel sympathy or compassion for this figure. As Frye recognized, satire places its audience in a position of judgment with respect to the satire's central characters, thus making identification impossible. The second thing that *American Psycho* achieves is the systematic collapse of our ability to say what is or is not "real" in the context of the film's actions. Despite the fact that we cannot say decisively what does or does not happen, we have to recognize that the events of the film are not *simply* a projection of Bateman's imagination. Instead, the film is a metaphorical presentation of the implosion of the values that had originally defined Bateman and his yuppie associates. Finally, *American Psycho* begins and ends with no intermediaries to help us respond to Patrick Bateman. His voice-over narration leads us through the film. We must make up our own minds about him, because there are no morally positive characters whose responses we can track.

But there is a question just how we go about making up our own minds about Bateman. *American Psycho* deliberately violates the convention of providing a satisfying resolution to its chief dramatic questions—which are, roughly, "How are we to understand Bateman?" and "Will Bateman be stopped or punished?" It is true that we learn the answer to the second question—Bateman will not be stopped or punished—but to the extent that he functions as the horror monster, this is not a satisfying resolution. And we are as far from understanding Bateman at the film's conclusion as we were at the beginning. The film's final shot pulls in slowly to frame Bateman's face in extreme close-up as he says in voice-over that there is no hope for a better world, no escape, no catharsis, that his punishment continues to elude him, and that he will gain no deeper knowledge of himself. He finishes with the chilling observation that his confession has meant nothing. Chilling not just because the confession hasn't changed him, but because he cannot change. We end as we began, with Bateman presented as an unresolvable contradiction, his normal public exterior masking a dark, psychotic mind. Not only are we denied explanatory closure (since Bateman is as much of a mystery as ever,) but we are denied the epistemic basis for such an explanation. The final aspect of the film that connects *American Psycho* with the tradition of psychological horror exemplified by *Psycho* and *The Silence of the Lambs* is that our protagonist remains unknowable. Even in Carroll's terms, that makes Patrick Bateman a monster.

Notes

1. Noël Carroll, *The Philosophy of Horror; or, Paradoxes of the Heart* (New York: Routledge, 1990).

2. George M. Wilson, *Narration in Light: Studies in Cinematic Point of View* (Baltimore: The Johns Hopkins University Press, 1986), 40. Wilson here sets out his own two conditions that classical narration satisfies. His second condition differs from ours, however.

3. Seymour Chatman, *Coming to Terms: The Rhetoric of Narrative in Fiction and Film* (Ithaca: Cornell University Press, 1990), 132. Chatman's discussion seems to make unreliable narration a function only of homodiegetic narrators, whereas like Wilson, we argue that primary visual narration can in specific cases be systematically unreliable.

4. Cynthia A. Freeland, "Realist Horror," in Freeland and Wartenberg, eds. *Philosophy and Film* (London and New York: Routledge, 1995), 126–42.

5. "Art-horror" is Carroll's term intended to distinguish between horror as an affect relative to artforms, and horror as a response to real-life situations.

6. Carroll, 39.

7. Noël Carroll, "Horror and Humor," *Journal of Aesthetics and Art Criticism* 57, no. 2 (Spring 1999): 145–60.

8. Steve Neale, *Genre and Hollywood* (New York: Routledge, 2000), 96.

9. See Neale, 96, who refers to Mark Jancovich's *Rational Fears: American Horror in the 1950s* (Manchester, U.K.: Manchester University Press, 1996).

10. It is worth noting that point of view is used quite inconsistently in *Halloween*. Sometimes we see things "from" Michael's point of view, whereas other times a shot that might seem to be from his perspective turns out not to be.

11. Even the sorts of monsters that Carroll seems to prefer occasionally accomplish this, for instance Dracula (most notably in *Bram Stoker's Dracula*).

12. Barry Keith Grant, "Rich and Strange: The Yuppie Horror Film" in *Contemporary Hollywood Cinema*, ed. Steve Neale and Murray Smith (New York: Routledge, 1998), 286.

13. Grant is quoting from Marissa Piesman and Marilee Hartley's *The Yuppie Handbook: The State of the Art Manual for Young Urban Professionals* (New York: Long Shadows Books, 1984). The quote appears in Grant, 280.

14. Grant, 286.

15. This last sequence of the film is the one most usually misunderstood in popular reviews. For instance, Bruce Kirkland's otherwise positive discussion in the *Toronto Sun* (April 14, 2000) says the film "veer[s] off track for a few seconds in its final climax, a mindless killing spree that sets up the movie's most dynamic plot twist." See Kirkland, "Psycho a killer," available online at

www.canoe.ca/JamMoviesReviewsA/americanpsycho_kirkland.html (June 15, 2001).

16. Northrop Frye, *The Anatomy of Criticism: Four Essays* (Princeton: Princeton University Press, 1957), 163–86.

17. Neale, 31–39.

Real Horror

Robert C. Solomon

Since September 11, 2001, there is no forgetting or avoiding the awful visions we all shared. It was just before 9 in the morning that a plane hit the World Trade Center (WTC) in New York. On CNN, a few minutes later, we watched as United Airlines Flight 175 plowed into the second (south) tower, followed by that awful ball of flame. It happened that we were watching, horrified and helplessly, from 1,300 miles away. But for a glitch in our travel plans, we might well have been in New York that morning, watching even more horrified and helplessly from a short distance away. In any case, we spend a lot of time in New York. I have spent hours in the upper floors of the WTC. We've had drinks at Windows on the World. It took no leap of imagination for me to think of our being there, in the midst of the horror.

Compared to that haunting vision, other examples of horror, especially art-based horror, pale by contrast. Witticisms aside, art imitates life, not the other way around. Plato was right at least about this: Our imitations are poor copies of reality, whatever their other virtues. Horror is, first of all, a very real emotional experience, whether or not it is provoked by very real horrors. But I will argue that pretend horror, or what Noël Carroll nicely calls "art-horror," is derivative.[1] And the horror films that provoke laughter and make-believe screams, including horror films about horror films (*Young Frankenstein* [1974], the *Scream* movies, etc.) are quite literally imitations of imitations. (So, too, we might construe Carroll's suggestion that movie viewers' horror mimics the horror of the characters in the story.) Regarding such movies (and theater and novels), it is all well and good to ask what pleasure people find in the

230

fear or horror that otherwise would seem to be a most unpleasant emotion ("the paradox of horror pleasure"). But it makes no sense at all, or else it takes a very sick sense, to ask such a question of real-life horror. To be sure, the image of that second jetliner crashing into the tower is awesome, and one might argue that awe carries with it a certain horrified pleasure. But in this case, the overwhelming emotion is horror, not pleasure.

With this in mind, I would like to analyze the emotion of horror.[2] But I want to depart from the voluminous literature on horror in books and movies (sometimes in paintings and poems) by focusing first of all on real horror, that is, horror in real life, and only then considering the nature of art-horror, horror provoked by the make-believe. Sometimes prominent authors on horror allude to real-life horror. (Cynthia A. Freeland has a persuasive essay on "Realist Horror," and in *The Naked and the Undead* she at least refers to "real life kind of horror."[3] Daniel Shaw talks about "realistic horror" in his essay on David Cronenberg's *Dead Ringers* (1988).[4] Carroll, however, interestingly dismisses all such films from his consideration.) But real horror more often than not seems to resemble the Platonic form in which all horror movies, books, and such only "participate" but which (according to Plato) is not grasped directly and would be too overwhelming if so experienced. As the Socratic moviegoer who emerges from the dark of the theater and leaves the reflections on the screen for the harsh sunlight of the street, I want to first get some appreciation and understanding of real-life horror, leaving the analysis of "art-horror" as a secondary concern.

Now, what I want you to notice about my all too real example of real-life horror is that:

- The experience was in no way pleasurable, delightful, or enjoyable. There was nothing fun or funny about it.
- It did not involve any distinctive narrative (although there is an enormous amount of background knowledge that was required to experience the horror *as* a horror).[5]
- It did not involve any monsters (leaving aside the metaphors by which the terrorists would soon be described).[6]
- It did not involve epistemic uncertainty or suspense.[7] (There was not much question *what* was happening. There were a few moments of uncertainty after the first attack [Was it an accident? Could it be terrorism?], but these questions were quickly answered with the second attack.)
- The experience was not essentially metaphorical (with apologies to George Lakoff, who thinks, with good reason, that metaphors

"go all the way down"). Metaphor too easily cheapens and denies the horror rather than clarifies it (consider, e.g., "We have witnessed a visual metaphor for an impossible act of procreation: the silver phallus penetrating the petrified sphincter; an anal orgasm."[8])

- There were no sexual overtones or implications, no references to gender, no picking on females, no relation to incest or more modest forms of illicit sex.[9]

- Disgust played no role in the experience (however much disgust may have come to dominate the scene of carnage afterward).

- The dominant emotion, for those of us watching from a safe distance, was not fear. It was horror. To be sure, there was fear and uncertainty regarding the possibility of subsequent attacks, and for those at Ground Zero the dominant emotion was terror. There were no doubt paranoids watching in Austin and Omaha who feared that their cities (in fact, their very homes) were next, but their most appropriate emotion, I would argue, was horror.

- Everyone watching was powerless to do anything.[10] (The experience of those *in* the buildings was otherwise. It was all they could do to get out and/or help others do so. Their dominant emotion, as opposed to ours, was indeed fear. But for those of us who watched, the experience was one of helplessness and horror.)

- Watching the horror was not just a matter of passivity or "Darwinian emotions." It took quite an active imagination to "digest" what was happening.[11]

- The fact that we were transfixed by what we saw had nothing to do with satisfying our curiosity about anything (not even the sick curiosity that wondered what would happen if a fully loaded jetliner were to hit the WTC).[12]

- There was no "aesthetic form" to be appreciated[13] (although a grudging awe at the ingeniousness of the plot was unavoidable).

- It did not leave us with the thought that life is meaningless. (If anything, the overwhelming recognition was the preciousness of life.)

Such considerations have dominated discussions of art-horror, starting with the "paradoxical" observation that horror can be pleasurable. Well, in books and films, perhaps. There we *choose* to be horrified. (On some interpretations, we not only choose to read or to watch but we also choose to engage in a game of "make-believe," which is obviously not the case in real-life horror.[14]) In real life, horror forces itself upon us unbidden. And that plain fact undermines most of the aesthetic accounts of horror as a more or less pleasurable emotion. Carroll argues persuasively that art-horror involves a narrative about a monster. Well, sometimes it does. But the literary sense of narrative as plot need play no role in real-life horror, and the "interstitial" or "uncanny" experiences provoked by monsters only occasionally account for real-life horror (and then often trivial varieties, such as looking at your reflection in a mirror just after a slightly disfiguring accident or after a bad haircut). (Steven Schneider suggests that we might have some such experience walking home after seeing a horror movie, but unless one is addicted to the genre, this will not be a routine occurrence.) Horror may involve suspense, but it certainly need not do so, and often it is *knowing* what has happened and not epistemic uncertainty or curiosity that defines the moment of horror.

Real-life horror comes in many varieties. Some are intermingled with fear and disgust, while others involve shock and surprise. "Pure" horror, unmingled with other emotions, is probably hard to come by. But an all too familiar example is an automobile crash, not the horrendous yearly statistics but a particular accident with particular victims, lying there maimed and bleeding on the highway. It is one of the perplexities of the subject that we often go out of our way to experience horror, no matter how upsetting it may be. That explains, in part, why we would choose to go to horror films, though I would not leap from that to the conclusion that one therefore gets pleasure out of it. But the urge to "gawk" is so evident in such situations that the attraction of horror must surely count as one of its most tantalizing aspects. (This is *not* to deny that we would prefer that the horrible incident not occur. If it *has* occurred, however, we would rather see than not see.) But horror need not be so tantalizing. For some people, seeing a dead rat in the driveway or a squashed cockroach in the bathtub inspires horror. Think of looking down at a half-eaten worm in the apple you just bit into, or of gazing with some amazement at the remaining stub of one's bloody little finger after an accident with a sharp implement. Imagine a shocked family watching a loved one, totally "out of character," stage a psychotic tantrum or fly into a drunken rage. Real horror need not be viewed first-hand. It suffices that the horror is real (and one knows or at least believes that it is real.) Watching the WTC attack on television is an instance of real horror. I felt real horror watching the filmed scene (and the book photographs) of male lions killing the suckling cubs of other males in David Attenborough's *The Trials of Life* (1990).

It is impossible to imagine enjoying any such experiences, although to be sure we may derive perverse enjoyment from other people's experiences of horror. When fictionalized, what we enjoy in horror is other people's horror, including the characters on the screen or in the book (and this is the very contrary of empathy with them, as Carroll suggests). We can enjoy our own horror one step removed. We laugh at ourselves *after* we have screamed at the appearance of the man in the rubber Godzilla suit. We can even laugh at ourselves *as* we scream at the appearance of the man in the rubber Godzilla suit, perhaps. Insofar as we do seem to enjoy horror I would argue that it is not the horror as such that is enjoyed. When we laugh at ourselves *as* we scream at Godzilla it is not horror we feel but, echoing Ken Walton, something very much like "make-believe" horror, which I would argue is not any kind of horror at all.

To state the matter by way of a simple hypothesis, just in order to throw into question the basic presumption of the "pleasure-horror paradox" that is so much a part of the literature: If art-horror is or can be quite entertaining, it is precisely because it is not horror. Horror and entertainment are mutually exclusive, both logically and psychologically. Art-horror can give pleasure, but real horror blocks the very possibility of pleasure. Thus, there is a paradox of horror-pleasure only if we suppose that horror is the same in both art and reality and that it is the horror that is pleasure rather than something else. Of course, there are always cases of "mixed emotions," like mixed envy and pleasure when a friend wins the prize that you have worked so hard for or joy and despair when your long-lost dog comes running across your freshly paved sidewalk, but horror and pleasure seem not to be any such possible mix.[15] Horror is wholly absorbing. If in art we seek out horror and we find pleasure, it is because such an experience of art-horror (and the anticipation of horror) is somehow pleasurable, but not horror itself. When Orson Welles broadcast H. G. Wells' *War of the Worlds* in 1938, causing a nationwide panic, those who were panicking were in no way amused, and afterward, of course, they were (for the most part) furious. Looking back, it is hard to say why Welles or anyone else thought that people would be entertained.

And yet, it is well-known that public taste for horror increases with real horror in the background. There was an explosion of horror films during World War II. Interest dropped when the war ended, and by the 1950s the genre had momentarily dried up. Vietnam spawned *Night of the Living Dead* (1968), *Rosemary's Baby* (1968), and *The Texas Chainsaw Massacre* (1974). Again, the number dropped radically after the war's end. The biggest movie in the weeks following September 11th was *From Hell*. This suggests to many that art-horror is some kind of compensation or "release" from real-life horror. And that, in turn, is the source of its pleasure. Chip off the old bloody block Bela Lugosi Jr. is quoted as saying, "Imaginary horror is a way to escape real horror. It's a safe haven from real horror and takes your mind off of it."[16]

But art is not life, and art-horror is not real-life horror.

Delineating Horror (and Art-Horror)

What is horror? And what kind of emotion is horror? Again, there is some room for the challenge that horror is not an emotion at all, in the same way, perhaps, that vengeance, for example, is said not to be an emotion. That is, it does not name a discrete emotion but at best an emotion-related phenomenon (horror as the cause of certain emotions, vengeance as a consequence of certain emotions). Perhaps we could finesse the question by calling horror an "emotional phenomenon," but, as I noted, I think the boundaries of the category of "emotion" are sufficiently indistinct so as to make this not a very significant qualification. What is obvious is that horror *involves* emotion, indeed very powerful emotion. But it has often been argued (with reference to art-horror in particular) that horror involves *many* emotions although it is not itself a distinct emotion. (This is an argument I have often heard regarding love as an emotion as well). But again, while I think that this assumes a discreetness that is inapplicable in the analysis of emotions and even if indeed horror (like love) might *also* be manifested in any number of other emotions, it nevertheless deserves at least an attempt at analysis in its own terms. As readers of my other work will no doubt anticipate, my analysis will be predominantly (but not entirely) "cognitive" in nature.[17]

First, perhaps, we should distinguish horror from disgust, two emotions that are, not surprisingly, often found in tandem. Disgust is often cited as a "basic emotion" in the sense that it is (at least in part) a more or less automatic (or, more accurately, *autonomic*) reaction with "hardwired" manifestations in expression (for instance, the wrinkling of the nose and the extrusion of the tongue).[18] On the other hand, disgust has been argued to be too primitive to be a proper emotion, precisely because it is so automatic and inflexible.[19] Moral conceptions of disgust are accordingly designated as secondary and derivative uses of the word.[20] One can find roughly similar treatments of horror, notably in some of Jerry Levinson's work.[21] Levinson questions the strong cognitivist approach to horror, noting that Carroll (and Walton, too) neglect the significance of non-intellectual, perceptually based, cognitively impenetrable quasi-beliefs. I think that Levinson is right and horror can be like this. In fact, I would argue that horror is also a candidate for a "basic" emotion in that it has its origins in infantile helplessness and also displays characteristic, hardwired facial expressions (eyes wide open, mouth open as in a scream).[22] But I would not take infantile horror as exemplary of horror in the way that I would take physical disgust as exemplary of disgust. In art-horror, we may tap into and reactivate *real* emotions that are not themselves based on art at all, as Levinson argues. Real horror, by contrast, consists of real emotions, that is, nonintellectual, perceptually based, cognitively impenetrable quasi- or "Darwinian" emotions. Thus construed, horror might also be deemed "primitive" or "basic," and intellectualized horror (much of art-horror) might be deemed secondary and derivative.

I believe that there is much to support such an analysis, but I would argue that (1) horror is no less cognitive for all of that (where cognition and intellect must surely be distinguished) and (2) horror is nevertheless distinct and quite different from disgust. The support comes from neurological studies, going back to seminal work by William James, that place perception and hardwired" (autonomic) reactions at the heart of emotion. Recent studies show quite clearly that emotional response (fear is usually the emotion in question) is so quick and automatic that there is no time for involvement of the "higher" cerebral centers of the brain, in other words (as it is frequently stated these days) "emotion precedes intellect."[23] But cognition is not intellect, and the most primitive perception, if it is to count as perception at all, involves *recognition* (which is not to say that this involves anything like the recognition of a thing's full significance or attaching any sort of name to the object in question). In horror, the recognition might be as crude and nonspecific as "something horrible has happened (or is happening)" or it might be as fully specific as "my sister, who used to be such a beautiful person, has turned into a hideous, affect-less, murderous pod-person, one of those aliens from another planet" (with reference to one of my favorites, Don Siegel's 1956 *Invasion of the Body Snatchers*). In other words, horror is through and through cognitive, if only in that it recognizes something as horrible, whether or not it also involves (or requires) higher intellectual faculties.

This suggests at least one point of tension with disgust.[24] Disgust is indeed often very primitive, so primitive that it can be argued not to require recognition at all. But this depends at what point we identify the reaction in question. When a rotten tasting morsel is put in a baby's mouth, he or she shows the typical expression of disgust. When an adult sees blood and gore or smells decaying flesh, he or she experiences disgust (perhaps in the form of nausea) whether or not clearly displaying the stereotypic facial expressions. It could be argued that this does not or need not involve any recognition except in the utterly minimal sense of a physiological "registering" of some noxious stimulus. Horror, by contrast, depends on a much more sophisticated sense of *significance*, for instance, a comparison between what something is expected to be and the way it appears to be. The object might (in a straightforward ontological sense) be *the same* as the object of disgust, for instance, the same dead and decomposing body. But for the purposes of disgust, it does not matter *whose* or what body it is. It is just disgusting. In horror, by contrast, it matters very much what or whose body it is. One can imagine seeing a dead and decomposing body and then recognizing in horror that it is the body of one's professor or neighbor. This is not to deny that a sensitive person might be horrified (as well as disgusted) by *any* dead and decomposing body, but for horror it is nevertheless the differential between what one might have expected (e.g., that the person is still alive) and what (who) it is that makes for horror.

In the case of art-horror, I think the distinction between horror and disgust is particularly important because it is so often violated. Many so-called horror films might much better be designated disgust films, or what Carroll calls "splatter films." It doesn't take a talented director or scriptwriter to disgust an audience with gore (although to do so with subtlety takes considerable skill). Horror as opposed to disgust usually involves some plot development, some sense of suspense, however formulaic this may have become in the long tradition of horror films. Critics of Carroll are correct, however, in noting that not all art-horror involves plot development or narrative.[25] Certain *moments* in horror films are horrible, quite apart from any plot development or narrative. (These are the source of many of the stills that fill books on horror films.) There are also paintings which represent frozen moments in time that depict the horrible and provoke horror in those who look at them. (Consider works by Breugel and Bosch, and some of those ceremonial demon masks from Bali.) Some *thoughts* seem to be intrinsically horrible and horror provoking, particularly those with distinctively personal significance. But in any case, it is the significance of the object (whether in film, painting, or thought) that provokes horror, not any mere stimulus, and mere disgust is not enough to be horror.

Nevertheless, what is horrible is often also disgusting, and what is disgusting may also be horrible, especially when the disgust is not merely of the "visceral" kind. Moral disgust and moral horror are much akin, in fact one way to understand the phenomenon of moral disgust is to interpret it not as a secondary or derivative version of disgust but rather as a species of horror. (If disgust is limited to visceral feelings, as many have argued, horror is not so limited. One can be horrified by one's companion's immoral behavior without being nauseated by it. But then again, some authors (e.g., Levinson) might insist on a similarly "visceral" conception of horror. But horror and disgust, both in the case of real horror and in the case of art-horror, should be kept distinct. Horror has to do with significance, and this requires a complex kind of recognition. That is why disgust is a protective mechanism that is found fairly far down the phylogenetic ladder, while horror can be ascribed only to the most intelligent animals (apes, elephants, dolphins, dogs, and horses).[26] It is also how horror makes art-horror possible— because it can be artful in a way that disgust cannot be.

In the same way, we should distinguish horror from mere shock or what in psychology is called the startle reaction.[27] Carroll sometimes suggests that the horror experience typically involves shock, but he wisely catches himself and warns that shock alone is not an emotion and is not sufficient to characterize the horror experience.[28] Again, third-rate directors may well get a sharp physiological reaction out of an audience by having a creature (or for that matter almost anyone or anything) suddenly leap in front of the camera and into the faces of the unprepared audience or startle them with a sudden loud noise. But this has nothing to do with horror. Surprise is a bit more intriguing, for surprise is a fully cognitive emotion whereas being shocked or startled are not emotions at all. (Being startled is a straightforward physiological reaction without any cognitive dimension at all. Being shocked is more complex, ranging from a straightforward medical condition, a partial collapse of circulatory function following trauma, to something that is emotionally disruptive— but without itself being an emotion. Hearing that one's father has just dies is a shock, but the emotions [grief, dismay, etc.] follow.) Surprise, like horror, involves a contrast between expectations and what appears. Some emotion theorists (e.g., Keith Oatley) have insisted that *all* emotions depend on such a contrasting change in our experience, but I think this is wrong; as Martha Nussbaum has argued, it badly distorts such emotions as love, joy, and depression.[29] But clearly an emotion cannot be surprise if it is fully expected, and expected at that time and of that intensity. One is surprised by the "surprise party" given by one's friends, but only if one has not been forewarned. (Consider how difficult it can be to feign surprise under such conditions.)

So, too, horror involves a contrast, but it is not a contrast between what is expected and what is experienced in anything like the same sense. Instead, the contrast is between what is "normal" and what is monstrous. (Thus, many authors, notably Carroll and Schneider, take "the monster" to be at the heart of horror.) One *can* be both surprised *and* horrified by the same occurrence, but these are not the same. Surprise also shares with horror its passivity—we *are surprised*, we *are horrified*. The WTC tragedy caught the country by surprise, and the horror may have been heightened by this fact. But the surprise was not necessary to the experience of horror, and in the awful prospect of continuing terrorist attacks, there is no reason to suppose that the horror—as opposed to the surprise—will diminish.

Further along the line of cognitive sophistication we have surprise as wonder, which Descartes lists as one of his six "primitive" emotions. ("Wonder is a surprise if the soul which causes it to apply itself to consider with attention the objects which seem to it rare and extraordinary."[30]) But here, we begin to approach the notion of the sublime and with it the proper domain of aesthetics (though not necessarily of art-horror). The point is that while horror may also be shocking or a surprise and even startle us, horror is not shock or surprise or startle, although it does share with surprise (as with Descartes' wonder) at least an implicit recognition of the extraordinary.

Horror should most importantly be distinguished from fear. This is a point of considerable contention in the literature on art-horror. Kendall Walton, for instance, in his well-known article "Fearing Fictions" and in his book *Mimesis as Make-Believe*, talks almost entirely about fear (and make-believe fear), hardly about horror at all (although he is writing about horror films). Carroll, by contrast, writes almost entirely of horror, not fear, but the fact that he strictly limits his attention to art-horror is of considerable significance here. There is an intricate debate about whether the emotion evoked by art-horror is genuine emotion or not. (There is no such debate, of course, about

whether the emotion evoked by real horror is genuine emotion or not.)
But I think that before we enter into this debate, we ought to determine
what the emotion in question is. If the emotion in question were fear,
then paradoxical concerns arise immediately. If fear is (at least in part)
the strong urge to avoid or get away from danger (presupposing the
belief that there is danger), then the question hits hard how we can
have any such emotion when we *know* that there is no such danger.
The H. G. Wells/Orson Welles case is illustrative: the audience did not
know that the invasion from Mars was wholly fictional but believed
that it was in fact happening. There is no paradox of make-believe fear
there. It was fear, pure and simple. And for those who knew what
Wells was doing, there was no fear at all, only entertainment (or,
perhaps, intellectual disgust).

But horror should not be analyzed in terms of immediate or
proximate danger. One can be horrified by that which poses no threat
at all, for instance by the long dead body of one's cat who disappeared
months ago. Thus, we can appreciate what Stanley Cavell means when
he notes that "terror is of violence, of the violence I might do or that
might be done me. I can be terrified of thunder, but not horrified by
it."[31] My 14-year-old dogs, who have survived more than a hundred
thunderstorms, nevertheless still cower and whimper with each new
one. The thunder is fearsome but it is not in any sense *ghastly*. One
can also be horrified by that which one learns second-hand, for
example on the news or in conversation, although it suggests no threat
whatever to oneself or to anyone else one knows. Nor do we have to
retreat to the merely physiological (the "goosebumps" that give
"horror" its name: the word "horror" comes from the Latin "*horrere*"
and the French "*orror*"—to bristle or to shudder). It may well be that
such physiological symptoms of both fear and horror may be produced
by fictional representations, even when one knows that they are
fictional, but such symptoms alone are not any emotion at all. (Thus
the attempt to split emotion from cognition fails as a solution to the
paradox.) Nor need we retreat to "quasi-fear responses" in which there
is no inclination to act (flee or call the police, for example). In horror,
there is no inherent urge to flee; in fact, the "gawking" impulse would
suggest the very opposite. No "as if" behavior counts as any part of the
emotion and the absence of any urge to flee does not in any way
undermine the claim that the emotion is real. But again, there are few
instances of "pure" horror, and fear is often intermingled therein. In
this respect, perhaps, the horror movie is as close as one comes to
"pure" horror, but then, of course, it is mixed with entertainment and

any number of other "impurities" (granting that art-horror is indeed genuine horror).

In horror, one stands (or sits) aghast, frozen in place or "glued to one's seat." Of course, one can be frozen (or "paralyzed") by fear, but that is when fear becomes horror. Horror involves a helplessness which fear evades. The evasive activities of fear may be pointless, even self-defeating, but they are activities nonetheless, activities that can be feigned. Horror is a *spectator's* emotion, and thus it is especially well-suited for the cinema and the visual arts. But this does not yet solve the apparent paradox, that we are horrified by something that we know not to be real. If it is a problem that one fears what one knows not to be real then it would seem to be a problem as well that one is horrified by something that one knows not to be real. One is horrified at the bleeding body on the midnight asphalt of Interstate 35, but is that the same sense in which one is or seems to be horrified at the bleeding body of the victim depicted on the screen as a fictional victim of a fictional monster? The absence of action readiness in horror as opposed to fear is not yet an account of art-horror.

The difference between real horror and art-horror explains the difference between Dan Shaw and me on the perception of *power* in horror (that is, art-horror). He proposes "a genre analysis that posits a catharsis theory of horror-pleasure"[32] and appeals to one of my favorite authors and mentors, Friedrich Nietzsche, whose philosophy of the Will to Power suggests that power motivates all human (and nonhuman) behavior (although it is not always clear whether it is the acquisition of power, the feeling of power, or the discharge of power that serves as this ultimate motivation). Shaw argues that the pleasure we glean from horror films comes from

> our dual identification with both the threatening antagonists and human protagonists in such works. The astounding feats of the monster or human psychotic are what most attracts us to them, for they exhibit powers and abilities far beyond those of mortal men. It is precisely for this reason that we revel in their penchant for wreaking immeasurable havoc. Vicariously sharing in their superhuman acts, we are exhilarated and alarmed by our enjoyment of the forbidden.[33]

Perhaps, but thinking of the WTC catastrophe, however awesome the spectacle and however diabolically clever the plan, what horrifies us is not the power of the forces or the intelligence displayed but rather the sheer awfulness of what happened and the fact that we were utterly powerless to do anything about it. One might imagine an al-Qaeda operative watching his brethren's handiwork from a safe distance and getting considerable pleasure out of it as his takes in the awesome power of the forces unleashed. But, of course, he is not horrified at all. He identifies with the antagonists (Or are they, for him, the protagonists?) and their awesome display of power, and that may be a source of his pleasure. But it is not horror. So, too, in a horror film we may well identify with the protagonist and (as in a Freudian dream) with all of the other characters as well, and this may give us considerable pleasure. But insofar as we do so we are not horrified. Shaw's account may indeed explain at least some of our response to at least part of the genre of art-horror, but I find it quite misleading if it is extended to real horror as well.

The distinction between fear and horror also applies to the distinction between terror and horror. Terror is an extreme form of fear (and I would argue that it, like horror, necessarily excludes pleasure). Terror, too, requires a real danger, or at least the belief that a danger is real. When Cavell insists that "I can be terrified of thunder, but not horrified by it," he assumes that I—like my dogs— believe that it constitutes a real danger to me. (One might wonder how much of the emotional impact of thunder lies in the mere fact of surprise, however. Contrast the startling effect of a sudden "boom!" with the marauding presence of "rolling thunder.") Terror may sometimes result in panic, but panic and terror are still quite different (as are panic and fear). Panic is essentially a physiological reaction, an almost "mindless" urge to flee which, in the absence of restraints, results in fleeing. Patricia Churchland assures me that panic can be electrically stimulated (in a cat, for instance) even in the absence of any perceived danger. Thus, one might even say that panic differs from fear in that it lacks not only belief but an object, although this, I think, is going one step too far. Terror often results in panic insofar as it is rarely reflective and often obsessive. Horror, by contrast, may be overwhelming, but there is no reason to panic if only because there is nowhere to flee. (One can flee what is horrible, of course, but one does not flee the horror, which one carries away as one flees.)

So, too, we should distinguish horror from such emotions as anxiety and dread. Anxiety has also been argued to lack a proper object, notably by Freud, who defined "free-floating anxiety" in exactly that way. (The claim that the object—or the connection between the object and the anxiety—remained "unconscious" somewhat undermined the idea that the anxiety lacks an object). In any case, anxiety has an "obscure" object, but horror, by contrast, has a quite striking and specific object. So, too, with dread, another emotion whose object remains at a distance; thus Kierkegaard took this concept to refer to "the unknown" in an unusually profound way. Dread shares with fear a sense of imminent danger, though it shares with anxiety the obscurity of its object. But so again it differs from horror in two important ways: no imminent danger, and no specific object.

So what is horror? It can indeed be a "primitive" emotion, one that is barely articulatable and in that sense noncognitive (or "cognitively impenetrable," in the latest jargon). But it nevertheless consists of a horrified recognition that things are not as they ought to be, which in turn requires an implicit comparison (if only a "seeing as") and an evaluative judgment or appraisal.[34] The object of horror is concrete as opposed to abstract (although we may secondarily employ such phrases as "I am horrified by the idea that . . . "), specific rather than non-specific. Thus one might dread the unknown or be generally anxious but one is properly horrified only by a particular and more or less immediate event or object of perception. Horror is detached (or at least distanced from) action, however, which distinguishes it from fear. Thus, horror evokes no "action readiness," though one might react *to* the horror, as opposed to *from* fear (e.g., by turning away or screaming). In this sense, it is a spectator emotion, even in real life, and it thereby seems appropriate to talk without paradox about horror in the face of fictional events and objects, for example, in films and in art generally. (The complex state of mind involved in being moved by that which one knows to be make-believe is not a paradox.)

From Horror to Art-Horror

Art-horror is a historical phenomenon, and it has indeed a long history which preceded the advent of cinema and the first film depiction of *The Golem* shortly before World War I by hundreds or thousands of years. Real horror may to some extent depend on the time and the place (what horrifies depends on what is expected and what is believed, and what might be horrible in one circumstance might be routine in another), but art-horror is complicated by the added dimension of genre. Carroll traces art-horror back to the "Gothic" novels of the Enlightenment but before them there were real Gothic horror stories of all sorts, which Carroll too readily dismisses because people actually believed them.[35] This, I think, exaggerates the gap between art-horror and real horror. Moreover, I think that Carroll is wrong—or too much in a hurry to get to his preferred subject of movies—when he insists that the horror genre begins during and as a reaction against the Enlightenment. Before the explicitly depicted horrors of Hell and damnation, there was Petronius' *Satyricon* and the many monsters of the *Odyssey*, not to mention the horrifying manifestations of Shiva and Kali; the malevolent goddesses of the Solomon Islands and the devils of Bali; the monster Grendel in *Beowulf;* and later the perversities of Merlin in Malory's *Morte d'Arthur*. In every human society, there has always been art-horror as well as real horror, that is, depictions and/or stories about what is horrible. These depictions inevitably took on a life of their own, evoking art-horror in place of real horror, whether or not people also continued to believe them.

I also think that Carroll is mistaken in limiting his analysis to the peculiar contemporary experience of sitting in a theater or in front of a television watching one of a large but carefully delimited set of mostly inferior, often silly, and culturally pointless films. There is something to be said for his casual suggestion that horror novels depicting the "unnatural" presupposed the Enlightenment conception of an orderly nature, and I agree with him that the usual Manichean account of horror and much of Romanticism as the "dark side" of the Enlightenment depends on an image that is both inaccurate and obscure. But what Romanticism really represented does not seem to be of any interest to him, including its proclivity for original "Gothic" (i.e., medieval) and ancient pagan mysteries and monsters. What happened in the 18th and 19th centuries is but part of a story that goes back to pre-Biblical times, beginning no doubt when a few rather clever cavemen (or, more likely, cavewomen) scared the pelts off some of the youngsters, no doubt invoking the possible presence of prehistoric monsters which were by no means fictional at the time. Stoking the emotions with (more or less) make-believe horror on the basis of honest to goodness real horror seems to be one of those perennial but often neglected bits of human nature that makes our species both much more interesting and more perverse than it would be if we limited ourselves to real horror alone.

Within the genre of horror films, which (for obvious technological reasons) did not begin before this century, there is a multifaceted history that deserves some attention. It is not insignificant that the genre and all of the early classics began in Germany, despite the fact that the technology was developed in the U.S. and France. It is not incidental that America followed the (defeated) Germans into the genre only several years after the war, and then with a spoof—Paul Leni's *The Cat and the Canary* (1927)—rather than with "straight" horror. Whereas the Germans sought to stoke (or re-stoke) horror, the Americans evidently liked their horror buffered and limited, one step removed, so to speak. It is worth noting as well how "celebrity-bound" the American pictures and their never-ending sequels became. Eventually, Boris Karloff and Bela Lugosi became so identified with the parts they played that a viewing of *The Mummy* (1932), *Frankenstein* (1931), *Dracula* (1931), or any of their many variations became more like spending a few hours with an obnoxious but familiar and entertaining relative rather than subjecting oneself to horror. It is also significant that so many of the horror films made today are what Carroll correctly but disgustingly identifies as "splatter films"— movies where the primary and sometimes sole distinction are the gruesome special effects depicting bodies being mutilated in any number of ways. Our contemporary timidity about horror seems to have led to a propensity for the disgusting, for disgust is a much easier emotion to handle and get over than horror.

Seeking a definition of art-horror (as Carroll does) is an admirable enterprise, but it depends on how we circumscribe the scope of our examples. I think that Carroll makes some overly refined and historically misleading divisions between horror and fantasy, thrillers and monster pictures as such, and we lose a good deal of material that way. It matters a great deal, for example, whether one takes *Jaws* (1975), *King Kong* (1933), *The Blob* (1958), *Night of the Living Dead*, Jean Cocteau's *Beauty and the Beast* (1946), or (Carroll's own apparent favorite) *The Exorcist* (1973) as a paradigm. I join many critics in finding Carroll's exclusion of *Psycho* (1960) lamentable. How about Charles Laughton's *Night of the Hunter* (1955)? There may be no monsters, but there are plenty of tingles and sleepless nights. (How many people still had qualms about closing the shower curtain years after first seeing *Psycho*?) Then there is Walton's green slime, which fits Carroll's definition while the biologically more plausible monster (or rather, monstrous shark) in *Jaws* does not. That is, unless one interprets that particular shark as unnatural—impossibly huge, unusually intelligent and malicious, even sadistic. But I think such an interpretation misses the central point of the movie, which is to present the shark as perfectly possible. Its size is by no means unknown in nature, and I would guess that its behavior is not particularly unusual. But if we are temporarily entertained (hardly horrified) by the blob of green slime, there were certainly many people who continued to express and exhibit horror after Peter Benchley's remarkably well-timed shark attack novel and Steven Spielberg's subsequent movie. On the other hand, the sentimental if somewhat chauvinist giant ape film *King Kong* began as horror and evolved into soap opera, as did any number of other lovable monster movies, including, one could argue, the original (Mary Shelley's and Kenneth Branaugh's) *Frankenstein*.[36]

I do not want to take a stand on the issue of defining art-horror here, but I do want to highlight one particular kind of horror film (and literature) that seems to me most emotionally poignant. It is this sense of inner horror that *The Exorcist* badly mangles but is much better represented in Siegel's *Invasion of the Body Snatchers*, captured nicely by Ron Rosenbaum in his 1979 *Harper's* piece, "Gooseflesh." His is a quasi-religious analysis of horror but I do not think religion is essential to it. A secular paradigm would be the ideologically loaded "Cold War" threats of mind control, such as appear in *Invasion of the Body Snatchers* (the blatant propaganda has been excised from the movie), in Claude Rains' brilliant performance in *The Invisible Man* (1933), where his invisibility soon gives way to megalomania and psychosis,[37] and, more recently, in *Altered States* (1980) and *Alien* (1979). These are all, in one way or another, stories of possession. They may feature what is (currently) scientifically implausible—for instance, a formula to make a person invisible—but the subject of the film is a fundamental human fear, ultimately, the fear of oneself. For the possession need not come from the outside, as an invasion or a peculiar pharmaceutical. More horrifying (because more palpably real) is possession by our own powers.

We can trace a history of such narratives warning against the abuse of one's powers (whether magical, mythical, or alchemical) from the medieval and oriental enchanters and enchantresses who were caught up in their own wizardry to the modern genre of science fiction horror. *Frankenstein*, for instance, coincides with the beginning of the revolution in medical technology, and the horror films of the 1950s coincide with the fears and horrors of the nuclear age. One can also note the contemporary significance of the ancient horror tale of King Midas, which should certainly resonate in the world of Wall Street and now-bankrupt Enron today. Indeed, what the Midas story underscores is the significance of those horror stories without monsters at all, that is, without the sort of "unnatural" or "split" monsters discussed by Carroll. (In this sense, one might consider Oliver Stone's *Wall Street* [1987] a horror film as well as a cautionary tale.) But such examples and the paradigm in general suggest that we should not flat-footedly declare that the difference between art-horror and real horror is that art-horror's objects are fictional. Not only may they be "realistic" and even "based on a true story"; they may in every sense be very real. What makes art-horror art instead of just horror is the fact that it is presented or packaged for impact. Thus there is real merit in Levinson's suggestion that art-horror depends on real horror for its impact and significance, though I would amend his thesis in two ways. First, art-horror may not only depend on real horror for its impact and significance, but the *object* of art-horror may in fact be the object of real horror. Second, not all art-horror has to be based on real horror, if by "real horror" we mean only those non-intellectual, perceptually-based, cognitively impenetrable quasi-belief based emotions. Sometimes the real horror upon which art-horror is based is quite fully articulate and thoughtful, which makes it readily available for packaging and presentation as art-horror.

So Whence the Pleasure in (Art-) Horror?

I said that horror is by its very nature a spectator emotion, but I did not mean to imply by this that it is a detached or disinterested emotion, free from care or concern. On the contrary, horror is necessarily an overwhelming emotional response to what is horrible. But the fact that horror is overwhelming, I hypothesized, also means that it is not one of those emotions that can be "mixed," and, in particular, it does not mix with pleasure. While fear and pleasure readily combine in various ways, horror, by contrast, does not. The conditions under which fear and pleasure combine may be complex. (They need not include the belief that there is not really any cause for fear. On the contrary, the fear enjoyed by most "daredevils" depends on the danger being very real.) But although horror does not combine with pleasure, it may be *followed* by pleasure, for instance, when one is relieved to discover that the horrifying object or event was not as it seemed (e.g., when the apparently dead body of one's elderly but mischievous grandparent suddenly springs to life with a hearty laugh). Moreover, the anticipation of such pleasure may itself be pleasurable. But what is not pleasurable is the horror.

It can be argued that the response evoked or provoked by art-horror is first and foremost a response to the art, not to the horror. This would explain how we can appreciate art-horror rather than just be horrified by it, and why we can even enjoy it. It has often been argued that in art-horror we appreciate the skill of the presentation rather than the subject matter itself. This difference in focus at least diminishes or minimizes the paradox of horror pleasure with respect to art-horror, as it is not the horror but the art we are said to enjoy. Of course, a purely fictional work may evoke horrific memories of real horror (as Levinson argues is always the case), in which case the focus shifts back to the object of horror and away from the art, and pleasure becomes impossible. Thus, Carroll, having rejected religious, Freudian, and ideological accounts, retreats to a purely aesthetic explanation. Carroll claims that what we really find pleasurable in art-horror is the plot, on which he spends considerable time showing us the typical structures. We enjoy "the rhetorical framing of horror, and its narrative form."[38] Art-horror is "an aesthetic contrivance," and monsters are simply "natural subjects for curiosity."[39]

In many so-called horror stories and films, the horror is merely alluded to. The book or film in question is actually a comedy. Indeed, I would venture that the bulk of American horror films are clearly intended in just this way. I think that one problem with Carroll's book (corrected by him since[40]) is his separation of horror from humor. In terms of my earlier hypothesis, that humor and horror are incompatible, I thoroughly agree. But that is quite compatible with saying that horror films are not about horror at all.

Despite its predictably more somber origins in Germany, the horror film in America has almost always been tied up with comedy. The first Hollywood horror film was a spoof, and it was not long before Abbott and Costello and the Three Stooges were sharing the screen with Dracula, Frankenstein's monster, and Lon Chaney Jr. Roger Corman made his reputation with a sequence of films that were much more ludicrous than they were frightening (notably, the original 1960 version of *Little Shop of Horrors*, remade as a Lower East Side play in New York and then as a trendy film with Rick Moranis and Steve Martin.) King Kong is comic as well as cosmic, and Donald Sutherland carries echoes of *M*A*S*H.* (1972) into the podland with him. "Schlock-horror" has continued to be one of lower Hollywood's most prolific subgenres, and many (if not most) of the horror films produced in the last forty years have obviously been intended as laughable rather than terrifying. And this is to say nothing of the many rubber-suited Japanese monsters or the truly inspired horror-comedies of Tim Burton (*Beetlejuice* [1988], *Edward Scissorhands* [1990]), Roman Polanski's *Fearless Vampire Killers* (1967), or George

Hamilton as an implausibly sun-tanned Dracula in *Love at First Bite* (1979).

If art-horror involves mixed emotions, then in accordance with our earlier hypothesis we should insist that the object of pleasant emotions is something other than the object of horror (e.g., the skills required for the effectiveness of the presentation, the techniques displayed, the inter-textual references to other works of the same genre, the little jokes that punctuate even the "scariest" horror films). I do not want to make this an a priori claim, however, and I do not want to ignore questions about the status of intentional objects of emotion. On the contrary, the question of what the intentional object of horror (and art-horror) is will be crucial to understanding, among other things, those cases of art-horror in which we both want to insist and want to deny that the object is the same in both reality and fiction. But I will not address that complex issue here. What I want to suggest is only that the object of (art-) horror is not the object or source of pleasure.

Thus, in accordance with our hypothesis, we might suggest that people do not go to horror films (read books, etc.) to enjoy them, but do so for other reasons—to prove their mettle or to prepare themselves for some future potential horror or to satisfy their curiosity—and *this* they might enjoy. Teenage males go to horror films to prove their bravado and insensitivity. (The promotions challenge: "If you are brave enough to watch!") Their semi-willing girlfriends go along today for the same reason, though a decade or so ago they went along as an excuse to engage in the submissive helpless behavior that modern feminism has now bred out of them.[41] Tenured professors (male and female alike) may sit up late at night, watching once again one of so many mummies stagger back to the vault, but I doubt that the reason is to enjoy (or for that matter even to experience) the horror. More likely, it is in order to study this curious popular phenomenon (though the question "Why choose *this* phenomenon?" cannot be ignored). Watching horror films may be to continue an adolescent ritual. It may be to appreciate the art (though the proportion of films that rewards such an interest is notoriously small). It could even be to regain a youthful machismo or live those years again or, perhaps, to vicariously identify with power and evil (Shaw's Nietzschean interpretation). But sometimes a cigar is just a smoke, and the purpose may be nothing deeper than the desire to wile away a slow Saturday night and enjoy a beer or two, or a glass of wine.

Then, there is the more controversial theory that people use "make-believe" horror to *compensate* for real-life horrors such as those witnessed in New York on September 11th. (We should note that "compensation" is backward-looking, in law, an attempt to right a previous wrong. But what is often intended in this context is forward-looking, as if experiencing fictional horror will lessen future real horror.) But the mechanism for this "compensation" is by no means clear, nor is the similarity between the real horror and the pretend variety. Is the compensation like inoculation (a dose of bacterium B' to ward off an infection by bacterium B), or like homeopathic medicine (a tiny dose of C to ward off a pathogenic dose of C), or a kind of distraction (over-compensation) whereby a massive dose of D overwhelms a modest dose of A (e.g., the old Three Stooges routine where Moe stomps on Curly's right foot to distract his attention from the pain in his left foot?). (The last example is neither backward-looking nor forward-looking, suggesting instead two simultaneous horror experiences.) But in what sense, if any, can the fiction or fantasy of unspeakable horror lessen the horror of something painfully real?

It is a common supposition that exposure to horror, fictional or not, "desensitizes" people, especially children, to real horror; this is an argument that is most often made with reference to violence. To be sure, there is something to the habituation argument (repeated exposure to A lessens the shock of a new instance of A), but shock is not all there is to horror and, besides, it is not clear that any fiction serves to "compensate" for or lessen any real horror. Two instances of real horror may have such an effect on one another, but there is not much evidence that art-horror has much of an effect on the horror of real horror. With reference to violence, there is another, more troublesome set of considerations, that are often confused with the question of "compensation." Suggestible people, especially children, may well *imitate* violent behavior, even the relatively innocent antics of the Three Stooges, causing considerable harm. But this is a matter of *doing*, and as I have argued, horror is not a matter of doing anything so imitation is not relevant to the question of compensation.

It has often been argued that the object of art-horror must at least be a real possibility or at least be associated with an object of real horror. But art-horror cannot be *too* real. The scheduled release of "action" movies was seriously disrupted after September 11th. The reasoning was straightforward; depictions of plane crashes are rarely screened on airplanes, and not just because to do so would be a flagrant violation of taste. (A recent exception was Tom Hanks' *Cast Away* [2000] on transoceanic flights, despite the harrowing enactment of an airplane crash early in the film.) The depiction of an airplane crash too readily evokes the idea of a real airplane crash. To state the obvious: It is not the case that watching a movie about airline crashes, no matter how fictionalized, immunizes a nervous flyer before his or her upcoming trip. So, too, in the weeks following the attack on the WTC, Hollywood editors were busily editing out shots of the Twin Towers and even postponing new releases because they were "just too real" and evocative of the real-life horror. Thus, while one consideration for art-horror may be that its object must be close to a real object, another is that for there to be any pleasure at all, art-horror must remain at a safe distance. Getting these two demands in balance is the (rarely met) challenge of horror filmmakers.

One source of pleasure lies in the sheer fact that we *choose* to watch horror films and read books whose subject matter horrifies us. In control, there is pleasure. Just as it is the self-infliction of pain that brings with it the pleasure of control (though we do not thereby enjoy the pain), it is through the self-infliction of horror that we enjoy a certain amount of control (though we do not thereby enjoy the horror). There is for this reason something suggestive but also sanctimonious about the common complaint that the most effective horror films are "manipulative." *Jaws* was so accused, for example, even by some of the best reviewers in the business. But, of course, what you were paying three dollars for (back in 1975) was precisely to be skillfully manipulated and appropriately horrified. By the same token, however, making it too obvious how you are being manipulated (as in overly "tear-jerking" movies) undermines the effects of the manipulation. We are "willing," in Coleridge's phrase, whether or not we willingly suspend our disbelief. And our willingness itself is conducive to a certain pleasure. (The angry reactions of an unwitting companion, who accompanies you to *Carrie* [1976] or *The Silence of the Lambs* [1991] in the belief that the film will be a romance, provides a telling contrast.) But, again, it does not follow that it is the horror itself that we find pleasurable. What we enjoy is only our ability to choose, or to turn away.

Given that art-horror is by definition horror "mixed" and compromised, if only by being packaged and intentionally presented, several further suggestions present themselves. First, the pleasure lies in precisely the fact that it is make-believe, that it is *not real*.[42] The pleasure is thus not in the horror but in the absence of the horror.

(What we make of the status of make-believe objects or make-believe horror is not essential to this point.) Second, the pleasure comes from the fact that the horror is orchestrated, whether well or badly, such that one can (through identification with the hero or heroes) get some sense of power or control over the horror, which is what is so obviously absent in real-life horror.[43] I think that this point is independent of the many concerns over the nature of empathy and "identification" with fictional characters in fiction. Third, one can satisfy one's curiosity about a certain source of horror, knowing full well that it is only make-believe.[44] Again, the pleasure is not in the horror but in the absence of (or safe distance from) the horror, now mixed with a certain sense of familiarity (and in that sense mastery) of it. Finally, what is uncertain and mysterious is resolved and clarified in the course of the narration.[45] But once again, the pleasure is in the narrative satisfaction, not the horror.

Richard Gilmore tries to explain the pleasure obtained in art-horror with an utterly implausible evolutionary hypothesis, according to which horror is a feeling that originated—and had adaptive value—in children who watched with horror as their parents were killed by marauding beasts or unfriendly neighbors.[46] Thus, the pleasure in horror, he says, is the pleasure of surviving. This, I think, is an unbelievable stretch, first in attributing pleasure of any kind to the children whose parents are being slaughtered and who are obviously threatened themselves as well, and second in trying to derive the giddy amusement that often accompanies art-horror from something so horrible in real life. But the mistake here is not so much the utterly implausible evolutionary hypothesis as it is the much more common insistence that art-horror, as such, gives pleasure. Why else, the argument goes, would people voluntarily (and sometimes frequently) subject themselves to this?

There is a much more plausible analysis of this than a desperate and dubious search for a source of pleasure. Trauma demands repetition. This is not to say that a traumatized person wants the traumatic event itself to be repeated, of course. But James Pennebaker and other trauma psychologists have made much of the need for those who have suffered trauma to relive, revisualize, speak, or write about the trauma, and they have shown that writing or talking about one's experiences allows one to "work through" it.[47] As a consequence, not only do memories of the trauma become less painful, but there are all sorts of health benefits, including reduced stress, improved immune system, and so on.[48] There are some obvious but difficult questions about whether choosing to experience art-horror that is reminiscent of real horror has anything like the results of writing or talking about it. Then, there are all those questions about what precisely the actual or original object of horror might be (whether it is some specific trauma or trauma-type, or whether it is a general working through of trauma as such). But it is at least a plausible hypothesis that willfully exposing oneself to repeated fictional depictions of what once was real horror may have some salutary effects. Again, though, a decrease in pain and trauma should not be confused with pleasure.

In September, people around the world stayed "glued" to their television sets as CNN and other stations repeated the same gruesome scenes over and over and over. This was not just an attempt to get more information (although, to be sure, the networks abused their viewer's hunger for information by imposing those repetitive images on them). Art-horror is a good way to reiterate trauma in a safe and less upsetting way, if only because it (unlike the real horrors in the background) is obviously not real. By contrast, real horror repeated— like the continuous repetition of television images after September 11th—can contribute to and even cause mental illness. With this delicate balance in mind, we might better appreciate director Roman Polanski's translation of his own real-life childhood trauma into some of the most brilliant horror films ever made, including *Repulsion* (1964), *Rosemary's Baby*, and *The Tenant* (1976).[49] But our pleasure, again, is not in the horror. It is in the brilliance with which the art-horror is depicted and the real horror sublimated.

Here is yet another kind of explanation of the supposed pleasure associated with art-horror (and, perhaps, with horror too): *arousal* can be pleasurable, especially in the young.[50] This is not to say that all arousal is pleasurable, and being aroused by horror should not be pleasurable at all. But arousal is indiscriminate, without an essential object, and so it can be redirected from the object that initially provokes it (something horrible) to something else. Thus, Ovid, in his treatise on love, suggests taking ladies to the gladiatorial arena, where they will be sufficiently aroused (though horrified) that their arousal can readily be redirected to sexual passion, transferring that excitement from disgust to lust (just in case you wondered why taking dates to horror movies remains a favorite ritual among adolescents.) But Ovid's thesis has gained considerable empirical (that is, scientific) support in recent years; not to mention the testimonials of any number of seducers from the ancient world to the modern.

Because arousal as such can be pleasurable, one might suppose that horror—as a species of arousal—can be pleasurable. But not all arousal is pleasurable and arousal by horror is, I submit, *never* pleasurable. Sometimes, however (one might argue), the objects of real-life horror really do give pleasure. I hope we can agree that when this happens, it is morally repugnant and the moral repugnance lies precisely in the fact that those who enjoy the horrible no longer find that the horrible provokes horror. The Romans had their "circuses," in which gladiators disemboweled one another and wild animals devoured innocent and often unarmed religious martyrs. The people cheered, delighted by the "performances." They became sufficiently desensitized to suffering that blood and gore, and even screams and tears, could be viewed without compassion. Sadistic dictators in Chile and Argentina during their dark decades also displayed an inhuman insensitivity to their torturers' victims, enjoying and being amused rather than horrified by the horrors. There is some concern that art-horror may have this effect too, desensitizing viewers to suffering and allowing them to view real horror, too, as if it were merely pretend—just special effects. The evidence for this proposition, like the evidence for the thesis that watching violence prompts violence, remains inconclusive, but the pathology of enjoying what ought to provoke horror seems to me undebatable. In short, when people do take pleasure in horror, this is not a question in aesthetics. It is a question in psychopathology which, certain trendy movements aside, is not the same thing.

Conclusion

So, what is horror? Horror is an extremely unpleasant and even traumatizing emotional experience that renders the subject/victim helpless and violates his or her most rudimentary expectations about the world. This way of thinking about horror renders utterly inappropriate any question of enjoying or getting pleasure from horror. There is no "paradox of horror pleasure." Horror is not pleasurable. Aristotle, arguing against Plato, defended the theater and tragedy in particular as preparatory for the emotions and for life. That is why, he argued, we get pleasure from experiences that are not at all pleasurable, from depicted horrible events that evoke fear and pity. But the source of pleasure is not the horror (e.g., the self-mutilation of Oedipus). It is the excellence of the presentation itself, in accordance with the outlines that Aristotle so carefully laid out. Moreover, there is some satisfaction to be gained from the overall experience of having made ourselves face life's horrors. By confronting ourselves with the extremes of life on the page, in the theater, and on the screen, we open ourselves to life's contingencies and we may feel a certain satisfaction, but hardly pleasure, at having done so. But when it comes to real horror, there can be no satisfaction, much less pleasure. Real horror is, without exception, horrible. It is an emotional liability that we bear for the blessing of living, those of us who are so lucky, in a world in which real horror is sufficiently rare that we seek out its mere titillation.

Notes

1. Noël Carroll, *The Philosophy of Horror; or, Paradoxes of the Heart* (New York: Routledge, 1990).

2. Whether horror is an emotion rather than an emotional experience is not a question I want to take very seriously. The category of emotion is sufficiently indistinct, apart from a small set of "basic" emotions (including fear), that I do not think such a question is either interesting or decisively answerable. To muddy such worries even further, "horror" refers to the object of horror as well as to the emotional experience. Thus "horror movie" may refer both to the content of the movie and to the intended reaction of the audience (which Carroll conflates into a single definition of horror as that which provokes those intended effects). But it is the nature of that emotion— and not the content of such movies—that interests me here, insofar as those two questions can be treated separately.

3. Cynthia A. Freeland, "Realist Horror," in *Philosophy and Film*, ed. Cynthia A. Freeland and Thomas Wartenberg (New York: Routledge, 1995), 126–42; Freeland, *The Naked and the Undead: Evil and the Appeal of Horror* (Boulder: Westview Press, 2000), 3.

4. Daniel Shaw, "Determinism and *Dead Ringers*," *Film and Philosophy* 3 (Winter 1996).

5. Carroll, *The Philosophy of Horror*; Sara Waller and Chris Meyers, "Disenstoried Horror: Art Horror Without Narrative," *Film and Philosophy* Special Horror Issue (2001): 117–26.

6. Carroll, *The Philosophy of Horror*.

7. Waller and Meyers, "Disenstoried Horror."

8. Benjamin Halligan, "On The Interval Between Reality and Unreality," *Senses of Cinema* no. 17 (November–December 2001), www.sensesofcinema.com/contents/01/17/symposium/halligan.html (January 15, 2002). Thanks to Steven Schneider for this example.

9. Cynthia Freeland has done a fine job of bringing out the gender issues in a good many horror films, but I think it is okay to insist that men and women were indiscriminately victims in the WTC attack, and that this was an aspect of the horror. See also James Twitchell, *Dreadful Pleasures: An Anatomy of Modern Horror* (Oxford: Oxford University Press, 1985), who traces art-horror back to the supposedly universal horror of incest.

10. Noël Carroll, "Horror, Helplessness, and Vulnerability: A Reply to Robert Solomon," *Philosophy and Literature* 17 (1993): 110–18. But see also Daniel Shaw, "Power, Horror and Ambivalence," *Film and Philosophy*, Special Horror Issue (2001): 1–12; and Daniel Shaw, "The Mastery of Hannibal Lecter," this volume.

11. Jerrold Levinson, "Review of Carroll's *Philosophy of Horror*," *Journal of Aesthetics and Art Criticism* 49 (1991): 253–58.

12. Carroll, *The Philosophy of Horror*.

13. David Hume, "Of Tragedy," in *Of the Standard of Taste and Other Essays* ed. John Lenz (Indianapolis: Bobs-Merrill, 1965).

14. Notably Kendall Walton, in his *Mimesis as Make-Believe: On the Foundations of the Representational Arts* (Cambridge, MA.: Harvard University Press, 1990).

15. I am aware that I am taking on some giants in aesthetic theory with this hypothesis, notably Kant, who thought that the sublime (in nature) provided us with a realistic combination of delight and horror. My simple argument would be that it is not horror that he is actually discussing but simply the "awesome" ("the dynamically sublime"). The lost dog on the fresh sidewalk example is from Johnny Hart ("BC") in Andrew Ortony, et al., *The Cognitive Structure of Emotions* (Cambridge: Cambridge University Press, 1988).

16. *USA Today*, 25 October 2001.

17. I am not alone in this, needless to say. Carroll, Walton, and Freeland, just to name three, also defend a largely cognitivist account of horror. Carroll seems particularly attracted and attached to William Lyons' theory of emotion as a physiological disturbance caused by cognition. See Lyons, *Emotion* (Cambridge: Cambridge University Press, 1980). This theory has both its advantages and disadvantages. The most obvious advantage (in my not unbiased opinion) is that it places proper attention on the role of "beliefs" (or some sort of "cognition") in the constitution of emotion in general and horror in particular. The main disadvantage is that it puts too much attention on the sheer physiology of the experience, particularly on the shivers and shudders that are typically provided (even promised) as part of the price of horror movie admission. Carroll defines the horror experience, in part, as disgust, an exceedingly visceral sensation (though arguably not an emotion at all), and it is all too tempting to suggest that horror *is* just this set of sensations.

18. See, e.g., Paul Rozin, J. Haidt, and C. McCauley, "Disgust," in *The Handbook of Emotions* (2nd ed.), ed. M. Lewis and J. Haviland-Jones (New York: Guilford Press, 2000), 637–53. On disgust as a "basic emotion," see Paul Ekman, "An Argument for Basic Emotions," *Cognition and Emotion* 69 (1992): 169–200.

19. Edward R. Royzman and John Sabini, "Something It Takes to Be an Emotion: The Interesting Case of Disgust," *Journal for the Study of Social Behavior* 31, no. 1 (March 2001): 29-60.

20. Royzman and Sabini, "Something It Takes to Be an Emotion."

21. Notably in Levinson, "Review of Carroll's *Philosophy of Horror*"; and Jerrold Levinson, "The Place of Real Emotion in Response to Fictions," *Journal of Aesthetics and Art Criticism* 48 (1990): 79–80.

22. Paul Ekman, "All Emotions Are Basic" in *The Nature of Emotion: Fundamental Questions*, ed. Paul Ekman and Richard Davidson (Oxford: Oxford University Press, 1994).

23. Notably Joseph Ledoux, *The Emotional Brain: The Mysterious Underpinnings of Emotional Life* (New York: Touchstone, 1998); and Antonio Damasio, *The Feeling of What Happens: Body and Emotion in the Making of Consciousness* (New York: Harcourt Brace, 1999).

24. The definitive book on disgust is William Ian Miller's *The Anatomy of Disgust* (Cambridge, MA: Harvard University Press, 1997).

25. Sara Waller and Chris Meyers, "Disenstoried Horror." Steven Schneider argues that "Horror film monsters are best understood as metaphorical embodiments of paradigmatic horror narratives." See his "Monsters as (Uncanny) Metaphors: Freud, Lakoff, and the Representation of Monstrosity in Cinematic Horror," in *Horror Film Reader*, ed. Alain Silver and James Ursini (New York: Limelight Editions, 2000), 173.

26. *Readings in Animal Cognition*, ed. M. Bekoff and D. Jamieson (Cambridge, MA: MIT Press, 1996); Jeffrey Moussaieff Masson, *When Elephants Weep: The Emotional Lives of Animals* (New York: Dell Press, 1995).

27. Jenefer Robinson, "Startle," *Journal of Philosophy* 92, no. 2 (February 1995): 53–74. Cf. Robert Baird, "The Startle Effect: Implications for Spectator Cognition and Media Theory," *Film Quarterly* 53, no. 3 (Spring 2000): 12–24.

28. Carroll, *The Philosophy of Horror*, 36. Recent work in psychology on the "startle response" has tended to the same conclusion. Paul Ekman, for example, took shock and surprise as an emotional paradigm in much of his early work on the facial expression of emotion. He now rejects surprise as an emotion proper and classes it rather as a straightforward reflex.

29. Keith Oatley, *Best Laid Schemes: The Psychology of Emotions* (Cambridge: Cambridge University Press, 1992); Martha Nussbaum,

Upheavals of Thought: The Intelligence of Emotions (Cambridge: Cambridge University Press, 2001).

30. René Descartes, *The Passions of the Soul*, trans. S. H. Voss (Indianapolis: Hackett, 1989), Article LXX.

31. Stanley Cavell, *The Claim of Reason: Wittgenstein, Skepticism, Morality and Tragedy* (New York: Oxford University Press, 1979), 418.

32. Shaw, "Power, Horror and Ambivalence."

33. Shaw, "Power, Horror and Ambivalence."

34. By "evaluative judgment" and "appraisal," I do not mean the reflective varieties in which deliberation and articulation are predominant, but the "pre-reflective" versions which are essential to even the most primitive emotion and perception. See, e.g., Antonio Damasio, *Descartes' Error: Emotion, Reason, and the Human Brain* (New York: Putnam, 1994).

35. The Catholic church, for example, made a specialty of horror. In the name of "sexual renunciation," sexual organs were self-removed. In *The Body and Society: Men, Women, and Sexual Renunciation in Early Christianity* (New York: Columbia University Press, 1988), Peter Brown describes a wide variety of medieval self-castrations, one with a sickle. Today, we have movies like *Jaws* and a hundred lesser Saturday night specials, in which girls who "do it" are the first ones to go.

36. See Harvey Roy Greenberg, "Heimlich Maneuvers: On a Certain Tendency of Horror and Speculative Cinema," in *The Horror Film and Psychoanalysis: Freud's Worst Nightmares*, ed. Steven Jay Schneider (Cambridge: Cambridge University Press, forthcoming 2003).

37. See J. P. Telotte's chapter, this volume.

38. Carroll, *The Philosophy of Horror*, 179–81.

39. Carroll, *The Philosophy of Horror*, 182.

40. Noël Carroll, "Horror and Humor," *Journal of Aesthetics and Art Criticism* 57, no. 2 (Spring 1998): 145–60.

41. Cf. Linda Williams, "When Women Look: A Sequel," *Senses of Cinema* no. 15 (July–August 2001): www.sensesofcinema.com/contents/01/15/horror_women.html (June 3, 2003).

42. Walton, *Mimesis as Make-Believe*.

43. Shaw, "Power, Horror and Ambivalence."

44. Carroll, *The Philosophy of Horror*.

45. Waller and Meyers, "Disenstoried Horror."

46. Richard Gilmore, "Horror and Death at the Movies," *Film and Philosophy*, Special Horror Issue (2001): 127–42.

47. James Pennebaker, *Opening Up: The Healing Power of Confiding in Others* (New York: Guilford, 1996).

48. Roger Booth and James Pennebaker, "Emotions and Immunity," in *Handbook of Emotions*, ed. Michael Lewis and Jeannette M. Haviland (New York: Guilford, 2001), 558–70.

49. See Aaron Smuts, "Sympathetic Spectators: Roman Polanski's *Le Locataire* (*The Tenant*, 1976)," *Kinoeye: A Fortnightly Journal of Film in the New Europe* 2, no. 3, February 4, 2002: http://www.kinoeye.org/02/03/smuts03 .html (February 11, 2002).

50. Torben Grodal, *Moving Pictures: A New Theory of Film Genres, Feelings, and Cognition* (Oxford: Oxford University Press, 1997).

A Reply to "Real Horror"
Daniel Shaw

Imagine, if you will, that the filmmakers behind the original *Thirty Seconds Over Tokyo* (1944) abandoned its quasi-documentary style and added the following scene. Seeing the mission going awry, Colonel James Doolittle (Spencer Tracy) spots two highrise government buildings in the heart of the city. In a suicidal attack, he aims his B-25 directly at them, and (by some Hollywood miracle) manages to bring them both down. Audiences in 1944 America would have roared their approval.

As Bob Solomon admits, a member of al-Qaeda watching the crashes on CNN from his Hamburg hideaway, would have felt a similar, though much more intense, elation at the spectacle. The ability of his organization to strike at the primary symbol of the infidel's financial empire would have provided him with an exhilarating sense of power, a feeling (since he no doubt believes in the justice of his cause) relatively unhindered by any moral qualms about killing 3,000 innocent civilians. The horror that I felt watching the towers collapse was grounded in my sense of the almost unimaginable evil that was being perpetrated before my very eyes. Our experience of art-horror, on the other hand, is a far more ambivalent admixture of attraction to and repulsion from the evil force, which can be experienced as pleasurable only because it is clearly fictional.

Again, imagine watching the same sequence of WTC collapse images CGI-generated as part of an action film like *Speed* (1994) (I was struck by how much the original CNN footage looked like a movie anyway). If we are immersed in it, the horror we feel at seeing such a thing can be pleasurable precisely because we never suspend disbelief so thoroughly that we forget we are viewing a fictional film. Watching real people actually die is a radically different experience from watching fictional people only apparently doing so. But that doesn't mean that art-horror and real horror are totally different emotions.

Cynthia Freeland has convincingly argued in her book *The Naked and the Undead* that a confrontation with evil is at the heart of most horror films.[1] I agree, and have also made the notion an integral part of my power-centered theory of horror.[2] Briefly, I contend that most horror films have a power struggle between evil monsters and good human protagonists as their narrative engine, and that the pleasure we take in horror comes from the vicarious power we feel by identifying both with the monstrous force and with the humans trying to eradicate it. We can experience these confrontations with such evil forces as pleasurable precisely because of their fictional status. If Hannibal Lecter were running around loose and fixing to terrorize my family, I could no longer experience his character as such a cinematic delight.

But, of course, I felt real, unmitigated, and totally unpleasant horror in response to the WTC collapse because I knew it was actually happening to living persons. The same sequence, in a fictional film, could have been exquisitely pleasurable (I love old disaster flicks like *The Towering Inferno* [1974]), even if its perpetrators are portrayed as totally evil. So I don't see how the real horror we felt on 9/11 puts the lie to the notion that a feeling of vicarious power is the major cause of the pleasurable aspect of our experience of art-horror.

Our real feelings of horror are greater in proportion to the power of the horrific force. A hurricane that can wipe Galveston off the face of the earth is more horrifying than one that results in moderate property damage. The WTC attacks were more horrifying than the assault on the Pentagon, and not just because the latter is the headquarters of the military. Digging up the remains of over thirty young men in the crawlspace of the house of John Wayne Gacy was more horrifying than finding the bodies of two young girls crudely buried in somebody's backyard. In each case, the greater the power of the horrifying force, the greater the real horror that we feel in the face of it.

Professor Solomon grudgingly talks about feelings of awe that the WTC spectacle called up in us, but discounts these as being easily overwhelmed by the horror that was our predominant reaction. What was awesome was precisely the incredible impact of the two suicidal crashes, which far surpassed even the plotters' expectations. Our moral outrage at the injustice of the event precluded our enjoyment of its immensity; on that I completely agree with Bob. But, rather than refuting my proposed theory of the pleasures of art-horror, this fact serves only to illustrate it.

Why we could enjoy seeing the very same images CGI generated in an action flick and could not in real life is because of our awareness that the former would be fiction while the latter was decidedly not. Analogously, one would have to be mentally ill to delight in watching a Michael Myers-type serial killer enact his crimes in real life. But most theories of horror-pleasure do not so characterize the fans that revel in such cinematic attractions.

Furthermore, when Solomon traces the roots of horror back to mythology and religion, he talks about "stoking the emotions with (more or less) make-believe horror on the basis of honest-to-goodness real horror" as a perennial part of human nature. How can one "stoke" the other if they are not fundamentally similar? Indeed, he makes this claim in a passage where he faults Noël Carroll for drawing the line too strictly between the two. He even singles out for discussion a common type of horror film that warns against the abuse of one's powers. While this type of cautionary tale is rather prevalent, it seems to me that we enjoy it precisely because of the power of the overreaching transgressors (this is nicely illustrated by David Cronenberg's *The Fly* [1986]), as well as from seeing them get their comeuppance. The Frankenstein tale continues to fascinate us because it deals with that ultimate power, the creation of life.

Despite many able criticisms of Carroll's *The Philosophy of Horror*,[3] Solomon still fundamentally agrees with him that "the object of art-horror is not the object or source of pleasure." Both theorists deny that our horrified response is in any sense ambivalent, and both contend that horror *per se* is unmitigatedly unpleasant. Concluding from his analysis of our response to 9/11 that horror is not an emotion that mixes well with others, Solomon argues that people must be enjoying some other facet of the experience, either as satisfying their curiosity about impossible beings, as an astringent psychical preparation for (or reenactment of) real horrors, or as an adolescent rite of passage that gives young people an opportunity to prove their mettle in the face of what disgusts them. He even admits that some might be seeking the vicarious identification with powerfully evil entities on which my theory focuses. But he wants to say that all these are *different from* the feeling of horror *per se* and our immediate response to the horrific object that causes it.

My view is that, in horror films, we do enjoy the horrific objects *themselves*, and that this is possible only because of their clearly fictional status. Of course real horror isn't pleasurable, because our moral outrage is so great that it overwhelms any attraction we may have to its cause. But that doesn't prove that art-horror is different in kind from the real variety. Rather, art-horror is caused by a fictional object, which can be enjoyed for its sheer power, and without our attraction to what horrifies us being precluded by our ethical sensibilities.

As indicated by his description of the horror genre as forming a "large but carefully delineated set of mostly inferior, often silly and culturally pointless" productions, I suspect that Professor Solomon is not a true aficionado here. Horror films are not "culturally pointless"; indeed, recent work in the philosophy of horror has mined the genre for rich cultural and philosophical insights. They *are* mostly inferior and often silly, both because they are so popular that handsome profits can be made on low-budget productions, and because it is no small accomplishment to make a really terrifying film.

Solomon likens the experience of art-horror to the self-infliction of pain, contending that both give us a feeling of control. He observes as well that horror films convey a sense of control through our identification with the hero or heroes that overcome the monstrous force. They can also, on his view, serve as reenactments of real traumatic events, reenactments that are able to ease the painful impact of such events without making the cinematic experiences "pleasurable" in themselves.

Again, likening the experience of art-horror to the self-infliction of pain seems to indicate that Professor Solomon does not really enjoy it. Those of us who are obsessed with the genre do revel in its unique pleasures, and not with the sado-masochistic glee of a self-mutilator. But his latter comment sounds remarkably like what I have been contending, that our identification with the protagonists of horror give us a vicarious feeling of power or control by overcoming the monstrous force. While he clearly denies that we ever pleasurably identify with the monstrous force *per se*, he seems to embrace the second aspect of my dual identification theory.[4]

Notes

1. Cynthia A. Freeland, *The Naked and the Undead: Evil and the Appeal of Horror* (Boulder: Westview Press, 2000).

2. See my "Power, Horror and Ambivalence." *Film & Philosophy* Special Horror Issue (2001): 1–12.

3. Noël Carroll, *The Philosophy of Horror; or, Paradoxes of the Heart* (New York: Routledge, 1990).

4. An abbreviated form of Solomon's essay, and Shaw's reply, were first presented at the American Society for Aesthetics National Conference in Coral Gables, Florida in November of 2002.

Bibliography

Alderman, Harold. *Nietzsche's Gift* (Athens: Ohio University Press, 1977).

Alford, C. Fred. *What Evil Means to Us* (Ithaca: Cornell University Press, 1997).

Andrew, Dudley. *Concepts in Film Theory* (Oxford: Oxford University Press, 1984).

Aristotle, *Nichomachean Ethics*, trans. Martin Ostwald (Indianapolis and New York: Bobbs-Merrill, 1962).

———. *On Rhetoric*, trans. George A. Kennedy (New York and Oxford: Oxford University Press, 1991).

———. *Poetics*, ed. and trans. Stephen Halliwell (Cambridge, MA and London: Harvard University Press, 1995).

Auden, W. H. "The Guilty Vicarage" (1948). In *The Dyer's Hand, and Other Essays* (New York: Vintage, 1968), 150–53.

Badley, Linda. "The Darker Side of Genius: The (Horror) Auteur Meets Freud's Theory." In *The Horror Film and Psychoanalysis: Freud's Worst Nightmares*, ed. Steven Jay Schneider (Cambridge: Cambridge University Press, forthcoming 2003).

Baird, Robert. "The Startle Effect: Implications for Spectator Cognition and Media Theory." *Film Quarterly* 53, no. 3 (Spring 2000): 12–24.

Bansak, Edmund. *Fearing the Dark: The Val Lewton Career* (Jefferson, NC: McFarland & Co., 1995).

Barker, Martin. "Violence Redux." In *New Hollywood Violence*, ed. Steven Jay Schneider (Manchester, U.K.: Manchester University Press, forthcoming 2003).

Barker, Martin and Julian Petley (eds.). *Ill Effects: The Media-Violence Debate* (London: Routledge, 1997).

Barker, Martin and Kate Brooks. *"Judge Dredd": Its Friends, Fans and Foes* (Luton, U.K.: University of Luton Press, 1998).

Barratt, Daniel H. "The Paradox of Emotion Revisited: Uncovering the Emotional Foundations of Pictorial Representations" (unpublished manuscript).

Barzun, Jacques. "Romanticism." In *The Penguin Encyclopedia of Horror and the Supernatural*, ed. Jack Sullivan (New York: Penguin, 1986).

Baz, Avner. "What's the Point of Seeing Aspects?" *Philosophical Investigations* 23, no. 2 (2000).

Bazin, André. "The Ontology of the Photographic Image," (1945). In *What Is Cinema? Volume 1*, ed. Hugh Gray (Berkeley: University of California Press, 1967), 9–16.

Bekoff, M. and D. Jamieson (eds.). *Readings in Animal Cognition* (Cambridge, MA: MIT Press, 1996).

Bernay, Jacob. "Aristotle on the Effect of Tragedy." *Articles on Aristotle*, Vol. 4, ed. Jonathan Barnes, Malcolm Schofield, and Richard Sorabji (London: Duckworth, 1979).

Black, Joel. *The Aesthetics of Murder: A Study in Romantic Literature and Contemporary Culture* (Baltimore: The Johns Hopkins University Press, 1991).

Blanchot, Maurice. *The Gaze of Orpheus*, trans. Lydia Davis (New York: Station Hill, 1981).

Booth, Roger and James Pennebaker. "Emotions and Immunity." In *Handbook of Emotions*, ed. Michael Lewis and Jeannette M. Haviland (New York: Guilford, 2001), 558–70.

Bordwell, David. *The Films of Carl-Theodor Dreyer* (Berkeley: University of California Press, 1981).

Brown, Peter. *The Body and Society: Men, Women, and Sexual Renunciation in Early Christianity* (New York: Columbia University Press, 1988).

Buchan, John. *The Power-House* (London: Great Pan, 1961).

Carroll, Noël. "Disgust or Fascination: A Response to Susan Feagin." *Philosophical Studies* 65, nos. 1–2 (1992): 85–90.

———. "Enjoying Horror Fictions: A Reply to Gaut," *The British Journal of Aesthetics* 35, no. 1 (1995): 67–72.

———. "Horror and Humor." *Journal of Aesthetics and Art Criticism* 57, no. 2 (Spring 1999): 145–60.

———. "Horror, Helplessness, and Vulnerability: A Reply to Robert Solomon." *Philosophy and Literature* 17 (1993): 110–18.

———. "A Paradox of the Heart: A Response to Alex Neill." *Philosophical Studies* 65, nos. 1–2 (1992): 67–74.

———. *The Philosophy of Horror; or, Paradoxes of the Heart* (New York and London: Routledge, 1990).

Cavell, Stanley. "Aesthetic Problems in Modern Philosophy." In *Must We Mean What We Say?* (New York: Charles Scribner's Sons, 1969).

———. *The Claim of Reason: Wittgenstein, Skepticism, Morality, and Tragedy* (New York: Oxford University Press, 1979).

Cazeaux, Clive. *The Continental Aesthetics Reader* (London: Routledge, 2000).

Chatman, Seymour. *Coming to Terms: The Rhetoric of Narrative in Fiction and Film* (Ithaca: Cornell University Press, 1990).

Cherry, Brigid. "Refusing to Refuse to Look: Female Viewers of the Horror Film." In *Identifying Hollywood's Audiences: Cultural Identity and the Movies*, ed. Richard Maltby and Melvyn Stokes (London: BFI Publishing, 1999), 187–204.

Cioffi, Frank. *Wittgenstein on Freud and Frazer* (Cambridge: Cambridge University Press, 1998).

Clack, Brian. *Wittgenstein, Frazer and Religion* (London: Macmillan, 1999).

Clover, Carol J. *Men, Women, and Chain Saws: Gender in the Modern Horror Film* (Princeton: Princeton University Press, 1992).

Coleridge, Samuel Taylor. *The Statesman's Manual*, ed. W. G. T. Shedd (New York, 1875).

Counts, Kyle B. and Steve Rubin. "The Making of Alfred Hitchcock's *The Birds*." *Cinefantastique* 10, no. 2 (Fall 1980): 26.

Cowie, Elizabeth. "The Spectacle of Actuality." In *Collecting Visible Evidence*, ed. Jane Gaines and Michael Renov (Minnesota: University of Minnesota Press, 1999), 19–45.

Creed, Barbara. *The Monstrous-Feminine: Film, Feminism, Psychoanalysis* (London: Routledge, 1993).

Dalle Vacche, Angela. "F. W. Murnau's *Nosferatu*: Romantic Painting as Horror and Desire in Expressionist Cinema." In *Cinema and Painting: How Art Is Used in Film* (Austin: University of Texas Press, 1996).

Damasio, Antonio. *Descartes' Error: Emotion, Reason, and the Human Brain* (New York: Quill, 2000).

———. *The Feeling of What Happens: Body and Emotion in the Making of Consciousness* (New York: Harcourt Brace, 1999).

De Lauretis, Teresa, *Alice Doesn't: Feminism, Semiotics, Cinema* (Bloomington: Indiana University Press, 1984.

De Quincey, Thomas. "On Murder Considered as One of the Fine Arts" (1827). In *The Collected Writings of Thomas De Quincey, Volume XIII* (Edinburgh: Adam & Charles Black, 1890).

Debord, Guy. *The Society of the Spectacle*, trans. Donald Nicholson-Smith (New York: Zone Books, 1995).

Descartes, René. *The Passions of the Soul*, trans. S. H. Voss (Indianapolis: Hackett, 1989), Article LXX.

Dewey, John. *Art as Experience* (New York: Capricorn, 1958).

———. "The Live Creature and Etherial Things." In *The Philosophy of John Dewey*, ed. John J. McDermott (Chicago: University of Chicago Press, 1981).

———. *The Quest for Certainty* ed. Jo Ann Boydston (Carbondale: Southern Illinois University Press, 1990).

Dietz, Mary Lou. "Killing Sequentially: Expanding the Parameters of the Conceptualization of Serial and Mass Killers." Paper presented at the First International Conference on "Serial and Mass Murder: Theory, Research, and Policy," University of Windsor, Windsor, Canada (April 3–5, 1992).

Dobash, R. Emerson and Russell Dobash. *Violence Against Wives: A Case Against the Patriarchy* (New York: Free Press, 1979).

Doss-Davezac, Shehira. "Schopenhauer According to the Symbolists." In *Schopenhauer, Philosophy, and the Arts*, ed. Dale Jacquette (Cambridge: Cambridge University Press, 1996).

Durgnat, Raymond. *Franju* (London: Studio Vista Movie Paperbacks, 1967).

Dyer, Richard. *Se7en* (London: BFI Publishing, 1999).

Ebert, Roger. "Hollow Man." *Chicago Sun-Times* (August 4, 2000).

Ekman, Paul. "All Emotions Are Basic." In *The Nature of Emotion: Fundamental Questions*, ed. Paul Ekman and Richard Davidson (Oxford: Oxford University Press, 1994).

———. "An Argument for Basic Emotions." *Cognition and Emotion* 69 (1992): 169–200.

Eliot, T. S. *The Complete Poems and Plays of T.S. Eliot* (London: Faber & Faber, 1975).

Fahey, Paul Alan. "'Alfred Hitchcock's *Rope*': a director and his cast uncover Rupert's true sexual identity." *The MacGuffin* 28 (May 2002).

Feagin, Susan L. "Monsters, Disgust and Fascination." *Philosophical Studies* 65, nos. 1–2 (1992): 75–84.

Felleman, Susan. "Playing with Fire: Women, Art and Danger in American Movies of the 1980s." In *New Hollywood Violence*, ed.

Steven Jay Schneider (Manchester, U.K.: Manchester University Press, forthcoming 2003).

Fletcher, Angus. *Allegory: The Theory of a Symbolic Mode* (Ithaca: Cornell University Press, 1964).

Foucault, Michel. *Discipline and Punish*, trans. Alan Sheridan (New York: Vintage Books, 1979).

——. "Space, Knowledge, Power." In *The Foucault Reader*, ed. Paul Rabinow (New York: Pantheon Books, 1984).

Frazer, James. *The Golden Bough* (London: Macmillan, 1992).

Freeland, Cynthia A. *The Naked and the Undead: Evil and the Appeal of Horror* (Boulder: Westview Press, 2002).

——. "Plot Imitates Action: Aesthetic Evaluation and Moral Realism in Aristotle's *Poetics*." In *Essays on Aristotle's Poetics*, ed. Amélie Oskenberg Rorty (Princeton: Princeton University Press, 1992), 111–32.

——. "Realist Horror." In *Philosophy and Film*, ed. Cynthia Freeland and Thomas Wartenberg (New York: Routledge, 1995), 126–42.

Freud, Sigmund. *Beyond the Pleasure Principle* (1920). In *The Standard Edition of the Complete Works of Sigmund Freud, Volume 18*, trans. James Strachey (London: The Hogarth Press, 1953–74). Hereafter cited as *SE*.

——. *The Ego and the Id* (1923). In *SE, Volume 19*.

——. *Inhibitions, Symptoms and Anxiety* (1926 [1925]). *SE, Volume 19*.

——. "The 'Uncanny'" (1919). *SE, Volume 17*, 217–56.

Frye, Northrop. *The Anatomy of Criticism: Four Essays* (Princeton: Princeton University Press, 1957).

Fujiwara, Chris. *Jacques Tourneur: The Cinema of Nightfall* (Jefferson, NC: McFarland & Co., 1998).

Gaut, Berys. "The Enjoyment Theory of Horror: A Reply to Carroll." *The British Journal of Aesthetics* 35, no. 3 (1995): 284–89.

——. "The Paradox of Horror." *The British Journal of Aesthetics* 33, no. 4 (1993): 333–45.

Gelder, Ken. *Reading the Vampire* (New York: Routledge, 1994).

Gilmore, Richard. "Horror and Death at the Movies." *Film and Philosophy*, Special Horror Issue (2001): 127–42.

Graczyk, Michael. "Odyssey of Henry Lee Lucas." *Houston Chronicle* (August 15, 1993): 5D.

Grant, Barry Keith. "Rich and Strange: The Yuppie Horror Film." In *Contemporary Hollywood Cinema*, ed. Steve Neale and Murray Smith (New York: Routledge, 1998), 280–93.

Greenberg, Harvey Roy. "Heimlich Maneuvers: On a Certain Tendency of Horror and Speculative Cinema." In *The Horror Film and Psychoanalysis: Freud's Worst Nightmares*, ed. Steven Jay Schneider (Cambridge: Cambridge University Press, forthcoming 2003).

Grodal, Torben. *Moving Pictures: A New Theory of Film Genres, Feelings, and Cognitions* (Oxford: Oxford University Press, 1999).

Halligan, Benjamin. "On The Interval Between Reality and Unreality." *Senses of Cinema* 17 (November/December 2001).

Hantke, Steffen. "Monstrosity Without a Body: Representational Strategies in the Popular Serial Killer Film." *Post Script: Essays in Film and the Humanities* 22, no. 2 (Winter/Spring 2003): 32–50.

Harari, Roberto. *Lacan's Seminar on Anxiety* (New York: The Other Press, 2001).

Hardy, Phil. *Horror* (London: Aurum Press, 1985).

Harris, Thomas. *Hannibal* (New York: Random House, 1999).

——. *The Silence of the Lambs* (New York: St. Martin's Paperbacks, 1988).

Heidegger, Martin. *Being and Time*, trans. Joan Stambaugh (Albany: SUNY Press, 1996).

Hills, Matt. *The Pleasures of Horror* (London: Continuum, forthcoming 2003).

Hitchcock, Alfred. "Alfred Hitchcock on His Films," a discussion with Huw Wheldon. *The Listener* (August 6, 1964).

——. "Let 'Em Play God." In *Hitchcock on Hitchcock: Selected Writings and Interviews*, ed. Sidney Gottlieb (Berkeley: University of California Press, 1995). Essay originally published in *Hollywood Reporter* 100.47 (October 11, 1948, 18th Anniversary issue).

——. "Why Thrillers Thrive." In *Hitchcock on Hitchcock: Selected Writings and Interviews*, ed. Sidney Gottlieb (Berkeley: University of California Press, 1995). Essay originally published in *Picturegoer* (January 18, 1936).

Hoover, Michael and Lisa Stokes. "Enfant Terrible: The Terrorful, Wonderful World of Anthony Wong." In *Fear Without Frontiers: Horror Cinema Across the Globe*, ed. Steven Jay Schneider (Surrey, U.K.: FAB Press, 2003), 45-59.

Hume, David. "Of Tragedy" (1757). In *Of the Standard of Taste and Other Essays*, ed. John W. Lenz (Indianapolis: Bobbs-Merrill, 1965).

Humphries, Patrick. *The Films of Alfred Hitchcock* (London: Bison Books, 1986).

Jackson, Rosemary. *Fantasy: The Literature of Subversion* (London: Methuen, 1981).

Janaway, Christopher. *Schopenhauer* (Oxford: Oxford University Press, 1994).

Jancovich, Mark. *Horror* (London: Batsford, 1992).

———. *Rational Fears: American Horror in the 1950s* (Manchester, U.K.: Manchester University Press, 1996).

Kael, Pauline. "Are Movies Going to Pieces?" *The Atlantic Monthly* 214, no. 6 (December 1964): 61–81.

Kalat, David. "*Se7en* vs. *Dr. Phibes*," *Midnight Marquee Monsters* 61 (Fall 1999): 36–42.

Keesey, Pam. "*The Haunting* and the Power of Suggestion: Why Robert Wise's Film Continues to 'Deliver the Goods' to Modern Audiences." In *Horror Film Reader*, ed. Alain Silver and James Ursini (New York: Limelight Editions, 2000), 305–15.

Kierkegaard, Sören. *The Living Thoughts of Kierkegaard*, presented by W. H. Auden (Bloomington: Indiana University Press, 1963).

Kirkland, Bruce. "*Psycho* a killer." *Toronto Sun* (April 14, 2000).

Kristeva, Julia. "Ellipsis on Dread and the Specular Seduction" (1975), trans. Dolores Burdick. *Wide Angle* 3, no. 3 (1979): 42–47.

———. *The Powers of Horror*, trans. Leon Roudiez (New York: Columbia University Press, 1982).

Krohn, Bill. *Hitchcock at Work* (London: Phaidon, 2000).

———. "Le musée secret de monsieur Hitchcock." In *Cahiers du Cinéma* (juillet/août 2001): 66–71.

Krzywinska, Tanya. "Demon Daddies: Gender, Ecstasy and Terror in the Possession Film." In *Horror Film Reader*, ed. Alain Silver and James Ursini (New York: Limelight Editions, 2000), 247–67.

La Caze, Marguerite. "The Mourning of Loss in *The Sixth Sense*." *Post Script: Essays in Film and the Humanities* 21, no. 3 (Summer 2002): 111–21.

Lacan, Jacques. *The Ethics of Psychoanalysis*, trans. Denis Potter (London: Tavistock/Routledge, 1992).

———. *The Four Fundamental Concepts of Psycho-analysis*, trans. Alan Sheridan (Harmondsworth, U.K.: Penguin Books, 1979).

Laplanche, Jean. "Interpretation between Determinism and Hermeneutics." In *Essays on Otherness* (London: Routledge, 1999).

Lear, Jonathan. "Katharsis." In *Essays on Aristotle's Poetics*, ed. Amélie Oskenberg Rorty (Princeton: Princeton University Press, 1992), 315–40.

LeDoux, Joseph. *The Emotional Brain: The Mysterious Underpinnings of Emotional Life* (New York: Touchstone, 1998).

Leff, Leonard J. *Hitchcock and Selznick: The Rich and Strange Collaboration of Alfred Hitchcock and David O. Selznick in Hollywood* (London: Weidenfeld & Nicolson, 1987).

Leggio, Maria B., et al. "Representation of Actions in Rats: The Role of Cerebellum in Learning Spatial Performances by Observation." *Proceedings of the National Academy of Sciences, USA* 97, no. 5 (2000): 2320–325.

Levinson, Jerrold. "The Place of Real Emotion in Response to Fictions." *Journal of Aesthetics and Art Criticism* 48 (Winter 1990): 79–80.

——. "Review of Carroll's *Philosophy of Horror*." *Journal of Aesthetics and Art Criticism* 49 (1991): 253–58.

Lienhardt, Godfrey. *Divinity and Experience: The Religion of the Dinka* (Oxford: Oxford University Press, 1961).

Loban, Lelia and Richard Valley. "The Pictures of Dorian Gray." *Scarlet Street* 41 (n.d.).

Lowenstein, Adam. "Films Without a Face: Shock Horror in the Cinema of Georges Franju." *Cinema Journal* 37, no. 4 (Summer 1998): 37–58.

Lyons, William. *Emotion* (Cambridge: Cambridge University Press, 1980).

Masson, Jeffrey Moussaieff. *When Elephants Weep: The Emotional Lives of Animals* (New York: Dell Press, 1995).

Matravers, Derek. *Art and Emotion* (Oxford: Oxford University Press, 2001).

McConnell, Frank D. *The Spoken Seen: Film and the Romantic Imagination* (Baltimore: Johns Hopkins University Press, 1975).

McDermott, John. *The Culture of Experience: Philosophical Essays in the American Grain* (New York: New York, 1976).

McDonagh, Maitland. Interview with Julian Hobbs. *Time Out* (New York edition, October 26–November 2, 2000): 109.

Miller, William Ian. *The Anatomy of Disgust* (Cambridge, MA.: Harvard University Press, 1997).

Milton, John. *Milton*, 2nd edition, ed. Maynard Mack (Englewood Cliffs, NJ: Prentice Hall, 1961).

Modleski, Tania. "The Terror of Pleasure: The Contemporary Horror Film and Postmodern Theory." In *Studies in Entertainment: Critical Approaches to Mass Culture*, ed. Tania Modleski (Bloomington: Indiana University Press, 1986), 155–66.

——. *The Women Who Knew Too Much: Hitchcock and Feminist Theory* (New York and London: Routledge, 1989).

Mogg, Ken. *The Alfred Hitchcock Story* (London: Titan, 1999).

Morrison, Toni. *Beloved* (New York: Plume, 1998).

Moya, Carlos J. *The Philosophy of Action: An Introduction* (Cambridge: Polity Press, 1991).

Mulhall, Stephen. *On Film* (London: Routledge, 2002).

Mulvey, Laura. "Death Drives: Hitchcock's *Psycho*." *Film Studies* 2 (Spring 2000): 5–14.

Neale, Steve. *Genre and Hollywood* (New York: Routledge, 2000).

Needham, Gary. "Playing with Genre: An Introduction to the Italian *Giallo*." *Kinoeye: A Fortnightly Journal of Film in the New Europe* 2.11 (June 10, 2002).

Neill, Alex. "Empathy and (Film) Fiction." In *Post-Theory: Reconstructing Film Studies*, ed. David Bordwell and Noël Carroll (Madison: University of Wisconsin Press, 1996), 175–94.

——. "On a Paradox of the Heart." *Philosophical Studies* 65, nos. 1–2 (1992): 53–65.

Newman, Kim. *Cat People* (London: BFI Publishing, 1999).

Nietzsche, Friedrich. *Nietzsche Selections*, ed. Richard Schacht (New York: Macmillan, 1993).

Nobus, Dany. "Not Enough and Never Too Much: Closing Remarks of the 2nd Annual Congress of the Association for Psychoanalysis and Psychotherapy in Ireland (November 11, 1995)." *The Letter: Lacanian Perspectives on Psychoanalysis* 6 (Spring 1996): 110–17.

Nussbaum, Martha C. "Tragedy and Self-Sufficiency: Plato and Aristotle on Pity and Fear." In *Essays on Aristotle's Poetics*, ed. Amélie Oskenberg Rorty (Princeton: Princeton University Press, 1992), 261–90.

——. *Upheavals of Thought: The Intelligence of Emotions* (Cambridge: Cambridge University Press, 2001).

Oatley, Keith. *Best Laid Schemes: The Psychology of Emotions* (Cambridge: Cambridge University Press, 1992).

Ortony, Andrew, et. al. *The Cognitive Structure of Emotions* (Cambridge: Cambridge University Press, 1988).

Pennebaker, James. *Opening Up: The Healing Power of Confiding in Others* (New York: Guilford Press, 1996).

Perkins, V. F. "*I Confess*: Photographs of People Speaking." *CineAction* 52 (2000): 28–39.

Phillips, Jim. "Killeen Quiet, but Questions Are Disquieting." *Austin American-Statesman* (October 18, 1991).

Piesman, Marissa and Marilee Hartley. *The Yuppie Handbook: The State of the Art Manual for Young Urban Professionals* (New York: Long Shadows Books, 1984).

Pinedo, Isabel Cristina. *Recreational Terror: Women and the Pleasures of Horror Film Viewing* (Albany: SUNY Press, 1997).

Pirandello, Luigi. *Right You Are! (If You Think So), All for the Best, Henry IV* (Harmondsworth, U.K.: Penguin Plays, 1962).

Plato. *The Republic*, trans. Desmond Lee (Baltimore: Penguin, 1974).

Prince, Stephen. *Savage Cinema: Sam Peckinpah and the Rise of Ultraviolent Movies* (Austin: University of Texas Press, 1998).

—— "Violence and Psychophysiology in Horror Cinema." In *The Horror Film and Psychoanalysis: Freud's Worst Nightmares*, ed. Steven Jay Schneider (Cambridge: Cambridge University Press, forthcoming 2003.

Rebello, Stephen. *Alfred Hitchcock and the Making of Psycho* (New York: Harper Perennial, 1991).

——. "*Psycho.*" *Cinefantastique* (October 1986).

Rhees, Rush. "Wittgenstein on Language and Ritual." In *Wittgenstein and His Times*, ed. Brian McGuinness (Oxford: Blackwell, 1982).

Rivers, W. H. "Freud's Psychology of the Unconscious." *The Lancet* (June 16, 1917): 912–14.

Robinson, Jenefer. "Startle." *Journal of Philosophy* 92, no. 2 (February 1995): 53–74.

Rockett, Will H. *Devouring Whirlwind: Terror and Transcendence in the Cinema of Cruelty* (New York: Greenwood Press, 1998).

Rosenbaum, Jonathan. "Seeing Right Through Us." *Chicago Reader* (August 11, 2000).

Rothman, William. *Hitchcock—The Murderous Gaze* (Cambridge, MA: Harvard University Press, 1982).

Royzman, Edward R. and John Sabini. "Something it Takes to be an Emotion: The Interesting Case of Disgust." *Journal for the Study of Social Behavior* 31, no. 1 (March 2001): 29–60.

Rozin, Paul, J. Haidt, and C. McCauley. "Disgust." In *The Handbook of Emotions* (2nd edition), ed. M. Lewis and J. Haviland-Jones (New York: Gilford Pres, 2000), 637–53.

Russell, David. "Monster Roundup: Reintegrating the Horror Genre." In *Refiguring American Film Genres*, ed. Nick Browne (Berkeley: University of California Press, 1998), 233–54.

Sanjek, David. "Same as It Ever Was: Innovation and Exhaustion in the Horror and Science Fiction Films of the 1990s." In *Film Genre 2000*, ed. Wheeler Winston Dixon (Albany: SUNY Press, 2000), 111–23.

Santner, Eric. "History Beyond the Pleasure Principle: Some Thoughts on the Representation of Trauma." In *Probing the Limits of Representation: Nazism and the "Final Solution,"* ed. Saul Friedlander (Cambridge, MA: Harvard University Press, 1992), 143–54.

Sartre, Jean-Paul. *Situations 1* (Paris: Gallimard, 1947).

Schefer, Jean Louis. *The Enigmatic Body* (Cambridge: Cambridge University Press, 1995).

Schiller, Friedrich. "Reflections on the Use of the Vulgar and the Lowly in Works of Art" (1802). In *Aesthetical and Philosophical Essays, Volume 1,* ed. N. H. Dole (Boston: Aldine, 1910).

Schneider, Steven Jay. "Barbara, Julia, Carol, Myra, and Nell: Diagnosing Female Madness in British Horror Cinema." In *British Horror Cinema,* ed. Stephen Chibnall and Julian Petley (London: Routledge, 2001), 117–30.

———. (ed.). *Fear Without Frontiers: Horror Cinema Across the Globe* (Surrey, U.K.: FAB Press, 2003).

———. (ed.). *The Horror Film and Psychoanalysis: Freud's Worst Nightmares* (Cambridge: Cambridge University Press, forthcoming 2003).

———. "Kevin Williamson and the Rise of the Neo-Stalker." *Post Script: Essays in Film and the Humanities* 19.2 (Winter/Spring 2000): 73–87.

———. "Killing in Style: The Aestheticization of Violence in Donald Cammell's *White of the Eye," Scope: An Online Journal of Film Studies* (May 2001): www.nottingham.ac.uk/film/journal/articles/killing-in-style.htm (June 3, 2003).

———. "The Madwomen in our Movies: Female Psycho-Killers in American Horror Cinema." In *Killing Women: The Visual Culture of Gender and Violence,* ed. Annette Burfoot and Susan Lord (Waterloo: Wilfred Laurier University Press, forthcoming 2003).

———. "Manufacturing Horror in Hitchcock's *Psycho." CineAction* 50 (1999): 70–75.

———. "Monsters as (Uncanny) Metaphors: Freud, Lakoff, and the Representation of Monstrosity in Cinematic Horror." In *Horror Film Reader,* ed. Alain Silver and James Ursini (New York: Limelight Editions, 2000), 167–91.

——— (ed.). *New Hollywood Violence* (Manchester, U.K.: Manchester University Press, forthcoming 2003).

———. "'Suck . . . don't suck'. Framing Ideology in Kathryn Bigelow's *Near Dark."* In *The Cinema of Kathryn Bigelow: Hollywood*

Transgressor, ed. Deborah Jermyn and Sean Redmond (London: Wallflower Press, 2003), 72–90.

——. "Thrice-Told Tales: *The Haunting*, from Novel to Film . . . to Film," *The Journal of Popular Film & Television* 30.3 (Summer 2002): 166–76.

Schopenhauer, Arthur. *The World as Will and Representation, Volume II*, trans. E. F. J. Payne (New York: Dover, 1966).

Schulte-Sasse, Linda. "The 'Mother' of All Horror Movies: Dario Argento's *Suspiria*." *Kinoeye: A Fortnightly Journal of Film in the New Europe* 2.11 (June 10, 2002).

Sconce, Jeffrey. "Spectacles of Death: Identification, Reflexivity, and Contemporary Horror." In *Film Theory Goes to the Movies*, ed. Jim Collins, Hilary Radner, Ava Preacher Collins (New York: Routledge, 1993), 103–119.

Shaw, Daniel. "Determinism and *Dead Ringers*." *Film and Philosophy* 3 (Winter 1996).

——. "Power, Horror, and Ambivalence." *Film and Philosophy*, Special Horror Issue (2001): 1–12.

Shea, Chris and Wade Jennings. "Paul Verhoeven: An Interview." *Post Script* 12, no. 3 (Summer 1993): 3–24.

Siegel, Joel. *Val Lewton: The Reality of Terror* (New York: The Viking Press, 1973).

Sirigu, A., et al. "The Mental Representation of Hand Movements after Parietal Cortex Damage." *Science* 273 (1996): 1564–68.

Smith, Greg M. "Local Emotions, Global Moods." In *Passionate Views: Film, Cognition, and Emotions*, ed. Carl Plantinga and Greg M. Smith (Baltimore: The Johns Hopkins University Press, 1999), 103–26.

Smith, Murray. "(A)moral Monstrosity." In *The Modern Fantastic: The Films of David Cronenberg*, ed. Michael Grant (Westport, CT: Praeger, 2000), 69–83.

Smuts, Aaron. "The Principles of Association: Dario Argento's *Profondo Rosso* (*Deep Red*, 1975)." *Kinoeye: A Fortnightly Journal of Film in the New Europe* 2, no. 11 (June 10, 2002).

——. "Sympathetic Spectators: Roman Polanski's *Le Locataire* (*The Tenant*, 1976)." *Kinoeye: A Fortnightly Journal of Film in the New Europe* 2, no. 3 (February 4, 2002).

Solomon, Robert C. *Continental Philosophy Since 1750: The Rise and Fall of the Self* (Oxford: Oxford University Press, 1988).

——. "The Philosophy of Horror, Or, Why Did Godzilla Cross the Road?" In *Entertaining Ideas—Popular Philosophical Essays: 1970–1990* (New York: Prometheus Books, 1992).

——. "Review of Noël Carroll, *The Philosophy of Horror.*" *Philosophy of Literature* 16 (1992): 163–73.

Spoto, Donald. *The Life of Alfred Hitchcock: The Dark Side of Genius* (London: Collins, 1983).

Stone, Martin. "Shellshock and the Psychologists." In *The Anatomy of Madness: Essays in the History of Psychiatry* (Cambridge: Cambridge University Press, 1985), 242–71.

Summers, Montague. *The Gothic Quest: A History of the Gothic Novel* (London: Fortune, 1938).

Suplee, Curt. "Serial Killers May Be Closer to Normal Than We'd Like to Believe." *Washington Post*. Reprinted in *Houston Chronicle* (August 7, 1991).

Tashiro, C. S. *Pretty Pictures* (Austin: University of Texas Press, 1998).

Taubin, Amy. "The Allure of Decay." *Sight and Sound* 6, no. 1 (January 1996): 22–25. Reprinted in *Action/Spectacle Cinema: A Sight and Sound Reader*, ed. Jose Arroyo (London: BFI Publishing, 2000), 150–53.

Telotte, J. P. *Dreams of Darkness: Fantasy and the Films of Val Lewton* (Urbana and Chicago: University of Illinois Press, 1985).

——. "Faith and Idolatry in the Horror Film." *Literature/Film Quarterly* 8, no. 3 (1980): 143–55. Reprinted in *Planks of Reason: Essays on the Horror Film*, ed. Barry Keith Grant (Metuchen, NJ: Scarecrow Press, 1984).

——. "Verhoeven, Virilio, and 'Cinematic Derealization'," *Film Quarterly* 53, no. 2 (2000): 30–38.

Todorov, Tzvetan. *The Fantastic: A Structural Approach to a Literary Genre* (Ithaca: Cornell University Press, 1975).

Truffaut, François. *Hitchcock*, updated edition (Frogmore, U.K.: Paladin Books, 1978).

Turvey, Malcolm. "Seeing Theory: On Perception and Emotional Response in Current Film Theory." In *Film Theory and Philosophy*, ed. Richard Allen and Murray Smith (Oxford: Oxford University Press, 1999), 431–56.

Twitchell, James. *Dreadful Pleasures: An Anatomy of Modern Horror* (Oxford: Oxford University Press, 1985).

Urbano, Cosimo. "Projections, Suspense and Anxiety: The Modern Horror Film and Its Effects." *Psychoanalytic Review* 85 (December 1998): 909–30.

Verhaeghe, Paul. "The Riddle of Canstration Anxiety: Lacan Beyond Freud. 'Mind The Gap. Mind The Gap. Mind The Gap . . . '." *The*

Letter: Lacanian Perspectives on Psychoanalysis 6 (Spring 1996): 44–54.

Virilio, Paul. *The Art of the Motor*, trans. Julie Rose (Minneapolis: University of Minnesota Press, 1995).

———. *The Vision Machine*, trans. Julie Rose (London: BFI Publishing, 1994).

———. *War and Cinema: The Logistics of Perception*, trans. Patrick Camiller (London: Verso, 1989).

Vorobej, Mark. "Monsters and the Paradox of Horror." *Dialogue: Canadian Philosophical Review* 36, no. 2 (Spring 1997): 219–46.

Waller, Sara and Chris Meyers, "Disenstoried Horror: Art Horror Without Narrative." *Film and Philosophy*, Special Horror Issue (2001): 117–26.

Walton, Kendall. *Mimesis as Make-Believe: On the Foundations of the Representational Arts* (Cambridge, MA: Harvard University Press, 1990).

Wasserman, Earl. *The Subtler Language* (Baltimore: The Johns Hopkins University Press, 1968).

Wilde, Oscar. *The Picture of Dorian Gray* (London: Penguin Classics, 1985).

Williams, Linda. "When the Woman Looks." In *Re-Vision: Essays in Feminist Film Criticism*, ed. Mary Ann Doane, Patricia Mellencamp, and Linda Williams (Frederick, MD: University Publications of America, 1984), 83–99.

———. "When Women Look: A Sequel." *Senses of Cinema* no. 15 (July–August 2001): www.sensesofcinema.com/contents/01/15/horror_women.html (June 3, 2003).

Williams, Tony. "Hong Kong Social Horror: Tragedy and Farce in Category 3." *Post Script: Essays in Film and the Humanities* 21, no. 3 (Summer 2002): 61–71.

Wilson, George M. *Narration in Light: Studies in Cinematic Point of View* (Baltimore: The Johns Hopkins University Press, 1986).

Wittgenstein, Ludwig. *Culture and Value* (Oxford: Blackwell, 1980).

———. *Philosophical Investigations*, trans. G. E. M. Anscombe (Oxford: Basil Blackwell, 1953).

———. *Philosophical Occasions 1912–1951*, ed. James Klagge and Alfred Nordmann (Indianapolis: Hackett, 1993).

Wolfreys, Julian. *Victorian Hauntings: Spectrality, Gothic, the Uncanny and Literature* (London: Palgrave, 2002).

Wood, Robin. "An Introduction to the American Horror Film." In *Movies and Methods, Volume II: An Anthology*, ed. Bill Nichols (Berkeley: University of California Press, 1985), 195–219.

——. *Hitchcock's Films* (South Brunswick, NJ: A. S. Barnes, 1965).

——. *Hitchcock's Films Revisited*, revised edition (New York: Columbia University Press, 2002).

——. *Hollywood from Vietnam to Reagan* (New York: Columbia University Press, 1986).

Worland, Rick. "Faces Behind the Mask: Vincent Price, *Dr. Phibes*, and the Horror Genre in Transition." *Post Script: Essays in Film and the Humanities* 22, no. 2 (Winter/Spring 2003): 19–31.

Index

About the Contributors

Curtis Bowman specializes in the history of German philosophy and aesthetics, and was most recently a visiting Assistant Professor at Haverford College. He has published articles on Immanuel Kant and Johann Gottlieb Fichte, as well as edited a three-volume set of the works of Johann Joachim Winckelmann. He is also one of the translators of the forthcoming volume thirteen of *The Cambridge Edition of the Works of Immanuel Kant*, to be titled *Notes and Fragments*.

Noël Carroll is Monroe C. Beardsley Professor of the Philosophy of Art at the University of Wisconsin-Madison. He is the author of numerous books, including *The Philosophy of Horror; or, Paradoxes of the Heart* (Routledge), *Theorizing the Moving Image* (Cambridge University Press), and *Philosophical Problems of Classical Film Theory* (Princeton University Press). He has also written scores of articles and reviews for academic journals and such publications as *The Village Voice*, *Art Forum*, and *The Boston Review*.

Elizabeth Cowie is Reader in Film Studies in the School of Drama, Film and Visual Arts at the University of Kent, Canterbury. She is the author of *Representing the Woman: Cinema and Psychoanalysis* (Macmillan), and the co-editor of *The Woman in Question: M/F* (MIT Press). Most recently she has written on the documentary film, and on memory and trauma in *Hiroshima mon amour*.

Angela Curran works on ancient Greek philosophy, philosophy of film, and aesthetics. Her recent publications include essays on feminism and film, Aristotle's theory of tragedy, and issues in Aristotelian essentialism. Her current projects include an introductory anthology on the philosophy of film (coedited by Thomas Wartenberg, contracted by Blackwell Press), an essay for this volume on *Stella Dallas* and critical spectatorship, and a manuscript in progress, *Aristotle on Essence and Human Nature*.

Cynthia A. Freeland is Associate Professor of Philosophy and Director of Women's Studies at the University of Houston. She has published widely on topics in ancient philosophy and aesthetics, is the author of *The Naked and the Undead: Evil and the Appeal of Horror* (Westview Press) and *But is it Art?* (Oxford University Press), and is the co-editor of *Philosophy and Film* (Routledge).

Michael Grant is Senior Lecturer in Film Studies at the University of Kent, Canterbury. Publications include studies of contemporary poets, essays on psychoanalysis and the horror film, a monograph on *Dead Ringers* (Flicks Books), and a collection he edited, *The Modern Fantastic: The Cinema of David Cronenberg* (Praeger). He is also the editor of *The Raymond Tallis Reader* (Macmillan).

Matt Hills is the author of *Fan Cultures* (Routledge) and is currently working on a research monograph entitled *The Pleasures of Horror* (Continuum). He has written for *Foundation—The International Review of Science Fiction*, *New Media and Society*, and *The Velvet Light Trap*. Matt is the co-editor of *Intensities: The Journal of Cult Media*, available at www.cult-media.com. He is a lecturer in the School of Journalism, Media and Cultural Studies at Cardiff University, Wales.

Deborah Knight is Associate Professor of Philosophy at Queen's University, Kingston, Canada. Her primary research is in aesthetics and philosophy of art. Recent publications include papers in *The Journal of Aesthetics and Art Criticism*, *Journal of Social Philosophy*, *Film and Philosophy*, *The Simpsons and Philosophy*, and *The Oxford Handbook of Aesthetics*.

George McKnight is Associate Professor of Film Studies at Carleton University, Ottawa, Canada. He is the editor of *Agent of Challenge and Defiance: The Films of Ken Loach* (Flicks Books). With Deborah

Knight he has co-authored papers in *Philosophy and Literature*, *Journal of Social Philosophy*, *Hitchcock: Centenary Essays*, and *The Matrix and Philosophy* (Open Court).

Ken Mogg edits the independent journal *The MacGuffin* and runs its Hitchcock website. He is the author of *The Alfred Hitchcock Story* (Titan Books). He lives in Melbourne, Australia, where he has taught Film Studies at the College of Advanced Education, Melbourne University.

Steven Jay Schneider is a PhD candidate in Philosophy at Harvard University and in Cinema Studies at New York University's Tisch School of the Arts. He has published widely on the horror film and related genres, and is the author of the forthcoming *Designing Fear: An Aesthetics of Cinematic Horror* (Routledge). Steven is the editor of *New Hollywood Violence* (Manchester University Press) and *The Horror Film and Psychoanalysis: Freud's Worst Nightmares* (Cambridge University Press), and the co-editor of *Understanding Film Genres* (McGraw-Hill) and *Horror International* (Wayne State University Press), all forthcoming 2003-04.

Daniel Shaw is Professor of Philosophy and Film at Lock Haven University of Pennsylvania. He is editor of the journal *Film and Philosophy*, and secretary-treasurer of its sponsor organization, the Society for the Philosophic Study of the Contemporary Visual Arts (SPSCVA). He has published several articles on film in such venues as *The Journal of Value Inquiry*, *Kinoeye*, and *Film/Literature Quarterly*. His reviews also appear periodically in the *Journal of Aesthetics and Art Criticism* and in *Choice* magazine.

Aaron Smuts studied philosophy in the Ph.D. program at the University of Texas at Austin. He has written on David Hume, contributed articles on Roman Polanski and Dario Argento to *Kinoeye: A Fortnightly Journal of Film in the New Europe*, and is currently working on the paradox of emotional response to fiction and the concept of violence "numbers." He is currently doing graduate work in film theory, philosophy, and cognitive science at the University of Wisconsin-Madison.

Robert C. Solomon is Quincy Lee Centennial Professor of Business and Philosophy and Distinguished Teaching Professor at the University

Texas-Austin. He is the author of *In the Spirit of Hegel* (Oxford University Press), *The Passions* (Hackett), *About Love* (Simon & Schuster), *A Passion for Justice* (Addison-Wesley), *It's Good Business* (Rowman & Littlefield), *Spirituality for the Skeptic* (Oxford University Press), and many other books.

J. P. Telotte is Professor of Literature, Communication, and Culture at the Georgia Institute of Technology. He is the author of *Dreams of Darkness: Fantasy and the Films of Val Lewton* (University of Illinois Press), *Replications: A Robotic History of the Science Fiction Film* (University of Illinois Press), *A Distant Technology: Science Fiction Film and the Machine Age* (University Press of New England), and *Science Fiction Film* (Cambridge University Press), and is the editor of *The Cult Film Experience* (University of Texas Press).